Intonation is a subject of increasing importance in fields from syntax to speech recognition. D. Robert Ladd provides an exceptionally clear presentation of the key ideas of the influential 'autosegmental–metrical' theory of intonational phonology associated with the work of Janet Pierrehumbert. He outlines the evidence for the theory's basic tenets and relates them to the ideas of competing approaches in a way that will allow sceptics to reach an informed opinion, and he presents a wealth of new material on the cross-language comparison of intonation (including melodic universals and accent/focus) couched in autosegmental–metrical terms. He also draws attention to problems in Pierrehumbert's version of the autosegmental–metrical theory, and offers some theoretical proposals of his own. This book will appeal to phonologists and phoneticians as an original contribution to the debate it discusses, and will be welcomed by a wide range of students and researchers as an ideal overview of recent work.

CAMBRIDGE STUDIES IN LINGUISTICS

Intonational phonology

In this series

Supplementary volumes

Earlier issues not listed are also available

INTONATIONAL PHONOLOGY

D. ROBERT LADD

Reader in Linguistics, Edinburgh University

CAMBRIDGE
UNIVERSITY PRESS

Published by the Press Syndicate of the University of Cambridge
The Pitt Building, Trumpington Street, Cambridge CB2 1RP
40 West 20th Street, New York, NY 10011-4211, USA
10 Stamford Road, Oakleigh, Melbourne 3166, Australia

First published 1996

Printed in Great Britain at the University Press, Cambridge

A catalogue record for this book is available from the British Library

Library of Congress cataloguing in publication data

Ladd, D. Robert, 1947–
Intonational phonology / D. Robert Ladd.
    p.   cm. – (Cambridge studies in linguistics ; 79)
Includes bibliographical references.
ISBN 0 521 47498 1 (hardback) ISBN 0 521 47575 9 (paperback)
1. Intonation (Phonetics).   2. Grammar, Comparative and general –
Phonology.   3. Autosegmental theory (Linguistics)   4. Metrical
phonology.   I. Title.   II. Series.
P222.L33   1996
414.6–dc20   95-52326   CIP

ISBN 0 521 47498 1 hardback
ISBN 0 521 47575 9 paperback

This book is dedicated to the memory of two men
who should have lived to see it completed:

Dwight L. Bolinger
1908–92

Dwight R. Ladd
1921–95

Contents

Figures

Acknowledgements

It is difficult to write a book that touches on as many different topics as this one does without running up a lot of debts of gratitude, both academic and practical. This is especially true when the book's gestation period has lasted as many years as this one's has lasted. In this note I would like to make public my thanks to those without whom *Intonational phonology* would not have finally seen the light of day. None of the people named here should be blamed for any of the book's shortcomings.

I am particularly indebted to six colleagues for many detailed discussions over many years, which have been central to the development of the ideas presented here. In something like chronological order, these six are Carlos Gussenhoven, Kim Silverman, Mary Beckman, Steve Isard, Haruo Kubozono, and Alex Monaghan. I hope I have not given any of them any reason to think that they could have made better use of the time they have spent talking with me.

Several people have read one or more chapters of the book in draft form. All of them have made useful suggestions for improvement, and some of them have spent hours (or pages) in discussion with me. Alphabetically, they are Sónia Frota, Esther Grabe, Martine Grice, Carlos Gussenhoven, Dik Hermes, Caroline Heycock, Will Leben, Marina Nespor, Francis Nolan, Willem Rump, Paul Taylor, Alice Turk, and Ann Wennerstrom; I thank them all. The list of others with whom I have discussed ideas germane to this book is potentially long enough to exceed my word limit, and I apologise for not including everyone. However, I must certainly acknowledge (again alphabetically) the contributions of Amalia Arvaniti, Steven Bird, Dwight Bolinger, Bruce Connell, Anne Cutler, Hans 't Hart, Heinz Giegerich, Nina Grønnum, Geoff Lindsey, Rachel Morton, Janet Pierrehumbert, Susanne Uhmann, Jacques Terken, Enric Vallduví, Jo Verhoeven, and Ron Zacharski. Thanks are also due to the participants in my courses at the European Summer School in Logic, Language, and Information (Lisbon, August 1993) and the Summer School on Field

Research and Language Description (Cologne, September 1993), who were subjected to earlier versions of many of the ideas presented here.

I also thank many speakers of the many languages discussed in the following pages for providing me with the grammatical intuitions and (in some cases) the live examples that form the basis of some of my empirical claims. Once again, it is scarcely possible to name everyone who has helped me in this way, but I would like to thank (this time alphabetically by language name) at least the following people: Aditi Lahiri (Bengali); Enric Vallduví (Catalan); Carlos Gussenhoven and Ineke Mennen (Dutch); Delphine Dahan (French); Esther Grabe, Christa Grewe, and Susanne Uhmann (German); Amalia Arvaniti (Greek); Anna Babarczy, Mária Józsa, and Szilvia Papp (Hungarian); Martine Grice and Antonella Sorace (Italian); Sónia Frota and Marina Vigário (Portuguese); Laurenţia Dascălu-Jinga (Romanian); Wayles Browne (Serbo-Croatian); Natasha Kostromskaya, Wayles Browne, and Jim Miller (Russian); Vedia Ceranoğlu (Turkish); and Femi Adéwọlé (Yoruba). I explicitly take responsibility for any misuse I may have made of the information with which they provided me.

On the practical side, I first of all thank Dominic Watt, Glyn Bottrell, Andrew Ladd, Ineke Mennen, Heather King, Diane Nelson, and Karen Kay, who together put in many hours of tedious editorial, computer, and library work on my behalf. I am especially grateful to Diane for her careful last-minute work on the bibliography and indexes, and to Karen for her unerringly ruthless way with mixed metaphors and excessively clever turns of phrase. Thanks are also due to the many colleagues near and far who answered last-minute requests for facts, examples, figures, and obscure references as the book neared completion. Finally, thanks are due to Judith Ayling of Cambridge University Press (for not losing patience with my repeated assurances that the book was indeed nearing completion), and to Jenny Potts, who copy-edited the entire typescript for the Press.

Sarah Hawkins and Tom Baer rented me a spare room in their house near Cambridge from January to March 1989, where I wrote much of an early draft of the book. René Collier and Jacques Terken helped arrange for me to spend six months (March–August 1994) as a Van Houten visiting research fellow at the Institute for Perception Research in Eindhoven, and Anne Cutler invited me to spend a month (July 1995) as a visiting researcher at the Max Planck Institute for Psycholinguistics in Nijmegen. The intellectual stimulation and the uninterrupted time for thinking and writing that I found at both institutes was invaluable for the book's development.

Closer to home, I thank my family – Antonella, Andrew, Marco, and latterly Carlo – for putting up with the long hours I spent at the office during the summers of 1993, 1994, and 1995. Nor should I neglect to mention the practical assistance during those summers of my parents-in-law, Carmelo and Luisa Sorace. I should particularly take appreciative note of Luisa's cooking, without which I would probably have stayed late at the office many more times than I did. I look forward to resuming something more closely resembling normal family life now that the book is finished.

Introduction

Research on intonation has long been characterised by a number of unresolved basic issues and fundamental differences of approach. Until recently, these have precluded the emergence of any widely accepted framework for the description of intonational phenomena, or even any general agreement on what the interesting phenomena are. Since the mid-1970s, however, several lines of research have converged on a set of broadly shared assumptions and methods, and studies on a variety of languages are now yielding new discoveries expressed in comparable terms. This emerging viewpoint – which it is perhaps only slightly premature to characterise as a standard theory of intonational structure – is the subject of this book.

As the book's title suggests, the heart of this theory is the idea that intonation, and pitch in particular, *has a phonological organisation*. This idea requires some justification, since pitch seems to pose problems for phonology. For one thing, pitch is somehow more relative than other phonetic properties. Instead of the complex constellations of articulatory settings or acoustic parameters that identify an [o] or a [t], we find only a simple sliding scale of up and down, which can differ conspicuously from speaker to speaker and from occasion to occasion. For another thing, pitch is clearly linked to a paralinguistic vocal code: sometimes against our will, it signals or helps signal information about our sex, our age, and our emotional state, as part of a parallel communicative channel that can be interpreted by listeners (even some non-human ones) who do not understand the linguistic message. For many investigators, these two properties are enough to set intonation beyond the reach of ordinary assumptions of phonological and phonetic theories.

We know, however, that in so-called tone languages (like Chinese or Thai or Yoruba) pitch has been captured for use in the phonemic system, and in all of these languages it is fairly simple to identify a small inventory of phonological elements ('tones') that are phonetically based on pitch but are otherwise quite analogous to segmental phonemes. For example, in

Standard Chinese ('Mandarin') there are four tone phonemes, conventionally numbered 1–4, whose phonetic realisations in isolation are respectively
high level, mid-high rising, low-dipping, and high–low falling. The four
tones contrast exactly like segmental phonemes, so that *huà* 'speech, language' and *huā* 'flower' are just as different as *huà* and *guà* 'hang up'.
Allophonic variation and neutralisation occur with tone phonemes in ways
that are exactly comparable to segmental phonology. Tone 3, which is low
dipping in isolation, has two variants (allophones or 'allotones') in connected speech: a low level variant preceding Tones 1, 2, and 4, and a mid-
high rising variant, identical to Tone 2, preceding another Tone 3. Tones
also condition allophonic variation in segmental phonemes; for example,
vowels with Tone 3 tend to be longer and in some cases more open than
with other tones.

   Yet pitch in tone languages also serves the paralinguistic functions mentioned above. Chinese-speaking men generally have lower-pitched voices
than Chinese-speaking women, and a voice raised in anger sounds much
the same in Chinese as it does in any other language. This means that pitch
per se has no intrinsic properties that prevent us from ascribing to it a
phonological structure. Rather, the principal peculiarity of pitch in language is that, in addition to any phonological organisation it may have, it
is also universally used for paralinguistic functions as well. The question is
not whether pitch *can* have phonological structure – we know that it can –
but whether it does have phonological structure in languages like English
or French. By claiming that it does, we are in some sense focusing on the
distinction between linguistic and paralinguistic functions of pitch, and
claiming that intonation belongs to the former.

   Two independent developments have led to the increasing acceptance of
this phonological view. The first of these is the growth of non-linear generative phonology. Beginning with Leben's and Goldsmith's work on African
tonal systems (Leben 1973; Goldsmith 1976) and Liberman's work on
stress and rhythm (Liberman 1975), 'autosegmental' and 'metrical'
phonology have at the very least provided descriptive insights and new ways
of thinking about suprasegmental phenomena that are in many cases
directly applicable to problems of intonation. The second development is
the rapid expansion of speech technology research, and the concomitant
recourse to instrumental phonetics as a source of data for phonological
theory ('laboratory phonology'; see Beckman and Kingston 1990).
Linguists are increasingly involved in developing quantitatively explicit
models of F_0 so that synthetic speech can progress beyond the caricature

monotone of science-fiction robots – and the most successful such models are based to a great extent on strings of phonological elements (e.g. Pierrehumbert 1981; Anderson, Pierrehumbert, and Liberman 1984; Ladd 1987). Even linguists who are not developers of speech technology are in some sense consumers of it: there is no doubt that laboratory phonology has been made possible by the availability of fast and easy computer speech analysis tools.

Without a doubt the single most influential contribution to current work on intonational phonology has been Janet Pierrehumbert's PhD thesis 'The phonology and phonetics of English intonation' (1980). Building on Liberman's metrical theory (Liberman 1975; Liberman and Prince 1977) and on Bruce's analysis of Swedish word accents (Bruce 1977), Pierrehumbert proposed a simple yet powerful theory of intonational phonology that effectively resolved the long-running 'levels vs. configurations' debate and focused the attention of investigators on certain well-defined questions that have occupied much of their time since. She also, by undertaking to explain *in a phonological description* various details of instrumentally measured F_0, set new standards of phonetic accountability, and (in effect) contributed to the credibility of linguists working on speech technology. Her theory has been directly adopted in more recent work on intonational pragmatics (Ward and Hirschberg 1985; Pierrehumbert and Hirschberg 1990), the syntax–phonology interface (Selkirk 1984), and the relation between word and sentence prosody in Japanese (Poser 1984; Pierrehumbert and Beckman 1988). It has also strongly influenced descriptions of intonation in European languages by, for example, Ladd (1983a), Gussenhoven (1984), Féry (1993), and Grice (1995a).

Yet despite the success of this approach among a small community of researchers, there exists no comprehensive account accessible to the outsider. The seminal article on metrical phonology – Liberman and Prince 1977 – appeared in *Linguistic Inquiry*, but Liberman's and Bruce's theses were published as monographs that are not widely available, and Pierrehumbert's thesis circulated only in photocopied form for several years. In any case, like many influential theses, none of these works is written for the non-specialist. Many linguists and speech researchers whose interests impinge on intonation are aware of the existence of the general Pierrehumbert 'school' of intonation, but are unsure how it relates to their own work.

The first goal of this book, therefore, is to set out the theoretical assumptions and empirical foundations of the general autosegmental–metrical approach to intonational phonology in enough detail to permit non-specialists (syntacticians interested in focus, say, or speech technologists interested in phonetic cues to parsing) to make intelligent use of this body of work. This is the focus of chapters 1–3. To accomplish this first goal adequately, I have had to include a certain amount of background material that some will find superfluous, and to provide definitions for terms (such as 'citation form' or 'spectral tilt') that may be unfamiliar to a significant number of potential readers.

The second, closely related goal is to demonstrate the potential of the theory, by discussing what is known about supposedly universal characteristics of intonation in terms suggested by the autosegmental–metrical point of view. I have made a point of including enough new illustrative material – in particular, the typological and descriptive work in chapters 4 and 5 – to allow readers from a wide range of language backgrounds to appreciate the relevance of this approach to problems in their own languages, and more generally to help demonstrate that this approach to intonational phonology holds the promise of providing a genuinely universal descriptive framework.

The third and most specialised goal of the book is to state the case for my own particular version of the general autosegmental–metrical theory. In a sense I have been writing this book ever since the summer of 1981, when I taught a summer course based in large measure on Pierrehumbert's newly appeared thesis. Specialist readers may recognise themes and arguments from a number of papers that I have published since 1981, criticising various aspects of the orthodox Pierrehumbert theory (in particular Ladd 1983a, 1990b, and 1993b). These focus particularly on the status of pitch range, and on the kinds of hierarchical prosodic structures that are needed in intonational description. What I have tried to do here – especially in chapters 6 and 7, but to some extent throughout the book – is to tie together these specific critiques into a more coherent overall picture. I have also – especially in chapters 1–3 – tried to distinguish what I see as the essential ideas of the autosegmental–metrical approach from the specific details of Pierrehumbert's analysis of English.

The conception of 'phonology' underlying this book is fairly elementary, and most of the theoretical issues discussed here are remote from current debates in phonological theory. The reader who wishes to know more about the relevance of intonational phenomena for Optimality Theory, for instance, will find little of direct interest here. There are at least three reasons for this. First, I have made a deliberate choice of how to present the material here: because the book is aimed at a wide audience, I cannot take familiarity with the latest phonological issues for granted. Second, I assume the validity of some sort of distinction between 'lexical' and 'postlexical' phonology, and I assume that intonation is postlexical; since many current issues in phonology (in particular those being dealt with in Optimality Theory) deal primarily with lexical phonology, they may simply not be relevant to the questions discussed here. Third and perhaps most important, I believe that much taxonomic work still remains to be done on intonation – in effect, the kind of phonemes-and-allophones work that is a basic part of fieldwork on an unfamiliar language – and that there are still fundamental uncertainties about the nature of intonational phenomena that do not arise in the study of segmental phonology.

Nevertheless, it is my hope that, if I am able to shed some light on the areas of fundamental uncertainty, the relevance of general phonological theory to the study of intonation may become more obvious. If I can at the same time clarify the relevance of studying intonation to general phonological theory, then I will have more than adequately accomplished my purpose in writing this book.

1 *Introduction to intonational phonology*

1.1   Intonation

One of the many difficulties of writing on the subject of intonation is that the term means different things to different people. It is therefore appropriate, right at the beginning of the book, to offer my own definition of intonation, or at least to try to delimit the area I propose to cover. One of the implicit goals of the book will be to show that the area so defined is a coherent object of study.

1.1.1   Three defining characteristics

Intonation, as I will use the term, refers to the use of *suprasegmental* phonetic features to convey 'postlexical' or *sentence-level* pragmatic meanings in a *linguistically structured* way. The three key points in this definition are the three italicised terms:

1   *Suprasegmental*: I follow phonetic tradition in restricting my attention to suprasegmental features – features of fundamental frequency (F_0), intensity, and duration, according to a common definition. Although this restriction is traditional, it is not without problems, which I will only mention here. First, there is a problem of definition. Lehiste (1970) defines suprasegmentals as features of 'pitch, stress, and quantity'. The difference between her definition and the one I have given raises the more general question of the relations among physical, psychophysical, and phonetic properties. 'Stress' is clearly a phonetic property (i.e. a complex perceptual amalgam only indirectly relatable to psychophysical and physical dimensions); 'loudness' is psychophysical; 'intensity' is physical. Similar distinctions can be drawn in the case of 'pitch' and 'F_0', or 'quantity' and 'duration'. In all these cases, it is often unclear which terms of reference are most appropriately used in talking about suprasegmental phenomena. For the most part I have avoided this issue in what I have written

here; in particular, I have made no attempt to distinguish rigorously between pitch and F_0. Strictly speaking, F_0 is a physical property and pitch is its psychophysical correlate, but in many contexts outside psychophysics little ambiguity arises if the terms are used interchangeably, and this accords with much recent phonetic work.[1]

The other problem with restricting our attention to suprasegmental features is that there are other phenomena that might otherwise be covered by the definition of intonation proposed here. For example, it has long been observed that many languages use segmental morphemes to convey the kinds of meanings that in other languages can often be signalled intonationally. Two obvious examples are question particles and focus particles (see König 1991); there are several reports of detailed similarities between typical intonational functions and the function of particles in certain languages, such as German (Schubiger 1965, 1980) or Russian (Arndt 1960). It may be that the functional similarity between such particles and intonation as defined here should outweigh the clear phonetic and syntactic differences. Similarly, research on sign language phonology has suggested a three-way distinction closely comparable to the lexical–intonational–paralinguistic distinction that I will attempt to justify below (see Liddell 1977; Wilbur 1994a, 1994b). If such a comparison is valid, it is clearly important not to define intonation solely in terms of phonetic suprasegmentals. As in other areas of phonology, sign language research may be able to yield important insights into what is essential about intonation in spoken language, and what is accidental. However, throughout the book I have deferred to phonetic tradition, and have excluded both particles and sign language from any detailed consideration.

2   *Sentence-level or postlexical:*[2] intonation conveys meanings that apply to phrases or utterances as a whole, such as sentence type or speech act, or focus and information structure. By this definition, intonation excludes features of stress, accent, and tone that are determined in the lexicon, which serve to distinguish one word from another. For example, English *permit* (noun) and *permit* (verb) are composed of identical strings of phonemes, and distinguished by whether stress falls on the first syllable or the second; Standard Chinese *huā* 'flower' and *huà* 'speech, language' are segmentally identical, but are distinguished by the fact that the

former has high level pitch ('Tone 1') while the latter has sharply falling pitch ('Tone 4'). Intonational features are, by definition, never involved in signalling such distinctions. Phonetically, of course, lexical features of stress, accent, and tone interact with intonational features in many ways. In general, however, the two types can be kept distinct in a description.

3   *Linguistically structured*: intonational features are organised in terms of categorically distinct entities (e.g. low tone or boundary rise) and relations (e.g. stronger than / weaker than). They exclude 'paralinguistic' features, in which continuously variable physical parameters (e.g. tempo and loudness) directly signal continuously variable states of the speaker (e.g. degree of involvement or arousal). Like lexical features, paralinguistic features interact with intonational features. Unlike lexical features, paralinguistic aspects of utterances are often exceedingly difficult to distinguish from properly intonational ones, and it is a matter of considerable controversy which aspects are which, or whether such a distinction is even possible. I will return to discuss this at length at the end of the chapter.

1.1.2   Tune and relative prominence

Formally and functionally, the phenomena covered by this three-part definition have two orthogonal and independently variable aspects, which I will refer to as 'tune' and 'relative prominence'. These two aspects are illustrated by the four intonational possibilities of the simple utterance *five pounds* informally sketched in (1.1).

(1.1)   relative prominence

		weak–strong	strong–weak
	falling	five POUNDS.	FIVE pounds
tune			
	rising	five POUNDS?	FIVE pounds?

Tune: The two pitch patterns shown are by no means the only possibilities in English, but they are clearly distinct. The 'falling' tune is the one that would normally be used in a straightforward reply to a question, for example in answer to a question like *How much does it cost?* The 'rising' tune would normally be used to convey doubt, uncertainty, or some other 'questioning' modality: it could be used to ask for confirmation that the speaker has heard correctly (*Did you say*) *five pounds?* In a common North American usage the 'rising' tune can also be used on *five pounds* in answer to a question like *How much does it cost?* This tune in this context signals that the speaker is not sure of the answer, or that the price seems unreasonable, or more generally to invite feedback from the questioner about whether the price is acceptable. This shows that it is not possible to identify tune types with sentence types in any simple way. It does not, however, undermine the point being made here, since the two tunes are still clearly distinct: even in the popular press notice has been taken of this use of questioning intonation with statements, suggesting that the distinction is obvious to the casual native-speaker observer.[3]

Relative prominence: The two prominence patterns are also clearly distinct. The first, weak-strong, is the 'normal' stress pattern, used when there is no particular reason to emphasise either *five* or *pounds*, or (to put it somewhat differently) when the focus is on the phrase as a whole. This is the stress pattern that would normally be found if the phrase were used to answer a wide range of questions, like *How much does it cost?* or *What did you give him?* or *What have you got there?* The second pattern of prominence, strong–weak, focuses on *five* for contextual reasons, and would normally only be used in a discourse context where a specific number of pounds was under discussion: that is, as an answer to a question like *Did you say four pounds?* It is possible to bring about perceptible gradual modifications of the phonetic 'prominence' of the individual words *five* or *pounds* by gradual changes in various acoustic parameters, but the prominence *pattern* of the utterance as a whole must fall into one of the two categories shown: either we have narrow focus on *five*, or we do not. Detailed differences of prominence on the individual words work within the framework of these two possibilities.[4]

The distinctions of tune and relative prominence shown in (1.1) fit all three points of the definition of intonation just presented above. First, of course, the features under discussion are obviously suprasegmental. Second, the meanings conveyed are clearly not lexical: the meanings of *five* and *pounds* are unaffected by the intonational changes, and the differences of tune and of relative prominence affect the meaning of the utterance as a whole. Finally, the distinctions are linguistically structured, in the sense that we are dealing with *categories* such as rising vs. falling or weak–strong vs. strong–weak. The extent to which a categorical structure is involved in intonation is, as I said, a point of some controversy, but in these specific examples it seems fairly clear that we are dealing with sharp rather than gradual distinctions. By our definition, then, tune and relative prominence are at the heart of intonation.

Nevertheless, two points require further comment. First, in much earlier work it is often assumed that there are three main aspects to intonation rather than two; in a three-way division of intonational function, the third major function of intonation is said to be the division of the stream of speech into intonationally marked chunks ('intonational phrases', 'tone groups', and related terms). In the American phonemic tradition, for example, the three aspects were called 'pitch', 'stress', and 'juncture' (e.g. Trager and Smith 1951); juncture phonemes were supposed to be phonetically definable boundary markers of one sort or another. Halliday (1967a) states explicitly that the intonation of an utterance involves features of 'tone' (my 'tune'), 'tonicity' (part of what I am calling 'relative prominence'), and 'tonality' (the division of the utterance into tone groups). Other writers have made similar distinctions.

I do not of course deny that there are phonetic cues to the division of the stream of speech into smaller chunks, but I regard this fact as following from the existence of *phonological structure*, of the sort that has been extensively discussed in the literature on 'metrical phonology' and 'prosodic phonology' (e.g. Selkirk 1980, 1984; Nespor and Vogel 1986).[5] That is, I assume that utterances have a phonological constituent structure (or prosodic structure), and that the prosodic constituents have various phonetic properties, both segmental and suprasegmental. Intonation has no privileged status in signalling prosodic structure – indeed, much of the work on 'prosodic phonology' (e.g. Nespor and Vogel 1986) deals with segmental sandhi rules (rules describing phonetic adjustments at word and morpheme boundaries, such as the palatalisation that yields *gotcha* from *got + you*). Moreover, I assume that constituent boundaries in prosodic structure are in the first instance abstractions, not actual phonetic events: intonational features of tune and relative prominence are distributed in utterances in ways *allowed by* the prosodic structure. In some cases this means that conspicuous phonetic breaks occur at major constituent boundaries, but this is neither the essence of the boundary nor the only factor governing the distribution of the intonational features. I will return to the issue of prosodic structure and its relation to intonational features in chapter 6.

The second point on which comment is required has to do with the relation between phonological and phonetic description. In distinguishing tune from relative prominence and treating the two aspects of intonation as 'independent' and 'orthogonal', we are making a phonological abstraction. As can be seen from (1.1), there is a great deal of phonetic interaction between the two sides of the intonational coin: in short utterances like *five pounds*, the relative prominence is actually cued perceptually primarily by the pitch contour (see section 2.2). However, the fact that the tune and the prominence pattern can vary independently shows that we are dealing with two distinct phenomena: that is, in a general account of intonation, it is useful to posit an abstract prominence pattern, distinct from the pitch contours that may serve to realise it phonetically. To put this distinction in fairly traditional terms, the 'sentence stress' or 'nuclear stress' on *five* or *pounds* can be referred to independently of the 'pitch accent' or 'nuclear tone' by which it is phonetically manifested.

1.1.3   Intonational phonology

This brings us to the term 'intonational phonology'. Until the late 1970s there was not really any such notion, and even now it is not obvious to many intonation researchers what intonational phonology might mean. It is therefore necessary to demystify this term quite explicitly.

At a minimum, a complete phonological description includes (a) a level of description in which the sounds of an utterance are characterised in terms of a relatively small number of *categorically distinct entities* – phonemes, features, or the like – and (b) a mapping between such a description and a physical description of the utterance in terms of *continuously varying parameters* such as an acoustic waveform or tracks of the movement of the articulators. I emphasise that this characterisation of phonology is not intended to be controversial, although admittedly it has a laboratory phonology bias that not all readers may share. I also emphasise that it is intended to apply to phonological phenomena of any sort, not just intonation. It obviously deals mostly with issues of 'postlexical' phonology and phonetic realisation, and consequently leaves out all sorts of aspects of morphophonemics or 'lexical' phonology that would be needed for a characterisation of phonology as a whole. Nevertheless, the parts it leaves out are, by the definition given in the previous section, irrelevant to intonation, and it will therefore serve as an adequate notion of phonology for our purposes here.

Minimal though such a phonology may be, it is not something that is very often encountered in past work on intonation. Until the late 1970s there were two essentially separate approaches to studying intonation, which both in their own way failed to include a description that we might call phonological according to the characterisation just given. The two approaches also largely ignored each other. For want of better terms I will refer to these as the 'instrumental' approach and the 'impressionistic' approach, though – anticipating my conclusions a bit – I might also designate the two views as 'phonetic' and 'proto-phonological'. It will be useful to sketch these two approaches briefly.

The 'instrumental' or 'phonetic' tradition was that of experimental psychologists and phoneticians interested in speech perception and in identifying the acoustic cues to intonational phenomena. An excellent review of this work up to the late 1960s is Lehiste 1970. Much of this work has focused on discovering the acoustic cues to several specific intonational phenomena, in particular: (a) syntactic/pragmatic notions like 'finality', 'continuation', and 'interrogation' (e.g. Hadding-Koch and Studdert-Kennedy 1964; Delattre 1965; Lieberman 1967); (b) emotional states such as anger, surprise, and boredom (e.g. Lieberman and Michaels 1962; Williams and Stevens 1972); and (c) word and sentence stress (e.g. Fry 1958; Lieberman 1960). In none of these cases can clear understanding have been said to result, though there are some fairly general findings that are well established, such as the fact that active emotions like anger or surprise are generally signalled by higher overall pitch (Uldall 1964; Williams and Stevens 1972), or that the duration of pauses at intonational breaks correlates well with the syntactic 'strength' of the boundary (Cooper and Paccia-Cooper 1980). But more conclusive findings are elusive, and fundamental uncertainty remains about such questions as the acoustic nature of stress.

The 'impressionistic' or 'proto-phonological' approach was that of linguists and language teachers who were interested in describing intonation either for practical ends (improving the pronunciation of foreign speakers of a language, in particular English) or as part of the general development of phonemic theory. This approach is represented by the work of the American structuralist school (Pike 1945; Wells 1945; Trager and Smith 1951; and others) and those of the British school (Palmer 1922; Kingdon 1958; O'Connor and Arnold 1973). Descriptions in this tradition treat intonation in terms of a small number of categorically distinct elements – pitch phonemes, nuclear tones, etc. – and in this sense may be said to be investigating 'intonational phonology'. However, in most cases the authors of these descriptions had no ambitions to go beyond data that could be gathered by traditional auditory methods and written down as impressionistic pitch curves. Moreover, for reasons that I will discuss further below, within the impressionistic tradition there were always significant disagreements about the inventory of categorically distinct elements, and there was no obvious standard of evidence for settling such disagreement.

Because of the general lack of agreement and the notable absence of instrumental evidence for impressionistic descriptions, adherents of the instrumental approach have often felt that their work is somehow more rigorous or more scientific, or at the very least more complete. The following quotes are indicative of some widely held attitudes:

> Lieberman and Michaels (1962: 248) state that 'most current systems of linguistic analysis of intonation seem incomplete in that they merely note gross changes of fundamental frequency, minimize the role of amplitude and phonetic variations, and entirely ignore the fine structure of the fundamental frequency . . . these additional dimensions are responsible for a large fraction of the total emotional information transmitted in human speech.'
>
> Ohala (1975: 737f.), discussing different approaches to the study of suprasegmentals, contrasts the 'facile inventions by taxonomic linguists' with 'what scientists of language have proven and demonstrated empirically about the behavior of speech sounds'.
>
> Maeda (1976: 18) argues that a 'serious disadvantage of the studies based on auditory impressions of speech sounds is the lack of experimental means for checking whether or not the analysis is correct'.

As I have argued elsewhere (Ladd 1980a: ch. 6), such criticisms largely miss the point. The difference between the two approaches is not primarily one of methodology, nor one of completeness, but of theoretical assumptions. It is perfectly true that impressionistic descriptions until the 1970s made little attempt to relate their findings to instrumental work, and it is quite fair to treat this as a failing. Nevertheless, it is important to recognise that the impressionistic descriptions involve phonological categories that could *in principle* be related to instrumentally validated acoustic or articulatory parameters. More importantly, critics of impressionistic descriptions often fail to recognise that the instrumental approach also involves theoretical assumptions which can be examined and evaluated, and which do not always stand up to close inspection.

In any case, before writing an entire book on the subject of intonational phonology, it seems appropriate to address the views of those who question whether intonational phonology even exists. The remainder of the chapter is an attempt to do just that. In section 1.2, I discuss a theory of intonation that is 'phonological' according to the characterisation given just above, but whose scientific and methodological credibility among 'instrumental' researchers is impeccable. In section 1.3, I identify and discuss two theoretical issues on which phonological and non-phonological approaches clearly disagree, and present evidence for the phonological point of view. Finally, in section 1.4, I explore some of the reasons why it has been so difficult for impressionistic descriptions and their current intellectual descendants to arrive at a widely agreed-upon set of phonological categories in the intonation of any given language.

1.2   The IPO theory of intonational structure

This section sketches the approach to describing intonation developed since the mid-1960s at the Institute for Perception Research (IPO) in Eindhoven. Though originally motivated by the search for a model of the intonation of Dutch for use in speech synthesis, the IPO approach has subsequently developed into a general theory of intonational structure ('t Hart, Collier, and Cohen 1990). It has served as the basis of a pedagogical description of Dutch intonation (Collier and 't Hart 1981), and has been extended to the description of intonation in other languages, including English (de Pijper 1983; Willems, Collier, and de Pijper 1988), German (Adriaens 1991), Russian (Odé 1989), and most recently French (Beaugendre 1994) and Indonesian (Odé and van Heuven 1994). The IPO tradition is in many ways the first to make a serious attempt to combine an abstract phonological level of description with a detailed account of the phonetic realisation of the phonological elements.

1.2.1   *Phonological structure*

In the IPO approach, contours are idealised as sequences of pitch movements and connecting line segments. The model assumes that certain pitch movements 'are interpreted as relevant by the listener' and that these movements are 'characterised by discrete commands to the vocal cords and should be recoverable as so many discrete events in the resulting pitch contours, which may present themselves at first sight as continuous variations in time' (Cohen and 't Hart 1967: 177f.). Moreover, although the idealisation was not clearly stated as such in the earliest IPO work, these pitch movements are modelled on the assumption that 'the most elementary aspect of pitch variation is the difference between a relatively high and a relatively low pitch level' and that 'speech melody is characterised by the continual alternation between relatively high and relatively low pitch levels' (Collier and 't Hart 1981: 15; my translation). This notion of a basic distinction between relatively high and relatively low is a clear foreshadowing of the two-level phonologies of Bruce and Pierrehumbert, a point to which I will return in chapter 2.

Pitch movements in the IPO model are said to be of two types. The model follows Bolinger (e.g. 1958) in claiming that prominence of a particular word in a sentence is brought about by the occurrence of a pitch movement on the lexically stressed syllable of the word. Pitch movements used in this way are called 'prominence-lending'; Dutch prominence-lending pitch movements include both a rise and a fall occurring relatively early in the stressed syllable, an extremely late rise, and a kind of half-fall. These are distinguished from certain other pitch movements that are 'non-prominence-lending'. Non-prominence-lending pitch movements include a rise and a fall that occur at phrase boundaries, plus a rise and a fall that (unlike the other pitch movements in the model's inventory) may span several syllables. The non-prominence-lending pitch movements are clearly phonologically distinctive, in the sense that they may turn one contour type into a different one – for example, one of the important functions of the boundary rise is to distinguish a question from a statement – but they do not pick out a word or syllable as prominent. Cohen and 't Hart found it curious that the boundary rise, though clearly distinctive, 'need not occur in dominant words or even in prominent syllables' (1967: 189), but such an association of distinctive pitch movements with boundaries is now well established as a characteristic of intonational phonology (see sections 2.1 and 3.2.2.1).

The assumptions just outlined are well illustrated by the 'hat pattern', the best-known construct of the IPO model. This pattern consists minimally of a 'Type 1 Rise' (low to high early in accented syllable) followed by a 'Type A Fall' (high to low early in accented syllable). The two movements may occur as part of the same accent, in which case we have a 'pointed hat', or as separate accents, in which case we have a 'flat hat'. The stretches of contour preceding the rise and following the fall – and the stretch in between the two in the 'flat hat' – are idealised as straight line segments notated ∅ (for the upper line) and 0 (for the lower). All these aspects of the hat pattern can be seen in figure 1.1.

The hat pattern can be represented abstractly as

(1.2)   (0) 1 (∅) A (0),

that is, as an obligatory 1 and an obligatory A, with optional stretches of ∅ and 0 on any non-prominent syllables. *This is the phonological description.*[6] It is expressed in terms of categorically distinct entities (Type 1 Rise, etc.) that occur, in sequence, at well-defined points in the utterance. It abstracts away from differences that arise because the contour is applied to utterances of different lengths: it makes it explicit that the two contours in figure 1.1 are specific realisations of the same abstract linguistic unit, realisations that differ in predictable ways just as allophones of a phoneme differ predictably. In theory, the phonological formula in (1.2) tells us all we need to know about the physical properties of the hat pattern for 'higher-level' linguistic purposes: a linguist interested in the syntactic and pragmatic uses of the hat pattern would not need to be concerned with continuous F_0 parameters, only the phonological formula.

1.2.2   *Phonetic realisation*

As I noted above, a complete phonological description does not consist of abstract formulas alone, but must also specify how the abstract formulas are realised; that is, it must describe the mapping from the categorical phonological elements to the continuous acoustic parameters. The IPO researchers have devoted considerable effort to this task, and the theory has been used successfully as the basis of a model for synthesising Dutch intonation contours by rule. All the phonological elements of the model have been described in considerable phonetic detail (for example, there are phonetic specifications of how pitch movements are aligned with respect to the stressed syllable). These phonetic descriptions are based on experiments that attempted to set the limits of perceptible variation (i.e. how different can two pitch movements be physically and still count as perceptually the same?). For more detail on this entire aspect of the IPO model, the reader is referred to 't Hart and Cohen 1973 and 't Hart, Collier, and Cohen 1990.

Perhaps the best-known feature of the IPO approach to phonetic realisation is the notion of *declination*. This term was coined by Cohen and 't Hart (1967: 184) to describe the downward trend of F_0 observable in many utterances, and has since been adopted by a wide variety of authors. In the

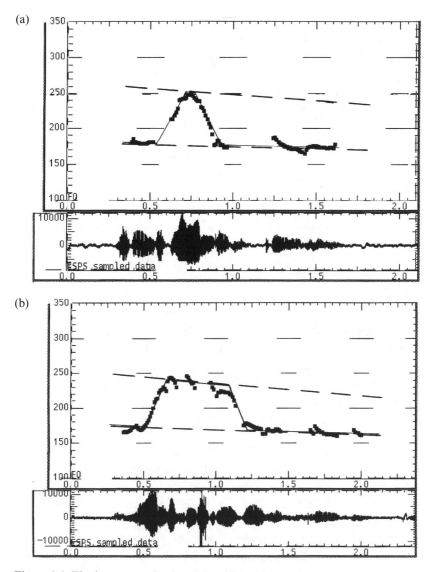

Figure 1.1 The hat pattern in the IPO model of intonation. Panel (a) shows the 'pointed hat', with the Type 1 Rise and Type A Fall on a single accented syllable, applied to the Dutch sentence *Zij is maandag gekomen* ('She came on Monday'). Panel (b) shows the 'flat hat', with the Type 1 Rise and Type A Fall on separate accented syllables, applied to the Dutch sentence *Maandag is zij naar Rome gevlogen* ('On Monday she flew to Rome'). The irregular dotted lines show the actual F_0 contours and the straight solid lines show the idealised contour. The straight dashed lines show the Ø-line (topline) and Ø-line (bottomline).

IPO model, declination refers specifically to the trend of the top and bottom lines that define the limits of the local pitch movements – the lines notated ∅ and 0 in the abstract phonological formulas that represent contours. This means that even when nothing is 'happening' phonologically in the contour, F_0 continues to go down slightly; it also means that a pitch movement at the beginning of a phrase will be higher than the same pitch movement later in the phrase. This aspect of the model can also be seen in figure 1.1.

A considerable amount of research has gone into discovering the phonetic details of declination within the IPO framework, and the notion of declination itself has been extensively studied by investigators with a wide variety of backgrounds, interests, and theoretical assumptions. Work within the IPO theory includes 't Hart 1979, Cohen, Collier, and 't Hart 1982, and Terken 1991; reviews from different perspectives include Vaissière 1983 and Ladd 1984, 1993c. I will return to discuss this issue again in section 2.4.

1.2.3   Key theoretical assumptions of the IPO approach

What makes the IPO approach phonological? There are two important properties of the elements of an IPO description that distinguish them from the analytical constructs of most other 'instrumental' work on intonation. These are *phonetic definition* and *linearity*.

Linearity is obvious: an IPO description of a contour consists of a string of discrete intonational elements. To be sure, the significance of this fact is disputed. In particular, Grønnum has suggested (e.g. Thorsen 1985) that my emphasis on the linearity of the IPO work is misleading: she considers declination to be an equally central feature of the IPO theory, and points out that the concept of declination has been widely adopted in many instrumental phonetic models of intonation that do not share any corresponding phonological abstractions. I do not think that this objection is valid, however. The distinction between the abstract elements and the details of their phonetic realisation is discussed very explicitly in 't Hart and Collier 1975. The abstract description clearly involves only a string of events in sequence, and declination is treated as a matter of phonetic detail, not as part of the abstract description. Declination in the IPO model certainly resembles the 'phrase components' of numerous non-phonological studies – about which more shortly – but it is part of the phonetic background, not something that is moulded to communicative ends.

As for phonetic definition, this is intended to mean that the elements of the IPO system – Type A Fall, Type 2 Rise, etc. – are defined in terms of their phonetic realisation. *Meaning or function plays no role in the analysis.* The elements are identified solely on the basis of the fact that they are perceptually distinct from other elements, and are defined solely in terms of the phonetic properties that distinguish them. There is no necessary reference to any supposed functions of intonation, and terms like 'continuation rise' are seldom used. As 't Hart and Collier (1975: 254) put it: 'we have deliberately restricted ourselves to the *melodic* aspects only. So far we have not said anything about the *functional* aspect of intonation, for example we cannot offer any explanation for the motives of the speaker that lead to the choice of a particular intonation pattern.'

Yet the question still remains: what makes the IPO work phonological? Why are linearity and phonetic definition crucial concepts in intonational phonology? This question has a certain amount of force, because the IPO researchers themselves have tended to present their own work as being basically about speech perception, not phonology. But the significance of linearity and phonetic definition becomes clear when we consider segmental analogues of what the 'phonetic' approach to intonation involves.

Consider first phonetic definition. In segmental phonetics, instrumental research is devoted to studying the physical cues to properties like voicing or vowel quality or nasality. Phoneticians do not try to study the physical cues to properties like plurality or verb aspect or negation – it seems obvious that it would be pointless to do so. The segmental categories investigated by instrumental phonetics are *phonological*, not lexical or grammatical. Yet one of the characteristic features of traditional instrumental research on intonation is that in many cases it attempts to identify direct physical correlates of meanings or linguistic functions. The anomaly is seldom commented on or even recognised, but this anomaly is precisely what the IPO model avoids when it deals in 'Type 2 Rises' rather than 'continuation rises'.

Now consider linearity. As an object of phonetic investigation, the 'F_0 contour' is actually quite problematic. Phoneticians who try to describe the shapes of F_0 contours would never treat 'second formant contours' in the same way. In segmental phonetics, it is taken for granted that the course of the second formant through an utterance is a function of the sequence of segmental sounds of which the utterance happens to consist. The second formant – like other formants – is often modelled phonetically as a sequence of locally specified targets or steady states and transitions between them. These are the assumptions that the IPO approach brings to the task of modelling F_0: the 'F_0 contour', like the 'second formant contour', arises from a linear sequence of categorically distinct elements.

Finally, of course, we come to the most important question: who is right? It is all very well to identify the underlying theoretical assumptions of the IPO approach, and all very well to argue that these assumptions are in line with the great body of instrumental phonetic work on segmental properties of speech: it remains the case that the IPO assumptions could be wrong. In the next section, therefore, I discuss the evidence for describing intonation in terms of linear strings of elements that are not defined in terms of their function.

1.3   Evidence for phonological assumptions in describing intonation

1.3.1   *Intonational meaning in experimental research*
As I just noted, segmental phonetic research almost never looks for things like 'acoustic correlates of negation', but in intonational work comparable quests are commonplace. 'Acoustic correlates' have been sought for a variety of meaningful aspects of utterances, including surface constituent structure, the discourse status of referring expressions, and speaker emotion and attitude. For the most part the authors of such studies make no attempt to identify phonological categories. Instead, they simply take a set of intonational functions for granted, and assume that the most appropriate description of how these functions are expressed is in terms of the continuously varying parameters of speech – in particular, the suprasegmental parameters of F_0, duration, and intensity.

Good examples of this approach are found in the work of William Cooper and his associates. For example, in their study of cues to surface constituent structure, Cooper and Paccia-Cooper assume that 'boundary strength' (defined in terms of the depth of the node in the syntactic tree that dominates the words on either side of the boundary) is directly reflected in various acoustic parameters, such as pause duration and the depth of F_0 valleys in the 'fall–rise' patterns; related work is reported by Cooper and Sorensen (1981). (Note that the 'fall–rises' in the work of Cooper and his associates are not usually the same as those of the British tradition.) In the same vein, Eady and Cooper and their collaborators (Cooper, Eady, and Mueller 1985; Eady *et al.* 1986) attempt to identify the acoustic correlates of notions like 'focus', 'contrast', and the distinction between questions and statements. Their procedures treat these notions as independent variables, and the various acoustic parameters they measure (such as duration and peak F_0 of focused word) as dependent variables. They take it for granted that functions like focus will have acoustic correlates, as the title of one of their papers ('Acoustical characteristics of sentential focus') makes clear.

A number of other more recent studies have attempted to find direct acoustic correlates of the 'givenness' of referring expressions. For example, Fowler and Housum (1987) and Shields and Balota (1991) found that 'second mentions' of nouns in a discourse were shorter than 'first mentions', while Koopmans-van Beinum and van Bergem (1989) found spectral and F_0 effects of givenness but no durational effects. To be sure, these are in the first instance psycholinguistic studies, concerned primarily with the *intelligibility* of referring expressions when presented out of context. The acoustic properties of the referring expressions are measured as part of an effort to explain the observed differences of intelligibility. Nevertheless, these studies fit the mould discussed in this section, in the sense that the measured acoustic properties are treated as direct correlates of givenness.

By directly relating phonetic detail to categories of meaning, the approach taken in these studies presupposes that intonation is unlike the rest of language, because it has no place for a phonological level of description. This presupposition is implicit, of course. Intonational phonology is simply not an issue in much of this research. It seems fair to say that in virtually all of these studies the main motivation for treating suprasegmental features in terms of continuous physical parameters is laudable: to avoid the seemingly unverifiable speculation of 'impressionistic' work, and to permit the use of familiar parametric statistical approaches. But the use of rigorous methods is no guarantee of useful findings if the conceptual foundations of the research are flawed.

The absence of any attention to phonological structure was discussed at some length by Pierrehumbert and Liberman (1982: 691) in their review of Cooper and Sorensen (1981). They comment on Cooper and Sorensen's treatment of the relation between syntactic boundary strength and the depth of F_0 valleys as follows:

> The consensus of the linguistic sources cited is that the basic fall–rise patterns fall into two categories. One pattern, which has a fall to the bottom of the speaker's range, occurs at the boundary between one intonation phrase and the next. The other, which involves a less extreme fall, occurs within a single intonation phrase . . . At a given syntactic boundary, an intonational boundary is typically optional. Its probability of occurring is influenced by phrase length, speech rate and style, and the information structure of the discourse . . .

> Cooper and Sorensen present a different picture, although they do not
> note that it differs from that developed by linguists. Under their account,
> the depth of the valley in fall–rise contours varies continuously, reflecting
> syntactic boundary strength . . . Unfortunately, the experimental data pre-
> sented to support Cooper and Sorensen's position are compiled in a way
> that cannot discriminate between it and the alternative . . . [Their] proce-
> dure would give a reasonable picture of data that varied continuously, but
> it would also make data that fall into two categories with varying proba-
> bility look as if they varied continuously.

Pierrehumbert and Liberman's criticism, in short, is that the constructs of
linguistic analyses of intonation have simply not been given a chance to
demonstrate their validity.

This brings up a further point: we are not dealing only with philosophi-
cal foundations, but with fairly clear assumptions that can be made explicit
and used as the basis of testable experimental questions. Whether we
should adopt a 'phonological' approach to intonation is not primarily a
matter of taste but an *empirical question*. Nothing in the phonological
approach requires us to use the impressionistic methods of half a century
ago, just as nothing in segmental phonetics requires us to limit ourselves to
IPA transcription. It is possible to work with the ideas of intonational
phonology and still do methodologically rigorous instrumental and experimental work. When we do so, we often find that hypotheses based on puta-
tive phonological categories stand up to empirical tests.

For example, none of the works cited above on the acoustic correlates of
givenness makes any attempt to control for the presence or absence of pitch
accent. They proceed as if there were no categorical distinction
accented–unaccented, and they treat the acoustic differences that they find
as a direct reflection of discourse status. This neglect of pitch accent was
called into question by Hawkins and Warren (1991), who performed the
same sort of study as Fowler and Housum (1987) (i.e. testing the intelligibility of words excised from context). Hawkins and Warren showed that
accentedness, not givenness *per se*, was the main source of differences in
intelligibility. Duration correlates with accentedness, and accentedness correlates with givenness, but the continuous acoustic properties measured by
Fowler and Housum are properly seen as a reflection of accentedness, and
hence only indirectly of givenness. In fact, more recently, Bard and her colleagues (e.g. Bard *et al.* 1991) have shown that, when accent is duly controlled for, there is still a direct effect of givenness on the duration and
intelligibility of referring expressions; that is, it appears possible to distinguish categorical or linguistic reflexes of givenness, such as accentedness,

from paralinguistic or continuous correlates, such as duration and precision of articulation.

For a more extended illustration of the potential usefulness of phonological constructs in explaining the function of intonation, consider a series of experiments on intonation and emotion by Scherer and his collaborators (Scherer, Ladd, and Silverman 1984; Ladd *et al.* 1985; Ladd, Scherer, and Silverman 1986). This is an area of study in which instrumental approaches have been widely adopted. In particular, there are many studies in which investigators identify a list of 'emotions' in advance and then set about trying to identify acoustic parameters that correlate with the chosen emotions (e.g. Lieberman and Michaels 1962; Kramer 1964; Apple and Hecht 1982). Instead of following this procedure, Scherer *et al.* based testable hypotheses on two different sets of assumptions broadly corresponding to the instrumental and the impressionistic approaches.

Scherer *et al.* refer to these two approaches as the 'covariance view' and the 'configuration view'. These terms (which are admittedly not the most memorable) are based on statistical notions. The 'covariance view' involves the claim that there are direct acoustic cues to emotional messages, independent of any linguistic message being expressed, and that these cues are continuous or parametric variables that *covary* with the message. The 'configuration view' is the idea that intonation has a linguistic structure involving contrasting categories such as rise and fall, and that in statistical terms the emotion is conveyed at least in part by *configurations of category variables*. In the terms we are using here, the covariance view is the one underlying most instrumental work, while the configuration view presupposes a notion of intonational phonology.

In order to evaluate the validity of these two views, Scherer *et al.* had judges rate the emotional force of a set of ordinary utterances. The utterances were all questions, and were all taken from recordings of spontaneous speech. One set of conditions was designed to test the assumptions of the 'covariance' or non-phonological approach. In some of these conditions, the utterances were modified in various ways to render the words unintelligible, and in one condition the judges rated only transcripts of the sentences. Not surprisingly, there was good agreement among the judges on the emotional force of the modified utterances, and little agreement on the transcripts. This part of the experiment thus shows very clearly that some of the emotional message of an utterance is indeed non-phonological, or (in Scherer *et al.*'s terms) works according to the assumptions of the 'covariance' view.

In a subsequent part of their study, however, Scherer *et al.* had judges rate the sentences in their original form, without any acoustic manipulations, and analysed the results looking for categorical effects. Such effects appeared unambiguously. Even on a very crude phonological categorisation of the intonation contours by final pitch movement (boundary rise vs. boundary fall), and a categorisation of the utterances as either yes–no or WH (question-word) questions, Scherer *et al.* showed that the judgements were affected by certain combinations (or in their terms, 'configurations') of categories. For example, yes–no questions with a final fall were judged strongly 'challenging', while none of the other three combinations was. In the same way, there was a strong interaction of contour type and question type in the extent to which utterances were rated 'agreeable' and 'polite': rising yes–no questions and falling WH questions (i.e. the combinations of intonation and sentence type that are commonly supposed to be normal) were rated high on these scales, while falling yes–no questions and rising WH questions were rated low.

Scherer *et al.*'s findings suggest that, in order to understand how intonation conveys emotion, it is not enough to look for continuous acoustic variables that directly signal the strength of some emotional message. In addition, it is also necessary to consider the categorical presence or absence of certain intonational elements at specific points in the contour (e.g. boundary rise vs. boundary fall) in conjunction with other categorical linguistic properties of utterances (e.g. question type). Experiments that ignore the phonological structure of the suprasegmental cues may simply fail to address part of the problem.

1.3.2   *Linearity and superposition in modelling F_0*

A more specific point of contention between phonological and non-phonological approaches to intonation is the question of what I have elsewhere (Ladd 1988) called *overlay* models of F_0. Overlay or superposition models treat the linguistic pitch contour as if it were some sort of complex function, which can be decomposed into simpler component functions. Many descriptions of intonational systems of individual languages are expressed in such terms, with local 'bumps' (e.g. for accent on a prominent word) overlaid or superimposed on global shapes or slopes (e.g. for the distinction between a statement and a question). Bolinger has expressed the basis of this view metaphorically (1964 (1972a: 19f.)):

> The surface of the ocean responds to the forces that act upon it in movements resembling the ups and downs of the human voice. If our vision

could take it all in at once, we would discern several types of motion, involving a greater and greater expanse of sea and volume of water: ripples, waves, swells, and tides. It would be more accurate to say ripples *on* waves *on* swells *on* tides, because each larger movement carries the smaller ones on its back . . . In speech . . . the ripples are the accidental changes in pitch, the irrelevant quavers. The waves are the peaks and valleys that we call *accent*. The swells are the separations of our discourse into its larger segments. The tides are the tides of emotion.

Mathematical implementation of the metaphor was apparently first attempted by Öhman (1967), but is perhaps best known in Fujisaki's F_0 model (e.g. Fujisaki 1983; Fujisaki and Hirose, 1982). Fujisaki's model posits two components to F_0, a *phrase component* and an *accent component*. The phrase component is modelled as an impulse response: graphically, it rises rapidly to a peak and then decays exponentially towards an asymptote. The accent component is modelled as a step function, which creates a string of steps up and steps down that represent the local rises and falls of pitch at accented syllables. The step function is smoothed by the addition of a time constant and is then added to the phrase component to create the contour. This is shown in figure 1.2.

The overlay approach, like the metaphor on which it is based, is intuitively appealing, and is almost certainly the most suitable model of certain aspects of F_0. For example, so-called microprosody – the local perturbations in the F_0 contour that are due to the effects of certain segment types – can best be seen as local 'ripples' on the contour that results from the speaker's linguistic intentions.[7] Similarly, the 'tides of emotion' that raise or lower the overall level of the voice can also perhaps best be factored out of the description of the contour. But most overlay models do not deal in detail with either microprosody or overall level. Instead, their main concern is the relation between local F_0 events (pitch movements on individual syllables or words due to accent and lexical tone) and F_0 trends that extend over somewhat larger domains (such as 'declination'). This is true of Fujisaki's model, and of quite a number of others, including the work of O'Shaughnessy and Allen (1983) on English, Grønnum (e.g. Thorsen 1980a, 1985) on Danish, and Gårding and her colleagues (e.g. Gårding 1983, 1987) on various languages including Swedish and Chinese. In all of these models, the emphasis is on the superposition of contour shapes for short domains (sentence or accent group) on contour shapes for longer domains (phrase or utterance). Microprosody and overall raising of the voice are considered only in passing. I will therefore focus the following remarks on the notion of the 'phrase component' (or its equivalent) and the

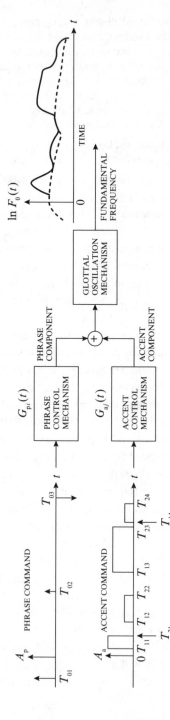

Figure 1.2 Basic features of Fujisaki's model of intonation. The output of the accent component (a string of rise–level–fall sequences of varying height and duration, lower left side of figure) is added to the output of the phrase component (a series of one or more impulses, upper left side of figure). The impulse response decays asymptotically and the result of adding the two components is a detailed model of a pitch contour (right side of figure).

way it is used in overlay models generally. Quite apart from the general question of whether it is sensible to attempt to model an overall contour shape (see my comments on the 'second formant contour' in the previous section), there are empirical and theoretical problems with phrase components that have never been successfully dealt with.

The most conspicuous problem with these models is that they have difficulty providing a quantitative definition of the phrase-level components that they presuppose. Even something as apparently straightforward as the slope of 'declination' has resisted quantitative characterisation. In Vaissière's words, 'declination is a general tendency easily detected from a visual inspection of relatively long stretches of F_0 curve, but calculation of the exact rate of declination is a difficult task' (1983: 56). Components with more complex shapes, which are posited in some overlay models, are correspondingly more difficult to define. For example, in the model proposed by Gårding (1983), a 'grid' is fitted to the tonally or accentually determined 'turning points' of the contour, as shown in figure 1.3. The shape of this grid is then taken as an indication of the global properties of the contour, and is related to, for instance, the distinction between questions and statements. As a rough expression of the relationship between global and local properties of contours, Gårding's model, like overlay models in general, makes intuitive sense. But if the 'grid' is to be something more than an impressionistic smoothing of graphically presented data, then it will have to be defined as a mathematical function. Moreover, if the mathematical function is to have any predictive value, it will have to generate a variety of distinct realisations (e.g. for utterances of different length), and, most importantly, it will have to provide a common characterisation of contour shapes that are perceived to have the same linguistic function. For example, if Chinese questions and statements are distinguished by the slope and width of the grid, then the function will have to provide a quantitative characterisation that distinguishes question grids from statement grids, so that the model can be tested against empirical data. As far as I know, Gårding has not attempted any such definitions for any of the profusion of grid types that she posits.

Even for overlay models without such a rich inventory of possible global components, the problem of explicit definition remains substantial. Grønnum, for example, makes a strong empirical case for a three-way distinction of overall slope across a phrase contour in Danish: the shallowest slope is interrogative, the steepest slope is complete (final) declarative, and intermediate slopes are incomplete (non-final) declarative (Thorsen 1980a)

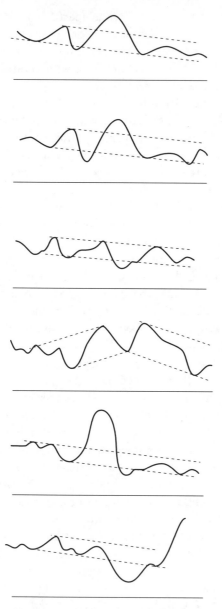

Figure 1.3 The 'grid' in Gårding's model of intonation. One or more straight lines are fitted to most of the local minima and most of the local maxima of a pitch contour to give an approximation of its overall range and direction. The figure shows grids applied to several different renditions of the Swedish sentence *Hon gick inte och la sej* ('She didn't go to bed'). From Gårding 1983. See further figure 4.3.

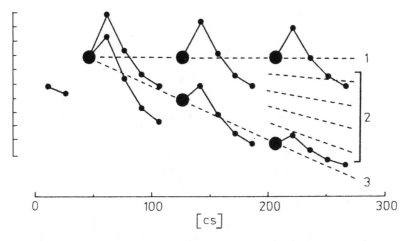

Figure 1.4 Grønnum's model of Danish sentence intonation. The sentence intonation component is modelled as a straight line of variable slope (nearly level for interrogative (line 1 on the figure), steeply declining for completed declarative (line 3), intermediate for incomplete declarative (four lines labelled 2)). The local low–rise–fall accentual configurations are fitted to the sentence intonation line. From Thorsen 1983.

(see figure 1.4). On this basis she argues that global slope is a distinctive element of an adequate model of intonation. But she makes no attempt to define the slopes except relative to other possibilities in the system: that is, she does not attempt to explain how, given a specific slope, a listener (or an investigator) can say with some certainty 'That was an interrogative contour'; she gives no quantitative characterisation of what is distinctive or invariant about any of the three slopes.

One specific aspect of the quantitative definition problem is the problem of advance planning or *lookahead*. Part of the reason it is difficult to provide quantitative descriptions of F_0 trends is that in general such trends are quite plainly dependent on the length of the domain to which they apply. Specifically with respect to declination, it has been found in numerous studies that the longer the domain over which declination can be observed, the less steep the declination slope. (An alternative way of stating this is that the amount of F_0 drop across a declination domain is relatively constant, irrespective of the length of the domain.) This means that any speech production model – or any F_0 generation model for speech synthesis – must know in advance how long a declination domain is in order to start the declination going at the appropriate slope. This degree of lookahead may be psycholinguistically implausible, and for speech synthesis models is certainly computationally expensive. This problem has been discussed at some length by Liberman and Pierrehumbert (1984: 220ff.).

As it happens, the quantitative definition problem has been solved by Fujisaki. There is only one type of shape for the phrase component, and it is generated as a decaying impulse response so there is no need for look-ahead. Indeed, one might with some justification regard Fujisaki's model as a possible phonetic realisation model of a linear phonological description: several people have suggested to me that there is no deep incompatibility between Fujisaki's approach and a linear phonology. Both the accent commands and the phrase commands 'happen' at specifiable times, like the events in the linear string of the IPO model. The basic compatibility can be seen in Möbius's work on German intonation, in which many of the assumptions of linear intonational phonology are integrated with a Fujisaki-style realisation model (Möbius 1993; Möbius, Pätzold, and Hess 1993).

But there *is* a problem with Fujisaki's model, and it has to do with the intended relation between the phrase component and the prosodic struc-ture of an utterance. Phrase commands are supposed to reflect phrasing in some way – say, a phrase command at the beginning of each intonational phrase. Empirically, however, this condition cannot always be met. In some cases, the result of a phrase command where it would be expected yields a contour of the wrong shape; to get the right shape, we have to put phrase commands in places that make no sense linguistically. Obviously, the appropriate goal of Fujisaki's model (or any model) is not just to model the F_0 contour as a physical signal, but to be able to relate the location of sig-nificant events in the contour to linguistic variables. Möbius (1993) has dis-cussed various problems in providing plausible linguistic motivation for the location of certain phrase commands that are 'needed' to make the contour come out the right shape.[8]

1.3.3   Intonation and lexical pitch features

The overlay approach is based not only on Bolinger's wave metaphor, but on a widespread (and partially justifiable) view of the relation between into-nation and lexical features such as tone or accent. A traditional way of thinking about this relation is that all languages have 'intonation', and that in addition some languages have local pitch perturbations for 'word accent' or 'tone' overlaid on the global intonation. There is, as we will see at several points throughout the book, some phonetic basis for this idea, and in fact I believe it is an important challenge for linear phonological theories of intonation to deal with tone–intonation relations of this sort.

Where the traditional view is not justified, however, is in the corollary it draws for the relation between intonational function and intonational phonetics. Overlay models assume not only that all pitch features extend over some domain, but also that the domain to which a pitch feature applies functionally must be the domain over which it extends phonetically. That is, they assume that *the phonetic extent of a pitch feature should reflect its function.* In one common formulation (e.g. Pike 1948: ch. 1; Laver 1994: ch. 15), 'tone' is a feature of syllables, 'pitch accent' ('word pitch', 'word tone', etc.) of words, and 'intonation' of phrases or sentences. But there is empirical evidence that this is not true, and that pitch features whose function is clearly 'intonational' can nevertheless be quite precisely localised in the utterance. This was first clearly demonstrated in Gösta Bruce's work on Swedish word accent (Bruce 1977). Bruce's specific concern was to develop an account of how lexical accent distinctions in Stockholm Swedish are manifested phonetically in different sentence contexts, but his solution to this problem lays the foundation for a more general theory of how word-level and sentence-level features interact.

Swedish, like Norwegian and a handful of other European languages, has a morphologically and lexically conditioned distinction of *accent type.* The main stressed syllable of each word, in addition to being stressed, bears one or the other of two accents, called acute and grave or simply Accent 1 and Accent 2. The classic Swedish minimal pair is *anden* 'the duck' (Accent 1, morphologically *and + -en*) and *anden* 'the spirit' (Accent 2, morphologically *ande + -en*).[9] The phonetic difference between the two accents is very striking in some environments and exceedingly subtle in others, but it typically involves a difference in the pitch contours of words and is therefore often described as a difference of 'pitch accent' or 'word accent'. Figure 1.5 shows pitch traces for the 'citation forms' (the forms in which words are typically spoken in isolation) of two segmentally similar words that differ in accent type.

As can be seen from figure 1.5, the phonetic difference between the two accent types is superficially a difference between single peaked (Accent 1) and double peaked (Accent 2) pitch contours that span the whole word. This is generally true of citation forms in Stockholm Swedish. However, Bruce established that the genuinely distinctive feature for the two accent types is the *alignment of an underlying pitch peak with the stressed vowel*: in

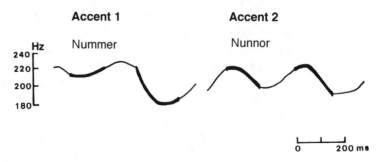

Figure 1.5 The Swedish word accent distinction. Citation form contours are shown for the words *nummer* ('number', Accent 1) and *nunnor* ('nuns', Accent 2). From Bruce 1977.

Accent 1 the peak precedes the onset of the stressed vowel by a consider-able extent, so that if there are no preceding unstressed syllables the stressed vowel simply begins low, while in Accent 2 the peak and the subsequent drop in pitch more or less coincide in time with the stressed vowel and are therefore always present in the phonetic F_0 contour.

The apparent distinction between single- and double-peaked word con-tours actually results from the interaction of word accent features and sen-tence intonation features in citation forms. There are two relevant features of sentence intonation, a peak and a final low. The peak or 'phrase accent' is theoretically aligned late in the prominent word, while the final low accompanies the end of the utterance, but of course in a citation form both the peak and the final low occur on the same word as the accentual fall. When these intonational features occur after Accent 2, in which the accent has already produced a clear peak on the accented vowel, the result is a 'second' peak. But when they follow Accent 1, in which the accentual peak may not be realised as such, the result is a phonetic rise across the accented vowel to the single peak in the utterance. The single peak/double peak man-ifestation of the distinction in citation form thus depends crucially on sen-tence intonation features, because citation forms of words are also complete utterances and hence contain sentence-level intonational features as well. In other contexts, as Bruce amply proved, the accentual distinction based on early and late alignment of the fall is invariably present, whereas the intonational features occur only on certain words in a sentence and there-fore affect the F_0 contour associated with the two accent types only in certain contexts.

In addition to providing an elegant and convincing solution for a long-standing problem of Scandinavian phonology, Bruce's analysis provides clear evidence of a case in which pitch features whose function relates to domains of different sizes (viz. the word accents and the sentence-level intonation features) interact as a *sequence of phonetic events* rather than by overlaying small-domain features on large-domain ones. This does not, of course, establish that phonological structure more in keeping with the wave metaphor is impossible, but it strengthens the argument for a rigorously linear phonological model, because it shows that such a model provides an accurate account of a case that *prima facie* might be expected to support the overlay approach.

1.4   Paralanguage and intonation

In the preceding section I have tried to show that traditional 'instrumental' approaches to studying intonation are based on assumptions of questionable validity. I have also argued that one can recognise the existence of phonological structure in intonation, in the manner of the 'impressionistic' descriptions of the 1940s and 1950s, and nevertheless produce methodologically sound work that accounts for the same general range of instrumental data. However, there is still certainly a problem in determining the phonological structure of intonation. The problem arises from the close link between intonation and 'paralinguistic' features in speech.

1.4.1   Relation between linguistic and paralinguistic features
The terms *paralanguage* and *paralinguistic* appear to have been coined in the 1950s to cover aspects of vocal communication that are clearly meaningful but not apparently organised along linguistic lines. (The basic reference is Trager 1958; for a good discussion of the history of the terms and the related ideas see Crystal 1969: ch. 2.) Paralinguistic messages deal primarily with basic aspects of interpersonal interaction – such as aggression, appeasement, solidarity, condescension – and with the speaker's current emotional state – such as fear, surprise, anger, joy, boredom. They are non-propositional and difficult to paraphrase precisely, and yet in many circumstances they communicate powerfully and effectively. Paralinguistic cues can be consistently interpreted even in the absence of the linguistic message; for example, paralinguistic meaning comes through when the linguistic message is experimentally obscured by such means as acoustic filtering, when the linguistic message is in a language that the listener does not

understand, and in some cases even when the listener is non-human. That is, stretches of speech can be produced in such a way as to convey, *irrespective of the linguistic message*, that the speaker is relaxed or impatient or aggressive or whatever.

The relation between paralinguistic and linguistic features is, by and large, unproblematic. The paralinguistic signals represent a parallel channel or channels of information, and do not for the most part alter or obscure the identity of the linguistic elements. Someone may call my name angrily, or hesitantly, or with surprise, but it is still unambiguously my name. Nevertheless, a few comments about the relation between the two types of information are in order.

First, the parallel paralinguistic channels are often tightly coordinated in time with the linguistic channel. Much research (e.g. Kendon 1972; McNeill 1992) has shown that nods, hand gestures, and eye contact coincide very precisely with events in the spoken message. For example, hand movements often coincide with stressed syllables, and gestures frequently accompany, for example, the introduction of a new entity into the discourse (Levy and McNeill 1992).

Second, the paralinguistic message obviously affects the interpretation of the utterance as a whole. Pike's formulation from half a century ago can scarcely be improved on:

> the hearer is frequently more interested in the speaker's attitude than in his words – that is, whether a sentence is 'spoken with a smile' or with a sneer . . . If one says something insulting, but smiles in face and voice, the utterance may be a great compliment; but if one says something very complimentary, but with an intonation of contempt, the result is an insult. A highly forceful or exciting statement in a very matter-of-fact intonation may, by its lack of balance, produce one type of irony. (1945: 22)

In interpreting any utterance, in other words, we take into account all the communicative channels, not just the linguistic one. But that fact does not mean that the identity of the channels is confounded; on the contrary, Pike's reference to mismatches between the linguistic message and the attitude with which it is conveyed suggests that the two remain clearly distinct.

Finally and most importantly, we need to mention the nature of the phonetic interaction between linguistic and vocal paralinguistic cues. While I have just argued that the identity of the linguistic and paralinguistic is not normally confounded, it is certainly true that some paralinguistic messages are carried on the same acoustic signal as the linguistic message. How do the two interact?

I believe that, at a fairly low level of analysis, paralinguistic cues should be regarded as *modifications of the way in which phonological categories are realised*. Such modifications do not normally affect the categorical phonology. For example, it is known (Tartter 1980) that smiling has an effect on vowel formants, and that this effect can be detected by listeners in recorded speech (i.e. without seeing the speaker's face). The paralinguistic message modifies the acoustic realisation of the vowel categories, but does not modify them so much as to distort their identity. Closer to the topic of this book, we may note that paralinguistic modifications of pitch range – such as raising the voice in anger – modify the realisation of lexical tones in languages like Yoruba or Chinese, but do not normally obscure their identity. This is true even in languages in which the tone phonemes are distinctive levels (such as High, Mid, and Low in Yoruba); in some way that we do not entirely understand, the phonological essence of the levels must be invariant relative to a phonetic frame of reference that can be modified for paralinguistic purposes.

Distortion of phonological identity is not impossible, however. In some cases paralinguistic modification may cause instances of a given phonological category to sound like instances of some other. A clear example of this is provided by a paralinguistic lip-pursing gesture which is very characteristic of German speech; it seems to convey something like friendliness or reassurance or some other kind of empathy with the hearer. The acoustic effects of this gesture are, not surprisingly, rather similar to those of phonologically specified lip rounding, and a phonologically unrounded vowel spoken with paralinguistic lip pursing may sound more like a rounded vowel than like a typical unrounded one. This is sometimes represented orthographically in written dialogue by using the letters for rounded vowels. In German comic books I have observed both *nöö* and *mööönsch* as representations of pursed-lips pronunciations of, respectively, *nee* ('no', colloquial) and *Mensch* ('man!', colloquial interjection). In Kurt Vonnegut's novel *Slaughterhouse-Five*, German railway guards are reported as lazily saying 'Yo, yo' (presumably *Ja, ja* 'Yes, yes' with paralinguistic lip pursing) to American prisoners of war who have just reported that one of their fellows has died in transit.

Nevertheless, such cases are relatively rare, and the only people who seem to notice the phonetic 'neutralisation' involved are non-native speakers, and dialogue writers who have the freedom from orthographic convention allowed by the comic book medium. Normal listeners hear the phonological categories and the phonetic modifications in their separate channels.

Moreover, languages seem not to allow many such ambiguities to arise: for example, Yoruba in general seems not to use paralinguistic modifications of pitch range to signal greater emphasis on a particular word or phrase (see Rowlands 1969: 24ff.), presumably because this would result in too many occasions where lexical identity could be obscured or neutralised.

1.4.2   Defining properties of paralanguage

While the distinction between linguistic and paralinguistic as just described seems fairly clear, there is one area where it breaks down quite substantially. This is in the area of intonation. The most obvious paralinguistic cues are global properties of the speech signal such as loudness, voice quality, and pitch range. The properties involved in intonation are therefore also involved in conveying paralinguistic messages. This means that in analysing intonation we are faced with the task of distinguishing linguistic and para-linguistic aspects of the same signal. In principle, as we just saw, this is not a problem, but in practice, in a language like English, it can be very tricky to separate paralinguistic effects on F_0 from what I am calling intonational effects. It is therefore important to try to understand the difference between paralinguistic and linguistic signalling before we tackle intonational phonology.

The central difference between paralinguistic and linguistic messages resides in the *quantal* or *categorical* structure of linguistic signalling and the *scalar* or *gradient* nature of paralanguage. In linguistic signalling, physical continua are partitioned into categories, so that close similarity of phonetic form is generally of no relevance for meaning: that is, /θ/ and /f/ are different phonemes in English, despite their close phonetic similarity, and pairs of words like *thin* and *fin* are not only clearly distinct but also semantically unrelated. In paralinguistic signalling, by contrast, semantic continua are matched by phonetic ones. If raising the voice can be used to signal anger or surprise, raising the voice a lot can signal violent anger or great surprise. Paralinguistic signals that are phonetically similar generally mean similar things. This feature of paralinguistic signalling is often referred to as 'gra-dience' (Bolinger 1961a); in my view it is the defining characteristic. The difference between language and paralanguage is a matter of *the way the sound–meaning relation is structured*.

I emphasise this in order to draw attention to three aspects of paralan-guage which may at first appear to be defining characteristics but on closer inspection are not. First, paralanguage is not a matter of specific acoustic properties. Voice quality is commonly, perhaps even universally, used paralinguistically, but there are numerous examples of lexical 'phonemic' distinctions of voice quality as well. For example, in Hindi and certain other Indo-Aryan languages the series of stops often called 'voiced aspirates' are actually produced with a special type of voicing: Ladefoged (1982: 132ff.) describes them as 'murmured' stops and states that they involve a period of murmur or breathy vibration of the vocal folds during and immediately following the release of the stop. In many varieties of Chinese, some tone phonemes are distinguished not only by characteristic F_0 patterns but by differences of voice quality as well (e.g. Rose 1989, 1990). As Ladefoged noted in a slightly different context (1983: 351), 'what is a pathological voice quality in one language may be phonologically contrastive in another. Putting it more colloquially, "one person's voice disorder is another person's phoneme".' There is nothing intrinsically paralinguistic about voice quality, and *mutatis mutandis*, the same applies to other common paralinguistic cues as well.

Nor is the difference between language and paralanguage a matter of the domain over which a particular acoustic property is present. Some paralinguistic features are indeed a matter of what Laver (1980) has called 'long-term settings', such as an overall raising of the voice to express active emotions like anger or surprise. But it is important not to equate 'paralinguistic' with 'long-term': paralinguistic features may also be linked phonetically to individual parts of the message and their effect accordingly localised. Indeed, by coupling paralinguistic cues to individual words or phrases we can achieve a level of expressiveness that transcends the signalling power of either words or paralanguage functioning separately. (Imagine, for example, an unsympathetic lecturer attaching paralinguistic cues for sarcasm to a single word repeated from a naive question by a student.) Crystal's transcriptions of English natural speech (in e.g. Crystal 1969) contain many indications of paralinguistic markers attached to single words or phrases.

Finally, the difference between linguistic and paralinguistic signalling is not simply a matter of the kind of message conveyed. Obviously, it is impossible to express propositions like '$e = mc^2$' or 'Do you remember the great 1947 Burgundies we used to drink in Poitiers?' without resorting to true language, but it does not follow that it is impossible to use true language to convey subtle emotional or interpersonal messages. Probably all languages contain lexical items and grammatical categories whose main function is to convey nuances of doubt, irony, surprise, condescension, solidarity, and the like. These include categories of modality in verb inflection (e.g. the choice between the subjunctive and indicative in relative clauses in French or Italian); derivational categories like diminutives, augmentatives, and pejoratives (in Italian and many other languages); and 'particles' like German *doch, wohl, eben, ja*, and the like. These can be every bit as effective as strictly paralinguistic cues for conveying emotional or interpersonal meanings.

On all three of the criteria just discussed – its acoustic nature, the domain over which it extends, and the messages it conveys – intonation clearly 'feels' paralinguistic. First, the suprasegmental features that are used in intonation are commonly used in paralinguistic signalling: overall pitch range, loudness, and duration are almost certainly used paralinguistically in all languages. Second, at least some intonational features seem to spread over longer stretches of speech, and it is tempting to view the pitch contour of a sentence as a 'long-term setting' for the sentence as a whole. Third, intonational meaning is unquestionably affective and interpersonal, and almost never propositional: there are not many cases where intonation can reasonably be said to affect the truth value of an utterance.[10] But the claim made here is that none of these three factors is decisive. The real issue is whether intonation involves a categorical structure.

1.4.3   *Intonational meaning*
Let us return in closing to the issue of 'instrumental' and 'impressionistic' approaches to intonation. With the foregoing discussion behind us, it is now possible to see more clearly what the problems with these two approaches are. The difficulty with the 'instrumental' tradition is straightforward: traditional instrumental research of the sort discussed above *treats all intonational meaning as paralinguistic*. It looks for continuously variable phonetic properties of utterances that can be directly related to aspects of the utterance's meaning. While this approach is clearly appropriate for truly paralinguistic meaning (such as overall raising of the voice to convey greater emotional arousal or interest), it is clearly inappropriate for linguistic meaning (as the very idea of 'acoustic cues to negation' or 'acoustic cues to tense' makes clear). By approaching all of intonational meaning in this way, the traditional instrumental approach rules out *a priori* the possibility of finding evidence for phonological structure in intonation.

The problem with the 'impressionistic' tradition is more subtle. This approach starts from the assumption that there is phonological structure in intonation. The most basic task of any phonological analysis, as I suggested above, is to identify the categorical or quantal elements in a phonological system and to account for the ways in which the realisation of these elements varies. If intonational and paralinguistic messages are indeed distinct, then one of the sources of variation in the realisation of intonational categories is paralinguistic modification, and the basic task of analysing intonational phonology is to tell intonation and paralanguage apart.

In certain cases, there is broad agreement about which is which. For example, in an accent contour that rises to a peak and then falls to the bottom of the range, it is widely agreed that the height of the peak can vary paralinguistically to convey greater emphasis without affecting the linguistic identity of the contour; that is, the difference between the following two utterances:

(1.3)

He   didn't.   He   didn't.

would generally be treated as paralinguistic only. But in many cases one description presents as an intonational contrast what another treats as the result of paralinguistic variation. To continue with the example, in some descriptions (e.g. Schubiger 1958; O'Connor and Arnold 1973) there is said to be an intonational difference between a 'high fall' and a 'low fall', as in the following pair:

(1.4)

He   didn't.   He   didn't.

In other analyses (e.g. Palmer 1922; Crystal 1969) these are treated as paralinguistic variants of the same basic intonational category 'fall'. Since it is genuinely difficult to tell paralinguistic and intonational messages apart, and since there is no obvious independent body of theory nor standard of evidence to which one might appeal in order to decide issues like this, these disagreements have tended to remain unresolved. I have elsewhere (Ladd 1993a) referred to such disagreements as 'paralinguistic stalemates'.[11]

Despite these problems, we should not overlook the extent of the common ground in adherents of phonological approaches to intonation. In particular, I think it is legitimate to identify something that we might call the 'Linguist's Theory of Intonational Meaning' (see Ladd 1987a: 638). The central idea of this view is that *the elements of intonation have meaning.* These meanings are very general, but they are part of a system with a rich interpretative pragmatics, which gives rise to very specific and often quite vivid nuances in specific contexts. This view contrasts sharply with the assumptions underlying the instrumental approach, in which it is generally assumed that quite specific meanings, such as interrogation, anger, and incompleteness, are conveyed by rather general phonetic properties, such as overall raising of pitch, and that context-dependent pragmatic inference plays little role in the interpretation of intonational features.

The Linguist's Theory of Intonational Meaning is extremely widespread among linguists of otherwise diverse outlooks. Bolinger and Gussenhoven, for example, have extensively developed the idea of 'intonational morphemes'; much of their work on intonational meaning (especially Gussenhoven 1984; Bolinger 1986, 1989) consists of detailed explications of specific intonational nuances on the basis of postulated general meanings for specific elements of intonational analysis. Brazil (1975) presents some interesting preliminary ideas on the discourse function of the various nuclear tones of the British tradition, ideas that influenced Gussenhoven's analysis and are developed to some extent in more general work on discourse analysis by Brazil, Coulthard, and Johns (1980). Liberman (1975: section 3.2.5) discusses the general properties of intonational meaning at some length, emphasising the generality of the basic meanings and the vividness of specific nuances in specific contexts. My own work on 'stylised intonation' (Ladd 1978) is a concrete application of this general point of view; the same can be said of Pierrehumbert and Hirschberg 1990, which attempts to provide basic meanings for the elements of Pierrehumbert's description of English, some of which are strikingly reminiscent of Bolinger's analyses.

In short, linguists may have markedly different views about what the phonological categories of intonation are, but by and large they agree on how those categories contribute to the meaning of an utterance. The fact that this common understanding has not led to detailed agreement about the analysis of intonation does not mean that the Linguist's Theory is wrong, but is rather an indication of the difficulty of unravelling intonation from its paralinguistic context.

1.4.4   Prospect

The close acoustic and semiotic connection between intonation and paralinguistic cues is unquestionably the most important conceptual problem in studying intonation. My goal in this chapter has been, in effect, to show that this is only a problem, not an insurmountable hurdle. I have argued that there are good scientific reasons for trying to draw a clear distinction between paralinguistic uses of suprasegmental features and intonation in the sense that I have defined it here. More specifically, I have suggested that intonation has a categorical linguistic structure, consisting of a linear sequence of phonological events that occur at well-defined points in the utterance. The remainder of the book is devoted to exploring the consequences of that view.

2 *Fundamental concepts of the autosegmental–metrical theory*

Beginning in the late 1970s, an explicitly phonological approach to intonation began to develop, based on PhD theses by Liberman (1975), Bruce (1977), and Pierrehumbert (1980). This theory – which I will refer to as the autosegmental–metrical (AM) theory – is the subject of the rest of the book. Like the IPO theory, which was used in chapter 1 to illustrate the assumptions of a 'phonological' but none the less phonetically accountable approach to intonation, the AM theory adopts the phonological goal of being able to characterise contours adequately in terms of a string of categorically distinct elements, and the phonetic goal of providing a mapping from phonological elements to continuous acoustic parameters. However, unlike the IPO theory, which has its roots in work on speech perception, the AM theory grows out of theoretical problems in phonology. As a result there are certain differences of emphasis and several matters on which the two views substantially disagree.

This chapter sets out four basic tenets of the AM approach to intonation, comparing them where appropriate to divergent ideas from IPO and other theories. The four can be stated as follows:

1   *Linearity of tonal structure*: tonal structure is linear, consisting of a string of local *events* associated with certain points in the segmental string. Between such events the pitch contour is phonologically unspecified and can be described in terms of *transitions* from one event to the next. In languages like English, the most important events of the tonal string are *pitch accents*, which are associated with prominent syllables in the segmental string, and *edge tones*,[1] which are associated with the edges of prosodic domains of various sizes.

2   *Distinction between pitch accent and stress*: pitch accents, in languages that have them, serve as concrete perceptual cues to stress or prominence. However, they are in the first instance *intonational*

features, which are *associated with* certain syllables in accordance with various principles of prosodic organisation. The perceived prominence of accented syllables is, at least in some languages, a matter of *stress*, which can be distinguished from pitch accent.

3   *Analysis of pitch accents in terms of level tones*: pitch accents and edge tones in intonational languages can be analysed as consisting of primitive *level tones* or pitch targets, High (H) and Low (L).

4   *Local sources for global trends*: the phonetic realisation or *scaling* of any given H or L tone depends on a variety of factors (degree of emphasis, position in utterance, etc.) that are essentially orthogonal to its identity as H or L. Overall trends in pitch contours (e.g. gradual lowering of overall range) mostly reflect the operation of *localised* but *iterated* changes in scaling factors.

The chapter concentrates on the empirical motivation for these four tenets, and on showing how they contribute to a coherent theoretical whole. The discussion is, from the point of view of an adherent of Pierrehumbert's system, deliberately elementary; the style of presentation has a twofold goal. First, I aim to defend the AM approach in terms that will be accessible to anyone concerned with intonation, not just to adepts of generative phonology. Second, I wish to identify what I see as the essential ideas of the approach, and to distinguish them from the specific details of Pierrehumbert's analysis of English intonation. Closer consideration of Pierrehumbert's description of English will be undertaken in chapter 3.

2.1   Linearity of tonal structure

Like the IPO theory and the other phonologically oriented precursors mentioned in chapter 1, the AM theory represents pitch contours phonologically as sequences of discrete intonational events. For languages like English and Dutch, there are assumed to be two main types of such events, pitch accents and edge tones. In tone languages and other languages with lexically specified pitch features, the events may have different functions, but, as we shall see in section 4.4, the basic phonological structure is the same.

It is not difficult to demonstrate the usefulness of distinguishing between pitch accents and edge tones. Consider, for example, the rising–falling–rising tune that can be used in English for a strongly challenging or contradicting echo question, as in the following exchange:

(2.1)   A: I hear Sue's taking a course to become a driving instructor.

B: Sue!?

(In order to appreciate the point of these examples it is important to get the intonation right on B's reply. We are not interested in the more or less steadily rising contour that conveys surprise or merely a request for confirmation. The relevant tune is one that, on the monosyllabic utterance *Sue*, rises and falls and rises again. This is what is shown in the impressionistic pitch contour given in the example.) In the traditional British analysis, this contour would be described as a 'rise–fall–rise' nuclear tone, and on the basis of the monosyllabic utterance the rising–falling–rising melody appears as the essence of the contour type under consideration. However, we are not dealing with a global rise–fall–rise *shape* that applies holistically to an entire utterance. This can be seen when we put the same tune on a longer utterance:

(2.2)   A: I hear Sue's taking a course to become a driving instructor.

B: A driving instructor!?

The rise–fall–rise shape that spanned the entire one-syllable utterance in *Sue!?* is not simply stretched out over the six-syllable utterance here. Instead, the contour is seen to consist of a sequence of at least two discrete events, an accentual feature consisting of a rise through a prominent syllable (here *driv-*) followed by a fall, and an edge tone consisting of a rise during the last few tenths of a second of the utterance. The low level stretch on the syllables *-ing instruct-* is simply a transition between these two events, which can be vanishingly short (as on the monosyllable *Sue*) or as long as needed. For the identity of the tune it is the accentual rise-plus-fall and the boundary rise that 'count': they are the distinguishing features that lead us to describe the contour on *Sue!?* and that on *A driving instructor!?* as 'the same'. A description in these terms gives us a simple but accurate way of describing how the tune in question is applied to texts with varying numbers of syllables and different stress patterns.

By breaking down the contour into component parts in this way, we do not, of course, preclude the possibility of referring to larger units. In particular, most of the nuclear tones of the British tradition can be readily translated into combinations of pitch accents and edge tones (cf. Gussenhoven 1984; Roach 1994). In the example just given, we have not questioned the existence of a 'rise–fall–rise' nuclear tone in English, but have simply been more explicit about its internal structure. The rise–fall–rise nucleus in English can be seen as a composite or superordinate unit, a status comparable to that of the 'hat pattern' in the IPO model. As we shall see in chapter 3, the basic intonational taxonomy of the British tradition is not for the most part rendered obsolete by the theoretical framework presented here, only cast in a new light. There is no necessary contradiction in recognising both the functional unity of 'nuclear tones' or other such 'tunes' and the phonological separateness of their component parts.

On the other hand, by distinguishing accents from edge tones we may be able to resolve some long-standing problems in the traditional British taxonomy. In particular, much of the difficulty with the variety of falling–rising tunes in English (see e.g. Lee 1956; Sharp 1958; O'Connor and Arnold 1973: 29; Gussenhoven 1984: ch. 3) can be seen as a consequence of failing to make this distinction: there does seem to be a characteristic rise–fall–rise intonational unit in English, but it can probably be distinguished from essentially adventitious sequences of a falling accent and an independently selected boundary rise. Moreover, the AM theory does diverge significantly from most past work in drawing an explicit distinction between *events* and *transitions*. It recognises that some parts of contours are linguistically important, and others are merely what happens between the important parts. Furthermore, it assumes that the important parts are localised 'events', not long stretches of contour. This is an important point of difference between the AM theory and the IPO theory: the latter allows linguistically specified line segments (in particular, the 'Type 4 Rise' and 'Type D Fall' in the IPO analysis of Dutch) that may span several syllables, like the 'heads' of the traditional British description. From the point of view of the AM theory, as has been pointed out by, for example, Ladd (1983a: 747ff.) and Cruttenden (1992a), such line segments can simply be treated as the gradual transition from a high level at the end of one local event to a low level at the beginning of the next.

2.2   Pitch accents, prominence, and tune–text association

As we just saw, the phonological elements of the pitch contour that accompany certain stressed syllables in languages like English or Dutch are known in the AM theory as pitch accents. A pitch accent may be defined as a local feature of a pitch contour – usually but not invariably a *pitch change*, and often involving a local maximum or minimum – which signals that the syllable with which it is associated is *prominent* in the utterance. This use of the term 'pitch accent' was first proposed by Bolinger (1958) and resurrected by Pierrehumbert (1980),[2] and is now in general use.

Bolinger originally proposed the notion of pitch accent as a way of making sense of experimental data (in particular the findings of Fry 1955, 1958) showing that pitch change is a major cue to the perception of stress. In Bolinger's view, 'stress' is an abstract lexical property of individual syllables, while 'pitch accent' is actual prominence in an utterance. If a word is prominent in a sentence, this prominence is realised as a pitch accent on the 'stressed' syllable of the word. Much the same view was put forth early in the development of the IPO model, where pitch accents are known as 'prominence-lending pitch movements', and little consideration is given to supposed differences of prominence not involving pitch movement. In the AM view of pitch accent, beginning with Liberman (1975) and Pierrehumbert (1980), there is a shift of emphasis: pitch accents are viewed in the first instance as building blocks of pitch contours, and stress is treated as a separate feature of the phonological organisation of utterances. In order to clarify the significance of this change of outlook, it will first be necessary to take a more detailed look at the whole problem of stress.

2.2.1   The phonetic nature of stress

Probably no topic in the general area of intonation and suprasegmentals has posed such a puzzle as stress. A great deal of experimental work going back many decades has sought to establish both physiological and acoustic correlates of stress as a phonetic phenomenon. Lehiste, writing in 1970, says that 'of the three suprasegmental features [quantity, tonal features, and stress], stress has for a long time been the most elusive one' (p. 106).

A simple example makes clear the extent of the problem. Consider a stress minimal pair from English, like *permit* (noun) vs. *permit* (verb). In citation form, the stress contrast is signalled most conspicuously by differences in pitch contour:

(2.3)

a. p e r m i t   (noun)   b. p e r m i t   (verb):

The pitch rises to a peak on the stressed syllable, followed by a rapid fall. There are also differences of vowel quality, intensity, and especially syllable duration between the two words, but, as we just saw, Fry (1958) showed that the pitch differences are the cues that listeners use most reliably to make judgements about stress in isolated words when the suprasegmental features are manipulated experimentally. Yet if we change the citation forms into questions, the pitch contours are much less distinct:

(2.4)

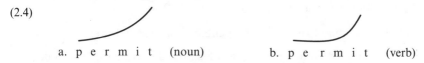

    a. p e r m i t (noun)   b. p e r m i t (verb)

Moreover, the question contours are completely different from the statement contours; we can no longer say that the stressed syllable is cued by a pitch peak. And if we put the words in context after the main intonational peak of an utterance, there may be no pitch distinction at all, yet we still clearly perceive the different stress patterns of the noun and the verb:

(2.5)

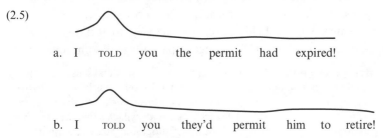

  a. I TOLD you the permit had expired!

  b. I TOLD you they'd permit him to retire!

Fry's results, taken at face value, suggest that 'stress' – in the sense of perceived prominence on a syllable – is a complex amalgam of F_0, duration, and intensity, with F_0 generally the most important but with uncomfortable exceptions made for certain intonational contexts such as (2.4) and (2.5). This view has remained remarkably widespread in certain quarters since the time of Fry's experiments, and a good deal of instrumental work has concentrated on trying to find better characterisations of the correlation between acoustic cues and perceived prominence (e.g. Gay 1978). From the point of view of the AM approach, though, much of this work is misdirected, and ignores basic theoretical problems with the idea that 'stress' is simply a scalar phonetic property of individual syllables. The AM view – like any view that incorporates the notion of 'pitch accent' – assumes that 'pitch accent' and 'stress' are (in some sense that is still not entirely clear) not the same thing.

Pierrehumbert expresses the difference between the two views as follows:

> In the wake of Fry's classic study . . . the impression grew up that F_0 can be viewed as a transducer of stress: the higher the stress, the higher the F_0

> (or the greater the F_0 movement). In the [autosegmental–metrical] frame-
> work . . . the relation of F_0 to stress is not as direct as this. Rather, a . . .
> given F_0 pattern could be compatible with more than one conclusion
> about the location of stress, if more than one assumption about where the
> accent is located was consistent with a well-formed intonational analysis
> for the contour. (1980: 103)

Halliday comments on the same theoretical issue as follows:

> It is thus a little misleading to ask anyone if he can 'hear the four degrees
> of stress'. The answer may well be that he can hear, and tell apart, what
> are being *called* four degrees of stress, but would analyse them as some-
> thing else; but the question is so framed as to preclude this answer. (1967a:
> 14n.)

The outlines of a theory in which stress is not treated as a single scale of
'degrees of prominence' have been growing clearer for some time. In the earliest versions, the distinction is drawn between 'abstract' word stress and
'concrete' sentence stress. Lehiste ascribes this view to Weinreich (1954),
and supports this position herself, though apparently with some reluctance:

> It appears probable that word-level stress is in a very real sense an abstract
> quality: a potential for being stressed. Word-level stress is *the capacity of
> a syllable within a word to receive sentence-stress when the word is realized
> as part of the sentence* . . . The fact that not all syllables that are perceived
> as stressed are associated with peaks of subglottal pressure supports the
> idea that what is realized phonetically is sentence-level stress rather than
> word-level stress. In other words, our knowledge of the structure of the
> language informs us which syllables have the potential of being stressed;
> we 'hear' the underlying phonological form. (1970: 150; emphasis sup-
> plied)

More or less the same view was taken by Abercrombie (e.g. 1991), who distinguished *accent* (word-level abstraction) from *stress* (actual phonetic
manifestation in an utterance). This view helps with cases like (2.5) above,
but in some sense still leaves us with the same question: instead of 'What
are the acoustic correlates of stress?', we have 'What are the acoustic correlates of actual sentence-level stress?' Further theoretical refinement is
needed.

Bolinger's pitch accent theory, first published in 1958, is the first proposal
for such a refinement. For Bolinger, as for Lehiste or Abercrombie, lexical
stress is a phonological abstraction, and the 'stressed' syllable of a word is
simply the place where actual sentence-level prominence occurs, if the word
is prominent in a sentence.[3] Where Bolinger differs from Abercrombie and
probably from Lehiste is in claiming that actual sentence-level prominence

is more or less *exclusively* a matter of intonational pitch movement. When there is no intonational pitch movement, there is, Bolinger claims, no prominence and no consistent phonetic correlate of lexical stress. As speakers of the language we think we hear the lexical stress because we recognise the word. Thus in the citation forms in (2.3) above, the peak and fall are intonational pitch features that attach to the lexically stressed syllable when the word is prominent in the utterance (which it is, more or less by definition, in a citation form). The situation in (2.4) is similar, in that the lexically stressed syllable attracts the intonational pitch movements, though these movements are very different for reasons having to do with sentence intonation rather than anything directly to do with stress. In (2.5), where there is an emphatic stress on *told* and consequently no sentence-level prominence on *permit* at all, the stress difference we hear between the noun and the verb in this context is due entirely to our knowledge of the language, and not to any consistent phonetic cues.

Bolinger's view, which is essentially the view of the IPO theory, succeeds in making some sense of the relationship between stress and pitch in languages like English or Dutch. In particular, it helps explain why pitch can be an overwhelmingly reliable cue to stress in some contexts (like (2.3)) and virtually irrelevant in others (like (2.5)). However, it does little to explain the existence of phonetic cues to stress other than pitch accent – cues such as duration, intensity, and spectral composition – and it does little to explain the existence of a fairly consistent impression on the part of analysts that there are *degrees* of relative stress, although Bolinger does note that vowel reduction could provide the basis for another 'degree of stress' (e.g. 1964: 285 (1972a: 22)).

A somewhat more complicated system, proposed in two variant forms by Halliday (1967a) and Vanderslice and Ladefoged (1972), and given a textbook presentation in Ladefoged 1982, says in effect that there are *two* sentence-level prominence features, not just pitch accent. (This view, like Bolinger's, allows for vowel reduction as a third sentence-level phonetic feature that can interact with the others.) In what follows I will call the two sentence-level features *stress* and *accent*.[4]

In this view, both stress and accent are either–or categories: syllables are either stressed or not, and if stressed they can be either accented or not; but both are phonetic characterisations, not abstractions. 'Accent' covers a subset of the cases that Bolinger referred to as accented, and is explicitly linked to the structure of the intonation contour. 'Stress' includes the rest of Bolinger's cases but also others as well: Halliday emphasises rhythmic

considerations in his definition of stress, while Ladefoged emphasises physiological facts such as an increase in respiratory energy. All versions of this
view involve the claim that 'the intonation system interacts with the accentual [i.e. stress] one so as to account for what some observers have analysed
as a difference in degree of stress' (Vanderslice and Ladefoged 1972: 820;
see also the quote from Halliday above). In effect, then, this view accepts
Bolinger's idea that intonational accent is a distinct phenomenon from
stress, but disagrees with Bolinger by assuming that stress has a separate
phonetic reality of some sort and is not merely a lexical abstraction.

The view incorporated into the AM theory takes the idea of a distinction
between utterance-level stress and intonational accent one step further:
instead of allowing a single binary distinction of 'stress' in actual utterance
prominence, it assumes that utterances have a 'stress pattern', which may
involve several different degrees of perceived prominence. This stress
pattern reflects a set of *prominence relations* between the elements of the
utterance. The stress pattern is manifested in a variety of phonetic cues,
which are admittedly not well understood. In addition to the stress pattern,
there is an intonation pattern for the utterance, which is composed of a
string of pitch accents and edge tones, and the pitch accents are 'lined up
with the text on the basis of the prominence relations' (Pierrehumbert 1980:
102). General conditions of prosodic well-formedness stipulate that pitch
accents must occur with prominent stressed syllables, and the occurrence of
a pitch accent therefore serves as a *cue* to the location of prominence, as Fry
and others have found. The essential nature of pitch accent, however, is not
'prominence-lending', as suggested by Bolinger and the IPO researchers,
but merely 'prominence-cueing' (a term suggested to me by Francis Nolan,
personal communication).

This theoretical view has begun to influence instrumental work on stress,
and evidence is accumulating that duration, intensity, and spectral properties, if measured appropriately, can actually serve as reliable indicators of
stress in English. For example, Beckman (1986) argues that the traditional
distinction between melodic accent ('pitch accent') and dynamic accent
('stress accent') is valid; she shows experimentally that in Japanese pitch
change is essentially the *only* acoustic cue to accent, whereas in English
duration, intensity, and vowel quality all play a significant role. More recent
work by Campbell (e.g. 1993) lends substance to this view by providing a
way of quantifying duration that identifies stressed syllables reliably even in
the absence of any intonational pitch features. Most recently, a study by
Sluijter and van Heuven (forthcoming) explicitly starts from the assump-

tion that accent and stress need to be distinguished, and shows that, if accent is controlled for, then spectral tilt (the relative energy in different parts of the spectrum) can be used as a reliable indicator of whether a syllable is stressed (see also Huss 1978).

2.2.2 Tune–text association

If, as just suggested, utterance-level prominence patterns ('stress') can be characterised independently of the distribution of pitch accents, then a complete account of intonational phonology within the AM approach will have to incorporate a theory of stress or linguistic prominence. The search for such a theory is the focus of much work within what has come to be known as metrical phonology. Metrical phonology begins with Liberman's notion that linguistic prominence crucially involves a *relation* between nodes in a binary-branching tree structure (Liberman 1975, Liberman and Prince 1977). According to Liberman and Prince, in any such relation one node is strong and the other weak:

(2.6)
```
      /\              /\
     w  s            s  w
  p e r m i t (verb)  p e r m i t (noun)
```

It is important to emphasise (because this is a point on which there has frequently been misunderstanding) that no absolute degree of prominence is implied by the labels 'strong' and 'weak'. There is no direct phonetic interpretation whatsoever of either label, but only of whole structures. What the notation means is that one node is *structurally* stronger than the other; this relative strength may be manifested phonetically in a great variety of ways. This abstract structural understanding of 'strength' – explored in depth by Beckman (1986: chs. 2 and 3) – is crucial for the metrical interpretation of experimental studies of the perception of stress.

For example, consider the two words in (2.7) as separate words.

(2.7)
```
    /\            /\
   s  w          s  w
   baby          sitter
```

In citation form, the 'strong' syllables of these two words are phonetically very prominent, with substantial pitch excursions, and the 'weak' syllables are conspicuously less so, with energy dropping off very rapidly and the pitch trailing away to the bottom of the speaker's range. But now let us combine them into a single compound:

(2.8)

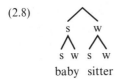

baby   sitter

(This representation says that *ba-* is stronger than *-by*, *sit-* is stronger than *-ter*, and *ba-* is stronger than *sit-*.) The phonetic realisation of this more complex structure, unlike the simple case, allows no single phonetic interpretation of the notion 'strong' syllable. However, it is still possible to state reasonably clearly how the prominence relations are realised. The structure in (2.8) defines a single strongest point or peak of prominence for the phrase as a whole, on *ba-*. (In Liberman and Prince's terminology, this peak of prominence is known as the *Designated Terminal Element* or DTE.) Like the citation forms, the compound has a single DTE, and, as in the citation forms, the sole pitch accent occurs at the DTE. This means that in the compound only *ba-* is marked by a pitch accent. We can still identify *sit-* as stronger than *-ter* in the compound, but the phonetic cues are a great deal more subtle, and certainly do not involve any significant pitch change. Pitch change, in other words, serves as a cue to prominence when the structure allows it, but prominence relations can also be cued in other ways.

The idea that pitch accents are elements of an intonational tune, and occur at syllables whose prominence in the utterance is somehow independently definable, is an aspect of what Liberman called 'tune–text association'. This notion can be motivated by analogy to the relation between musical tunes and song texts. In setting texts to music, linguistically stressed syllables are not necessarily associated with long or high-pitched or saliently loud notes – as would be expected if stress is primarily a matter of specific acoustic cues. Rather, what is crucial is for linguistically stressed syllables to be associated with notes at musically strong positions – 'on the beat', roughly speaking. Liberman's example is the 'children's chant':

(2.9)

Johnny   has   a   girlfriend

As Liberman points out, ill-formed associations of texts to this tune must be defined in terms of the position of stressed syllables relative to the metrically strong locations in the tune (the notes immediately preceded by bar lines). We cannot chant:

(2.10)

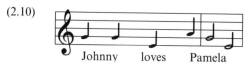

but must adjust note durations and syllables as follows:

(2.11)

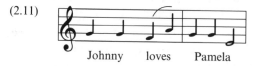

so that the stressed syllable *Pam-* comes out on the beat. All of this is at least consistent with the idea that linguistic stress is primarily a matter of phonological strength, and of association with features of the tune; local acoustic properties of individual syllables are not necessarily interpreted locally but as part of an overarching metrical structure.

This general view may seem perversely abstract to those whose interest is in perceptual cues. However, comparable distinctions are well motivated in music theory. In fact, in music we may clearly distinguish between the structural strength or prominence of the 'downbeat' (the main beat of each bar), the actual acoustic prominence of an 'accent' (added loudness, duration, added percussion, etc.), and the occurrence of salient features of the melodic and harmonic structure. For example, some musical styles are characterised by accents (added loudness, etc.) on weak beats (e.g. the 'backbeat' in rock and roll, or the striking off-the-beat accents in reggae). Similarly, in order to define 'syncopation' in music we must distinguish between the structural strength of the underlying beats and the prominence of melodic events occurring 'off the beat'. Obviously, the very fact that music theory has terms for things like 'backbeat' and 'syncopation' suggests an expectation that acoustic prominence and prominent melodic events will go together with underlying beats. In speech, too, major pitch movements generally coincide with other cues to prominence. But the importance of distinguishing structural strength from melodic events and acoustic prominence is also clearly shown by the musical analogy.[5]

2.2.3 Alignment of F_0 features with segmental features

Metrical phonology, in the view advanced here, is thus a theory of the prominence relations in an utterance. These prominence relations are in the first instance phonological abstractions, but they may be manifested in at least two distinct phonetic aspects of utterances: actual acoustic salience of individual syllables ('stress'), and the location of pitch accents. In simple cases both stress and pitch accent coincide with metrical strength, but it is possible, as in music, for dissociations to occur. Because the constructs of metrical phonology and the notion of tune–text association are abstract, they can readily accommodate these dissociations.

Perhaps the clearest and most successful case of the way such dissociations can be dealt with in the AM approach involves the *alignment* of F_0 features with the segmental string. Recall (section 1.3.3) that the essence of the Swedish word accent distinction, according to Bruce, is the way the H of the accent contour is aligned with the stressed syllable: the peak of Accent 1 is always aligned earlier than that of Accent 2. Earlier accounts had concentrated on the pitch contour of the accented syllable itself, and had tried to explain the extreme variability of this contour, without much success. Bruce saw that the F_0 contour on the accented syllable is merely a consequence of which tones occur and how they are aligned with the segmental string: if the H is aligned at the beginning of the accented syllable, the accented syllable will have a falling contour, whereas if the H is aligned at the end of the accented syllable, the syllable will show a rising contour. The H of the accent – the accent peak – is an independent element of the structure, and the invariant phonetic cue to the word accent distinction lies in the temporal alignment of the peak with the accented syllable.

In Ladd 1983a I proposed that this notion of alignment could be used to describe intonational distinctions in other languages, such as English and German, in the context of a Pierrehumbert-style tonal analysis. Specifically, I suggested that the 'rise–fall' or 'scooped' falling accents in English (see e.g. Vanderslice and Ladefoged 1972: 822; Ladd 1980a: 35 and 110–12) are identical in tonal composition and differ only in the alignment of the H tone with the accented syllable. Specifically, both are tonally H*+L, but in the ordinary fall the peak is aligned early in the syllable, whereas in the 'scooped' fall the peak is aligned considerably later, sometimes well into the following unstressed syllable ('delayed peak'). I argued that this analysis expresses the functional similarity between the two accent types (which is reflected in the failure of traditional analyses to distinguish them consistently), yet at the same time provides a phonetically explicit account of the difference.

In fact, this analysis was almost certainly wrong (cf. section 3.5.1 below), but the point I wish to emphasise here is that the notion of 'alignment' is a natural consequence of the general AM viewpoint. The AM theory does not treat F_0 as a 'transducer of stress', but as the manifestation of an overarching structure in which elements of a tune are associated with elements of a text in ways that reflect the prominence relations in the text. A high F_0 peak is no longer seen as a phonetic property of a prominent syllable, but as an element of the phonological structure of the utterance, on a par with the prominent syllable itself. Given this shift in point of view, it makes sense to investigate the phonetic details of the association between the F_0 peak and the syllable, and one of the most obvious phonetic properties of that association is the alignment in time of the peak relative to the syllable.

I am therefore drawing a distinction (as I did in Ladd 1983a) between alignment and *association*. Alignment must be defined as a *phonetic* property of the relative timing of events in the F_0 contour and events in the segmental string. Association, on the other hand, is the abstract structural property of 'belonging together' in some way. The fact of association entails no specific predictions about alignment: if a H tone is associated with a given prominent syllable, we may expect to find a peak of F_0 somewhere in the general vicinity of the syllable, but the peak may be early in the syllable or late, and indeed it may be outside the temporal limits of the syllable altogether. For example, it is particularly common in accented syllables at the beginning of an utterance to see the high F_0 peak aligned in time with the following unstressed syllable. These kinds of cases are difficult to reconcile with a strict 'prominence-lending' interpretation of pitch accent, but can readily be accommodated in a view which says only that the F_0 contour must have an interpretation as the realisation of a pitch accent in a well-formed prosodic structure.

It should be emphasised that alignment data have a clear theory-neutral interpretation. Since the early 1980s there has been a great deal of research on alignment, not all of it even presupposing the AM theory (e.g. Kohler 1987; Silverman and Pierrehumbert 1990; Caspers 1994; Verhoeven 1994; Arvaniti and Ladd 1995; see further section 2.3.3.2 below). Virtually all of this work has led to clear robust findings (for example, the clear phonetic conditioning of alignment as a function of prosodic context reported by Silverman and Pierrehumbert (1990)). It cannot be claimed that the AM theory was necessary in order to make the significance of alignment clear: in the case of the Scandinavian word accents, Bruce's analysis is hinted at by Haugen and Joos (1952), and in the case of intonational pitch accents the early IPO work established the relevance of alignment differences for a variety of perceptual distinctions. But the AM theory, by eliminating the idea that pitch accent is a transducer of stress, suggests a reason why alignment might be expected to vary as it does.

2.2.4   *Metrical strength and phonetic stress*

We might summarise the foregoing discussion by saying that the 'elusive' nature of stress, on which Lehiste commented, is primarily a theoretical problem and not an empirical one. I believe that metrical phonology, combined with the notion of tune–text association, goes a considerable way to solving this theoretical problem. In particular, it permits us to distinguish three facets of 'stress' that have often been conflated in earlier accounts: abstract prominence relations ('metrical strength'), concrete acoustic prominence or salience ('stress'), and the location of prominence-related intonational events ('pitch accent'). However, within metrical phonology itself little effort has been made to account for older instrumental findings about 'stress'. Consequently, the AM theory has not been widely accepted by many experimental phoneticians.

For example, objections have been raised to analysing some kinds of syllables as metrically 'strong' because they are phonetically indistinct or in any case much less phonetically salient than other syllables in a constituent. A case in point is the utterance-final syllables of French, which are regarded by metrical phonologists as the 'strongest' syllables of their constituents. For many phoneticians, what is striking about these syllables is that they are so often acoustically indistinct, especially compared to the *accents d'insistance* that are so prevalent in reading style. Indeed, it has been argued (e.g. by Beckman 1986: 33) that French does not have stress at all, but only 'demarcative' cues to the edge of a phonological word or phrase. Yet it has been convincingly shown by Dell (1984) that the distribution of tonal properties of French intonation contours can only be accounted for by assuming that the last full-vowel syllable in a French phonological word has some special status – by assuming that it is metrically strong, in the terms used here. Dell's arguments are based crucially on the tonal behaviour of sentences in which the final schwa or *e muet* is realised. If we assume that accent tones in French go to the edge of the phonological word, then we would expect them to attach to schwa as readily as to any other syllable, but, as Dell shows, this is not what happens. For example, consider the rather emphatic statement intonation that falls (sometimes only slightly) from a high peak on the final syllable of a phrase (the *intonation d'implication* of Delattre 1966). This is illustrated by Dell in the following examples (slightly modified from Dell's originals, but preserving Dell's impressionistic indication of a 'mid' tone):

(2.12)

T'étais pas au courant.
'You didn't know what was going on.'

(2.13)

Il met la tab'.
'He's setting the table.'

When this contour is applied to a sentence with any of various kinds of tags
– such as vocatives or right-dislocated constituents[6] – the final L spreads to
the whole tag constituent, which forms a separate prosodic phrase
(*tronçon*); the H remains anchored to the last syllable of the first prosodic
phrase:

(2.14) L   M H L

Il met la tab', Mercier.
'Mercier's setting the table.'

As Dell points out, if the final schwa of *table* is realised in this context, it
does not count as the last syllable of the first prosodic phrase, but rather the
H is still anchored to the syllable *ta-*:

(2.15) L   M H L

Il met la table, Mercier.
'Mercier's setting the table.'

The last full-vowel syllable has some special status as an anchor for
tune–text association; we cannot simply say that the tones go to the edge of
the phrase.

Given the approach put forward here, we can identify the 'special status'
of the last full-vowel syllable as 'accent' or 'metrical strength'; the fact that
in other respects this 'accented' or 'strong' syllable may be phonetically not
very salient is irrelevant. In Dell's words,

> the criteria that determine the position of the key syllables [= DTEs]
> within an intonational phrase are exclusively accentual (and not syn-
> tactic). It is true that the relevance of accentual factors . . . is not as strik-
> ing in French as in some other languages. This is because in works on
> intonation one normally starts by investigating the phrase-final melody
> that precedes silence. In this context, as a result of certain peculiarities
> of the phonology of schwa, words are always accented on their last syl-
> lable. Consequently, certain melodic events may give the illusion of

being associated with the right edge of constituents, whereas in fact they are associated with accented syllables. (Dell 1984: 67f.; my translation)

In this connection it may also be useful to note the difficulties encountered by Odé (1994) in investigating Indonesian intonation within the IPO framework. In keeping with IPO assumptions, she attempted to get listeners to identify 'prominent' words, but her subjects – described as 'graduate linguists' – found the task very difficult and disagreed considerably among themselves. Among her conclusions is the claim that 'prominence in Indonesian cannot be described in terms of stressed or accented syllables' (p. 63). Yet acoustic phonetic descriptions of Indonesian intonation reported or discussed in the same volume (Halim 1984; Ebing 1994; Laksman 1994) all agree that characteristic pitch movements in Indonesian can readily be defined, mostly with respect to the penultimate syllable of the word.

This means that in the terms proposed here, the penultimate syllable in Indonesian is 'accented' or 'metrically strong', because it is the anchor for the events of the intonational string. However, it is not necessarily 'stressed' or 'prominent' in the sense of having some clear phonetic salience, because that is a separate phenomenon, which apparently does not occur very consistently in Indonesian. For example, among the facts discussed in Laksman's paper is that pitch patterns are identical in two-syllable words regardless of whether the first syllable has a schwa or some other vowel. This is confusing from an English or Dutch point of view, because a schwa is by definition unstressed and must therefore be unaccented. However, it makes perfect sense from the point of view of, say, Japanese, in which it is known that accent can occur on syllables that are voiceless or elided between voiceless obstruents (Sugito and Hirose 1988). If we simply abandon the assumption that the anchor point for tonal events must be a phonetically 'prominent' syllable, then the presence of a pitch accent on a schwa ceases to be a problem.

2.2.5   Summary

The foregoing discussion of stress and accent in the AM theory can be summarised as follows. In at least some languages, certainly including English and Dutch, there is a phonetic phenomenon of stress that can usefully be distinguished from pitch accent. Stress in this sense might be glossed as 'acoustic salience': it is a complex of properties that can be related to greater force of articulation, including increased intensity and duration, and shallower spectral tilt.

The stress pattern of an utterance reflects the organisation of the syllables into a hierarchical metrical structure. This structure specifies abstract
relations of prominence or strength between syllables, and between larger
constituents such as words and phrases. The way in which words and
phrases are fitted into a well-formed metrical structure is dictated in part
by the lexically specified stress pattern of words.

By and large, syllables that are prominent in the abstract metrical structure are also phonetically stressed, but the theory does not preclude the
occurrence of systematic dissociations. A syllable can be metrically strong
or prominent without necessarily being stressed. Such a dissociation is
comparable to those found in music: for instance, dissociations between
rhythmical prominence (defined by the underlying beat) and melodic or
dynamic prominence (defined by harmonic changes, note durations, added
loudness, etc.).

Metrically strong syllables in a language like English or French are sometimes accompanied by pitch accents. However, pitch accents are elements
of the intonation contour and do not in themselves represent the acoustic
realisation of stress. They serve as an indirect cue to syllable prominence,
because they must be associated with strong or prominent syllables, but
(*contra* the Bolinger–IPO view) they do not in and of themselves constitute
the prominent syllable's prominence. In some languages (like English or
Dutch), the metrically prominent syllables to which pitch accents are associated are also stressed. In other languages (like French or Indonesian)
pitch accents may associate to syllables which are not necessarily stressed
and which may not seem 'prominent' either to native speakers or to phonetically trained listeners.

2.3   Analysis of pitch accents in terms of level tones

So far we have discussed pitch accents as the most important of the phonological events into which pitch contours can be analysed. However, one of the
most conspicuous features of AM descriptions of intonation is that in many
cases pitch accents are themselves further analysed as sequences or combinations of High (H) and Low (L) tones. At first glance this makes it appear that
the AM theory takes a clear stand in what was long known as the 'levels-vs.-
configurations' controversy – the debate between those who analysed contours in terms of distinctive pitch levels and those who took the primitives of
intonational analysis to be pitch movements or 'configurations'. In fact, I
think it is fairer to say that the AM theory successfully resolves this debate.

2.3.1   *The levels-vs.-configurations debate*

The levels-vs.-configurations controversy was without a doubt the premier theoretical issue in intonation research from the early 1950s to the early 1980s. The issue was first posed in these terms by Bolinger (1951), who drew attention to a variety of problems with the then widely accepted American structuralist analyses of Pike (1945), Wells (1945), and Trager and Smith (1951). The most striking characteristic of these descriptions was that intonation was analysed in terms of four-level 'pitch phonemes' (Low, Mid, High, and Overhigh),[7] which were said to occur at certain structurally salient points in the utterance (see further Hockett 1955, 1958; Trager 1964). Bolinger pointed out that this four-level system is, in effect, both too rich and not rich enough: on the one hand, it predicts the existence of intonational contrasts that do not seem to occur; and on the other hand, it is unable to provide an analysis for various contours that clearly do occur. He attributed these problems to the use of pitch levels as primitives, and argued that the distinctive functional units of intonation were really 'configurations' like rise or fall.

In retrospect, it is clear that many of the problems Bolinger discussed were the consequence of certain general theoretical precepts of American structuralist linguistics, not just of the 'levels' idea (this point is discussed at length in Ladd 1983b). Throughout the debate, one of the problems that nagged at many 'configurationists' (e.g. Sledd 1955; Ladefoged 1967) was the need to be able to refer to actual F_0 levels in an explicit phonetic description of intonation, which seems to require some phonological notion of pitch level, and which suggests that there is some flaw in the dichotomy posed by Bolinger. Nevertheless, for roughly thirty years the levels-vs.-configurations debate was an issue that intonation researchers felt they had to take sides on, and it certainly influenced the way individual researchers viewed their own work.[8]

The AM theory effectively resolves this debate. Two theoretical claims are central to this resolution. These are, first, the reduction of the number of distinctive levels to two (viz. High and Low), and second, the acknowledgement of the existence of pitch accents.

By reducing the number of distinctive levels to two, the AM theory avoids the problem of predicting more contrasts than there are. For example, the four-level analysis of English predicts the existence of six distinct falling contours /21/, /31/, /41/, /32/, /42/, and /43/. It is almost certain that these sharp distinctions are of no relevance to the linguistic system of English, even if contours corresponding roughly to the six phonetic possibilities might be found. By analysing all falling contours as HL, and ascribing variations in the height of the H or the L to orthogonal factors, a two-level theory seems to strike the right balance between phonological contrast and paralinguistic variation.[9]

By acknowledging the existence of pitch accents *at some level of analysis*, the AM theory can use the primitive H and L tones to refer to pitch level in phonetic realisation, while at the same time acknowledging that pitch accents are in some sense distinctive pitch configurations. In this, the theory crucially diverges from the original 'levels' view, which directly analysed utterance contours in terms of levels. In fact, with respect to pitch accents and phonetic realisation there is little practical difference between the AM view and the IPO theory. The IPO theory regards the pitch configurations as units, and emphasises the primacy of 'configurations', but in modelling actual contours the theory nevertheless specifies starting and ending levels for each local configuration, defined with reference to the upper and lower declination lines. These starting and ending points are effectively equivalent to tonal targets in the AM approach.

The most important respect in which the levels-vs.-configurations debate might still be said to be unresolved is in the realm of perception. One of the central arguments of, for example, the IPO researchers has always been that movements are crucial to the perception of intonational distinctions. We cannot hear that something is high, so the argument goes, except relative to something else in the context that is lower (cf. section 7.1.1 below). To some extent this is clearly true, but it seems likely that the case has been overstated. The best evidence that the case has been overstated is the existence of languages like Yoruba in which it is uncontroversial that the system of lexical tones is based on distinctive levels: in an utterance that consists only of H tones, there is nothing lower in the context to serve as a point of comparison. A general (i.e. in this case non-Eurocentric) theory of pitch perception will need to make clear how listeners are able to perceive the 'highness' of the H tone in the absence of syntagmatic comparison to M or L. Once we have such a theory, it is plausible to assume that it will apply to English or Dutch as well. In any case, the argument from perception is not by itself enough to sustain the 'configurations' position in the levels-vs.-configurations debate.

2.3.2 The African example
The development of ideas about intonational structure in the AM theory has clearly been influenced by the tonal phonology of African languages.

In these languages it is well established that two 'level' lexical tones (such as H and L) can occur on the same syllable and yield a phonetically falling or rising contour. It will be useful to provide a few sample cases, so that readers unfamiliar with tone languages may have a clearer idea of the kinds of phenomena that are involved.

There are two main kinds of motivation for analysing syllable contours as sequences of level tones. The first type of case involves segmental elision. In many African languages, the vowel of a syllable may be elided phonetically while leaving its tone to be realised. In this case one of the syllables adjacent to the elided syllable is realised with two tones. If the two tones are different, the result may be a contour or pitch change on the syllable. This can be seen in the following example from Yoruba:

(2.16)   M L H   M   M LH M
         | | | | | ⋁ |
         Ayọ (o) lọ ⟶ Ayọ lọ 'Ayọ goes'

Here the H tone on *o* ('he/she/it') remains in the tonal string even though the vowel to which it is underlyingly associated is completely elided.[10] The H tone reassociates to the preceding syllable -*yọ*, which then has two tones, L and H. This two-tone sequence is realised as a rise on -*yọ*.

The second motivation for analysing contours as sequences of levels in many African languages involves economy of description. For example, in Efik (as described by Ward 1933) monosyllabic verb stems have one of three distinct tonal patterns, High, Low or Rise. Thus:

(2.17)   dep (High) 'buy'   du (Low) 'live'   ka (Rise) 'go'

If we infer from this that there are three separate tone phonemes – High, Low, and Rise – then for two-syllable verb stems we predict nine possibilities: Low–High, Low–Rise, Rise–Low, and so on. In fact, there are only three possibilities for two-syllable stems, exactly as for one-syllable stems. These are High–High, Low–Low, and Low–High:

(2.18)   kere (H–H) 'think'   dori (L–L) 'put'   fehe (L–H) 'run'

An obvious account of these facts is to say that there are only two tone phonemes, High and Low, and only three permitted tonal patterns for verb stems, namely High, Low, and Low–High. The surface realisation then depends on the association of the tonal pattern to the syllables available in the stem:

(2.19) H   L   LH
        | | V
        dep   du   ka

        H   L   LH
        ∧   ∧ | |
        kere   dori   fehe

The description with only H and L tones has a smaller inventory of basic units, and predicts exactly which two-syllable patterns are possible.

Examples of these two kinds are to be found in language after language throughout sub-Saharan Africa (for good further background reading see Welmers 1973; for the autosegmental interpretation of examples like (2.19) see Leben 1973; Goldsmith 1976; Williams 1976). This makes it clear that a place for 'level tones' must be found in our general understanding of linguistic pitch systems. Whether level tones are present in European languages is of course a separate question, to which we now turn.

2.3.3   Phonetic evidence for distinctive levels

While the example of African tone systems has undoubtedly influenced the development of AM intonational phonologies, there are other more direct empirical foundations for the view that pitch movements may be represented as sequences of tones. The most important of these is Bruce's discovery that a precisely aligned peak, not a rise or a fall, is the most reliable correlate of word accent in Swedish (see sections 1.3.2 and 2.2.3). Certain pitch movements that might ordinarily be taken as distinctive – specifically, the rise on the accented syllable in citation forms with Accent 1 – are shown by Bruce's work to be *transitions* from one phonologically specified point to another. That is, the F_0 configurations that happen to span the accented syllables play no useful role in phonetic description of the overall contour; the invariant features of the pitch system appear to be the *turning points* in the contour rather than the transitions that connect them.

Bruce's data show very clearly that the 'word accent maximum' is the most reliable anchor for the phonetic description of contours: it always occurs at the same time relative to the accented syllable, and its F_0 level in a given utterance context is effectively constant. In order to account for these regularities, it is appropriate to treat the word accent maximum as a phonological entity. In Bruce's words, we need to 'represent the tonal commands induced by the prosodic features in terms of two pitch levels, which are considered to be linguistically relevant: a LOW and a HIGH . . . These tonal points can be viewed as ideal F_0-targets and give a rough picture of the essential tonal characteristics of an utterance' (1977: 130f.). Bruce concludes that in modelling accentual pitch configurations 'reaching a certain pitch level at a particular point in time is the important thing, not the movement (rise or fall) itself' (*ibid.*, p. 132). He also goes on to state the principle that the actual phonetic scaling of the idealised Hs and Ls is a separate problem: 'this tonal representation has to be further elaborated to fit actual F_0 data . . . by the operation of F_0 rules'.

For a long time one of the most important arguments in favour of 'configurations' rather than 'levels' was that it is all a matter of how the analyst looks at the problem: in Bolinger's words (1986: 225f.), 'it makes no difference, in describing a movement, whether one says "first you are going to be up and then you are going to be down" or "you are going to go down"'. But the implication of Bruce's findings is that it does matter. Moreover, since Bruce's work, there is now abundant evidence that speakers control the level and temporal alignment of certain *F_0 target points* with considerable precision, and that hearers can perceive the differences. By contrast, in several experiments on both production and perception, hypotheses based unambiguously on the notion of pitch movement (i.e. hypotheses not re-interpretable in terms of levels) have failed to predict the results. This experimental evidence is reviewed in the following subsections.

2.3.3.1   Consistency of target levels in production

Production experiments in which speakers read controlled texts consistently reveal regularities of F_0 level at particular points in utterances. Maeda (1976) found that the low pitch at the end of sentence-final fall varied little for any given speaker, and this finding has been replicated in many studies since (e.g. Menn and Boyce 1982; Liberman and Pierrehumbert 1984; Anderson and Cooper 1986; Connell and Ladd 1990; Ladd and Terken 1995; the studies by Menn and Boyce and by Anderson and Cooper are based on spontaneous or semi-spontaneous speech). Similar consistencies in the height of accentual peaks are less readily observed, because peaks can vary so much for other reasons (emphasis, place in utterance, etc.). In general, though, when other factors are carefully controlled the height of peaks seems to be as regular as that of final low endpoints.

The study that drew attention to the control of peak height was Pierrehumbert's experiment on pitch range modification in two specific contours of English (Pierrehumbert 1980: ch. 3; Liberman and Pierrehumbert 1984: section 2). The two contours studied, and appropriate contexts for their use, are illustrated in the following exchanges:

(2.20)   a. *'Background–answer (BA) contour'*
Question: What about Anna? Who did she come with?

Answer: Anna came with Manny.

b. *'Answer–background (AB) contour'*
Question: What about Manny? Who came with him?

Answer: Anna came with Manny.

As can be seen, both contours consist of two accents, but the accents differ according to whether the accented word is (in Pierrehumbert's terminology) the *answer* to the question or part of the discourse *background* that is presupposed. In Pierrehumbert's analysis both accents are L+H* followed by a L phrase tone (see section 3.2.2.1), and the background accent is followed by a further H boundary tone. In British terms the answer accents are (rise–)falls and the background accents are fall–rises (or rise–fall–rises). More importantly for the point under discussion, the two accents may have peaks of different heights: in the AB contour, the peak of the background accent on *Manny* is markedly lower than that of the answer accent on *Anna*.

Pierrehumbert had speakers produce multiple repetitions of these contours, with ten different 'degrees of overall emphasis'. She then measured the F_0 levels of several presumed tonal targets, including the peaks of both accents. For each of the two contours, all four speakers showed virtually constant relationships between the height of the two accent peaks, irrespective of the pitch range. This is shown in figure 2.1, in which data from both contours for one speaker are plotted. The plots for the other speakers are comparable. It is difficult – though not impossible – to avoid the conclusion that the relationship between the two peaks is being rather carefully controlled.[11]

While the *Anna/Manny* experiment focuses our attention on the *relation* between two peaks, the consistencies it reveals are evident even in studies where pitch range is not experimentally manipulated. For example, if we

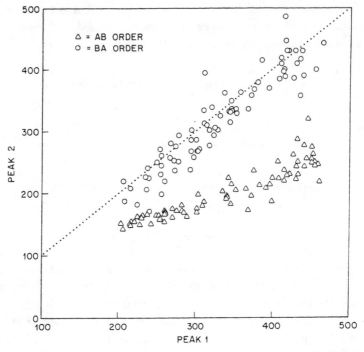

Figure 2.1 Data for one speaker in Pierrehumbert's *Anna/Manny* experiment. For each individual utterance, the figure plots the F_0 value of the accent peak on *Anna* against that on *Manny*. The 'AB' order has the 'answer' before the 'background', and the 'BA' order is the reverse (for more detail see text). From Liberman and Pierrehumbert 1984.

look at the mean values of sentence-initial accent peaks for individual speakers in the data reported by Ladd (1988), we find that standard deviations average only 7.5 Hz (ranging from 3.7 Hz to 11.5 Hz), suggesting rather considerable consistency in speakers' productions. To put this finding in perspective, it is instructive to compare it with results from a methodologically similar study of Yoruba (Connell and Ladd 1990), since we might expect that speakers of Yoruba, which has three lexical level tones, would control F_0 level rather carefully. Standard deviations on sentence-initial H tone question particles in this study averaged 14.8 Hz, with a range from 8.3 to 31.4 Hz. We can conclude that, under roughly similar conditions, English speakers control pitch level at least as precisely as Yoruba speakers. Similar consistency in the final high pitch of questions in French is reported by Grundstrom (1973).

2.3.3.2   Invariance of temporal alignment of targets

Related to findings of consistent pitch level are findings that certain identifiable points in the F_0 contour are aligned with the segmental string in extremely consistent ways. As noted in section 2.2.3, Bruce (1977) found that the distinction between Accent 1 and Accent 2 is reliably cued by the timing of a high peak early in the accentual configuration: before the beginning of the accented syllable for Accent 1 and just after the onset of the accented vowel for Accent 2. Normally this high peak is followed by a fall, but Bruce found that the fall can be abbreviated or lost altogether under certain conditions; only the high and its alignment are invariant. This is the basis of Bruce's view that 'reaching a certain pitch level at a particular point in time is the important thing' (1977: 132). On the basis of this conclusion, Bruce and Gårding (1978) have produced a prosodic typology of Swedish word accents, showing that the accentual distinction is always signalled by the earlier alignment of the peak of Accent 1, even though the peaks of *both* accents may be aligned relatively earlier or later in different dialects, and even though there may be other concomitant phonetic or phonological differences.

Similar consistencies in the alignment of F_0 turning points were noted (with surprise) by Ashby (1978). Ashby was investigating the acoustic correlates of the 'high-fall' and 'low-rise' nuclear tone configurations of the traditional British analysis of English intonation. He had three phonetically trained speakers read a long randomised list of sentences, with no instructions on how to produce them except to specify one or the other nuclear tone. While there was a good deal of variation in the prenuclear stretches of the sentences, the nuclear tone realisations were extremely consistent. For the high-fall tones, for each speaker considered separately, both the level and the alignment of the peak showed very little variation: for example, one male speaker had peaks of about 200 Hz aligned about 35 ms after the onset of the vowel. The final low of the high-fall tones on sentence-final nuclear monosyllables was also extremely constant. The same male speaker reached a low of about 100 Hz 150 ms after the vowel onset. The rises were characterised by a low, very slightly falling 'plateau whose length is a linear function of the total voicing time after vowel onset' (p. 334), followed abruptly by a rise of fixed slope (6.7 octaves/sec.) that continued to the end of voicing. The abrupt onset of the rise and the predictability of the location of the rise onset is certainly consistent with the idea of a clearly defined low target aligned with the stressed vowel in a clearly defined way.

A study by Silverman and Pierrehumbert (1990) demonstrates the existence of typical phonological conditioning factors on alignment. They show, for example, that the peak of a non-final accent occurs proportionally later in a syllable when the speech rate is slower, and that it occurs proportionally earlier the closer it is to the end of the accented word. In fact, this study merely exploits the assumed consistency of target alignment: Silverman and Pierrehumbert were actually interested in the entirely separate issue of whether nuclear and prenuclear accents are phonologically the same. But the timing of peaks is so consistent, and so consistently influenced by prosodic context, that they were able to use it as the basis for drawing conclusions about other things.

In all three of these studies, then, there is clear evidence that the alignment of F_0 targets is carefully controlled. This fact fits simply and naturally with a theory in which F_0 targets are the phonetic manifestation of underlying static tones. It is not completely incompatible with a phonological theory that treats pitch movements as primitives, but as more and more evidence for precise target alignment accumulates (see e.g. Arvaniti and Ladd 1995), it is increasingly difficult to maintain that F_0 targets are nothing more than the point where the pitch movements begin and end. The burden of proof, in my opinion, has shifted to proponents of the 'configurations' view.

2.3.3.3   Failure of predictions based on pitch excursion

It is not necessarily easy to distinguish predictions based on peak F_0 from those based on F_0 excursion size. That is, given a pair of contours of the idealised form shown in figure 2.2, it is equally plausible to describe the difference between a and b in terms of level – x' is higher than x – or in terms of excursion size – (x'–y') is greater than (x–y). In every case where the distinction can be made clearly, however, the level description better expresses the regularities in experimental data. For example, in Pierrehumbert's *Anna/Manny* experiment, we saw that the relationship of peak F_0 at the two accent peaks was constant under changes in overall pitch range. Liberman and Pierrehumbert (1984) also analysed the same data from the point of view of excursion size: that is, they looked at the relation between the excursion sizes of the two accent configurations. While there was, not surprisingly, a substantial correlation between overall pitch range and excursion size, the *relation between excursion sizes* in any given utterance was far less regular than the relation between peak heights. (For details, the reader is referred to Liberman and Pierrehumbert 1984: 210–15.)

Work in progress by myself, Amalia Arvaniti, and Ineke Mennen has

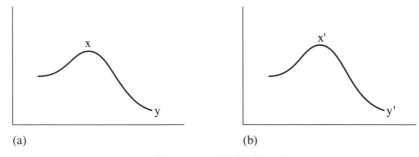

(a)   (b)

Figure 2.2 Two different approaches to quantitative definition of the 'prominence' or 'pitch range' of accent peaks. The relative prominence of the two idealised accent peaks in the figure could be described in terms of relative peak height, or in terms of the size of the 'pitch excursion' or amount of pitch movement. In many cases (as here) the two kinds of definitions are difficult to distinguish empirically.

yielded a similar finding. We have measured the L and H targets of prenuclear pitch accents in Greek, and find small variability for both. This means that there is little variation in the size of the excursion. If the L and H were simply the endpoints of a distinctive pitch excursion, we might expect some correlation between the L and H of a given accent: slight variations in overall pitch height would have similar influence on both ends of a pitch excursion of constant size. If, on the other hand, L and H are two distinctive targets, we would expect the variability of the two targets to be independent, and we would not expect to find any correlation between the L and H of a given accent. In accordance with the latter prediction, we find no correlation.

Perception data tell a similar story. Experiments by 't Hart (1981) and by Rietveld and Gussenhoven (1985; see also Gussenhoven and Rietveld 1988) suggest that listeners attend to target level, and are, in fact, exceedingly poor at judging excursion size *per se*. The experiment by 't Hart (1981) is particularly interesting, as it was avowedly motivated by the theoretical assumption that excursion size is perceptually relevant. In 't Hart's words, 'insofar as pitch movements may lend prominence, one could ask, in the case of an utterance in which two syllables are made prominent by means of similar pitch movements, how much larger either of the two pitch movements should be in order to make that syllable more prominent than the other' (1981: 812); that is, 't Hart assumed that excursion size is correlated with degree of prominence, and set up his experiments to exclude the influence of peak height.

Specifically, 't Hart prepared pairs of stimuli with synthesised rising or falling accents of different sizes, and asked listeners to judge whether the first or the second had a larger pitch movement. To make it unambiguous that subjects were judging interval size and not peak height, the members of each stimulus pair were frequently in different 'registers', that is, of different overall pitch level, and subjects were given an explicit 'warning against a certain type of stimulus pair . . . where the first item has the highest pitch peak, but the second one [in a lower register] the larger pitch movement' (pp. 814–15). Under these conditions, the subjects' performance was very poor; 't Hart found it necessary to distinguish 'discriminators' and 'non-discriminators'. The non-discriminators (a majority of subjects in certain conditions) were able only to discriminate differences greater than 4 or 5 semitones (st); even the discriminators showed a mean discrimination threshold in the area of 2.5 st, which, as 't Hart notes, is 'much higher than would be expected on the grounds of known data about the just noticeable difference in pitch of speech sounds' (p. 815). Yet despite what he calls a 'rather complicated' outcome to his study, 't Hart does not question his assumption 'that speech pitch can best be described in terms of pitch movements rather than pitch levels' (p. 820). Instead, he concludes that, for the purposes of speech synthesis, differences of 3 st in excursion size of neighbouring pitch movements are probably the minimum we may expect 'to be heard with any certainty as differently large, and even then not by every listener'.

This specific conclusion was challenged by Rietveld and Gussenhoven (1985), who show that a difference of even 1.5 st reliably correlates with different prominence judgements. Their experimental task was broadly similar to 't Hart's, but they used a fairly complex statistical procedure to establish an implicit prominence scale for their stimuli, on the basis of the relative prominence judgements for the individual stimulus pairs. Even stimuli whose pitch excursions differed by only 1.5 st had significantly different scale values. It thus seems unlikely that a threshold of 3 st for reliable discrimination of the prominence of accents is the whole explanation for the results of 't Hart's original study. More plausible, in my view, is that pitch level must somehow be taken into account.

2.3.4   Scaling of tonal targets as an empirical issue

If we accept the conclusion that distinctive pitch levels are involved in languages like English, we must acknowledge that we do not understand how the distinctiveness of pitch level works. One of the virtues of the AM approach is that it insistently draws our attention to pitch level as a problem for investigation.

Previously, one of the objections to analysing pitch contours in terms of levels, rather than configurations such as rise or fall, had been that the levels do not reflect phonetic reality. Bolinger (1951) suggested that the number of levels in any given analysis is merely a matter of how finely the analyst divides up what is essentially a gradient, while Lieberman (1965) showed that the pitch levels of the American structuralist analysis do not correspond systematically to actual observed levels in the instrumentally determined pitch contour. For the two-level analysis proposed by Bruce or Pierrehumbert, these objections are essentially irrelevant. With only two levels, the levels cannot possibly have any direct correspondence to phonetic reality; anyone can see that contours are more varied than that.

In the two-level view, that is, H and L are phonological abstractions, comparable to phonemes, and there is no reason to expect them to be realised always in the same way. Rather, the phonetic realisation of H and L – like the phonetic realisation of any other phoneme – is subject to a variety of conditioning factors, which may make any given occurrence of H or L come out phonetically in a quite different way from some other occurrence. Consequently, the description as a whole must have theoretically interesting things to say about the mapping from abstract Hs and Ls to actual F_0 levels in contours. It thus seems fair to say that the phonological analysis of intonation in terms of only two distinctive levels implies a genuine attempt to come to grips with questions of phonetic realisation in pitch systems generally.

Bruce (1977: 131–43) makes some preliminary suggestions about the phonetic realisation of the H and L tones. He suggests that the phonetics of intonation might be represented in an idealised way in terms of four F_0 levels, numbered from 1 (lowest) to 4 (highest). Any given H or L tone is realised at one of these levels. Bruce's discussion brings out the distinction between abstract phonology and concrete phonetic realisation very explicitly:

> F_0-level 1 is considered to the base level and is the true representative of the LOW pitch level [i.e. L tone]. The F_0 movements can roughly be described as positive deviations . . . from this base level . . . In certain contexts the LOW pitch level will also be specified as F_0-level 2 (and occasionally as F_0-level 3). The HIGH pitch level [i.e. H tone] can be specified as F_0-levels 2, 3 or 4, depending on the context. This means that F_0-level 2 can represent both a HIGH and a LOW pitch level, which may seem paradoxical. But the pitch levels HIGH and LOW are to be conceived of as relative and contextually specified for each case as a particular F_0-level. (1977: 137)

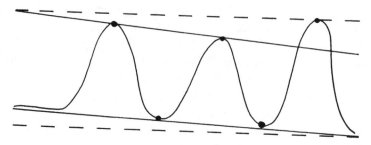

Figure 2.3 Phonetic realisation of pitch features in the model proposed by Bruce and Gårding 1978. The limits of the utterance range are shown by the horizontal 'focal lines', and the range within which most pitch accents are realised is shown by the gradually declining 'statement lines'. After Bruce and Gårding 1978.

Bruce goes on to note that he idealises the four F_0 levels as unchanging throughout the utterance, though he acknowledges that there is some evidence that they actually decline or drift lower. In subsequent work (Bruce and Gårding 1978), the idea of four F_0 levels is dropped and declination is built into the realisation model in terms of a distinction between 'statement lines' and 'focal lines'. The statement lines are a 'topline' and a 'baseline', which connect the peaks and valleys, respectively, of the *non-focal* word accents of the phrase; these lines decline gradually. The focal lines show the level of the word accent maxima and minima for the *focused* word or words of the phrase; these lines are nearly horizontal, and roughly reflect the top and the bottom of the speaker's range for any given utterance. The Bruce and Gårding realisation model is shown in figure 2.3.

There is an obvious similarity between the Bruce and Gårding model and the IPO model discussed in section 1.2. The IPO model has theoretical reference lines that get tilted downwards in actual phonetic realisation – just like the 'statement lines' in Bruce and Gårding's model. This provides further confirmation of the comment I made above in connection with the levels-vs.-configurations debate: there is little practical difference between describing intonation in terms of distinctive 'pitch movements' that move between topline and baseline, and describing it in terms of distinctive pitch accents composed of 'level tones' scaled at well-defined levels in the speaker's range. That is, though Bruce and Gårding's model is based on Bruce's theory that makes use of H and L level tones, it can be compared rather directly to the IPO model, which in theory deals in pitch movements and ascribes no theoretical significance to the beginning and ending levels of those movements.

On the other hand, by distinguishing the statement lines from the focal lines, the Bruce and Gårding model incorporates a notion of what I have elsewhere (Ladd 1992a) called *tonal space*. Tonal space is a subset of the overall speaking range which is available for realising tonal distinctions at any given point in the utterance. In Bruce and Gårding's model, the tonal space is defined by the 'statement lines', and changes throughout the course of the utterance. The larger range is the one defined by the 'focal lines', which does not change.

The term 'tonal space' is my own, intended as a name for a construct that is crucial to making AM intonational phonology work, but which is not always clearly recognised as a construct of the models in which it appears. The key features of the tonal space idea are, first, that the phonetic realisation of pitch features is defined relative to the tonal space, and second, that the actual phonetic value of the tonal space may change or evolve continuously during the course of the utterance (e.g. as a result of 'declination'). In my view, Clements's 'tone level frame' (1979), Pierrehumbert and Beckman's 'transform space' (1988: 182), and the 'register' of Poser 1984 or Connell and Ladd 1990 are all instantiations of the tonal space idea. I shall return to discuss various aspects of the tonal space view in the next section, in section 4.4, and especially in chapter 7.

The point with which I wish to conclude here is the following: the AM view, by describing contours in terms of only two distinctive levels and by treating phonetic realisation – 'scaling' – as a separate problem, has virtually eliminated the levels-vs.-configurations debate as an active issue in intonation research. In languages with lexically specified level tones, such as Yoruba, it is entirely uncontroversial that we need some sort of description with abstract phonemic levels and concrete phonetic realisation rules. The innovative idea in Bruce's and Pierrehumbert's work lies in seeing that the same idea of phonologically conditioned variation in the realisation of lexical tones can be extended without difficulty to the elements of a level-tone phonological representation of intonation. Once this is accepted, the basic opposition between high and low emerges naturally as a description of how intonation works. In place of the unresolvable levels-vs.-configurations conundrum, the AM theory has spawned the much more tractable empirical issue of how tonal targets are scaled.

2.4 Phonological interpretation of global F_0 trends

It has been clear at least since Pike (1945) that F_0 tends to decline over the course of phrases and utterances, both in tone languages and in languages like

English or Dutch. It has also been noted that in a number of languages this 'declination' is suspended or reversed in questions (see e.g. the especially clear evidence from Hausa in Lindau 1986 and Inkelas and Leben 1990, as well as the data from Thorsen 1980a discussed in section 1.3.2). Observations like these are easy to incorporate into an overlay model of F_0; if we reject overlay models, we must nevertheless offer some account of such global trends.

The solution to this problem is in two parts. The first part involves drawing an explicit distinction between the abstract phonological specifications and their phonetic realisation. In the terms just introduced, that is, it involves treating the problem of declination and other global trends as part of the more general question of how tonal targets are scaled. The second part involves generating global trends by a sequence of local (i.e. phonologically controlled) modifications of the phonetic realisation parameters. This is the subject of this section.

Given the notion of 'tonal space' just introduced in the preceding section, then 'local modifications of the phonetic realisation parameters' may be thought of as discrete localised changes to the tonal space. By modelling the 'evolution of the tonal space' (to use the terminology introduced in the previous section) by means of a sequence of localised changes, AM models part company with the IPO model. In the IPO model, the evolution of the tonal space is purely a matter of declination, and the downward slope of the declination lines is directly specified as such. There is a standard formula for computing the starting level and the rate of declination, based on the length of the utterance (for quantitative details of the IPO declination model see 't Hart 1979). By directly specifying a slope, the IPO model blurs the line between a segmented model and an overlay model – as I noted earlier in my presentation of the IPO model in section 1.2.3.

In all AM work since Pierrehumbert 1980, by contrast, the evolution of the tonal space is treated in a way more in keeping with the idea of a sequence of localised phonological events. Specifically with regard to declination, Pierrehumbert (1980) advanced the hypothesis that most or all of declination can be accounted for as the result of *downstep* – the stepwise lowering of pitch (or of the tonal space) at specific pitch accents.[12] Figure 2.4 shows the difference between describing an idealised downtrending contour in terms of global declination and treating it as the result of the repeated localised occurrence of downstep.

Inspiration for the notion of downstep in English comes from the tonal systems of many languages of sub-Saharan Africa. In many such languages, the second High tone in a sequence High–Low–High is realised at

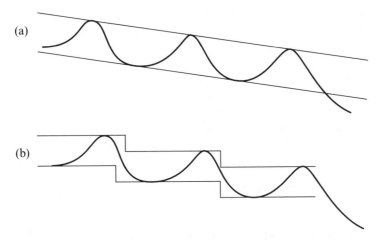

Figure 2.4. Two different ways of describing the overall downward trend of a pitch contour. Idealised contour and 'tonal space' diagrams show the overall downward trend as the consequence of (a) gradual declination, (b) downstep at specific points in the utterance.

a lower level than the first High, and the level of the second High sets a new ceiling for the realisation of High tones until the end of a phrase or some other relevant prosodic unit. Similar phenomena have since been shown to occur in Japanese (Poser 1984; Kubozono 1989), conditioned by the presence of lexical accent: the H tone of a phonological word, whether accented or unaccented, will be lower if it follows an accented word than if it follows an unaccented word. The use of local downstep to generate global trends in English entails the claim that English has a distinction between downstepped and non-downstepped accents: a downstepped accent is realised at a lower F_0 level than a corresponding non-downstepped one.

Although the notion of downstep is crucial for a linear account of global trends, the justification for drawing the distinction between downstepped and non-downstepped accents in English can be demonstrated most clearly on the basis of short utterances with only two accents. Consider a phrase like *my uncle's notebooks*. First, recall (section 1.1.2) that there is a distinction between the two possible prominence patterns strong–weak and weak–strong (i.e. *my UNCLE'S notebooks* and *my uncle's NOTEBOOKS*). In the strong–weak version, the focus is on *uncle's* (e.g. my uncle's notebooks, not my aunt's), while in the weak–strong version, the focus is either on *notebooks* (my uncle's notebooks, not his files) or on the whole phrase (my uncle's notebooks, not any of the family furniture). Now, with an ordinary declarative intonation, the pitch contour on the strong–weak version will show a peak on *uncle's*, and *notebooks* will be realised quite low in the speaking range:

(2.21)

my uncle's notebooks

But there are two distinct ways of realising the weak-strong version that both nevertheless remain roughly within the realm of ordinary declarative intonation. First, we can have

(2.22)

my uncle's notebooks

with the accentual peak on *notebooks* equal to or higher than that on *uncle's*. But second, we can also have

(2.23)

my uncle's notebooks

which has a downstepped accent on *notebooks*. Though (2.23) is very similar phonetically to (2.21), there is an unmistakable difference: (2.21) focuses on *uncle's*, and (2.23) does not. Phonetically, that is, a downstepped accent on *notebooks* is very similar to the absence of accent, but pragmatically it is clearly an accent.

In order to account for these observations, we need to be able to say that *notebooks* in (2.23) is metrically stronger than *uncle's*, even though it is scaled considerably lower. This is achieved by postulating a distinction between downstepped and non-downstepped accents. The downstepping adds a nuance like finality or completeness, but does not make the accent 'less prominent' in the way it affects the focus of the phrase: both downstepped and non-downstepped accents can manifest the underlying prominence pattern weak–strong. Since 1980 there has been considerable debate over the appropriate phonological analysis of English downstep, but Pierrehumbert's basic descriptive insight – that there is such a distinction – has been widely accepted (see e.g. Ladd 1983a; Hirst 1983; van den Berg *et al.* 1992). This, in turn, makes it plausible to account for at least some global downtrends in English in terms of the repeated occurrence of downstep.[13]

Pierrehumbert and her colleagues (Pierrehumbert 1980; Liberman and Pierrehumbert 1984; Pierrehumbert and Beckman 1988) have devoted a great deal of attention to the detailed phonetics of downstep in English. The details of the model have changed – in particular, the 1988 version of the model much more clearly incorporates a tonal space than the original 1980 model – but one of the main points remains unchanged; namely that, given an appropriate scale in which to express F_0 values, the steps in a downstep sequence like that shown in figure 2.4 are of equal size. More precisely, the value of each accent peak in a downstep series is a *constant proportion* (in terms of the model's parameters) of the previous peak. Similar results have been obtained for Dutch by van den Berg, Gussenhoven, and Rietveld (1992).

This is an important finding, because, like Bruce's data on Swedish word accents, or like the results of the *Anna/Manny* experiment, it is consistent with the view that target levels are actively controlled by the speaker and are therefore appropriately represented in a phonological description of intonation. It is also important because it calls into question a significant motivation for overlay models: if target values can be generated from left to right, with only a small 'window' looking back to a previous value, it is possible to generate overall trends in contours without incorporating them as actual components of the model.

In fact, the downstep model is discriminating enough to permit Liberman and Pierrehumbert to distinguish downstep from what they call 'final lowering' in production data. In an experiment in which speakers produced utterances containing a series of from two to five downstepping accents, Liberman and Pierrehumbert found that the final accent was invariably lower than would have been predicted by the constant proportion in the phonetic model of downstep. The amount by which it was lower was consistent across utterances and across experimental conditions. Liberman and Pierrehumbert therefore suggested that the scaling of the final accent was subject to two distinct effects, downstep and final lowering, each of which makes its own distinct contribution. This interpretation of the instrumental data is in line with observations of tone languages, in which the last tone in an utterance is often realised at a much lower level than would otherwise be expected (cf. Pike 1948: 28). It is difficult to see how such specific effects on specific accents could be accounted for in an overlay model with anything like the same simplicity.[14]

A great deal remains to be explored in this general area. Many experiments are being done that make sense to one investigator but are subtly out of focus from the point of view of another. Many ideas are being proposed that are broadly similar in spirit but mutually incompatible in detail. A great deal of essential quantitative data about global trends is simply missing. But I think that the idea of tonal space, recognised as a feature of how pitch range is controlled, has a great deal of potential for clarifying the empirical questions that need to be asked.

3 *Phonological representation of pitch in the autosegmental–metrical theory*

Now that we have explored the theoretical and empirical foundations of the AM approach to intonation, we can move on to consider the technical details of the AM description of the intonational phonology of specific languages. The obvious starting point for any such discussion is Pierrehumbert's analysis of English. There are actually three distinct versions of the Pierrehumbert analysis: the original version presented in Pierrehumbert 1980; a revised version, intended to supersede the original, developed by Pierrehumbert in collaboration with Mary Beckman (Beckman and Pierrehumbert 1986; Pierrehumbert and Beckman 1988); and a modified and simplified version of the revision that forms part of the ToBI transcription system (Silverman *et al.* 1992). The discussion in this section attempts to take account of all three. I will sketch the main claims of the original analysis, trace the development from one version to the next, and discuss several issues that have arisen in the past fifteen years.

3.1   Pierrehumbert's notation and the structure of tunes

It will be useful to begin with a few remarks about notation. For those who are largely unfamiliar with Pierrehumbert's system, the notation may be its most striking novelty, and it is important to distinguish mere notational conventions from the theoretical innovations that the notation system expresses.

Pierrehumbert's notation represents the contour as a string of pitch accents and edge tones. All pitch accents consist of a single H or L tone or a combination of two tones. The central tone of a pitch accent is indicated with an asterisk, as either H* or L* (hence 'starred tone'). In addition to this central or starred tone, a pitch accent may contain a 'leading' (preceding) or 'trailing' (following) tone.[1] This notation is used, for example, in cases where the pitch accent is characterised by rapid local F_0 movement rather than just a local maximum or minimum; more detail is given in the next section.

79

In the original notation, leading and trailing tones are written with a following raised hyphen (H⁻ or L⁻), and the two tones of a bitonal pitch accent are joined with a plus sign (e.g. L*+H⁻). In some systems based on Pierrehumbert (e.g. Féry 1993; Grice 1995a), both the plus sign and the raised hyphen are dispensed with, and one writes simply L*H. In what follows I retain the plus sign, to avoid any ambiguity over which is the starred tone: it is clearly important to distinguish 'starred tones' (which we can write generically as T*) from 'unstarred tones' (T⁻), as the two types may differ in their phonological and phonetic behaviour. However, I omit the raised hyphen except when it is essential for clarity.

Pierrehumbert's original analysis posited seven possible pitch accent types, H*, L*, L+H*, L*+H, H+L*, H*+L, and H*+H. In the revised standard (Beckman and Pierrehumbert 1986) the H*+H accent has been eliminated. The remaining six are all those logically possible combinations of the two tones and the star that do not contain two like tones. The motivations for eliminating the H*+H involve larger issues having to do with the treatment of pitch range, and I will postpone discussion of the H*+H until chapter 7. The presentation in this chapter is based largely on the six pitch accent types of the revised standard.

Tonal events at the edges of prosodic domains – edge tones – are divided into two types in Pierrehumbert's original analysis, *phrase accents* and *boundary tones*. Boundary tones in this strict sense are single tones – either High or Low – associated with the end of an intonational phrase. In Pierrehumbert's notation they are indicated as H% or L%. Phrase accents (or, in more recent work, 'phrase tones', which is the term I shall use here) are free-standing unstarred tones H or L (i.e. unstarred tones that do not serve as leading or trailing tone in a bitonal pitch accent) occurring between the last pitch accent and the boundary tone. In Pierrehumbert's original analysis, every intonation phrase ends with a sequence of a phrase tone and a boundary tone. This claim has been modified somewhat in the revised version of the analysis, as discussed below in 3.3.2.

This notation expresses several of the theoretical claims about intonational phonology that were outlined in the previous chapter. First and most obviously, it embodies the basic phonological claim that contours are to be analysed as strings of elements occurring at well-defined points in the utterance. Second and more specifically, it clearly distinguishes between two types of elements, pitch accents and edge tones. Third, it further analyses pitch accents as consisting of one or more H and L tones.

The notation also embodies several ideas about the *structure* of tunes.

These are summarised by Pierrehumbert (1980) in the following finite-state grammar, which can be used to generate all the legal tunes of English.

(3.1)

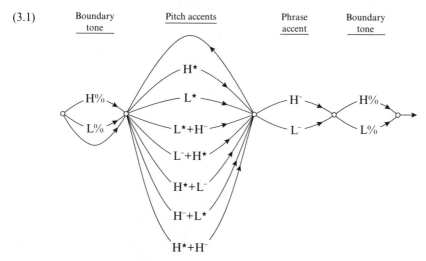

| Boundary tone | Pitch accents | Phrase accent | Boundary tone |

This grammar says that tunes are made up of one or more pitch accents, followed by an obligatory phrase tone and an obligatory boundary tone. It implies two interrelated theoretical claims about the structure of tunes that are worth highlighting here. First, the grammar implies that all possible combinations of pitch accents and edge tones are legal, an implication that Pierrehumbert explicitly endorses (1980: 30 (1988: 13)). Second, it implies that there is no constituent structure to the contour, in particular no analogue to the 'head' and 'nucleus' of the traditional British analysis. Together, these mean that there is no difference between 'prenuclear' and 'nuclear' accents, except – trivially – their position: for Pierrehumbert, the 'nuclear accent' is merely the last accent of the phrase. This general cluster of issues has a long history, and I will return to discuss them at length in chapter 6.

3.2   Basic intonational taxonomy

Despite appearances, there is much in the basic Pierrehumbert taxonomy of English intonation that is comparable with earlier analyses, in particular those of the British tradition. While denying any theoretical status to the notion of nuclear accents, Pierrehumbert (1980, in the Appendix to the Figures) illustrates the realisation of the twenty-two occurring combinations of pitch accent, phrase tone, and boundary tone in a way that invites

Table 3.1. *Correspondences between Pierrehumbert 1980 and British-style nuclear tones*

Pierrehumbert			British-style
H*	L	L%	fall
H*	L	H%	fall–rise
H*	H	L%	stylised high rise
H*	H	H%	high rise
L*	L	L%	low fall
L*	L	H%	low rise (narrow pitch range)
L*	H	L%	stylised low rise
L*	H	H%	low rise
L+H*	L	L%	rise–fall
L+H*	L	H%	rise–fall–rise
L+H*	H	L%	stylised high rise (with low head)
L+H*	H	H%	high rise (with low head)
L*+H	L	L%	rise–fall (emphatic)
L*+H	L	H%	rise–fall–rise (emphatic)
L*+H	H	L%	stylised low rise
L*+H	H	H%	low rise
H+L*	L	L%	low fall (with high head)
H+L*	L	H%	low fall–rise (with high head)
H+L*	H	L%	stylised high rise (low rise?) with high head
H+L*	H	H%	low rise (high range)
H*+L	H	L%	stylised fall–rise ('calling contour')
H*+L	H	H%	fall–rise (high range)

comparison to traditional British nuclear tones. (There are actually twenty-eight logically possible combinations of seven pitch accents, two phrase tones, and two boundary tones, but six – including all four that contain the doubtful H*+H pitch accent – are said to be indistinguishable from other sequences as a result of neutralisation brought about by the implementation rules.) Table 3.1 summarises the twenty-two combinations and gives a possible British-style description of each. Some of the equivalences suggested are open to argument, but the existence of clear correspondences in most cases can be taken as some indication of the validity of the basic taxonomy of intonational contrasts.

It is, however, pointless to attempt to state a complete correspondence between the two systems. For one thing, the 'British tradition' covers a range of divergent analyses of certain phenomena, notably the 'heads' or patterns of prenuclear accents, but also the distinctions between, for example, 'high fall' and 'low fall' (see the discussion in section 1.4). This means that there is no single agreed inventory of nuclear tone types that we can compare item by item against the Pierrehumbert analysis. For another thing, Pierrehumbert's approach is intended to provide a new foundation for analysing intonational distinctions, not merely a new notation for the same old description. The divergence between the two approaches is most obviously reflected in the way the nuclear tone types are grouped in table 3.1: these groupings make sense in the Pierrehumbert system but not in the British system. The grouping based on the Pierrehumbert analysis shows five completely parallel sets of four types, plus two additional ones, whereas from the point of view of the British tradition certain types like 'low rise' and 'high rise' show up rather unpredictably at several different places in the table,[2] and references to pitch range or to the type of preceding head are required here and there to describe certain distinctions.

The following subsections present the basic claims of Pierrehumbert's analysis more or less on its own terms. Comparisons to the constructs of other approaches, in particular the British and IPO traditions, are drawn where appropriate.

3.2.1 Accent types

First consider the phonetic interpretation of the H*, L*, and L*+H accents. H* is a local peak aligned with the accented syllable and L* is a local valley, and L*+H is an accent contour that is low for a good portion of the accented syllable and then rises sharply, often into the following unstressed syllable if there is one. Recall that there is no distinction in the theory between the 'nuclear' and the 'prenuclear' uses of these accents. This means that non-final H* is often used for what British analysts would treat as various sorts of prenuclear stressed or accented syllables. Figure 3.1 shows both H* and L*+H accents in both nuclear and prenuclear position. Recall also that the choice of accent type is theoretically independent of the choice of edge tones. Figure 3.2 shows the L*+H accent followed by two different edge tone sequences, yielding contours that are completely different in British terms.

Two further pitch accent types, L+H* and H+L*, are typically characterised by movement from a preceding syllable, rather than (as is the case with L*+H) movement to a following one. This is exactly what the notation suggests: the starred tone of these two accents is the central one, aligned with the accented syllable, while the unstarred tone is a 'leading' tone, which will normally determine the pitch of a preceding syllable if there

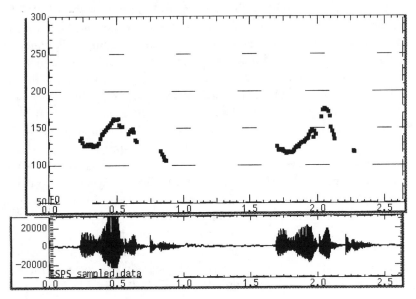

Figure 3.1 Comparison between the H* (left side of figure) and L*+H (right side of figure) accents. The figure shows the two as nuclear accents followed by a L..L% edge tone sequence. In British terms these are respectively 'fall' and 'rise–fall'. The text in both cases is *I wanted to*.

is one. However, L+H* and H+L* bring to light rather different problems, and it will be useful to discuss them separately.

L+H* is basically like H*, that is, a local peak, but it rises from a much lower level. The difference between L+H* and H* is particularly clear if there is a preceding syllable to display the level of the leading L. On a phrase-initial accented syllable, L+H* and H* can be difficult to distinguish.[3] Otherwise the phonetic interpretation of L+H* is fairly unproblematical. In fact, in a sense it is the interpretation of H* that is the problem: the presence of a local peak in figure 3.1 might seem to suggest the presence of a leading L before the H*. In the phonetic realisation model developed by Anderson, Pierrehumbert, and Liberman (1984), the problem is avoided by generating a small local peak for any H*, thereby eliminating the need for a leading L and reserving the L+H* accent for cases with a more distinct rise from a lower level. Nevertheless, the distinction between the H* and the L+H* clearly raises the more general question of how to identify which points in a contour reflect the occurrence of tonal targets. If both H* and L+H* are characterised by a rise in pitch at the beginning of the accented syllable, on what basis do we decide

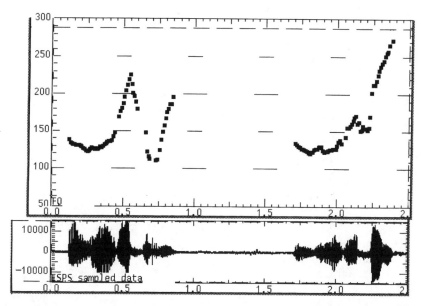

Figure 3.2 The L*+H accent followed by different edge tone sequences. On the left is the sequence L*+H..L..H%, in British terms a rise–fall–rise nuclear tone, applied to the text *I watered them*. On the right is the sequence L*+H..H..H%, in British terms a low–rise nuclear tone, applied to the text *You watered them?* In the system of Beckman and Pierrehumbert 1986 the latter contour is reanalysed as L*..H..H%.

that the beginning of the rise is a L tone in one case and no tone at all in the other? We will return to this point in section 3.5 below.

The H+L* accent is superficially comparable to L+H*. As L+H* involves a local rise to a peak from a preceding syllable, so H+L* involves a local drop from a preceding syllable. The relationship between H+L* and L* is thus analogous to that between L+H* and H*. However, the parallelism is not perfect, because the 'low' target of H+L* is not a local valley or F_0 minimum. Instead, it is scaled at the level of a 'downstepped' or locally lowered *high* tone: that is, the pitch drop indicated by the H+L* notation is from one high pitch to another high pitch that is slightly lower, not from a high pitch to a level that would independently be described as low. The main use of this accent type in Pierrehumbert's original analysis is in describing 'terraced' downstepping contours in English, which are illustrated in figure 3.3. Arguments for this analysis are presented in Pierrehumbert 1980: chapter 4.[4]

The last of the six pitch accent types, H*+L, indicates a high accent that triggers downstep in the following H tone. In the revised Pierrehumbert

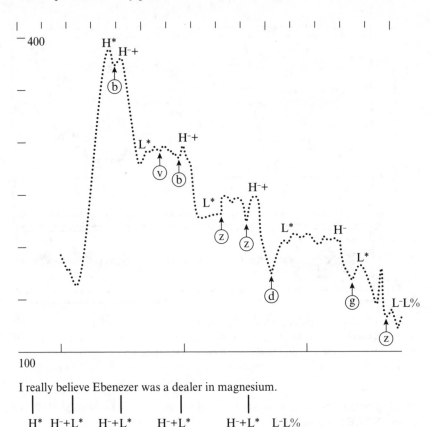

Figure 3.3 Terraced downstepping contour in English on the text *I really believe Ebenezer was a dealer in magnesium*, analysed by Pierrehumbert as a H* on the first accent followed by a series of H+L* accents. From Pierrehumbert 1980.

system, all bitonal pitch accents (viz. H*+L, H+L*, L*+H, L+H*) trigger downstep, but in the last three of these, as we have just seen, the bitonality also indicates some pitch movement in the vicinity of the accented syllable. In the H*+L, by contrast, the L has no phonetic interpretation other than as a downstep trigger. In all other respects H*+L is like H*. The distinction between a H*+L..H* sequence and a H*..H* sequence is shown in figure 3.4.

3.2.2   Edge tones

To some extent we have already considered the use of phrase tones and boundary tones in comparing the Pierrehumbert taxonomy to the

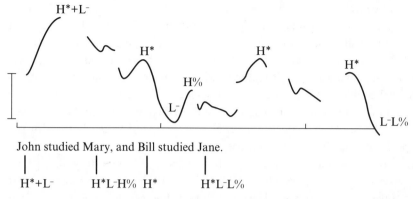

Figure 3.4 Difference between H*+L and H* in Pierrehumbert's analysis. The first half of the utterance has the accent sequence H*+L..H*, with the peak of the H* downstepped from the peak of the H*+L. The second half of the utterance has two H* accents, with peaks of approximately the same height. From Pierrehumbert 1980.

traditional British one. However, as we have seen, in theory the edge tones represent an independent choice, and British-style 'nuclear tones' are merely specific combinations of accents and edge tones (cf. table 3.1. and section 2.1). Therefore the edge tones can and should be described independently of the accents that they follow.

3.2.2.1 Boundary tones

The H% boundary tone always indicates a final rise. This is straightforward after the L phrase tone, but requires an 'upstep rule' (Pierrehumbert 1980: section 4.5) after the H phrase tone. That is, the final rise is what one would expect phonetically from a sequence of L and H, but from a sequence of H and H one might expect only a sustained level, and the upstep rule ensures that the level of the H% boundary tone is higher than that of the immediately preceding H phrase tone. In either environment, the final rise typically takes place at the very end of the phrase or utterance.

H% is clearly to be identified with the Type 2 Rise of the IPO analysis of Dutch, which is a 'non-prominence-lending' pitch movement occurring at the ends of phrases. As noted in section 1.2.1 above, Cohen and 't Hart (1967) originally found it odd that a pitch movement could be so distinctive and so unambiguously localised and yet not be prominence-lending. It now seems beyond dispute that 'distinctive, localised, and non-accentual' is precisely the nature of boundary tones, and that the recognition of

discrete pitch movements at boundaries is a concrete advance in our understanding. In the British tradition, there is no analogue to H%, and as a
result British nuclear tones such as fall–rise conflate the pitch movement on
the last accent (e.g. fall) with the pitch movement at the end of the phrase
(e.g. rise). The taxonomy of falling–rising contours is a long-standing unresolved problem in the British tradition (see section 2.1).

The L% boundary tone can best be described as indicating the absence
of final rise. After L phrase tone, it indicates a fall to the bottom of the
speaking range, but after H phrase tone it indicates a level sustention of the
previous tone. The sequence of H phrase tone and L boundary tone is how
Pierrehumbert analyses what Ladd (1978) called 'stylised' intonation, that
is, tunes ending with a level sustained pitch. The best example of a stylised
tune is the 'calling contour' or 'vocative chant':

(3.2)
Ma–
ry–

Pierrehumbert analyses this as H*+L..H..L%. (This contrasts with the
sequence H*+L..H..H%, which has a rise at the end instead of a sustained
level.) Note how in this analysis the H*+L pitch accent downsteps the H
phrase tone, yielding the characteristic stepping-down of the calling
contour. For the other stylised tunes see table 3.1.

3.2.2.2   Phrase tones

The idea of the phrase tone is borrowed from the 'phrase accent' of Bruce's
analysis of Swedish. As we saw in section 1.3.3, Bruce showed that a
Stockholm Swedish intonation contour can be analysed as a sequence of
one or more 'word accents' (the lexically specified accent patterns), followed by an additional peak at the end of the focused word of each phrase,
followed at the end of the utterance by a fall to the bottom of the speaker's
range. The peak at the end of the focused word of each phrase is the 'phrase
accent'.[5] Pierrehumbert's proposal was that in English, as in Swedish, the
last pitch accent of each phrase is followed by two distinct tonal events. This
analysis is motivated most clearly in the case of the rising–falling–rising
nuclear accent contour of English, where the first rise is analysed as a
L*+H pitch accent, the fall is the reflex of a L phrase tone, and the final
rise reflects a H% boundary tone.

The details of the phrase tones in Pierrehumbert's analysis are as follows.
The L phrase tone can be straightforwardly interpreted as low pitch following the final pitch accent of the phrase. The fall to this low level takes

place fairly soon after H* or any bitonal pitch accent, and the pitch remains low until the final boundary tone, at which point it either rises abruptly (H%) or drops off to the bottom of the speaker's range (L%). The stretch of low pitch can span several syllables, as in a sentence like (3.3):

(3.3)

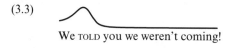

We TOLD you we weren't coming!

This extended span of low pitch is described by Pierrehumbert (1980: ch. 5) in terms of a 'tone-spreading' rule of the sort found in many African tonal systems.

The H phrase tone represents a high pitch following the last pitch accent, but the details require some comment. As we saw in the preceding subsection, the H phrase tone is put to good use in the representation of stylised tunes, where it represents the pitch level that is sustained until the end of the phrase. In ordinary tunes, however, the phonetic interpretation is less transparent. The main problem is with tunes that begin rising at the last accent and continue to rise until the end, such as the high-rise and low-rise nuclear tones of the British tradition. In a sequence H*..H..H% there is no obvious phonetic basis for saying where in the contour the H phrase tone 'occurs'.

3.3 Modifications to the original analysis

3.3.1 *Downstep and the L phrase tone*

In Ladd 1983a, I discussed several problems with Pierrehumbert's analysis of English, while at the same time supporting the overall idea of a linear tone-based description of intonational tunes. My overall argument was that the Pierrehumbert analysis is needlessly complex, and fails to express certain cross-classifying similarities between contour types. The source of the needless complexity, I argued, is Pierrehumbert's phonological analysis of downstep and its delicately balanced relation to her use of Bruce's concept of 'phrase accent'.

The problem revolves around the use of the notation H*+L. Given the way Pierrehumbert uses other bitonal accents (L+H*, L*+H, and H+L*) to indicate local pitch movements, the most natural interpretation of H*+L would be to indicate a local fall from a peak or other high level: a H peak and a trailing L. Since 'local fall from a peak or other high level' is a straightforward description of the ordinary declarative falling accent or falling 'nuclear tone', we might expect to find this most common accentual pattern represented as H*+L. Instead, as we saw above, Pierrehumbert uses H*+L to represent a high accent that is followed by another – downstepped – high, while the ordinary declarative fall is represented as a H* accent followed by a L phrase tone. In Ladd 1983a, I argued that both these analytical decisions were flawed.

Let us consider downstep first. Pierrehumbert sees downstep in English as a phenomenon of phonetic realisation which is 'triggered' by certain sequences of tones. For example, in a sequence of accents H*..H*, the second accent is realised at the same level as the first (other things being equal), whereas in a sequence H*+L..H* the sequence of tones H..L..H triggers downstepping of the second H*. This analysis is motivated in part by lexical tone and pitch accent languages that are known to have downstep, such as Yoruba or Japanese. In these languages, as we saw in chapter 2, downstep is often triggered on the second H of H..L..H sequences. Pierrehumbert tries to preserve this aspect of downstep in her analysis of English.

I argued that, for English, this view of downstep fails to express the fact that downstep is an independent intonational choice. In effect (as we saw in section 2.4), downstep *means* something, something like 'finality' or 'completeness'. Moreover, this meaning is orthogonal to the meaning of certain other intonational choices. Pierrehumbert herself points out that there are several different types of downstepping contours in English (see figure 3.5); I showed in Ladd 1983a that each of these downstepping contour types is matched by a contour in which the shape of the pitch accents is the same but in which the peaks do not downstep. Pierrehumbert's analysis, based on the notion that downstep is a mere phonetic consequence of an underlying sequence of tones, represents the various possible contours of English in ways that obscure both the orthogonality of downstep and the similarities between downstepped and non-downstepped accent types.

This is the point at which Pierrehumbert's analysis of downstep becomes intertwined with her adaptation of Bruce's 'phrase accent' concept. Pierrehumbert's representation, I argued, is driven entirely by the self-imposed requirement of providing enough distinct combinations of H, L, and * to create the H..L..H sequences that will trigger downstep. Because of the need to use H..L..H sequences to trigger downstep, the representation H*+L is preempted to describe a peak followed by a downstepped accent. Consequently Pierrehumbert needs a different way to describe the fall in pitch that follows the peak in the nuclear falling accent. It is for this

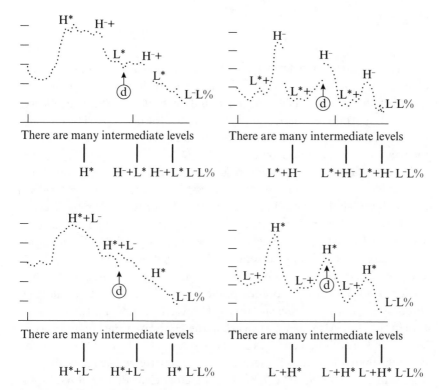

Figure 3.5 Four different downstepping contours in English, applied to the text *There are many intermediate levels*. From Pierrehumbert 1980.

reason that she proposes to analyse the fall as the reflex of a low 'phrase accent', that is, a separate phonological event from the accentual peak.

We eliminate this entire tangle of problems, I argued, if we recognise the phonological independence of downstep. The *shape* of accents can be expressed by means of the tonal analysis (H*+L, H*, L*+H, etc.), but downstep must be treated as an independently selected 'feature' of each accent that can be present or absent independently of the choice of accent type itself. For example, we might have two H* accents in sequence, either with downstep or without it. For the case without downstep, we would write H*..H*, like Pierrehumbert, but in the case with downstep, instead of Pierrehumbert's H*+L..H*, we would write H*..!H*, using the downstep diacritic /!/ frequently encountered in the Africanist literature. In terms of the 'features' I proposed in Ladd 1983a, the two possibilities are:

(3.4)   H*..H*   and   H*..H*
                                    |
                              [+ds]

By directly representing downstep with a feature or diacritic on the affected accent, we express the idea that downstep is an independent linguistic choice with an identifiable meaning and identifiable phonetic effects. Equally important, we leave ourselves free to use the notation H*+L transparently, to indicate a falling accent, and thereby to do away with the phrase tone and its attendant difficulties.

Those difficulties are considerable. It seems fair to say that the phonetic evidence for the phrase tone analysis is less compelling in English than in Swedish. In Swedish, as we saw, the phrase accent can be directly observed as a distinct peak in the contour separate from the lexical accent. In English, this is never the case. This is particularly apparent in the case of the H phrase tone, as just noted above (section 3.2.2.2 and note 2). To be sure, there are some contours where the phrase tone marks a clear turning point, notably the L phrase tone in the three (rise–)fall–rise nuclear tones H*..L..H%, L*+H..L..H% and L+H*..L..H%. Also, as we saw earlier, the H phrase tone creates a clear 'elbow' in the stylised contours L*..H..L% and H*+L..H..L%, and may do so in some other cases if there are enough unstressed syllables following the last accent (e.g. H* L L%). It is therefore clear that, in some cases, there is another tonal target following the starred tone of the accent. The question is whether this tonal target is to be identified as a distinct type of phonological event – the 'phrase tone' – which is always present in the structure of the contour, or whether it is part of a bitonal accent such as H*+L. This question was one of the main issues addressed by Beckman and Pierrehumbert (1986).

3.3.2   The 'intermediate phrase'

Beckman and Pierrehumbert (1986), in their presentation of a slightly revised standard AM analysis of English intonation, reject the entire line of argument in Ladd 1983a. With regard to downstep, they point out that whatever the flaws of the original Pierrehumbert analysis, the 'downstep feature' has serious problems of its own. The worst of these is the fact that a downstep feature could be applied to the first accent in a series. That is, in addition to the sequences shown in (3.4) above, there is nothing to prevent the feature system from generating a meaningless sequence like (3.5):

(3.5)   H*..H*
        |
        [+ds]

The original Pierrehumbert analysis, by contrast, is unable to generate a meaningless 'downstep the first accent' contour.[6] Beckman and Pierrehumbert present a slightly modified analysis of downstep, but retain the basic idea that downstep is 'triggered' by specific sequences of tones and could therefore never apply to the first accent in a series.

More importantly for our sketch of the phonology of English intonation, Beckman and Pierrehumbert (1986) propose a revision to the permissible structure of tunes in English (see section 3.1 above). This revision grows out of their work on applying the AM theory to Japanese (Pierrehumbert and Beckman 1988). The centrepiece of their proposal is the explicit formulation of a distinction between *intonation phrase* and *intermediate phrase* as levels of prosodic structure in English. Similar distinctions between larger and smaller phrase-like domains have frequently been made (see Ladd 1986: section 1.2). Beckman and Pierrehumbert's motivation for this particular distinction is the view that English does *not* have an 'accentual phrase' of the sort found in Japanese, that is, a prosodic unit based on a single pitch accent. There is a phrase-like prosodic unit in English that is smaller than an intonation phrase, but it can still have more than one accent, and is merely 'intermediate' between the intonation phrase and the prosodic word.

Beckman and Pierrehumbert relate this proposal to the issue of separate phrase tones. They suggest that the edge of an intermediate phrase is marked by a phrase tone, while the edge of an intonation phrase is marked by both a phrase tone and a boundary tone; that is, each type of domain has its own type of edge tone. This proposal, of course, provides new theory-internal motivation for analysing the falling nuclear accent as a sequence of a H* accentual peak and a separate L phrase tone: the phrase tone is now seen as a separate entity that marks the edge of the intermediate phrase. This in turn means that there is no pressure to stop using H*+L for an accent that downsteps a following accent, and consequently less reason to find an alternative phonological analysis of downstep.

The notion of the intermediate phrase has been adopted by numerous authors, though the term 'intermediate' poses a problem if for no other reason than that it makes it difficult to come up with unambiguous abbreviations for intermediate phrase and intonation phrase. Hayes and Lahiri (1991) suggest that the intermediate phrase is equivalent to the 'phonological phrase' of Nespor and Vogel (1986) and others. They also propose a potentially useful notational device, based on Beckman and Pierrehumbert's idea that the phrase tone is the edge tone for the phonological phrase and the boundary tone that for the intonational phrase; in place of Pierrehumbert's T for phrase tone and T% for boundary tone, they write T_p and T_i respectively. A similar notation is used by Grice (1995a), who writes T_b for intermediate phrase edge tones (phrase tones) and T_B for intonation phrase edge tones (boundary tones). However, neither notation has so far been widely adopted, and as long as there remains doubt about the proper analysis of falling nuclear accents (and more generally about the status of the phrase tone), the notational question seems likely to remain unsettled.[7] We will return to these issues in section 3.5 and in chapter 6.

3.3.3   ToBI

The third and most recent distinct version of the Pierrehumbert analysis is the one incorporated into ToBI (Silverman *et al.* 1992; Beckman and Ayers 1994; Beckman and Hirschberg 1994; Pitrelli, Beckman, and Hirschberg 1994), a proposed standard for labelling prosodic features of digital speech databases in English. A complete ToBI transcription contains several 'tiers' – strings of symbols anchored in time to specific points in the waveform of an utterance – including the orthographic transcription and a tier reserved for comments on disfluencies and the like. The two most important tiers are those indicating the *tones* (To) in the F_0 contour and the *break indices* (BI) that label the strength of each word boundary, and it is these two tiers that give the system its name.

Before discussing the ToBI tonal analysis, it may be worth sketching the background to the development of the system. ToBI was the joint initiative of a group of American researchers whose primary interest was in establishing a common system to indicate prosodic features in labelled computer corpora of speech. Two of the principal groups involved in this initiative had developed their own partial labelling systems. Those we may refer to as the 'To' group were more interested in intonation in the narrow sense of utterance melody, and had worked with Pierrehumbert's tonal analysis of English. The 'BI' group were more concerned with phrasing, prominence, and prosodic structure generally, and had developed the notion of 'break index' as a way of impressionistically indicating the strength of word and phrase boundaries (e.g. Price *et al.* 1991). The development of the system involved not only compromises between these two main groups, but also detailed discussion with potential users of labelled corpora (for research in speech technology or the study of dialogue). Once a preliminary system was in place, there was further discussion with representatives of certain other schools of prosodic transcription (in particular IPO and traditional British) before the agreed standard was finally published in 1992.

It is important to point out that ToBI is first of all a set of conventions for labelling prosodic features – analogous to a set of conventions for transcribing the segmental features of dialogue and connected speech – aimed at making large corpora of speech more useful for research. As such, a good deal of what has gone into the creation of ToBI is software development (ToBI is designed to be used in conjunction with the waves+ speech analysis and signal processing software produced by Entropic Research Laboratory Inc.; see Shore 1988; Talkin 1989) and the production of training materials (to teach potential labellers not only to hear the relevant prosodic distinctions but also to train them in the use of the labelling software and the agreed transcription conventions). It is also important to emphasise that ToBI is specifically a transcription system for English, and not, as some seem to think, a kind of high-tech IPA alphabet for intonation generally. However, labelling systems based on similar principles are being developed for a number of other languages (Batliner and Reyelt 1994; Grice and Benzmüller 1995).

The ToBI standard for transcribing tonal features is, as noted above, essentially a version of the Pierrehumbert analysis of English. However, certain modifications were made to the revised standard proposed in Beckman and Pierrehumbert 1986, with which the developers started. Interestingly, the issues discussed in the preceding sections, downstep and the phrase tone, were among the most contentious.

With respect to downstep, the Pierrehumbert representation was largely abandoned, and downstep is indicated by the traditional Africanist downstep diacritic /ᴵ/ before the affected tone. This was done for two reasons: first, because in actual auditory transcription it is not always clear whether an accent is to be regarded as downstepped; and second, because some of the contributors to the system found the standard Pierrehumbert notation difficult to use even when there was no doubt about the presence of downstep. There were two specific cases that arose frequently enough to cause problems, the H*+L accent and the H+L* accent.

The H*+L, which in the standard Pierrehumbert system downsteps the *following* accent, was merged with H*. The distinction between a down-stepping sequence H*+L..H* and a non-downstepping sequence H*..H* is now indicated by applying the /ᴵ/ diacritic to the *affected* (downstepped) accent. A downstepping sequence is therefore transcribed H*..ᴵH*. As for the H+L* accent, which in the standard Pierrehumbert system indicates a downstepped accent that steps down locally from the preceding unstressed syllable, this is now written H+!H*. As observed in note 4 above, this makes it clear that the level of the accented syllable is not necessarily low in the speaker's range, but only lower than what precedes. Both these changes were motivated by the desire to make the labels more phonetically trans- parent (and thus more usable by labellers not thoroughly versed in Pierrehumbert's theory), but they also have the theoretically interesting effect of making downstep a largely orthogonal phonological variable, specifiable independently of the choice of accent type, as proposed in Ladd 1983a. The downstep diacritic can also be applied to several other elements of the ToBI system, both accents and phrase tones.

Unlike the Pierrehumbert approach to downstep, the notion of the phrase tone as the edge tone for an intermediate phrase is preserved in the ToBI analysis. However, this too gave rise to difficulties in formulating the standard. The principal problem was posed by F_0 contours which, accord- ing to the Pierrehumbert analysis, can arise only through a sequence of accents and phrase tones, but which do not contain an audible boundary. For example:

(3.6)   a.
              Edinburgh's the capital of Scotland.

This must be analysed in Pierrehumbert's system as involving a phrase tone and hence an intermediate phrase boundary:

(3.6)   b. H*   L   L+H* L L%
              Edinburgh's the capital of Scotland.

Yet it is perfectly possible for there to be no cues to the presence of a bound- ary between *Edinburgh's* and *the* except for the phrase tone itself.

Cases like these create a problem because of the coordination between the tonal tier and the break index tier of a ToBI transcription. In the ToBI version of the break index system, there are five possible boundary strengths, from 0 (the greatest degree of phonetic integration between two words, i.e. the weakest boundary) to 4 (boundary between intonation phrases), with break index 3 being used for an intermediate phrase bound- ary in the Beckman and Pierrehumbert sense. This requires a coordination between the labels on the tonal tier and those on the break index tier: a con- sistent ToBI transcription indicates an intermediate phrase boundary (break index 3) on the break index tier any time a phrase tone is indicated on the tonal tier. Yet cases like (3.6) involve no audible boundary which might justify the use of break index 3! To those unconvinced of the very validity of the phrase tone analysis, this use of break index 3 seemed circular at best, and at worst misleading about the phonetic reality that the labelling was intended to reflect.

The problem was solved in the ToBI standard by permitting break index 2 to be used in conjunction with a phrase tone on the tonal tier in cases precisely like these. That is, break index 2 can indicate the absence of cues to the presence of a boundary other than those required by the tonal analysis. Thus:

(3.6) c. H*   L   L+H* L L%
       Edinburgh's the capital of Scotland.
              0 2 1   1 1   4

Break index 2 is also used in the converse way, to indicate an audible break between words that has no apparent tonal correlates. A technical solution for the problem is thus provided and the phrase tone analysis preserved.

A related but less serious problem has to do with the actual alignment of the phrase tone. As noted above, what Pierrehumbert analyses as the L phrase tone is probably timed a fairly constant interval after the H* of the accentual peak; it certainly occurs close to the accentual peak rather than close to the edge of the intermediate phrase if the two are some distance apart. This is what creates the 'elbow' in contours like (3.7a):

(3.7) a.
       That was the whole POINT of the exercise!

If the location of such elbows were noted in a ToBI transcription, we would once again have a paradoxical combination of tonal tier and break index tier, as in (3.7b):

(3.7) b. H*   L+H* L   L%
       That was the whole POINT of the exercise!
            1   1 1   1   1 1 1   4

Here the word *of* has a phrase tone (L) attached to it, but is not followed by a 3 break index, because of course the intermediate phrase boundary actually coincides with the intonational phrase boundary at the end of the utterance.

So long as the L is regarded as a phrase tone rather than part of the accentual contour, and so long as close coordination of the tonal and break index tiers is required, such paradoxical transcriptions will arise any time there are unstressed words following the last accent in a phrase. The solution to this problem was to treat sequences of phrase tone and boundary tone as a single choice, and therefore in effect to require the labeller to align the phrase tone with the break index corresponding to the intonation phrase boundary, in this case

(3.7)   c. H*   L+H*   L L%
         That was the whole POINT of the exercise!
              1   1   1   1   1 1   1   4

The precise location of the elbow is ignored, but there is no paradox at the word *of*. This solution is in keeping with ToBI's goal of providing a phonological rather than a detailed phonetic prosodic transcription.

3.4   Intonational meaning in Pierrehumbert's analysis

While the emphasis of this chapter, and of the book as a whole, is on phonetic and phonological issues, it should be noted that Pierrehumbert's analysis of English intonation has led to a line of research attempting to describe the 'meaning' of intonational tunes. This includes both the work of Hirschberg and her colleagues, which is anchored firmly in Pierrehumbert's analysis of English, and the work of Carlos Gussenhoven and myself, which is essentially a critique of that analysis. While this work has many implications for the study of intonational meaning in general, the most important point for our purposes here is that analysts are taking recourse to facts about intonational *meaning* as a way of shedding light on issues of intonational *form*. That is, Hirschberg and Pierrehumbert have used analyses of the meaning of, for instance, the H phrase tone in part as a way of arguing that the H phrase tone exists, while Ladd and Gussenhoven have used analyses of the meaning of, for instance, delayed peak to argue that a peak delay feature (or some other direct phonological representation of peak alignment) exists. These issues are briefly reviewed in this section.

I think it is fair to say that this line of work begins with the critique of Pierrehumbert's intonational phonology presented in my own paper on 'peak features' (Ladd 1983a). Essentially, the 'peak features' were intended as a kind of cross-classifying device for accent types: accents, in addition to being high or low, can be downstepped or non-downstepped, delayed or non-delayed, raised or non-raised, and so on. I presented this system as an exercise in 'insightful taxonomy', arguing that such features

make it possible to combine 'phonetic specification and linguistic generalization'. For example, as discussed in section 3.3.1 above, I suggested
that the impressionistic similarities among downstepping contours are
directly expressed by the use of the [±downstep] feature to represent the
occurrence of downstep. In Pierrehumbert's analysis, by contrast, downstep is merely the phonetic consequence of the occurrence of a 'triggering'
sequence of tones, and downstepping contours share no single phonological property. I argued that the phonological taxonomy underlying
Pierrehumbert's tonal descriptions was inadequate, because it represented
impressionistically similar contours very differently, and impressionistically very different contours very similarly (cf. the commentary on table
3.1 above).

In Ladd 1983a, I referred only vaguely to 'linguistic generalization' and
'impressionistic similarity' and the like; however, the idea of cross-
classifying features is extensively developed in Gussenhoven's work on
English intonation, and the relation of the cross-classifying analysis to a
theory of intonational meaning is made explicit.[8] Gussenhoven proposes
that English has three basic 'tones' (roughly equivalent to accent types in
Pierrehumbert's analysis), namely HL or fall, LH or rise, and HLH or
fall–rise. These 'tones' are subject to various 'modifications' such as styli-
sation (see section 3.2.2.1) and delay (see section 2.2.3). Each of the categories of this phonological taxonomy – both the tones and the
modifications – is then assigned a basic meaning, on the basis of which specific nuances and specific functions of intonational distinctions can be
described. For example, Gussenhoven states that each of the three basic
tones (i.e. accent types) has a different basic discourse function: the fall is
used to introduce an entity into the 'background' or shared knowledge of
the interlocutors (hence its use as basic statement intonation); the rise is
used to be non-committal about whether a mentioned entity is part of the
background (hence its use as basic question intonation); and the fall–rise is
used to 'select' an entity from the background. Similar analyses are provided for each of the proposed 'modifications'; for example, peak delay is
said to signal that the utterance is in some way very significant or non-
routine. While meanings such as these are obviously extremely general,
Gussenhoven provides extensive discussion of how they might (given
various reasonable assumptions about the nature of pragmatic inference)
give rise to specific nuances in specific contexts. Furthermore, Gussenhoven
(1984: ch. 7; see also Gussenhoven and Rietveld 1991) backs up his analyses with the results of perceptual experiments, in which speakers of English

were asked to judge the similarity between contours on otherwise identical utterances. With some exceptions, these experiments show that contours which Gussenhoven's analysis represents as similar are perceived as similar by listeners.

In a related development, Ward and Hirschberg (1985) provide an account of the semantics and pragmatics of the English rise–fall–rise nuclear contour (Pierrehumbert's L*+H..L..H%). Ward and Hirschberg assume a single basic meaning for the contour, which can be paraphrased as 'uncertainty'. They show how, by principles of pragmatic inference, listeners arrive at specific nuances in specific contexts. In subsequent work, Ward and Hirschberg show how this meaning can give rise to distinct interpretations such as qualification and incredulity. Like Ladd or Gussenhoven, then, Ward and Hirschberg are adherents of what we characterised in section 1.4.3 as the 'Linguist's Theory of Intonational Meaning'. The most important difference between Ward and Hirschberg and Ladd or Gussenhoven is the former's serious attempt to express their analysis in terms familiar to practitioners of formal semantics.

By itself, Ward and Hirschberg 1985 is not intended as a defence of Pierrehumbert's analysis of English. It uses the Pierrehumbert notation L*+H..L..H% to refer to the contour in question, but does not attempt to extend the analysis to other elements of Pierrehumbert's system. In a sense, by its very concern with a whole contour rather than a single pitch accent, it tends to undermine Pierrehumbert's insistence on the independence of the individual pitch accents and edge tones. Subsequent work by Pierrehumbert and Hirschberg, however, has combined Ward and Hirschberg's standards of formal explicitness with a concern to describe the basic meanings of the elements of Pierrehumbert's system in particular – the six pitch accents, the two phrase tones, and the two boundary tones. Ultimately, this means that the Ward and Hirschberg analysis of the meaning of the L*+H..L..H% contour must be derivable from the meaning of the L*+H accent, the L phrase tone, and the H% boundary tone.

The most accessible account of this subsequent work is Pierrehumbert and Hirschberg 1990. Pierrehumbert and Hirschberg present what they call a 'compositional approach to tune meaning'. They suggest that 'the components of tune – pitch accents, phrase accents, and boundary tones – are each interpreted with respect to their distinct phonological domains' (p. 286). Pitch accents, they state, 'convey information about the status of the individual discourse referents, modifiers, predicates, and relationships specified by the lexical items with which the accents are associated' (p. 286).

Phrase accent type expresses 'the degree of relatedness of one [intermediate] phrase to preceding and succeeding intermediate phrases . . . [If a phrase ends in] a H phrase accent, for example, it is more likely to be interpreted as a unit with a phrase that follows' (p. 287). Boundary tones, finally, 'contribute information about the intonational phrase as a whole' (p. 287). A significant portion of the paper is devoted to the interpretation of different pitch accent types; for example, they suggest that H* accents 'convey that the items made salient by the H* are to be treated as "new" in the discourse' (p. 289), while L* accents mark items that are intended 'to be salient but not to form part of what [the speaker] is predicating in the utterance' (p. 291).

Because the 'Hirschberg–Pierrehumbert theory of intonational meaning' has been seen in some quarters as a major innovation made possible by the AM approach (e.g. Hobbs 1990), it is worth emphasising that the principal novelty of Pierrehumbert and Hirschberg's work is the attempt to provide intonational meanings *for the elements of the Beckman–Pierrehumbert analysis of English intonation*. In other respects it is based, like the other work we have just sketched, on the Linguist's Theory of Intonational Meaning. Pierrehumbert and Hirschberg abundantly acknowledge their indebtedness to Gussenhoven, Bolinger, and others; their intended innovation is the claim that intonational meaning is compositional, and specifically that the compositionality can be best understood in terms of the Beckman–Pierrehumbert analysis. In a sense, their paper can be regarded as a response to the Ladd–Gussenhoven critique: Pierrehumbert and Hirschberg (pp. 282f.) accept Ladd's and Gussenhoven's idea that similarity of meaning should be reflected by similarity in phonological representation, and they seek to show that the elements of Pierrehumbert's analysis do indeed share meaning in common. That is, they accept the Ladd–Gussenhoven premise, but reject the conclusion that Pierrehumbert's analysis needs revision.

Despite the different opinions here, and despite the fairly clear results of Gussenhoven and Rietveld (1991) suggesting that the Gussenhoven analysis gives a better account of listeners' similarity judgements than does the Pierrehumbert analysis, there has been very little real debate on this issue. I think this is primarily because we know too little about pragmatic inference for the debate to be conclusive. On their own terms, analyses like Gussenhoven's, Ladd's, or Hirschberg and Pierrehumbert's can all be evaluated as reasonably plausible – or reasonably implausible, depending on who is doing the evaluating. However, there is no theoretical framework within which we can do a comparative evaluation that would command general agreement. For the present, proposals about intonational meaning are not a reliable source of evidence on intonational phonology.

3.5   Some unresolved issues

Pierrehumbert's analysis of English has been extremely influential, and the autosegmental–metrical theory of intonational structure that underlies it has been widely adopted in work on other languages. My own early response (Ladd 1983a), though in some respects a critique, showed how the theory could be used to understand the phenomena of Hungarian question intonation, and to overcome certain difficulties in the IPO analysis of Dutch. Gussenhoven and his colleagues (Gussenhoven 1984, 1993; Gussenhoven and Rietveld 1991; van den Berg, Gussenhoven, and Rietveld 1992) have applied the theory extensively to Dutch, while Wunderlich (1988), Uhmann (1991), and Féry (1993) have all analysed German in AM terms. Pierrehumbert and Beckman (1988) have treated numerous aspects of Japanese accent and intonation in the same general framework. Hayes and Lahiri (1991) provide a succinct and elegant application of the theory to the intonation of Bengali. Within the last few years AM descriptions of intonation in a variety of other languages have begun to appear, such as Sosa 1991 on American Spanish, Mennen and den Os 1993 and Arvaniti 1994 on Greek, Grice 1995a on Palermo Italian, Post 1993 on French, Frota 1995 on European Portuguese, and King 1996 on Dyirbal. Some of these analyses are essentially critiques of Pierrehumbert, while others are applications, but all accept the basic assumptions outlined in chapter 2.[9]

At the same time, when we consider this body of work as a whole, we can see more clearly the point of distinguishing the basic assumptions in chapter 2 from the specific details of the analysis of English in the present chapter. That is, the extensive application of Pierrehumbert's theory makes it possible to identify certain areas of disagreement over how the theory is to be extended past its original application to English. The specific issues we have been discussing in this chapter – downstep and the phrase tone – can be seen to depend on three basic questions that have yet to be answered in any widely accepted way.

The first of these questions has to do with the status of pitch range. This is such a fundamental problem – and has been such a fundamental problem for theories of intonation for so long – that I will postpone any discussion of it until chapter 7. The other two issues might be summarised succinctly as 'What is a tone?' and 'How are tones organised phonologically?' These two questions are discussed briefly in this section.

3.5.1 What is a tone?

As we saw in section 2.3, one of the central claims of the AM approach is that pitch accents are composed of combinations of H and L tones. Yet fundamental questions remain about how tones are to be recognised: by what criteria do we decide that a given pitch accent consists of one or two tones? How do we determine that there is or is not a tone at any given point in a string?

In Bruce's original version of the AM approach, tones are identified with turning points in the F_0 contour. Local maxima correspond to H tone and local minima to L tone. This is a very 'concrete' conception of tone, and leaves little room for argument about what the tones are in a given contour. It does leave a little room, because local maxima and local minima that are present physically in the contour may be attributed to segmental perturbations of F_0 or other non-intonational causes. Also, Bruce (1977: ch. 5) explicitly discusses the possibility that tonal targets may be undershot in, for example, a H..L..H sequence where the targets are very close together. On the whole, however, identifying tones with turning points puts severe limits on the range of possible phonological interpretations of a given contour.

This concrete conception of tones as turning points is implicitly abandoned by Pierrehumbert. In Pierrehumbert's approach, as we have seen, tones need not always correspond to turning points, and turning points need not always reflect the phonetic realisation of a tone. We saw an example of the latter case in section 3.2.1: the low turning point before a H* accent is not taken to reflect a L tone of any sort, but instead is accounted for by phonetically modelling the H* as a local pitch jump rather than merely a peak. We have seen several cases where posited tones do not correspond to turning points. For example, the L in an H*+L accent is never realised as a low target or turning point, but serves only to trigger downstep on the next H tone (see sections 3.2.1 and 3.3.1). In the same way, the L% in Pierrehumbert's analysis of English stylised contours does not represent a final low target, but only the absence of a further rise following the H phrase tone (see section 3.2.2.1 and table 3.1). The L* in a H+L* accent probably represents a target, but never a low turning point: it is an accentual target, lower than the immediately preceding context, but scaled at the level of a downstepped H tone (see sections 3.2.1 and 3.3.3).

A priori there is no reason to reject Pierrehumbert's approach, or to prefer Bruce's. It is abundantly clear from the tonal phonology of many African languages that we must allow for the possibility that tones in the underlying phonological string may not be realised phonetically as distinct F_0 targets. The clearest cases, as in Pierrehumbert's analysis of English, involve downstep. In many languages, the L in a H..L..H sequence may have no independent realisation as a turning point, but be manifested only in the lowering of the second H relative to the first. Other cases are less clear but still definitely involve a more complex relation between tones and targets. For example, Laniran (1992: ch. 3) shows that in Yoruba, the sequences L..H..H..H and H..L..L..L are not realised with abrupt steps from L to the first H or H to the first L, but rather involve a gradual transition from L to the third H and from H to the third L, almost as if the intervening syllables are tonally unspecified. There is much we do not understand about the relation between phonological tones and F_0 targets, but it is clear that the simple equation 'tone = turning point' is too restrictive to serve as a universally valid principle of tonal realisation.[10]

At the same time, in dealing with intonation languages, there are reasons not to proceed too enthusiastically to posit tones that are realised in indirect ways. For one thing, by abandoning Bruce's simple equation we throw away a powerful empirical check on our theorising. In languages with lexical tone, we often have independent evidence for postulated tones that do not surface as target points, because we can observe alternations in the shape of individual morphemes and words in different phonological contexts. In languages with only postlexical or intonational uses of tone, we have no such ready way of constraining our descriptions.

A clear illustration of the problems of abandoning the identification of tone and turning point is provided by my proposal for a 'delayed peak' feature, discussed in section 2.2.3 above. In suggesting that the 'scooped' or 'delayed peak' falling contours are tonally identical to non-delayed falls and that the only difference is one of alignment, I ignored the fact that the delayed contours often involve a slight stepping down to the accented syllable before beginning the rise to the (delayed) peak and subsequent fall. This slight stepping down is almost certainly to be interpreted as a low accentual target aligned with the accented syllable, namely a L*; that is, the delayed peak contour should be treated as L*+H, followed by a further L target (e.g. a phrase tone). By concentrating on the alignment of the peak and on my arguments for treating the falling accent contour as H*+L, I allowed no way to account phonetically for the accentual low.

A more extensive illustration is provided by the case of the 'sagging transition' between H* targets in Pierrehumbert's analysis of English. In Bruce's original conception, transitions between tonal targets are simply straight-line interpolations. Pierrehumbert's own work has shown the value of this idealisation in describing tonal realisation in Japanese (Pierrehumbert and Beckman 1988: esp. ch. 4). But in her analysis of English, as we have seen (section 3.2.1), Pierrehumbert proposes that the transition from one H* accent to the next is not a straight interpolation between the peaks, but gradually sags or declines after the first H* until just before the second H*, at which point there is a local rise to the level of the second peak.

This analysis, on its own, has a certain amount to recommend it, but considered in the light of the overall description makes for problems with the interpretation of turning points, as Pierrehumbert herself acknowledges. For example, in a two-accent sentence like *Their mother's a lawyer*, with identical high peaks on both accents, Pierrehumbert's analysis posits three possible contours, which she notates as H*+H..H*, H*..H*, and H*..L+H*.[11] The sequence H*+H..H* would have a high level transition between the two accent peaks; the sequence H*..L+H*, with a supposedly more emphatic second accent, would have a smoothly dropping transition from the first peak to a fairly low level immediately before the second peak; while the third type of sequence, H*..H*, shows the transition that falls gradually until just before the second H*, at which point it rises slightly but abruptly. These three contours are illustrated in figure 3.6.

The obvious question raised by this analysis is why the gradual fall and abrupt rise represent a L target (the leading tone of the L+H* accent) in one case, but no target at all, only a 'sag', in the case of the H*..H* sequence. Pierrehumbert recognises that the sagging transition is an unfortunate feature of her theory, and states that she 'made a serious attempt to get rid of it by developing an account under which the dip in [such contours] arises from a L tone' (1980: 70). However, given her other analytical decisions, none of the possible sources of L was satisfactory. Perhaps most obviously, she is once again confounded by her analysis of downstep. The sequence of tones otherwise most suited to describing the sagging transition, namely H*+L..H*, is preempted for use in triggering downstep. Pierrehumbert might also have explored the possibility of treating all H* accents as L+H*, with different degrees of emphasis affecting the depth of the leading L, but unfortunately, the sequence L+H*..L+H* is supposed to trigger downstep. If we assume an analysis in which the specification of

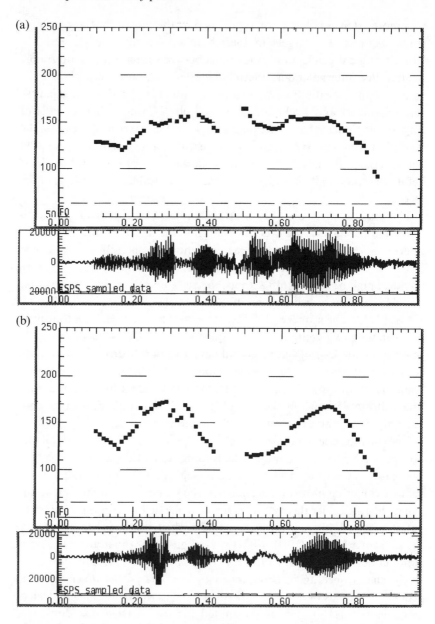

downstep is independent of or orthogonal to the string of tones, then this possibility becomes more attractive. Such a treatment of downstep is discussed in section 7.3.3.

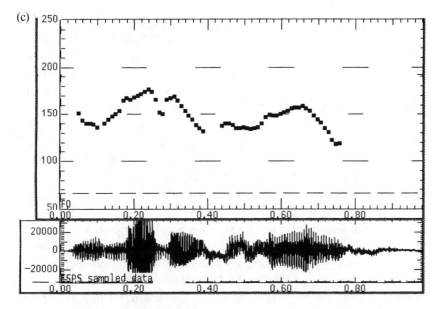

Figure 3.6 Three possible contours applied to the text *Their mother's a lawyer*, all with high accentual peaks on both *mother* and *lawyer*. Panel (a) shows the contour analysed by Pierrehumbert 1980 as having a sequence H*+H..H*, with a high level transition between the two peaks. Panel (b) shows the contour analysed as having a sequence H*..L+H*, with the second accent rising sharply from a low beginning and with a smooth transition from the H of the first accent to the initial L of the second. Panel (c) shows the sequence analysed as H*..H*, with a 'sagging' transition between the two peaks.

3.5.2   How are tones organised phonologically?

In any case, it is clear that decisions about what constitutes a tone are not made in an analytical vacuum. By concentrating only on what I saw as Pierrehumbert's failure to produce an 'insightful taxonomy', I failed to realise the potential of the AM approach for detailed modelling of phonetic targets. By giving priority to her analysis of downstep, Pierrehumbert was unable to make sense of the turning point preceding the second H* target in a H*..H* sequence. In both cases, the equation 'tone = turning point' was abandoned because other considerations came first.

In these two cases and in many others, the conflicting considerations in the phonological treatment of phonetic turning points mostly involve *phonological organisation*. One of the central claims of Pierrehumbert's work is that tones can be organised into larger structures – pitch accents, tunes, etc. At one level of description, the F_0 contour is the realisation of a simple linear string of tones, but at another level it is necessary to recognise that the string has internal structure. If we decide that a given phonetic turning point represents a tone, then, the very first thing we need to do is to decide how it fits into a larger phonological structure. For example, in order for Pierrehumbert to recognise the low turning point between H* accents as the reflex of a tone, she would have had to find a place for it in a pitch accent type. But the number of possible pitch accent types was extremely limited by her *independent* theoretical assumption that pitch accents never consist of more than two tones. It is because of this assumption that Pierrehumbert's analysis of downstep interferes with recognising the low turning point as a tone, and favours the 'sagging transition' analysis instead.

If we distinguish carefully between the identification of tones and the analysis of their phonological organisation, we can see more clearly which aspects of an AM analysis rest on fundamental assumptions and which are essentially hypotheses cast within a framework of such assumptions. Consider again the English rising–falling–rising contour that was applied to *Sue* and *a driving instructor* in examples (2.1) and (2.2). It is required by the basic assumptions of the AM approach that there are at least four tones in this contour: an initial L, a H peak, a valley L, and a final H. We might want to argue for the presence of two Ls in the valley, one immediately following the H peak and one immediately preceding the final H; we might also have more to say about the stretch of contour preceding the H peak; but four tones are a minimum. Given those four tones, however, it is a specific descriptive hypothesis that they are organised into a L+H* pitch accent, and L phrase tone, and a H% boundary tone. Other analyses are possible.

For example, a classical British-school analysis of this contour as applied to *a driving instructor* might be as a fall-rise 'nuclear tone' and a low 'prehead'. In effect, the H peak, valley L, and final H are grouped together into one unit, while the initial L is a reflection of a separate unit. There is actually a considerable lack of clarity within the British school about how nuclear tone contours spread to cover more than one syllable (in this case, the nuclear syllable *driv-* and the syllables *-ing instructor* of the 'tail'), but there is no disagreement that the fall–rise constitutes a single unit in the system, distinct from the prehead. We might therefore translate this British analysis into AM terms as involving a L prehead and a H*LH nuclear accent – which is essentially equivalent to the AM phonological proposals of Gussenhoven (1983a). Both analyses involve the same

L..H..L..H sequence of tones, but they structure the sequence in quite different ways.

The distinction between recognising the existence of a tone and hypothesising about its place in the phonological structure of the tune is explicitly discussed and clearly illustrated in the work of Martine Grice (Grice 1995a, 1995b). Grice shows that the nuclear or most prominent syllable of a short question in Palermo Italian is always marked by a high peak followed by a fall; she also shows that the peak (unlike peak + fall nuclear tunes in English, or statement tunes in Palermo Italian) must be preceded by a valley or a low level stretch of contour. We are therefore dealing with a tonal sequence L..H..L. As Grice points out, in the British tradition, the first L would inevitably be assigned to the 'head' (i.e. the stretch of contour preceding the nucleus), and the nucleus would be analysed as a fall or a rise–fall. She argues instead that the L is an essential part of the question intonation nucleus, and posits the following structure for the nuclear accent:

(3.8)

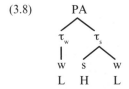

In the terms used here, the issue between Grice and the British tradition is not about the existence of the L tone before the nuclear H peak, but about its phonological status: does it belong to the nuclear contour, or to the preceding prenuclear stretch?

The issue is not limited to the constituency of the L tone, however. In proposing a structure like (3.8), Grice also breaks new theoretical ground within the AM approach, which she justifies at some length. That is, the issue between Grice and a standard Pierrehumbert-style analysis is not what the tones are, nor even whether the leading L is part of the nucleus, but how many tones can be organised into a pitch accent. Pierrehumbert proposes a flat structure for pitch accents, with one obligatory starred tone and at most one unstarred tone. If we adhere to this structure, the Palermo question nucleus will have to consist of a $L+H^*$ pitch accent followed by a L phrase tone. Grice proposes a more elaborate structure for pitch accents, which can accommodate three or even four tones in a single accent; in her analysis, all three tones of the Palermo question nucleus are part of the same pitch accent. It seems appropriate to describe both Grice's analysis and Pierrehumbert's as 'autosegmental–metrical', but there are considerable differences between the two analyses about which AM theory – so far – has little to say.

Related remarks can be made about Gussenhoven's notion of a 'tone linking' rule (Gussenhoven 1983a). (Note that this should be called a 'pitch accent linking rule' to be consistent with the terminology used so far.) Gussenhoven proposes that there are various possible realisations of any given sequence of accents, depending on phrasing and speech rate. Specifically, he suggests that it is possible to move or delete certain individual tones to link pitch accents more closely. In *partial* linking, the trailing tone of one pitch accent is reassociated as a leading tone to the following accent; in *complete* linking, the trailing tone is deleted. Gussenhoven thus proposes to relate the following three sequences as shown on his example sentence *Toronto is the capital of Ontario*:

(3.9)   H*L   H*L

    a.   basic form: Toronto is the capital of Ontario

                         H*   LH*L

    b.   partial linking: Toronto is the capital of Ontario

                         H*   H*L

    c.   complete linking: Toronto is the capital of Ontario

In the context of the present discussion, we can see that Gussenhoven's claim involves two separate aspects. First, he identifies three contours that differ with respect to the location of a particular L tone. Second, he proposes that the three contours are systematically related in the phonology – that they are in some sense different versions of the same thing. In an orthodox Pierrehumbert analysis, there would be no major disagreements over the surface tonal analyses of the three types; presumably these would be H*..L..H*..L for (3.9a), H*..L+H*..L for (3.9b), and H*..H*..L for (3.9c). However, no phonological relationships of the sort posited by Gussenhoven would be assumed; the contours are simply different.

Gussenhoven's analysis raises questions about the phonological organisation of the tune. In particular, his analysis of (3.9a) and (3.9b) focuses our attention on the L tone between the two H*s: what kind of tone is it, and where does it come from? For Pierrehumbert, it has two completely unrelated sources, and is underlyingly two different phenomena – in one case it is the phrase tone of a separate intonation phrase *Toronto*; in the other case it is the leading tone of the accent on *Ontario*. Gussenhoven, by relating the two contours in the phonology, suggests that in both cases we are dealing with the same thing: it is underlyingly the trailing tone of the first accent but can be moved around.

A broadly similar analysis of comparable data in German is discussed at length by Uhmann (1988 and 1991). Uhmann's approach, like Gussenhoven's, assumes that the L belongs underlyingly to the first accent. However, instead of moving the L to the following accent, she suggests that the L can spread rightward to a greater or lesser extent, with various specified consequences for phonetic realisation; for a case like (3.9a) Uhmann would have the L tone associated only with the immediately post-stress syllable in *Toronto*, whereas in a case like (3.9b) the L would spread to all the intervening unaccented syllables. She also explicitly allows the possibility of intermediate cases, which she relates to different possible focus structures; this suggests that some of what Uhmann discusses might be handled by Pierrehumbert in terms of the location of an intermediate phrase boundary.

There is clearly some kind of low tone in between the two H* accents in (3.9a) and (3.9b). The Pierrehumbert framework offers an unambiguous way to transcribe the low tone in both contours, making a clear distinction between phrase tones on the one hand and leading or trailing tones on the other. However, it provides no way to treat the contours as closely related. Gussenhoven's or Uhmann's analyses rather loosely exploit various kinds of phonological rules in ways that will probably not stand up to closer inspection. But they deserve attention none the less, because they question the sharp descriptive distinctions drawn by Pierrehumbert, and they suggest that phrase tones and trailing tones might be, in some way, different manifestations of the same thing. This idea, like Grice's idea that pitch accents have internal structure, is entirely heterodox from the point of view of Pierrehumbert's description of English intonation, but from a slightly broader perspective unquestionably falls within the general scope of the AM approach.

3.6   Conclusion

My goal in this chapter and the preceding one has been to show that the basic AM approach to intonational phonology has a great deal of promise, but that the Pierrehumbert analysis of English is, in effect, one possible AM analysis among several. There are many phonological analyses of intonation that are compatible with the AM assumptions outlined in chapter 2.

Pierrehumbert's description of English does not constitute an indivisible package, but rather gives us both a statement of fundamental assumptions and a set of specific descriptive proposals based on those assumptions.

I have identified four basic tenets that I think must form a part of any successful description of intonation. These four are linear structure (and the distinction between phonological events and transitions); the idea that pitch accent is an intonational phenomenon that is associated with certain stressed syllables, but not the phonetic essence of stress; the analysis of pitch accents into component level tones H and L; and the local specification of global F_0 trends. Furthermore, I have identified two specific problems with the Pierrehumbert analysis of English – the phrase accent and the analysis of downstep – that have been contentious in various applications of Pierrehumbert's approach and which, in my view, can be analysed in other ways. In chapters 6 and 7 I will return to present some additional proposals for modifications to current Pierrehumbertian AM ideas.

It is important, however, not to lose sight of the promise of the basic AM approach. Before proceeding to further theoretical discussion, therefore, I will attempt to apply AM ideas to the description of intonation across languages, and in particular to shed light on the question of intonational universals. This is the goal of the next two chapters.[12]

4   Cross-language comparison of intonation

4.1   Intonational universals and intonational phonology

A fundamental question in research on intonation across languages has always been whether intonation is universal. There are enough widely shared properties of intonation systems for many investigators to have hypothesised a universal common core of intonational signalling, a backdrop against which language-specific differences can be seen as minor variations on a single theme. At the same time, however, there are many obvious differences between languages, and between different dialects of the same language, differences that are often very striking to speakers of languages or dialects in regular contact. Without a generally agreed framework for describing intonation, it is difficult to compare intonation across languages and come to any reliable conclusion about the significance of the similarities, or of the differences. With such a framework, however, meaningful comparison ought to be possible. The goal of this chapter and the next is to illustrate the potential of the AM view in this regard.

4.1.1   The universalist view

The phenomena generally emphasised by those who assume a universal common core for intonation include declination (and more generally the association of low or falling pitch with completion), the association of high or rising pitch with both questions and non-finality, and the presence of local pitch movements on new or otherwise informative words. Among the names most prominently connected with these ideas is that of Dwight Bolinger. Bolinger's views, developed over roughly forty years of work on intonation, can be summarised as follows (for more detail see Bolinger 1978; 1986: ch. 9; 1989).

Intonation, according to Bolinger, has direct links to the prelinguistic use of pitch to signal emotion. Broadly speaking, high or rising pitch signals interest, arousal, and incompleteness, while low or falling pitch signals absence of interest and hence finality and rest. This fundamental opposition between high and low (or up and down) is clearly seen in the use of pitch range for obviously emotional expression – raised voice for active emotions such as anger or surprise and lowered voice for boredom, sadness, and the like. But the opposition also shows up in the apparently grammaticised uses of pitch – intonation – that turn up in language descriptions again and again. These include:

1   the tendency of pitch to drop at the end of an utterance, and to rise (or at least not to drop) at major breaks where the utterance remains incomplete;
2   the use of higher pitch in questions, since in questions the speaker expresses interest, and since the exchange is incomplete until the addressee answers;
3   the use of local pitch peaks (e.g. pitch accents) on words of special importance or newsworthiness in an utterance.

Bolinger argues that it is futile to attempt a phonological or grammatical account of intonation. His writings are full of phrases like 'around the edge of language' (Bolinger 1964) and figures like the wave metaphor cited in chapter 1. He comes very close to claiming that speakers are literally more aroused at an accented word than an unaccented one, and at a sentence-medial phrase boundary than at the sentence's end (1986: 203).

Other writers have put forth similar (if less poetic) views about intonation on the basis of more narrowly phonetic considerations. Lieberman (1967), for example, put forth a strong hypothesis relating intonational phrasing to the control of breath and subglottal pressure in speech production, in connection with which he made broadly similar claims about universal functions of intonation to those made by Bolinger. Specifically, he suggested that all linguistically significant[1] uses of intonation in all languages could be reduced to a distinction between 'marked breath group' and 'unmarked breath group' (corresponding roughly to phrase-final rise and fall respectively), plus local prominence for accent on individually informative words; lexical tone was seen as overlaid on the two breath group types. Lieberman's ideas are thus expressed in terms of an 'overlay' model of the phonetics of intonation, of the sort discussed in 1.3.2. It is probably not a coincidence that the same features of intonation – local pitch movements for accentual prominence, and declination or its absence as a signal of finality/statements or non-finality/question – are the focus of attention in many other overlay models. Many proponents of such models seem to assume that these features are more or less universal, though some (notably Grønnum on Danish) are careful to avoid making claims of universality.

While it would be foolish to deny the existence of these broad generalisations about intonation, there are good reasons for scepticism about the universalist view. For one thing, most of its generalisations are so broad or so vague ('high or rising pitch') that it is virtually impossible to falsify them. For another, they are often expressed (at least implicitly) in terms of an overlay model of intonational phonetics, and as we saw in chapter 1, there are independent problems with the overlay view. Indeed, many intonational differences between languages seem to reside precisely in those phenomena that are central to the AM approach, and which are difficult to describe in overlay terms – matters such as the alignment, association, and scaling of targets.

4.1.2   The case of Hungarian question intonation

As a concrete example of the kind of comparison that is made possible in an AM analysis, I will here review the facts of Hungarian question intonation, based on the presentation in Ladd 1983a (see also Gósy and Terken 1994). These facts have been fairly well established for several decades, but they have often been presented as extremely puzzling because of the conspicuous differences between the Hungarian pattern and question intonation in many Western European languages. It is not overstating the case to say that many Hungarian questions sound like emphatic statements to native speakers of English, which is *prima facie* something of a problem for a straightforward theory of intonational universals. Less conspicuously, the relation among lexical stress, focus, and pitch excursion is quite unlike what one might be led to expect on the basis of the Western European languages alone.

From an AM viewpoint, there are two major differences between Hungarian question intonation and the kinds of rising contour one finds in English or French. First, in Hungarian (as in many languages, including Russian, Romanian, and Turkish) the neutral location for the nuclear accent in a yes–no question is on the finite verb.[2] Second, though the pitch on the verb is low, the question tune ends with a high-falling pitch movement, which sounds to speakers of many Western European languages like a declarative falling accent, but which is not necessarily even associated with a stressed syllable. Dealing with the second of these differences first, we may say that the Hungarian question tune consists minimally of a L* pitch accent followed by a H..L% edge tone sequence. The L* is associated with the lexically stressed syllable (which is invariably the initial syllable) of the nuclear-accented word; if there are at least two syllables following the nucleus, the H edge tone is associated with the penultimate syllable and the L% with the final syllable. For example:

(4.1)   L*   H L%
          | | |
         Beszél a tanár?
         'Is the teacher talking?' (lit. talks the teacher)

(The acute accent in Hungarian orthography indicates vowel length, not stress. Lexical stress is fixed on the first syllable of the word.)

In this example it happens that the penultimate syllable is also the stressed (initial) syllable of *tanár*, but that is coincidence, as we can see if we substitute a three-syllable noun:

(4.2)   L*   H L%
          | | |
         Beszél a miniszter?
         'Is the minister talking?'

If the penultimate syllable is also the nuclear syllable (e.g. if the verb is final, or if the question intonation applies only to a noun phrase), the whole tune is 'squeezed' to the right, so that the penultimate syllable is low-rising and the final syllable falling (what happens on monosyllabic questions will be discussed in 4.3.1). We might represent this as follows:

(4.3)   L*HL%
          | V
         A tanár?
         'The teacher?'

If there are prenuclear accents, they are normally are medium-range H* peaks:

(4.4)   H*   L*H L%
          | | / |
         A magyar nehéz nyelv?
         'Is Hungarian a difficult language?' (lit. the Hungarian difficult language)

Now let us consider the first difference mentioned above, namely that the 'neutral' location for the nucleus in a question is on the verb. Differences in focus and emphasis can be conveyed both by changing word order (as in Italian or Russian) and by changing the location of the nucleus (as in English or Dutch), but the nucleus goes on the verb if no special focus is intended.[3] Thus:

(4.5) a.   L*   H L%
            | | |
            Vettél szódát?
            'Did you buy soda (= mineral water)?' (neutral, out of the blue)

       b.   L*   H L%
            | | |
            Szódát vettél ?
            'Did you buy SODA?' (i.e. 'Was it soda that you bought?')

       c.   H*   L* HL%
            | | ⁄
            Szódát vettél ?
            'Did you buy SODA?' (i.e. 'What about soda? Did you buy that?')

It is not difficult to imagine how a phonetician of forty years ago, equipped only with a basic non-autosegmental idea of 'stress' as pitch prominence and of 'intonation' as global utterance contour, might be mystified by these effects. The contour in (4.5a), in which the phonetically most salient pitch excursion occurs on *szó-*, is precisely the contour that does *not* focus on 'soda'; if we want to focus on 'soda' we have to use a different contour such as the ones in (4.5b) and (4.5c). However, once we understand that we are dealing with a tonal sequence L*..H..L% that does not occur in most Western European languages, we can see that all the facts about focus and the location of the phrase-final pitch peak are exactly what we would expect. The basic structural division of the contour into accent tones and edge tones, the way in which the tune is associated with major stressed syllables and boundaries, and the consequent variation in the realisations of the tune depending on the number and location of major stressed syllables and the location of focus, are just like what we find everywhere else. The only differences between Hungarian question intonation and other better-known intonation patterns in the European languages are that (a) it involves a different tonal sequence and (b) 'neutral' accent is on the verb.

On the other hand, it is worth emphasising that both the neutral accent placement, and the question tune itself, really are different from what we find in the Western European languages. That is, while the AM analysis brings out the basic features that the Hungarian question tune shares with many others, it also makes it possible, in a principled way, to avoid treating all question contours as variations on the same theme. If we simply say that questions universally have high or rising pitch at or near the end of the utterance, then Hungarian question intonation could be (and has been; cf. Bolinger 1989: 57ff.) treated as evidence for the universal nature of question intonation. The AM analysis makes it possible to combine an explicit account of the phonology and phonetics of Hungarian question intonation with falsifiable statements about what is and is not an intonational universal.

4.1.3   *Two topics for intonational typology*

The differences between Hungarian and English question intonation – the different tonal sequence, and the difference of neutral accent location – illustrate two of the most important differences with which any comparative study of intonation will necessarily be concerned. The discussion in this chapter and the next is devoted largely to exploring these two topics: this chapter deals primarily with tonal or melodic differences, and the next with accent location. Both chapters present observations about the ways in which languages can differ intonationally – a kind of 'natural history' of intonation. In both cases my aim is to show, first, that a strong universalist view is not tenable, and second, that comparison of intonation systems based on AM phonological descriptions makes it possible to provide explicit characterisations of many subtle differences.

The sample of languages considered in this chapter and the next is unquestionably Eurocentric. In part this is because rather little is known about intonation in languages in other parts of the world, but it is also because the discussion is restricted to pure 'intonation' languages – languages with no lexical use of pitch – of which the European languages are almost certainly the richest and most varied sample in the world. Moreover, by and large the examples have been chosen to make points clearly rather than to provide a systematic discussion of any language or language group. I believe that the distinctions drawn here will be of use in considering the intonation of other languages so far uninvestigated, including languages that do have lexical pitch distinctions. However, at the end of this chapter I have also briefly considered the relationship between tone and intonation, and made some typological suggestions that go beyond the Eurocentric sample on which the chapter is mainly based.

4.2   Tonal differences between 'intonation' languages

4.2.1   A taxonomy of phonological/phonetic differences

It may be useful to begin by distinguishing four possible ways in which languages can differ intonationally.

1   *'Semantic' differences*: differences in the meaning or use of phonologically identical tunes.

2   *'Systemic' differences*: differences in the inventory of phonologically distinct tune types, irrespective of semantic differences.

3   *'Realisational' differences*: differences of detail in the phonetic realisation of what may be regarded phonologically as the same tune.

4   *'Phonotactic' differences*: differences in tune–text association and in the permitted structure of tunes.

This classification of intonational differences is based loosely on a well-established tradition within British linguistics for the description of differences in segmental phonology and phonetics in different varieties of the same language (see Wells 1982). Before discussing intonational differences, it may be useful to sketch the segmental basis of the traditional classification.

The terms used by Wells (1982) for the four types of segmental difference corresponding to the four types of intonational difference are *lexical–incidential*, *systemic*, *realisational*, and *distributional*. The least interesting from a phonological point of view are *lexical–incidential* differences, essentially unsystematic differences between varieties of a language in the choice or selection of phonemes in the lexical representation of specific words. Most often this affects foreign or learned words: thus *methane* has the vowel of *meet* in British English but the vowel of *met* in American; *yogurt* has the vowel of *boat* in American English but that of *pot* in British. There are some generalisations about these differences, specifically between British and American English, that can be traced to differences in the phonological systems of RP ('Received Pronunciation', i.e. Standard Southern British English) and General American (see Lindsey 1990), but by and large the essence of these differences is that they are unsystematic facts about individual lexical items.

Systemic differences are differences of 'system' or phonemic inventory: a contrast made in one variety of a language is systematically absent in another. The clearest examples of this are the absence of any distinction in

Scottish English between the vowels of, for example *pool* and *pull*, and the absence in many Northern English accents of any distinction between the vowels of *book* and *buck*. The loss of the distinction between the vowels of *Don* and *Dawn* in many (especially non-Eastern) American varieties gives rise to another example.

Realisational, by comparison to systemic, differences are differences of phonetic detail involving no effects on the inventory of phonological contrasts. A good example in English involves the three short front vowels in *bit*, *bet*, *bat*. These are distinct in all varieties of English (even in those American dialects that neutralise the /ɪ/–/ɛ/ distinction before nasals, as in *pin* and *pen*). However, the realisation of this three-way contrast varies substantially from variety to variety, so that, for example, the Australian pronunciation of *bat* is virtually identical to some American pronunciations of *bet*, while the Australian *bet* is very similar to RP *bit*, and some retracted Scottish realisations of *bit* are similar to retracted 'Northern cities' American pronunciations of *bet*. Such realisational features contribute a great deal to the regional and social identity of a given variety of a language, but leave the underlying system of phonological contrasts unaffected.

Wells distinguishes the two foregoing categories of difference from phonotactic or *distributional* differences. The most conspicuous such difference in English is the divide between 'rhotic' and 'non-rhotic' varieties, that is, between those that permit /r/ in syllable codas in words like *car*, *port*, *water* (Scottish, Irish, many Western English and most North American accents) and those that do not (most English accents including RP, Australian and other southern hemisphere varieties, and various East Coast American accents). Distributional differences do not involve a difference in the inventory of phonological contrasts, but rather a difference in permitted phonotactic distributions of a given element of the system.

With this brief summary, we now leave segmental differences and exemplify some analogous differences in intonation. I emphasise that no great theoretical significance should be attached to the taxonomy of differences; it will be apparent that it is not always easy to classify specific cases, as is indeed often true for the segmental differences on which the taxonomy is based. But there is certainly some heuristic value in being aware that there are different kinds of differences. Moreover, for those who believe in the universality of intonation, it may be revealing to see segmental and intonational differences between languages compared in the same terms.[4]

4.2.2 Semantic differences: English question intonations

The first kind of intonational differences we may note are those in the meaning or use of otherwise identical tunes. These differences are not perfectly analogous to the 'lexical–incidential' differences in Wells's scheme of segmental variation, but they are comparable in that they are of little direct phonological interest in the description of intonation. They are discussed here first, however, because they often loom large in the perception of speakers of different varieties of the same language. Two cases from English provide typically striking examples.

In a range of contexts, in North American and Antipodean (Australian and New Zealand) English, a high-rising 'question' intonation (probably H*..H..H% or L*..H..H%; cf. table 3.1), is used on utterances that are grammatically, and apparently also functionally, statements. Such high-rising intonation occurs in all varieties of English with certain kinds of questions, but in North America and Australia/New Zealand, the questioning use is generalised to contexts in which the speaker is making a statement but at the same time asking for feedback from the listener (see section 1.1.2). This use is not found in most British varieties, and it strikes many British speakers as wheedling or insistent. One common context for this use is in narrative or other monologue, in which speakers often repeatedly use a high-rising contour to invite acknowledgement from the listener; the intonation is a kind of shorthand for 'Do you follow me?' Two other contexts in which the high-rising intonation is often found with statements are transaction-openers and answers to WH-questions. Both can be seen in the following exchange:[5]

(4.6)
$$\text{H*} \qquad\qquad\qquad \text{H* H\%}$$
A: I have an appointment with Dr Macmillan.
B: What's your name?
$$\text{H*} \qquad \text{H*H\%}$$
A: William Jarvis.

In both A's opener and his reply to the explicit WH-question, the high-rising intonation means something like 'Are you expecting me? Have you got a record of my appointment?' Thus the general meaning of 'request for response' is present in this use of high-rising intonation as it is in clear syntactically marked questions; more importantly, there is to my knowledge no phonetic difference that depends on whether the high-rising contour is used with syntactically marked questions or with statements. It therefore seems reasonable to say that we are dealing with 'the same' tune across varieties of English. The only difference is in the meaning or function of the tune.

Another semantic difference within English is seen in polite yes–no questions like

(4.7)   a.   H*   H* L H%
                Could I have the bill please?

        b.   H*   L H%
                Is your mother there?

On sentences like these, it is quite common in RP but not in any North American variety to use the tune shown: a high level prenuclear stretch and a falling–rising nucleus, which we might analyse as a high H* prenuclear accent followed by a nuclear H*..L..H%.[6] In North American English such questions are most likely to have a high-rising nucleus, identical to the transaction-opening statement in (4.6). The RP tune tends to sound condescending or peremptory to North Americans, since in North American English, to the extent that it is used at all, it is largely restricted to use on echo questions without question syntax implying a strong measure of doubt or disbelief:

(4.8)   H*   H*LH%
            You bought a Mercedes??

It may be worth noting that the impression of condescension seems to be due to the intonation itself and not to anything else about RP pronunciation. As an American speaker resident in Britain I have long since adopted the RP tune for use in these contexts, and now find it rather difficult to switch off. Though my segmental phonetics and phonology are still almost completely American, I have on several occasions elicited chilly reactions in North America by unintentionally using the RP tune, which suggests that it is the intonation, not the overall RP package, that Americans hear as condescending.

In this connection it is also interesting to report the reaction of a native bilingual speaker of German and American English to a discussion of this tune. In German, as in RP, the high-prenucleus-plus-falling–rising-nucleus tune is normal – at least in southern Germany – with questions of this sort:

(4.9)   a.   H*   H*   LH%
            Haben Sie heute Weizenbrot?
            Have you got wheat bread today?

        b.   H*   LH%
            Ist deine Mutter da?
            Is your mother there?

The bilingual speaker shared the general American reaction when the tune was applied to English questions like (4.7), and was astonished to realise that exactly the same tune applied to comparable questions in German does not have the same force.

4.2.3 Systemic differences: 'Urban North British' statement intonation

The analysis of systemic differences is the area where the empirical benefits of the AM approach seem clearest. As we saw with the illustration of Hungarian question intonation, if we do not content ourselves with vague characterisations of the intonational phonetics ('high or rising pitch') based on preestablished ideas about supposed intonational universals in conveying certain functions ('question intonation'), then we can arrive at a much more precise characterisation of what is shared across languages and what genuinely differs.

A specific case in point is provided by the intonation typically used in statements in 'Urban North British' (UNB) English. UNB is the cover term proposed by Cruttenden (1994) for the varieties of English spoken in Belfast and Glasgow (and Northern Ireland and western Scotland generally), together with the varieties of several major English cities, in particular Birmingham, Liverpool, and Newcastle.[7] Intonationally, the most conspicuous characteristic of these varieties is that the ordinary intonation on statements is rising or rising–falling. Sample contours from Glasgow English are shown in figure 4.1 (see also McClure 1980). For Liverpool the reader is referred to Knowles 1974; for Belfast see Jarman and Cruttenden 1976. For a good general review of intonational variation within English, including the rising statement tunes discussed here, see Cruttenden 1986: chapter 5, and specifically for the rises see Cruttenden 1994.

As Cruttenden (1994) makes clear, the UNB rises are not at all the same as the rises used in North American or Antipodean English on statements requesting feedback, discussed in the previous section. There are both pragmatic and phonetic differences. Pragmatically, the American/Australian rising statements represent a linguistic choice: statement intonation in these varieties can be either rising or falling in many contexts, and the choice of contour conveys a nuance. This does not appear to be true for the UNB varieties: the rise is not, as in North American or Antipodean English, basically a question tune being used to add a nuance to a statement, but rather is simply the ordinary way to pronounce a statement. Phonetically, the American/Australian rises begin high on the accented syllable and keep rising to the end of the phrase. This differs in two ways from the UNB

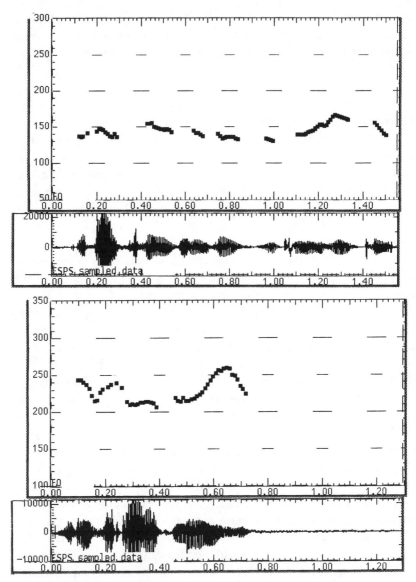

Figure 4.1. Glasgow English intonation contours from the HCRC Map Task Corpus (Anderson *et al.* 1991). Panel (a) shows the text of the declarative utterance *About three inches down from the caravan park*. The key features of the contour are a low valley immediately preceding the accented syllable and a high peak in the following unstressed syllable, followed by a gradual fall to the utterance-final low. Panel (b) shows the utterance *See the old mill?* The characteristic low–high–low pitch configuration is compressed onto the utterance-final accented syllable *mill*.

pattern: first, the accented syllable in the UNB rises begins quite low relative to what precedes, or is immediately preceded by a very low turning point; second and perhaps more importantly, the rise on the accented syllable is usually followed by a distinct fall, sometimes but not often all the way to the bottom of the speaker's range. In Cruttenden's terms (1986: 139ff.), this is a 'rise–plateau–slump', that is, a rising nuclear accent configuration, followed by a fall near the end of the phrase. It would appear that the most appropriate phonological analysis of this contour is therefore L*..H..L%, exactly like the Hungarian question intonation. This means we are dealing with a contour that does not occur in most other varieties of English.

This analysis disagrees with Bolinger's interpretation of UNB statement rises (Bolinger 1978: 510), both pragmatically and phonetically. Bolinger suggests that statement rises in UNB English (and other languages that have them) represent a fossilisation of a conventionalised but formerly meaningful questioning attitude – that the rise had 'a value at one time, now lost'. He bases this suggestion on the American rising tune discussed in the previous section:

> Many speakers of American English in giving a running acount of something will use exactly this kind of terminal rise at the end of practically every sentence – clearly a channel-clearing device that says, in effect, 'Are you listening?', for unless one gives a sign of attention, the monolog comes to a halt. It would not be hard to imagine such a habit becoming a contagion, after which, with interlocutors weary of giving the countersign, the language could be said to have a rising intonation as a mark of clause terminals in general.

In my view, this account stretches the explanatory value of the notion of 'intonational universals' past the breaking point; if UNB statement intonation does not count as a counterexample to the claim that statement intonation is universally falling, it is not clear what would. More importantly, by equating UNB rises with the rises used with statements in North American English, Bolinger glosses over the fact that the two kinds of rises are phonetically quite different. As we shall see later, he also fails to account for the fact that at least some UNB varieties have a clear distinction between question and statement tunes.

On the whole, then, I believe that the various rising statement intonations in different varieties of English present a clear illustration of the distinction between 'semantic' differences (North American and Antipodean English use the H*..H..H% contour in a way not found in British English) and 'systemic' differences (UNB statement intonation is L*..H..L%, a tonal sequence that does not occur in RP or American English). There are a number of interrelated complications that go beyond the scope of this brief discussion, to which I will return in section 4.3.4 below.

4.2.4   *A borderline case: focus and downstep in declarative intonation*

It should not be difficult in principle to distinguish semantic differences – different uses of the same tune – from systemic differences – different tunes for similar functions. However, a borderline case is provided by differences in peak height in declarative intonation in European languages.

In English, as we have already seen (2.4.2), the nucleus of a declarative tune may or may not be downstepped from the preceding accent. Downstepping adds a nuance of greater finality, but does not otherwise seem to affect the meaning of the contour. In particular, there seems to be no close relation with the focus of the sentence. Both downstepped and non-downstepped accents seem to be usable regardless of whether there is a narrow focus intended on the nuclear word:

(4.10)   a. A: What did John do yesterday?
              B: He painted the shed.

              b. A: John was supposed to paint the garage yesterday, wasn't he?
                 B: He painted the shed.

In (4.10a), a non-downstepped accent on *shed* would not in any way convey the impression of focus on that word, and in fact the use of the downstep-ping contour suggests a curious lack of involvement on the part of the speaker – as if B did not really want to talk to A. Conversely, in (4.10b), while a non-downstepped accent on *shed* is perhaps more likely, the down-stepping contour is quite possible and still in some sense conveys the narrow focus; the intonational nuance could be one of disgust or resigna-tion at John's inability to follow instructions.

In a number of other European languages, by comparison, there may be more of an association between downstepped nuclear accents and broad focus on the one hand, and between non-downstepped nuclear accents and narrow focus, on the other: that is, downstep on the final accent may be regarded as normal, while a non-downstepped accent tends to focus narrowly on the accented word. This has been explicitly claimed by Frota (1995) for European Portuguese. One of Frota's examples is the following:

(4.11)   a. A: E o Roberto e a Maria? ('What about Rob and Mary?')

B: Casaram. ('They got married.')

b. A: Eles separaram-se? ('Have they split up?')

B: Casaram

In (4.11a), B's reply has broad focus, and the accented syllable -*sa*- is downstepped from the utterance-initial pitch level. In (4.11b), B's reply focuses narrowly on 'married' as opposed to 'separated', and the accent peak is the highest point in the contour. In Italian there is no such strict association between downstep and focus as Frota claims for Portuguese, but it is certainly true that in all the Romance languages, at least in reading style, statement intonation normally involves downstepped final accents.

One defensible way to describe this difference between English and Portuguese would be as a 'semantic' difference: both downstepping and non-downstepping contours occur in both languages, but tend to be used in different ways. However, it should be noted that other languages have been reported to have fairly consistent associations between two different tune types and breadth of focus. These include Finnish (Välimaa-Blum 1993) and Bengali (Hayes and Lahiri 1991). If this turns out to be a common distinction cross-linguistically, it may not be appropriate to consider it in the same breath with unsystematic differences of nuance such as those in the English questioning contours discussed just above.

In this connection, it is relevant that recent AM works on Romance language intonation systems (Sosa 1991 on American Spanish; Post 1993 on French; Grice 1995a on Palermo Italian; Frota 1995 on European Portuguese) have all independently adopted a different analysis of what I have been calling downstepped and non-downstepped accents. Specifically, they distinguish between two different accent types, describing the 'downstepped' accent (as in 4.11a) as H+L* and the 'non-downstepped' accent (as in 4.11b) as H*+L. It is quite possible that this is a superior analysis on phonetic/phonological grounds, and it is certainly consistent with the idea that languages may have special tune types for narrow focus. This is clearly a matter for further investigation.

4.2.5   Realisational differences: differences of tonal alignment
Conceptually the idea of a realisational difference is rather simple – the
same phonological category is realised in different ways – although in practice it can be exceedingly difficult to define what we mean by 'the same' tune.
A fairly clear example can be based on the notion of the 'alignment' of
tones with the segmental string (see sections 2.2.3 and 2.3.3.2): two languages or dialects may have the same tonal sequence used in the same way,
but align the tonal targets differently with respect to the stressed syllable.
Details of alignment have been shown to vary within a single language, as
we saw above. For example, Bruce and Gårding's prosodic typology of
Swedish dialects (Bruce and Gårding 1978) is based to a considerable
extent on the alignment of the targets with the accented syllable. Grønnum
(1991) applies similar ideas to prosodic variability in Danish. Similar differences can be found in cross-language comparison of intonation.

Perhaps the clearest example of this is the ordinary declarative nuclear
fall which occurs in many languages of Europe in much the same form, and
which we might transcribe as H*..L..L% (in Italian and the Romance languages generally, as we have just seen, this is restricted to narrow focus contexts). In all cases we are dealing with a local peak associated with the
accented syllable, followed by a rapid fall to low in the speaking range, followed by a more gradual fall to the end of the phrase or utterance. However,
in different languages the local peak and the following rapid fall may be
aligned differently with the stressed syllable. In English and German the
peak tends to occur rather late, at or near the end of the stressed syllable,
so that the fall takes place between the stressed syllable and the following
unstressed syllable. In Italian, on the other hand, the peak occurs early in
the stressed syllable and the fall begins well before any following syllable
(see Delattre 1965: ch. 2).

Such phonetic differences can lead to phonological confusions in cross-
language or cross-dialect communication, just as Australian *bat* may be
confusable with American *bet*. When the English or German alignment of
the falling tune is transferred to Italian, it can lead to misperception by
Italian listeners of the location of the stressed syllable. If, for example, an
English or German speaker says an Italian word that is stressed on the antepenultimate syllable, such *Mantova* or *vongola*, the Italian listener may
interpret the resulting pitch contour as signalling that the foreign speaker
is incorrectly stressing the word on the penultimate (which is a common
learner's mistake in Italian). The reason for this percept is as follows: the

falling pitch that the Italian listener expects on the stressed syllable occurs near the beginning of the penultimate syllable, because the English or German speaker has placed the local peak near the end, rather than the beginning, of the antepenultimate – in order to stress it according to the phonetic habits of English or German. The difference is shown in figure 4.2. What is actually a phonetic error (misalignment of the falling contour with the stressed syllable) is thus interpreted as a phonological error (misplaced word stress).

The analysis of this specific difference between English and Italian seems not only valid but also potentially useful in language teaching. However, as discussed earlier (section 2.2.3), the more general place of 'alignment' in AM theory is still very unclear. Consequently it is often unclear whether a given difference between languages is to be described as a matter of phonetic alignment, or whether there are differences of tonal sequence and/or association.

4.2.6 Phonotactic differences: accents on lexically unstressed syllables
By and large, pitch accents must be associated with lexically stressed syllables. If something that looks like a pitch accent is associated with a lexically unstressed syllable, AM theory suggests we should call it something else. However, there is at least one type of case in which it may be appropriate to speak of language-specific differences in the association of pitch accents. In Italian, an additional emphatic falling declarative accent (H* or H*+L) may be placed on a lexically unstressed utterance-final syllable, so that the final word has two accents. This adds emphasis or conveys some sort of special emotional involvement on the part of the speaker. The following are two examples from my own observations:

(4.12)   a.   [context: scolding a child who had been insistently poking his mother]:

        H*H*L
      Mi fai male!
      You're hurting me!

    b.   [context: talking about watching New Year's Eve fireworks at a party attended by the speaker but not the addressee]:

        H*   H* H*   H*H*L
      . . . una terrazza da dove si vedeva tutta Roma!
      '. . . a terrace from which you could see all of Rome!'

In (4.12a) we might regard the extra accent as simply increasing the emphasis on the important word *male* ('evil, pain'). In (4.12b), however, the effect

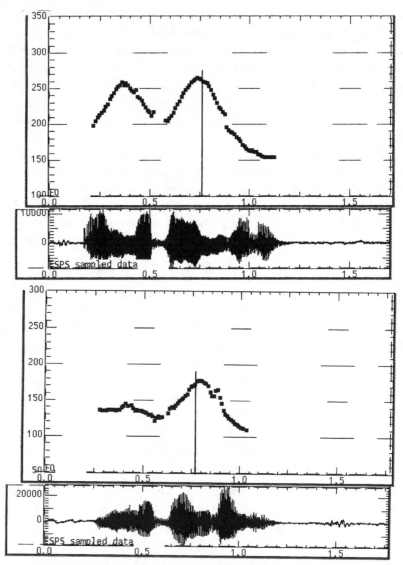

Figure 4.2 The Italian sentence *È una vongola* ('It's a clam'), produced with an emphatic accent by (a) a female native speaker of Italian and (b) a male native speaker of English who speaks Italian reasonably well. Word stress on *vongola* is on the first syllable. In the native speaker's rendition the F_0 reaches a peak during the stressed vowel and falls markedly during the following nasal; in the English speaker's rendition the F_0 continues to rise well into the nasal and most of the fall in pitch occurs during the following unstressed syllable. The vertical line in both panels marks the approximate boundary between the stressed [ɔ] and the [ŋ] of *vongola*.

clearly applies to the whole utterance, and emphasises, if anything, the magnificence of the view: there would have been no reason to emphasise *Roma*, since the conversation took place in Rome and both participants had just spent New Year's Eve there. That is, we seem to be dealing with a general strategy for increasing the emotional content of the contour by suspending the normal constraints on tune–text association.

This phenomenon does not seem to occur in other European languages in the same way as in Italian, but Bolinger (1958: 145 (1965: 52)) reports having heard the English word *No* pronounced emphatically with three accent peaks as

(4.13)
       N o – o – o

and I once knew an American speaker of English who often pronounced the single-word utterance *probably* with an extra accent on the final syllable. Beyond the European languages, King's description of Dyirbal intonation (King 1994), based largely on recorded narratives, cites three cases of additional final accent that seem identical to the phenomenon in Italian. One of King's examples (her figure 5.17) is as follows (the location of pitch accents is indicated by superscript asterisks):

(4.14)   *   *   * *
       jabuŋgu ŋajguna galgan da̱da̱
       'My mother left me as a baby' (lit. mother.ERG me leave.NF baby.NOM)

King (section 5.6.3.2.4) states that 'the extra emphasis on da̱da̱ "baby" may be intended to convey how young the speaker was when her mother left her. There is presumably some attitudinal information conveyed by the accenting but it is impossible to determine this without recourse to native speakers.'

4.3   Some extended illustrations

This section presents four 'case studies', illustrating the kinds of typological differences – and the kinds of theoretical and empirical issues – that we encounter when we compare intonation across languages in the terms just proposed. The aim is to exemplify the usefulness of the AM approach, not to provide definitive discussions of particular phenomena or particular language groups. As will become clear along the way, a great many new questions are raised for which there are at present no answers.

4.3.1   *'Compression' vs. 'truncation'*

Given that a distinctive tune consists at a minimum of a pitch accent and an edge tone, and given that tunes can apply to texts of any length, the situation frequently arises that two, three, or even more tones are associated with a single syllable in a monosyllabic phrase or utterance. Recall the example of the English rise–fall–rise tune applied to two different texts, which was used above (section 2.1) to illustrate the usefulness of the AM descriptive framework. In *Sue!?* the tune seems like a single continuous rise–fall–rise, whereas in *driving instructor!?* we can see that it consists of two clearly distinct parts, the rise–fall at the nuclear syllable and the final boundary rise. In AM terms, the tonal sequence is L*H..L..H%. In the longer utterance the tones will spread themselves out over the available syllables in something like the following way:

(4.15)   L*H L   H%

driving instructor!?

In the monosyllabic utterance, however, all are associated with the only available syllable:

(4.16)   L*H L H%

Sue!?

What happens phonetically in cases like the latter?

In English, as we saw, the pitch rises and falls and rises again during the monosyllable – in other words, all the tones are realised. (If this were not the case the comparison of *Sue* and *driving instructor* would be considerably less convincing!) In some languages, however, there seems to be a limit to the number of tones that can be realised on a single syllable, the most common limit being two. This can be illustrated with the Hungarian question intonation discussed above. As we noted, this is a tonal sequence L*..H..L%, where the first (H) edge tone is preferentially associated with the penultimate syllable; in two-syllable utterances the H edge tone is arguably squeezed over onto the final syllable, but in any case the distinctive low–rise–fall pattern is present in both cases. In monosyllables, however, the contour is reduced to a simple rise. In AM terms, this can be described by saying that no more than two tones can be realised on a single syllable. So, for example, in

(4.17)   ⌐
         sör?
         'beer?'

we may say that we have underlyingly

(4.18)   L* H L%
         sör

but that only the first two tones of the three-tone question tune are realised with the lone syllable of the utterance. The final L% is left unrealised, and the resulting contour is a rise.

It will be useful to have terms for these two types of behaviour with respect to multiple association. I will adopt the terms proposed by Grønnum in her typological description of Danish regional intonation (Grønnum 1991), namely *compression* (for the English type) and *truncation* (for the Hungarian type), and I will refer to languages as 'compressing' and 'truncating' languages according to the way they treat intonational tunes applied to monosyllables. English is a compressing language *par excellence*, and this is one of the things that makes English prosody distinctive in the ears of many other Europeans (see Delattre 1965: ch. 2). Hungarian and Palermo Italian (Grice 1995a) seem to be strongly truncating (Grice's term for truncation is *curtailment*).

Some languages, while not strictly ruling out compression, appear to avoid it in various ways. In German, for example, we may use a different tune rather than compress three tones onto a final accented syllable. Suppose someone has left a shopping bag or some money on the counter next to the cash register in a department store and is about to walk away. We might say any of the following using the high–fall–rise question intonation discussed in 4.2.2 above:

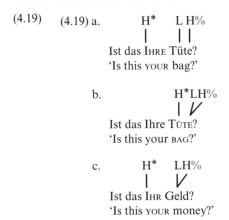

(4.19)   (4.19) a.   H*   L H%
                        | | |
                  Ist das IHRE Tüte?
                  'Is this YOUR bag?'

         b.   H*LH%
                        | ⱴ
                  Ist das Ihre TÜTE?
                  'Is this your BAG?'

         c.   H*   LH%
                 | ⱴ
                  Ist das IHR Geld?
                  'Is this YOUR money?'

Yet though it is perfectly appropriate pragmatically, it sounds odd phonetically to say

(4.20)   H*LH%

Ist das Ihr GELD?
'Is this your MONEY?'

with the three tones of the high–fall–rise compressed onto the final monosyllable. More natural would be a change of tune, to a high rise:

(4.21)   H*HH%

Ist das Ihr GELD?
'Is this your MONEY?'

or (somewhat less likely, because of the rather astonished sound it conveys), to a low rise:

(4.22)   L*HH%

Ist das Ihr GELD?
'Is this your MONEY?'

The same observation is made by Féry (1993: 91), who says that 'this tonal pattern usually occurs over several syllables. The realization of both movements [viz. the accentual fall and the boundary rise] on a single syllable is slightly marked.'

German also apparently exhibits truncation, but in this case it is the accent tone that is truncated rather than a final boundary tone. This can be seen in the tune used to answer the telephone. In German it is usual to answer the telephone with one's surname alone, with a 'stylised' low-rise tune:

(4.23)   L* H
          | |
        M ü l l e r

Considerably less polite is a stylised high rise (phonetically a mid-high level), which conveys boredom or distractedness:

(4.24)   H* H
          | |
        M ü l l e r

With a monosyllabic surname, however, either tune can be used without sounding impolite. The low rise involves compression:

(4.25) L*H

Schmidt

What seems to be happening in the second case is that we are not dealing with the bored high rise at all, but a kind of left-truncated low rise:

(4.26) (L*) H
           |
        Schmidt

Whether this analysis will withstand closer scrutiny I do not know, but it is consistent with the apparent fact that German tries to avoid compression, and explains why a phonetically mid-level contour can be used with a monosyllabic surname without sounding impolite.

Before leaving the subject of compression and truncation, I should briefly mention the fact that I have discussed truncation as a matter of phonetic realisation rather than a matter of phonological rules (in which case the entire phenomenon could be seen as a matter of 'phonotactic' differences; see section 4.2.6 above). That is, one could imagine writing a phonological rule to de-associate (or simply fail to associate) the truncated tone(s): for example,

(4.27) T* T Ⓣ
          V
          σ

Such tonal rules have often been posited in the autosegmental literature on African tonal systems, and Grice has discussed her Italian data in terms of such phonological rules (1995a: 171ff.). However, in Grønnum's original usage compression and truncation are clearly intended as phonetic descriptions, not phonological analyses. In both the Hungarian case and the German case just discussed, it would appear that we are dealing not with a clear-cut phonological difference between three tones and two, but rather with more likely or less likely phonetic realisations of the same basic phonological structure. In the German examples I have in any case presented the examples in terms of what is more likely, not what is possible or impossible. Even in the case of Hungarian, it is possible to get all three tones of the question tune realised on a monosyllable if the monosyllable is prolonged for paralinguistic reasons, for example to express amazement:

(4.28)   L* H L

│ ╱

sö-ör??

[you can't mean] beer?

However, for our purposes here, little hangs on the decision to regard this as a matter of phonetic realisation rather than phonological rules. The typological difference between compression and truncation is clear, and is essentially unaffected whichever way it is analysed.

4.3.2   The calling contour

In many European languages, in certain situations, people who are some distance away from a speaker can be called or hailed using a chanted tune on two sustained notes, stepping down from a fairly high level to a somewhat lower level. (The interval between the two notes is often, but by no means necessarily, three semitones.) However, this 'calling contour' exhibits subtle differences from one language to another, and provides a nice example of several of the types of differences discussed in section 4.2. It may also, as we shall see, shed light on the issue of 'What is a tone?' discussed in section 3.5.1 above.

The basic vocative use of the calling contour varies slightly from language to language. In North American English the stereotypical use is a parent calling for a child to come home, and this use is probably widespread. In German, however, the same tune is also used for calling between adults, usually with the notes less prolonged than in the North American variety, and with only [u u] or [hu u] as the segmental string. In the terms used in section 4.2, this comparison between English and German involves both realisational and semantic differences. In addition, German also uses the calling contour at close range – that is, for purposes other than calling – in a variety of contexts, such as greetings and leave-takings; such close-range uses are much less common in English.[8] For a detailed discussion of the use and realisation of the calling contour in English and German see Gibbon (1976: 274–87).

There are also significant 'phonotactic' differences among European languages with respect to the calling contour. Before we discuss these, however, we must briefly discuss the phonological representation of the calling contour. As noted earlier (3.2.2.1), the calling contour was analysed by Ladd (1978) as part of a subsystem of 'stylised' intonation contours, which are systematically related to non-chanted, non-stylised contours in English. As with Pierrehumbert's proposal that English has downstep, the basic 'stylised' analysis has generally been accepted, but details of the phonological representation are still a matter of disagreement. Part of the reason for the disagreement is the broader disagreement over the representation of down-step, because Pierrehumbert crucially depends on her analysis of downstep to represent the calling contour. Specifically, she analyses the higher level pitch of the calling contour as a nuclear pitch accent H*+L and the lower level as a phrase tone H, which is consequently downstepped in the resulting sequence H..L..H. Another part of the reason for the disagreement is uncertainty about how an AM analysis should represent the sustained, chanted quality of the tones. Pierrehumbert's analysis consistently uses the sequence of a H phrase tone followed by a L% boundary tone for the final sustained level, whereas I suggested in Ladd 1983a that stylised contours might have no boundary tone at all. I also suggested that they might involve a 'feature of sustained pitch', a suggestion I would prefer to pass over in silence. I now believe the sustained level pitches can best be accounted for by tone-spreading rules of the sort discussed in some detail by Leben (1976). In any case, for purposes of the discussion in this section, I will treat the calling contour as a sequence of a H tone and a downstepped H tone, since this much is agreed on by both Pierrehumbert's analysis and my own. (In the examples that follow I will use the *ad hoc* notation H* ꜜH for this analysis.) In section 4.3.4 I will return to the question of whether Pierrehumbert's more abstract analysis or my own more concrete one is to be preferred.

In English or German, the first H is clearly a starred (accentual) tone, because it must be associated with the nucleus or most prominent lexically stressed syllable of the utterance. Any syllables preceding the nucleus are a low L in a fully chanted version of the contour, though they may be at a fairly indeterminate mid level in a more 'spoken' version. If there is one syllable after the nucleus, the downstepped H goes with it; if there is more than one syllable after the nucleus, the location of the step down is determined by a variety of factors not treated here (but see 6.1.3 and cf. Leben 1976); if the main lexically stressed syllable is utterance-final, it is in effect split up into two syllables, to provide a place (a docking site, in autosegmental terms) for both the H and the downstepped H tone. This is shown in (4.29):

(4.29)   a. (English)

b. (German)

In Hungarian (see Varga 1989) and French, on the other hand, the H..'H sequence goes on the last two syllables irrespective of any accentual prominence, though if there is only one syllable, then, as in English or German, its vowel can be broken into two parts. Thus:

(4.30)   a. (Hungarian)

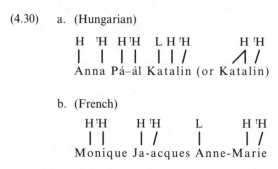

Anna Pá–ál Katalin (or Katalin)

b. (French)

Monique Ja-acques Anne-Marie

The difference between the English/German way and the Hungarian/French way of treating association of tones in the calling contour can perhaps best be appreciated by comparing the English and French versions on phonetically very similar names such as *Louise* or *Annie*:

(4.31)   a. (French)

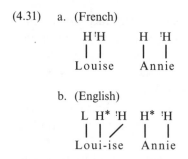

Louise   Annie

b. (English)

Loui-ise   Annie

French treats these two names identically, because both have two syllables. In English, on the other hand, the tune is associated with the two names in two different ways, because *Annie* has lexical stress on the first syllable and *Louise* has lexical stress on the second.[9]

A different kind of variability in the calling contour is found in Dutch: as in English or German, the first H is a H*, associated with the main accented syllable, but following the H* it is possible to have two or even more distinct downward steps, each of which seems to reflect the occurrence of a separate 'H tone. Thus a Dutch child calling others back to the den in a game of hide-and-seek may call

(4.32)   H* 'H   'H
          | | |
          uit– ko– men

(lit. 'come out'; in citation form the first syllable bears the main stress and the last syllable is reduced). A corresponding call in German (which might be used in hide-and-seek in the same way) would be

(4.33)   H*   'H
          | ⌐\
          raus– kommen

with only a single step. The principles according to which second and subsequent steps appear in the Dutch version are related to the overall metrical structure of the utterance and are treated in detail by Gussenhoven (1993).

In all of the languages discussed here it seems clear that we are dealing with the same tune. It also seems clear that the tune is associated with texts in ways that differ systematically between languages. A comparative study of intonation would obviously be incomplete if it failed to note the striking similarity of the calling contours across the languages of Europe; it may well be – as has often been suggested (e.g. Abe 1962) – that these similarities can be accounted for by functional principles such as the need to sustain high pitch to ensure audibility in calling at a distance. But the comparative study would be equally incomplete if it failed to note the differences of detail between languages. Like language universals of all sorts, that is, I believe that universal properties of intonation adapt themselves to the structural properties of individual languages.

4.3.3   *The French/Italian suspended-fall intonation*

French has a characteristic intonation pattern, common in everyday conversation, which may be used in place of ordinary statement intonation to convey an additional nuance. Phonetically the contour can best be described backwards from the final syllable. The final syllable is spoken on a fairly level mid-to-high pitch; the immediately preceding syllable is quite a bit higher; and any preceding syllables are very low. Fónagy, Fónagy, and Sap (1979) indicate the three pitches musically as follows:

(4.34)

On the basis of the phonetic form I have called this the 'suspended-fall contour'. Fónagy, Fónagy, and Sap call it the 'declarative triangle' (*triangle*

assertif), to distinguish it from the 'interrogative triangle' which they also discuss.

The additional meaning conveyed by the suspended-fall contour is exceedingly difficult to describe in words: it seems to be best characterised as the vocal equivalent of shrugging the shoulders. Its meaning may be similar to that of the English 'surprise–redundancy' contour discussed by Sag and Liberman (1975; see also Bolinger 1982): it seems to convey the idea that the propositional content of the statement is, or ought to be, obvious. Dell (1984: 66) says that the contour 'presents [the sentence] as an incredulous or disapproving reply to someone else's statements' (my translation). Fónagy, Fónagy, and Sap (1979) describe the nuance only by saying that it 'recalls the melodic schema of children's taunts (Na-na-na!)' (1979: 9; my translation). Some examples follow.

(4.35)

    a.   Alors il ne viendra plus.
           'Well, he won't come any more then.' (possible nuance: I wash my
           hands of this)

    b.   . Parce qu'il n'avait plus d'argent.
           'Because he didn't have any more money.' (nuance: why else?)

Dell (1984) represents this contour transparently as a sequence low–high–mid. Assuming a description without a distinctive mid tone, we would probably translate Dell's representation into L+H+!H*, that is, a downstepped H accent tone preceded by a L..H leading tone sequence. Thus:

(4.36)   L   H !H*

Parce qu'il n'avait plus d'argent!

There is of course no precedent in Pierrehumbert's analysis of English for accents that involve two leading tones, and it may well be possible to show that structurally the L is a left edge tone for the phrase, or belongs structurally to a prenuclear accent; I will not pursue this issue here. However, it is worth mentioning evidence for the H+!H* analysis of the final two tones. There are two main pieces of evidence for this analysis, one from within French and one arising from comparison with Italian.

French makes wide use of the syntactic device of right-dislocation (see ch. 2, note 6) for discourse foregrounding and backgrounding. The

following examples, with right-dislocated noun phrases, are quite unre-
markable in spoken French:

(4.37)　　a.　C'est pas joli, cette affaire.
　　　　　　　　'This business isn't very pretty.' (lit. it is not pretty, this matter)

　　　　　b.　Elle t'a rien donné, ta mère?
　　　　　　　　'Didn't your mother give you anything?' (lit. she didn't give you any-
　　　　　　　　thing, your mother)

　　　　　c.　Mais tu l'as, ton passeport!
　　　　　　　　'But you've got your passport!' (lit. but you have it, your passport)

The intonation of such right-dislocated constituents depends entirely on the
intonation of the matrix sentence: if the matrix sentence ends high, the right-
dislocated constituent is high, whereas if the matrix sentence ends low, the
right-dislocated constituent is low. (Delattre (1966) refers to these two possibilities for right-dislocated constituents as 'echo' (high) and 'parenthesis'
(low), and notes that they are in complementary distribution.) Thus:

(4.38)

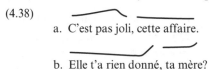

　　　a.　C'est pas joli, cette affaire.

　　　b.　Elle t'a rien donné, ta mère?

To this statement we must add the provision that matrix sentences ending
with an emphatic or exclamatory high peak (the 'intonation d'implication'
of Delattre 1966) are followed by low right-dislocated constituents, because
the intonation drops rapidly away from the peak:

(4.39)

　　　Mais tu l'as, ton passeport!

If we assume that this fall from the peak (which on a single syllable seldom,
if ever, reaches the bottom of the range) reflects an underlying intonation
pattern H*+L or H*..L, then the intonation of the right-dislocated constituent in all cases simply involves a copy of the last tone of the matrix sentence. Thus:

(4.40)

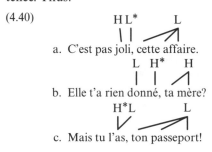

　　　　　　　H L*　　　L
　　　　　　　 | |　　 ↗
　　　a.　C'est pas joli, cette affaire.
　　　　　　　　L　H*　　H
　　　　　　　　|　 |　 ↗
　　　b.　Elle t'a rien donné, ta mère?
　　　　　　　H*L　　　　L
　　　　　　　 V　 ↗
　　　c.　Mais tu l'as, ton passeport!

Now consider what happens when the suspended-fall intonation is applied to a sentence containing a right-dislocated constituent. In this case, there is a second downstep: the right-dislocated constituent is lower than the final syllable of the matrix sentence (which in turn is lower than the immediately preceding syllable), but is not as low as the low right-dislocated constituent in (4.39). Thus:

(4.41)

Parce qu'il n'avait plus d'argent, Mercier.

This is exactly what we expect if the right-dislocated constituent copies the last tone of the matrix sentence, provided the last tone of the matrix sentence is !H*:

(4.42)   L   H !H*   !H
                         | | | ⁄|
          Parce qu'il n'avait plus d'argent, Mercier.

The second piece of evidence for the H+!H* analysis comes from Italian. Italian has a phonetically similar intonation pattern that is used in similar circumstances with a similar meaning to the French suspended fall contour just described. In utterances that end on a lexically stressed syllable, the contour is transparently the same as the French one:

                         L   H !H*
                         | | |
(4.43)   Perché non ne voglio più.
          'Because I don't want any more.' (nuance: as you should have noticed)

However, the normal position for lexical stress in Italian is penultimate, and earlier stresses are not unusual. When the contour under discussion is applied to sentences with non-final stressed syllables, the result may be a second downstepping level following the stressed syllable, exactly as in French sentences with a right-dislocated constituent. Thus both of the following are possible; the second seems more emphatic (and may be more characteristic of certain regional varieties than others):

(4.44)   L H !H*
                          | | |
          a. Allora lo dobbiamo buttare via.
              'Well, we'll have to throw it away then.' (possible nuance: you shouldn't have spoiled it)

          b.   L   H !H* !H*
                          | | | ⁄
              Perché non avevo più soldi.
              'Because I didn't have any more money.'

Up to the stressed syllable, in short, the Italian version of the contour is identical to the French version, that is, a sequence L..H..'H* beginning two syllables before the lexically stressed syllable. But given the Italian stress patterns, the 'full form' of the contour with the extra level may be seen in Italian any time the accented word ends in an unstressed syllable. In French, the full form shows up only in sentences with right-dislocation.[10]

One final point is worth mentioning. In French, it is not immediately obvious that there is a difference between the calling contour and the suspended-fall contour; that is, an utterance like

(4.45)   L   H 'H
          | | |
          Anne–Marie

appears phonetically ambiguous between the calling contour (see example (4.30b)) and the suspended-fall contour conveying a nuance like 'who else would you expect?'. The two contours certainly 'feel' different, and speakers are surprised when the similarity is pointed out, but it may nevertheless be that they should be given the same phonological analysis. In Italian, however, the distinction between the two is very clear; the first H tone is the starred tone in the calling contour while the downstepped 'H is the starred tone in the suspended-fall contour. Compare:

(4.46)   a.   *Calling contour*

               L   H* 'H
               ⌐\‾\ | |
               A n t o n e l l a

          b.   *Suspended-fall contour*

               L   H 'H* ('H)
               | | | |
               [Glielo devi dire a] A n t o n e l l a
               'You should tell Antonella' (possible nuance: it's not my problem)

Whether the phonological difference in Italian can be used to motivate a comparable analysis in French (which might therefore explain the French speaker's reaction that the two contours are different) is a matter for further investigation.

4.3.4   *UNB statement rises revisited*

In section 4.2.3, I used the 'Urban North British' statement rises as an example of systemic differences in intonation between varieties of English.

Specifically, I suggested that the UNB rising intonation is a sequence L*..H..L%, which does not occur in Standard British or American English. This analysis, however, raises a number of issues which I wish to discuss in more detail.

First, it is not clear whether there is a difference between ordinary statement intonation and ordinary question intonation in these varieties of English. Native speakers of Glasgow-area varieties among my students over the past several years have mostly maintained that there is not such a difference (e.g. Hastings 1990). Limited experimental investigation (e.g. Cole 1991; Huffman 1993) suggests that, in the absence of syntactic cues, the most reliable indicator of whether an utterance is a statement or a question is the height of the H – the higher it is, the more likely the utterance is to be perceived as a question. Second, there is considerable variation among the UNB varieties themselves, and it may not be appropriate at all to group them together. For example, there is some reason to think that Birmingham and Liverpool, though they have statement intonation similar to Glasgow, do have a clear distinction between statements and questions, with L*..H..L% a possible analysis of the statement and L+H*..L..L% a likely analysis of the question. As I am far more familiar with Glasgow than with the other UNB varieties, I will restrict the rest of the discussion to Glasgow. Finally, even if we could confidently decide that Glasgow does not have a basic question–statement distinction and that a single basic nucleus type does duty for both, it is still not clear that L*..H..L% is the correct phonological analysis. There are three problems: the alignment of the tones with the segmentals, the apparent variability of the contour, and the interpretation of the H..L% edge tone sequence.

The alignment of both the L* and the H (if that is indeed what they are) is rather unusual. Given enough unstressed syllables, the L* is usually aligned slightly *before* the accented syllable and the H is aligned slightly after it (see figure 4.1). This means that the contour typically rises throughout the entire accented syllable, and that neither target is aligned in time with the accented syllable. (The alignment of the tones can, of course, be modified if there are not enough unstressed syllables, because UNB is like other varieties of English in being 'compressing' rather than 'truncating'.) This makes it a little difficult to be certain that the L is the 'starred tone', or indeed to be certain that there *is* a starred tone; if we are dealing with a L*, it is unlike the L* of RP or Standard North American English. However, similar alignment of a L..H accentual sequence has been found for prenuclear accents in Modern Greek (Arvaniti and Ladd 1995; Ladd,

Arvaniti, and Mennen, work in progress). This means that there may be no problem at all in describing the Glasgow rise as L*..H; the problem may lie rather with the excessively narrow understanding of 'starred tone' based on Pierrehumbert's analysis of American English.

Second, in an extensive corpus of Glasgow speech (the HCRC Map Task corpus; Anderson *et al.* 1991), the alignment and scaling of the L* and H tones appear to be quite variable. It is not clear whether all this variation is phonologically conditioned (e.g. 'compression' conditioned by the number of available syllables), or whether any of it is meaningful. If any of it is meaningful, it is not clear whether it involves gradient paralinguistic variation within a single tune type (which, as we saw above, is suggested by the limited work done by students of mine over the past several years), or whether we can identify categorically distinct tunes such as L*..H..L%, H*..H..L%, and L*+H..H..L%.

The third problem with analysing the Glasgow intonation as L*..H..L% lies in the fact that the same tone sequence is used in Pierrehumbert's system for a rather different tune (the 'stylised low rise'; see table 3.1). Throughout her tonal inventory, Pierrehumbert uses the H..L% sequence to represent a phrase-final sustained level pitch ('stylised' in the terms of Ladd 1978; cf. the discussion of the calling contour in section 4.3.2 above). The question is whether Pierrehumbert's analysis of stylised intonation precludes the L*..H..L% analysis for Glasgow (or vice versa).

One possible answer would be that the two analyses are not incompatible. This was suggested by Pierrehumbert in discussion at the ToBI workshop at Ohio State University in June 1993. What counts, in this view, is the possible contrasts within any given dialect. In American English, after a H phrase tone, the pitch can either stay level or rise, but cannot fall. Therefore, for American English, a two-way opposition L% vs. H% expresses the phonological possibilities. If in Glasgow English there are similarly only two possibilities – either fall vs. level or fall vs. rise – then L% vs. H% will work equally well for Glasgow as for American. The difference between the two dialects would be one of phonetic realisation rather than of phonological system. That is, H..L% would represent final sustained level in American and final fall in Glasgow, while H..H% would represent final rise in American and either final level or rise in Glasgow.

Unfortunately, there probably are three possibilities after H phrase tone in Glasgow, namely rise, sustain, and fall. I say 'probably', because the distinction between sustained level and rise is perhaps not as clear as in most other varieties of English. One might, for example, argue that the only occurrences of actual rises in Glasgow represent dialect borrowing from RP, or that the only occurrences of sustained level represent incomplete utterances with no boundary tone. I do not think that these arguments can be maintained, but the situation is certainly not clear cut.

In any case, even if it should turn out that there is only a two-way distinction in Glasgow, there are other problems with Pierrehumbert's proposal. Most obviously, if we give markedly different contours identical phonological analyses, it makes cross-language and cross-dialect comparison of the sort I have exemplified in this chapter at best difficult and at worst meaningless. The whole discussion of 'semantic' and 'realisational' differences hinges on being able to treat identical phonological strings across dialects and languages as representations of the same tune. Specifically, if we analyse both the Glasgow statement and the American stylised low rise as L*..H..L%, with a difference in the phonetic realisation of the L%, we would have to treat the Glasgow statement contour and the American stylised low rise as the same contour conveying different nuances – a 'semantic' difference. Worse, we would have to give the Glasgow calling contour a different analysis from the American calling contour (because H..L% in Glasgow is phonetically falling, not sustained level). Yet the comparison in section 4.3.2 above depended on being able to use the same basic analysis of the calling contour in numerous languages of Europe. Unless it can be shown that Glasgow intonation is wildly deviant in a European context, it would seem preferable to assume that its calling contour is tonally like those in other European languages. More generally, if comparison of the sort presented in this chapter is of any value, it implies that we should not give identical phonological analyses to markedly different contours in mutually intelligible varieties of the same language.

The only way to avoid identifying Glasgow statements with American stylised low rises is to reanalyse one or the other. In my view it is clearly the latter that should be changed. Stylised intonation is quite special, and, in a way, marginal in the intonation system as a whole. This marginal status is not captured if we analyse it, as Pierrehumbert does, with a sequence of phrase tone and boundary tone that just happens to remain unused when the other contrasts of the system are taken care of. As I noted in section 4.3.2, I believe that the most likely representation of stylised contours generally is one without boundary tones, and with tone spreading to associate each syllable with a distinct level in the tonal string. Such analysis would leave us free to use the L*..H..L% for the UNB statement tune, and to analyse the UNB calling contour in the same way as in other European languages.

This is the point at which the discussion returns to the question raised at the end of the preceding chapter: what is a tone? The analysis L*..H..L% for Glasgow statements is phonetically transparent: the three tones can readily be identified as turning points or endpoints in the contour. By contrast, Pierrehumbert's analysis of the stylised contours as a group relies on her abstract analysis of downstep and on an abstract interpretation of the L%. Since her analysis demonstrably creates problems for cross-language and cross-dialect comparison, and given the independent reasons noted in section 3.5.2 to be cautious about abstract phonological analyses in intonation languages, I believe that the phonetically transparent analysis in this instance is clearly to be preferred. We cannot, as I said, rule out abstract tonal analyses *a priori*; we know we need them for the languages of Africa, and we may find evidence for them in European intonation languages as well. But at least in analysing the stylised contours, the case for the more abstract approach is, as they might say in Glasgow, not proven.

4.4   Melodic universals

One important topic remains to be discussed; so far we have said nothing about intonation in languages that have lexical tone. To the extent that the AM theory claims to provide a universal framework for discussing intonation, it is obviously important to establish that the intonational phenomena observed in tone languages can be accommodated in the theory presented so far. In particular, it is important to consider the relation between tone and intonation, or between lexical and postlexical pitch features, to use the terminology of chapter 1. The remainder of this chapter is a brief discussion of three specific topics in this general area.

4.4.1   The unity of pitch phonology

Perhaps the most important point to make at the outset of the discussion is that the AM theory, by analysing intonation contours as strings of phonological events in sequence, provides the basis for describing pitch phonology in all languages in the same terms. As we saw above (section 1.3.2), there is good reason to believe that the relationship between lexical and intonational features of F_0 need not be conceived of in terms of an overlay model, with lexical features superimposed on intonational trends. Rather, in at least some cases – as in the case of the Swedish word accent distinction as analysed by Bruce (1977) – the intonational aspects of F_0 are themselves localised events in a string of tones, exactly like the lexical aspects.

The AM approach makes sense of these findings by saying that, from the point of view of the phonology (as opposed to the lexicon or the grammar), pitch contours *in any language* are simply strings of tones or other phonological specifications. In languages like English, the most important tonal specifications are the pitch accents, which are postlexical or intonational features. In languages like Chinese, the most important events of the pitch contour are the lexically specified tones. In all languages, however, the pitch contour can be analysed as a string of phonological elements: that is, there is no fundamental difference in the phonological structure of pitch between 'tone languages' and 'intonation languages'. Linear tonal structure consisting of events and transitions is found in the pitch phonology of all languages. The function of the tones, and their internal organisation, is a separate issue.

Given this view, the conspicuous phonetic difference between the pitch contours of, for example, Chinese and English is simply a *consequence* of the functional difference, and involves no essential difference of phonological type. More 'happens' in pitch contours in Chinese, because the lexical tones occur at nearly every syllable and the transitions between them span only milliseconds, whereas in English the pitch accents occur mostly only on prominent words, and the transitions may span several syllables. But the specifications are the same kind of phonological entity regardless of their function, and transitions are the same kind of phonetic phenomenon irrespective of their length. There is no need to assume that tone languages involve an essentially different layer of phonological structure.

On the other hand, it may be useful to coin the term *core tones* to distinguish them from edge tones in a cross-linguistically valid way. For example, Japanese clearly has both pitch accents and edge tones; the former are associated with lexically accented syllables, while the latter occur at the left edge – and in some cases also the right edge – of prosodic domains of various types. The edge tones act as signals of phrasing and in some cases also cue the difference between statements and questions, while the pitch accents are lexically specified and only ever involve the tonal sequence HL (see Pierrehumbert and Beckman 1988 for a full discussion). In many respects, then, the structure of the pitch contour is exactly like the structure of the contour in English: the two languages share a clear distinction between the F_0 events that make up the body of the contour and those at the contour's edges. In English, however, both types of features have a sentence-level or postlexical function, while in Japanese, the accentual elements are lexically specified, and only the edge tones are postlexical. By emphasising the structural difference between core tones and edge tones, rather than the functional difference between lexically specified tones and intonationally specified ones, we emphasise the common features of tonal phonology – the phonology of F_0 – in all languages.

From this perspective, the fundamental difference between languages with and without lexical tone is primarily a matter of how the tonal specifications come to be where they are. Core tones in Chinese are part of the phonological shape of morphemes, whereas in English they signal intonational 'sentence accent' on selected words of a phrase, yet edge tones in both languages are intonational. In Tokyo Japanese, the core tones signal lexically specified accent, while the edge tones are intonational, but in Osaka Japanese some of the edge tones are lexically specified as well (McCawley 1978, Kori 1987). In Yoruba, meanwhile, there may not even be edge tones (or, if there are, they are completely predictable from the lexical specification of the last core tone).[11] Conversely, I would speculate that in some languages – the languages of western Siberia and the American Northwest are possible examples – there are no core tones at all, only edge tones. I have heard recordings of narratives in Chukchee and in an unidentified language of British Columbia, in which, impressionistically, the only salient pitch movements are rises at the beginnings of intonational phrases, after which the pitch remains level until the next phrase break; this could be analysed as an initial LH boundary tone. I emphasise that this statement is based on brief impressions, and I offer the speculative analysis only to show how readily such languages could be accommodated in the descriptive framework made possible by the linear phonological view.

4.4.2 Tone–intonation interactions

At least three kinds of phenomena have been cited as intonational features in tone languages. These are overall expansion or contraction of pitch range to express emotions (and/or to express intonational distinctions like question vs. statement or incompleteness vs. completeness); modification of specific tones, especially at the ends of phrases or utterances, to signal distinctions like question vs. statement; and modification of overall contour shapes to signify certain intonational messages, again in particular question vs. statement or incomplete vs. complete. The first two of these have straightforward explanations in terms of the theory presented so far, and I will argue that it is probably also possible to explain the third type – overall contour modifications – in terms that are compatible with the idea of linear tonal phonology.

First let us consider overall pitch range modification. In the view developed here, this is a paralinguistic effect that is orthogonal to the linear specification of tones. To take a hypothetical example, a tone sequence M..H..H..L..M might be realised as (4.47a) in a normal pitch range and as (4.47b) in a pitch range expanded to express anger or some other strong or active emotion:

(4.47)   a.

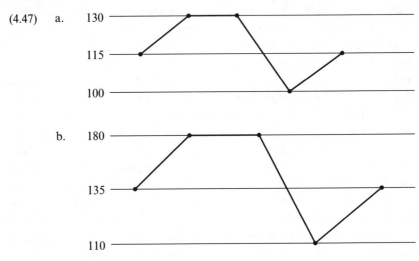

This kind of pitch range effect occurs in exactly the same way in intonation languages: in English as in Yoruba we can equally well distinguish a 'normal' and 'expanded pitch range' version of something that is in other respects the same tune. That is, the relation between paralinguistic pitch range modification and linguistic tonal specification is identical in tone languages and intonation languages. Consequently, the existence of paralinguistic pitch range modification does not constitute evidence against the AM theory, or indeed against any phonological theory of intonational structure: however we describe pitch range modification, we will describe it the same way in all languages.[12]

The second 'intonational' phenomenon in tone languages, phrase-final tone modification, is similarly unproblematical for the AM theory. It has frequently been reported that languages with lexical tone 'modify' the lexically specified tone at the end of a phrase or utterance to signal various utterance-level or postlexical effects (e.g. Abramson 1962 for Thai; Chang 1958 (1972) for Chengtu Chinese; and Lindsey 1985 for Hausa). For example, Chang (1958 (1972: 408f.)) reports the following 'perturbations' of the tone of the final syllable in questions ('naming tone' refers to the citation form):

Toneme I (naming tone: high-rising) remains high rising and often
ends higher than usual.

Toneme II (naming tone: low-falling) becomes low level.

Toneme III (naming tone: high-falling) becomes high level.

Toneme IV (naming tone: low-falling–rising) becomes low rising.

Chang herself refers to these changes as the result of superimposing the sentence melody on the sentence as a whole – that is, in terms of an overlay model – but given the fact that the perturbations are restricted to the final syllable, it seems equally plausible to regard them as being the result of associating the final syllable with a sequence of the lexical tone and a high boundary tone. That is, the basic shape of the contour is determined by the lexically specified tones on the morphemes that happen to make up an utterance; at the edge of the contour, there can be additional tones that affect the realisation of the final lexically specified tone or tones.

Potentially the most problematical intonational phenomenon in tone languages is the reported occurrence of meaningfully distinct overall contour shapes on which the lexical tones are superimposed. This is obviously the kind of evidence that would support Bolinger's wave metaphor and the 'overlay' view discussed in section 1.3.2. If we wish to maintain the view developed so far, namely that contour shapes are specified only in terms of local phonological events, then we need to examine this evidence carefully to see if it can be re-interpreted.

There are three fairly well-established types of cases that have been interpreted as evidence for the direct specification of overall shapes and therefore for the overlay view. These are:

1   suspension of downdrift in questions;
2   marking the location of focus;
3   signalling at least a three-way intonational distinction (yes–no question vs. WH-question vs. statement).

Let us consider each of these in turn.

The suspension of downdrift in questions has been demonstrated for Hausa by Lindau (1986) and Inkelas and Leben (1990). In Hausa, as in many African languages, the second H in a sequence H..L..H is normally realised at a lower level than the first H. Moreover, this effect can be iterated, so that in a sequence H..L..H..L..H..L..H each H tone is realised at a progressively lower level. This overall downward trend is clearly phonologically conditioned, however: in non-alternating sequences of tones like H..H..H..H..H, there is only a very slight 'declination', so that the slope of

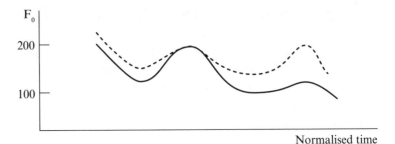

Figure 4.3 Overall contour shapes signalling location of focus in Chinese. The utterance in both cases is *Sòng Yán mài níuròu* ('Song Yan sells beef'), spoken by the same speaker. The dashed line shows the contour when the focus is late in the utterance and the pitch range remains more or less constant throughout; the solid line shows the contour when the focus is on the subject *Sòng Yán* and the pitch range narrows abruptly on the predicate *mài níuròu*. After Gårding 1987.

a 'topline' drawn through the H tones is much less steep than in the case of alternating sequences.

Now, this downdrift effect does not apply in questions. In a sequence H..L..H..L..H..L..H in a Hausa question, the H tones are all realised at approximately the same level, though there may be a slight amount of 'declination'. Obviously, this means that a postlexical or intonational factor influences the realisation of the lexically specified tonal string. However, it does so in a way that is entirely in keeping with the linear phonological view: rather than operating in terms of some preselected slope for questions or statements (which is what we might expect from, for example, Grønnum's model of Danish intonation; see figure 1.4), it is clear that the Hausa intonation patterns are produced *locally*, by the operation or non-operation of the downstep rule at successive points in a sequence of tones (see section 2.4). The slope of a line through a statement contour is very much dependent on the lexical tonal makeup of the contour, and *cannot* be specified as a global shape applying to statements. There *is* an interaction between intonation and lexical tone, but it must be described in terms of local phonological events. This is exactly what the AM theory would lead us to expect.

The second case is more problematical, but still not beyond the reach of the AM view. This is the reported use of overall contour shapes to signal the location of focus. Specifically, Gårding (1987) has suggested that 'early focus' sentences in Chinese have a 'grid' (see figure 1.3 and accompanying text) that narrows abruptly after the focus, whereas for normal 'late focus' sentences the grid remains wide. This is shown in figure 4.3.

The AM interpretation of such cases will have to involve modifications of pitch range for emphasis. This can be related to pitch range modification for emotional signalling, discussed above. The difference is that in the case of emotional modification of pitch range, the modification affects an entire utterance, where in the case of focus and emphasis it appears that the modification of pitch range can take place during the course of the utterance. Thus the early focus sentences would have an idealised 'tonal space' (see section 2.3.4) as follows:

(4.48)

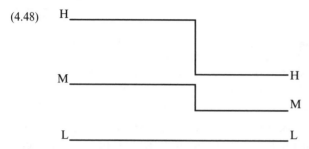

The normal late focus sentences, by contrast, would keep the tonal space unmodified throughout the utterance. As with the suspension of downdrift, we must obviously allow that in this case intonational or postlexical factors affect the realisation of the tones, but once again the intonational effects can be described as *occurring at a specific point or points in the utterance* rather than involving a contour shape that has to be specified as such in the phonology.[13]

Finally we come to the most difficult cases, in which it appears that overall contours with distinct shapes convey distinct intonational meanings. The most serious evidence for this comes from a proposal by Shen (1990) for Chinese, which has been applied to Kipare by Herman (1995). Shen claims that there are at least three distinct intonational tunes, which she calls Tunes I, II, and III. These are used, according to Shen, for yes–no questions (Tune I), WH-questions and alternative ('is it A or B?') questions (Tune II), and declaratives (Tune III). Herman suggests that the same three tune types are used in Kipare, for incredulous questions, ordinary yes–no questions, and declaratives respectively. Shen's graphic portrayal of the three tunes is shown in figure 4.4.

In order to accommodate these in an AM theory, one of two things will be necessary. The simplest possibility would be to interpret the overall shapes as involving local pitch range specifications – that is, to show that they result from successive expansions or contractions of pitch range that

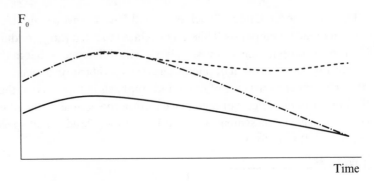

Figure 4.4 Chinese sentence-level 'tunes', from Shen 1990. The three tunes are intended to indicate the approximate overall shape of the utterance contour in declaratives (Tune I, solid line), alternative and WH-questions (Tune II, dash-dot line), and yes–no questions (Tune III, dashed line).

occur at well-defined locations. This kind of interpretation is not inconsistent with what Shen and Herman say about the three tunes. Shen's description is as follows (1990: 26):[14]

> *Tune I*: starting with a mid key, moving upward to a mid-high key at the highest peak, falling to a low register at the ending point.
>
> *Tune II*: starting with a mid-high key, moving upward to a high key at the highest peak, dropping, but not too low, ending in the high or mid-high register.
>
> *Tune III*: starting with a mid-high key, moving upward to a high key at the highest peak, stepping down and ending with a low key.

If we treat Shen's impressionistic descriptions of the different keys or registers as characterisations of the phonetic realisation of the tonal space, it is at least possible that we could show that the *changes* from one key to another happen at well-defined points in the contour. Herman's description of the three tunes is even more clearly consistent with this sort of interpretation: Tune I involves 'non-expanded pitch range with final lowering'; Tune II has 'expanded pitch-range with final lowering'; and Tune III exhibits 'expanded pitch range with final raising'. If such a description of these global tunes were possible, it would be comparable to the treatment of the pitch range effects involved in early focus sentences, discussed just above.

If this interpretation turns out not to be possible and it is necessary to describe the three overall shapes as global gestures, then this finding could be made compatible with the AM theory by showing that analogous effects on pitch range are found in intonation languages as well. For example, we might seek to show that English distinguishes contours in which the pitch accent peaks are of moderate height and gradually decline (Tune I) from contours in which the peaks are of much greater height and decline very little (Tune III). Such an interpretation might seem like an important theoretical concession, and in a sense it is; however, it is important to keep in mind that what the AM theory predicts above all is that *the phonological structure of pitch is comparable in all languages*. If it turned out that declination were meaningfully variable as such in all languages, then that fact would have to be built into our phonetic model. But in all languages it would still be possible to distinguish linear tonal specifications – English postlexical pitch accents or Chinese lexical tones – from pitch range modifications: that is, all languages would still require *both* tonal specifications and descriptions of how pitch range can be modified. Lexical tone would still not constitute an additional layer or special type of phonological specification, and the 'unity of pitch phonology' would remain unaffected.

4.4.3 'Pitch accent' languages

Finally we come to a third topic in the general area of tone–intonation interactions, namely the phonetic typology that Beckman (1986) has discussed under the title 'stress and non-stress accent'. Beckman's title unfortunately introduces a terminological confusion to which attention must be drawn from the outset (see notes 2, 3, and 4 in chapter 2). Her 'accent' might be defined as 'the special phonological treatment of a particular syllable or syllables in a word'. Given this definition, 'stress accent' and 'non-stress accent' are two ways in which the special treatment of the syllable can be manifested phonetically. 'Accent' is thus an abstract phonological feature specified in the lexicon; 'stress' is a phonetic description of one possible concrete realisation of the phonological abstraction.[15] In what follows I will refer to Beckman's sense of accent as *lexical accent*.

As we noted above (section 2.2.2), Beckman shows that in languages like English, lexical accent is regularly manifested by what we called stress, a cluster of phonetic properties that includes increased intensity and duration as well as various spectral correlates. *In addition*, stressed syllables are often accompanied by the major pitch movements we called pitch accent. Beckman compared English with Japanese, showing that in Japanese, lexical accent is marked only by pitch movement, and not at all by stress. On this basis she supports the traditional typological distinction between 'dynamic' and 'melodic' accent: dynamic or stress accent is lexical accent realised by stress (and often accompanied by pitch movement), while melodic or non-stress accent is realised always and only by pitch movement.

Because of Beckman's choice of English and Japanese for comparison, however, there is a potential for confusion that I wish to mention here. In English, pitch features are only postlexical or intonational, while in Japanese pitch features are specified in the lexicon. Nevertheless, the distinction between lexical and postlexical specification of pitch features is *independent of the distinction between stress and non-stress accent*. Stress vs. non-stress accent is a *phonetic* typological dimension (is lexical accent manifested by stress or not?). Lexical vs. postlexical specification of pitch features is a *phonological* or even morphological typological dimension (can pitch features be specified in the lexicon or not?). It is important not to assume that 'non-stress accent' is a matter of lexically specified pitch features, just because Japanese happens to work that way.

If the two typological dimensions are really independent, it ought to be possible to find four types of languages. In particular, we ought to be able to find languages that have lexically specified pitch features with stress accent, and languages that have only intonational pitch features and non-stress accent. I believe that this can be done: Swedish (like most of the European 'pitch accent languages') is an example of a language combining lexically specified pitch features with stress accent, while Bengali (and probably most of the languages of India) is an example of a language with non-stress accent and no lexical specification of pitch. This typological conjecture is summarised in (4.49)

(4.49)   Phonetic typology

		Stress accent	Non-stress accent
	Lexical pitch	example: Swedish	example: Japanese
Lexical typology			
	Postlexical pitch only	example: English	example: Bengali

In this connection we should explicitly mention the appropriate analysis of the European 'pitch accent' languages like Swedish and Serbo-Croatian. To my knowledge, all such languages clearly have 'stress' in

Beckman's phonetic sense, and at least some of them have the possibility (like English or Bengali, and unlike Japanese) of selecting different pitch accent types to convey different pragmatic meanings. (In the clearest such example, Serbo-Croatian has a different pitch accent type for use in questions – the 'reverse pattern' of Lehiste and Ivić (1980, 1986) – from the pattern used in statements and citation forms.) Where such languages differ from languages like English is in the fact that the choice of pitch accent type seems to be influenced by lexical considerations as well as postlexical ones. Thus Swedish distinguishes between Accent 1 words and Accent 2 words, Serbo-Croatian distinguishes falling and rising accents, and so on.

The correct tonal analysis of these languages is by no means clear, however. There have been a number of suggestions for these languages that the accentual contour itself is constant (say, HL), and that what varies is the alignment of the accentual contour with the segments on the accented word. Perhaps the most noteworthy of these analyses is Bruce's work on Swedish, which we have extensively discussed above (sections 1.3.3 and 2.3.4), but similar analyses have been given for other languages, such as Browne and McCawley's (1965) analysis of Serbo-Croatian accent. However, recent AM analyses, together with some recent phonetic data on Swedish, seem to point to the conclusion that the pitch accent configurations represent a combination of lexical and postlexical specifications. For example, Inkelas and Zec (1988) analyse the Serbo-Croatian accent distinction as based on the location of a prelinked lexically specified H tone: the falling accents have a lexically associated H tone on a word-initial syllable, and the rising accents have a lexically associated H on a non-initial syllable. The latter are then subject to leftward spreading, and in some cases to a postlexical final-lowering rule, while the former are not. Gussenhoven and van der Vliet (ms.) propose a roughly similar analysis for the word accent distinction in Venlo Dutch: the basic distinction is between the presence and absence of a lexical H tone on the stressed syllable, and the actual spoken contours depend on the interaction of any lexical tones with other tones that are assigned postlexically.

Such analyses are broadly consistent with new evidence about what happens to the Swedish word accents when they are emphasised (Fant and Kruckenberg 1994). Recall that Swedish citation-form contours comprise a sequence of an accentual fall and a 'phrase accent' peak. For Bruce, the fall is HL and the phrase accent is H, and the only difference between Accent 1 and Accent 2 is that the HL is aligned earlier with Accent 1.

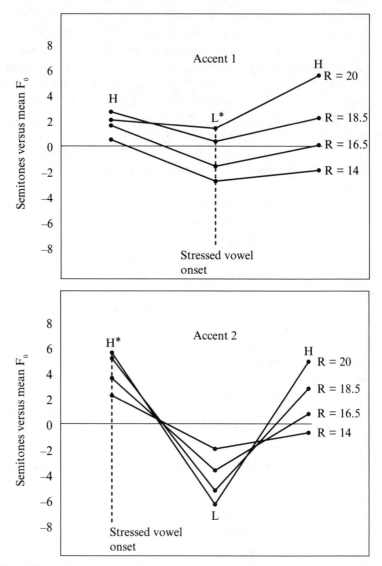

Figure 4.5 Effect of increasing emphasis on the pitch configurations of the Swedish word accents. In Accent 1 the accentual H and L and the phrase tone H are all raised with increasing emphasis. In Accent 2 the L is *lowered* and only the H tones are raised. From Fant and Kruckenberg 1994.

However, by asking speakers to pronounce the word accents with different degrees of overall emphasis, Fant and Kruckenberg showed that the L in Accent 2 is not the same as the L in Accent 1. When the overall emphasis was increased on Accent 1, all three turning points – accentual H and L and phrasal H – increased in F_0. By contrast, when overall emphasis was increased on Accent 2, the H tones were raised and the L tone was lowered. This is shown in figure 4.5. While it is by no means clear exactly how to translate these findings into lexical representations, it is not implausible to suggest that the L tone is somehow more 'real' in Accent 2 than in Accent 1. If we interpret 'real' as meaning lexically specified, then the Fant and Kruckenberg data could be seen as consistent with Gussenhoven and van der Vliet's analysis of Venlo Dutch.

Once again, we see here the importance of assuming what I called the unity of pitch phonology. The AM approaches to pitch accent sketched here draw no fundamental distinction between tones that are assigned in the lexicon and tones that are assigned or modified postlexically. Earlier, I suggested a distinction for Chinese and Japanese between lexical core tones and postlexical edge tones, but in the case of the European pitch accent languages it appears that lexical and postlexical tones may be interspersed. The distinction between the two is phonetically irrelevant; for all pitch contours in all languages, the input to phonetic realisation is a string of tones.

5 Patterns of prominence

We began the previous chapter with a characterisation of the 'universalist' view of intonation. The phenomena emphasised by this view, as we saw, are (a) the tendency to declination, (b) the association of high or rising pitch with questions and non-finality, and (c) the presence of local pitch movements – pitch accents – on new or otherwise informative words. We have now dealt in detail with the melodic aspects of intonation cross-linguistically, but we have yet to discuss the location of pitch accents except incidentally. The goal of this chapter is to show that, as in their melodic features, languages differ systematically in their patterns of utterance-level accentuation.

5.1 Prominence and focus

5.1.1 'Normal stress' and 'focus-to-accent'

It is now generally accepted that sentence accentuation reflects – in some way – the intended *focus* of an utterance. However, there remain a number of disagreements about *how* focus is conveyed by accent, and in many ways these disagreements represent the continuation of a decades-old debate about 'normal stress'. It will therefore be useful to review this issue briefly first.

In one conception, which goes back at least to Newman (1946), there is one pattern, commonly known as *normal stress*, which can be specified by rule for every sentence. Importantly for later sections of the chapter, this pattern includes a single primary stress or sentence stress. Normal stress has no meaning or function: it is simply the result of the operation of phonological rules on surface syntactic structures. Only 'contrastive stress', which is seen as essentially unpredictable and beyond the scope of normal stress rules, can be said to mean something. The normal stress view was dominant, at least in American linguistics, until the 1970s, finding perhaps its definitive expression in the Nuclear Stress Rule of Chomsky and Halle (1968: ch. 3).

The normal stress view was repeatedly criticised by Bolinger (e.g. 1958, 1972b). Bolinger argued instead that words in utterances can be 'focused' or 'highlighted' to signal newness, contrast, or some other special informativeness, and that focused words are marked by pitch accents. What speakers decide to highlight is not a matter of grammar but a matter of what they are trying to say on a specific occasion in a specific context; all accents are individually meaningful. Bolinger does not assume that one of the pitch accents is primary, and he explicitly rejects the idea that one particular pattern of pitch accents is assigned by rule. His view was succinctly summed up in the title of his paper 'Accent is predictable (if you're a mind-reader)' (1972b). Similar ideas – in particular, the relevance of discourse context and of speaker and hearer presuppositions – have been put forth by a number of others, including linguists of the Prague school (e.g. Daneš 1967), Halliday and his followers (Halliday 1967b; Halliday and Hasan 1976), and Chafe (1973, 1974, 1976).

Some of Bolinger's concerns – in particular, the notion of 'focus' – were brought into the mainstream in work on semantics in generative grammar (Chomsky 1972; Jackendoff 1972; Bresnan 1971, 1972), and his specific ideas on focus and accent were explored and developed in subsequent work on intonation by, for example, Schmerling (1976), Ladd (1980a), and Gussenhoven (1983a). All these works, in various ways, developed the idea that there is such a thing as 'broad focus' (the term was suggested in Ladd 1980a: ch. 4) – focus on whole constituents or whole sentences, not just on individual words. Given the idea of broad focus, 'normal stress' rules can be seen as a description of where accent is placed when focus is broad. Yet this view is also compatible with the idea that in cases of narrow focus – focus on individual words – accent goes on the focused word.

Pierrehumbert (1980) adopted Bolinger's notion of pitch accent, essentially for phonetic and phonological reasons, but in doing so she set the seal on the theoretical rehabilitation of his ideas about focus. Since the early 1980s virtually all work on sentence-level accentuation has accepted some version of what we might call, following Gussenhoven (1983a), the 'Focus-to-Accent' (FTA) approach. In very general terms, the FTA theory is that words and constituents in utterances can be focused for various reasons, and that focused words and constituents are marked by pitch accents. However, this general formulation of the FTA theory masks a deeper divergence of views over broad focus, and, in a sense, over the definition of focus itself. These issues are discussed in the next sections.

5.1.2   Narrow and broad focus

Let us begin with some central phenomena about which there is little disagreement. These can be illustrated in terms of a purely intuitive notion of focus and an impressionistic notion of accent. The discussion is based on the appropriate matching of accent patterns and discourse contexts.

Consider the phrase *five francs*. This could be used in a specific context where the number of francs was at issue, in which case we may say that the focus is on *five*:

(5.1)   I didn't give him three francs, I gave him five francs.

In this case, there would normally be a pitch accent on *five* and none on *francs*, and thus a direct relation between accent and focus. A simple notation for this pattern is FIVE *francs*. The same phrase could also be used in a context where the unit of currency was at issue, in which case we may say that the focus is on *francs*:

(5.2)   I didn't give him five marks, I gave him five francs.

In this case there would often be a prominent accent on *francs*, and either no accent on *five* or only a weak one. Once again there is a direct relation between accent and focus, and we can notate this pattern informally as *five* FRANCS. (The details of what happens on *five* are relevant to a number of issues to which we will return in section 5.3 and again in chapter 6.)

Finally, in relatively unusual circumstances there is also what we might call a 'double-focus' pattern, with very prominent accents on both *five* and *francs*. This might be found in very deliberate speech in a context like (5.3):

(5.3)   I didn't give him SEVen GUILDers, I gave him FIVE FRANCS.

The first clause of this example – *I didn't give him seven guilders* – also illustrates a basic feature of pitch accents, namely that when a pitch accent occurs on a word containing more than one syllable, the accent occurs on the lexically stressed syllable of the word (*sev-* of *seven* and *guil-* of *guilders*).

Continuing in just this informal way, we can illustrate the need for a notion of broad focus. In addition to the three fairly specific contexts just sketched, it is also possible for the phrase *five francs* to be used in a wide variety of other contexts in which the focus is not on either word alone but as it were on the whole phrase:

(5.4)

$$
\text{I didn't give him } \left\{ \begin{array}{l} \text{a dollar} \\ \text{fifty centimes} \\ \text{my notebook} \\ \text{your camera} \\ \text{the car keys} \\ \text{a sandwich} \\ \text{a lot of money} \end{array} \right\} \text{, I gave him five francs.}
$$

This is clearly distinct in meaning from any of the first three examples: in those cases one or both of the words in the phrase *five francs* is contrasted to other possible words from fairly specific sets of numbers and currency names. Here, the phrase *five francs* is contrasted *as a unit* to some other phrase from a more or less unlimited set of possibilities. This is what is meant by broad focus.[1]

While the broad focus meaning seems quite distinct from the various narrow focus meanings, the accentual pattern that signals broad focus may be similar or identical to the one that signals narrow focus on *francs*, namely *five FRANCS*. Actually, the claim that the two patterns are identical requires some non-trivial phonetic and phonological justification, but we will return to that matter in section 5.3 below. For the moment, let us assume, with many authors over the past three decades (e.g. Chomsky 1972; Jackendoff 1972) that patterns like *five FRANCS* are potentially ambiguous between narrow focus and broad focus readings.

This ambiguity requires comment within the FTA view, because it makes it difficult to assume a straightforward bidirectional correspondence between focus and accent. Simply put, it makes it difficult to assume that whatever is focused is accented and whatever is accented is focused. Given ambiguity, interpreting accent patterns is not simply a matter of perceiving individual focused words, but of identifying focused *constituents*. Signalling focus is not simply a matter of putting accents on individual highlighted words, but of applying the principles that decide which word takes the accent *when a given constituent is focused*. The problem may be stated in two interrelated questions: 'Where do we place accent, given focus?' and 'How do we determine the breadth of focus, given accent?' These questions have been approached in two conflicting ways.

5.1.3   *Structure-based and highlighting-based accounts of broad focus*

Within the FTA theory, there are two possible ways of dealing with broad focus, which we may call structure-based and highlighting-based. The first approach was sketched by Ladd (1980a, 1983c) and Gussenhoven (1983a, 1985), as part of their attempt to reconcile the notion of focus with traditional descriptions of normal stress. This view deals with the problem of broad focus by distinguishing between the distribution of *focus* and the distribution of *accents*. That is, the linguistic description of accent patterns involves two complementary but essentially separate aspects: a statement about which parts of an utterance are focused, and a statement about how a given pattern of focus is conveyed by the location of the accent. The speaker's decision about what to focus is subject to all kinds of contextual influences which are at best poorly understood: these are the factors with which Bolinger, Chafe, Halliday, and others have always been concerned. However, once the focused part of the utterance is specified, the accent pattern follows more or less automatically by language-specific rules or structural principles such as Gussenhoven's 'Sentence Accent Assignment Rule' and 'Minimal Focus Rule': these cover much of the ground that was dealt with by traditional 'normal stress' rules. The structure-based FTA view has no trouble accommodating narrow focus on individual words, but it also allows for the existence of 'unmarked' or 'default' patterns that specify the location of accent in cases of broad focus on whole constituents or sentences.[2] For example, in a simple sentence like *John painted the shed*, we might (for contextual reasons) have narrow focus on any one of the three constituents subject, verb, and object, in which case accent would go on the focused constituent; but we might also have broad focus on the whole sentence. In this case, according to Gussenhoven, two 'focus domains' are created, one on the subject and one comprising the verb and the object. Each focus domain then gets one accent, which means that there is only one accent available to signal the focus on the verb + object domain. By Gussenhoven's rules, this one accent goes on the object, yielding the accent pattern *JOHN painted the SHED*. The absence of accent on *painted* does not necessarily signal that *painted* is not focused, but only that it is part of a larger focus constituent that is marked by an accent somewhere else (viz. on the object).

The structure-based view may be said to underlie a good deal of recent work on the semantics of focus (e.g. Rooth 1985 or Krifka 1991 on the interpretation of the scope of logical operators like *only* and *even*) and on how focus interacts with syntactic and phonological organisation (e.g. Selkirk 1984; von Stechow and Uhmann 1986; Steedman 1991). The work of these authors is in many cases directly relevant to the description of how accent signals broad focus, and to the identification of any unmarked or default accent patterns that may exist. However, the emphasis in recent years has mostly been on formal semantics, not on phonology (an exception is Cinque 1993, which deals primarily with syntax). While I assume that a structure-based FTA theory is desirable, I believe that it needs to pay more attention to phonology and phonetics – and to pragmatics – than has been the case in this recent work. I will sketch a number of ideas on this topic in chapter 6.

The alternative to a structure-based FTA theory is to assume that broad focus requires no special account, but follows from the general principles relating focus to discourse context and speaker intentions. As we have just seen, the structure-based approach distinguishes clearly between the designation of certain constituents as focused, which is assumed to depend on poorly understood pragmatic factors, and the distribution of accents within focused constituents, which is assumed to depend on structural factors that may be language-specific. In highlighting-based FTA approaches, the distribution of accents within focused constituents is assumed to depend on the same kinds of pragmatic factors as the designation of focused constituents itself. In effect, this is a 'radical FTA' theory, which rejects the distinction between focus distribution and accent distribution, and maintains the validity of the bidirectional relation between focus and accent. In this view, if a word is focused, it is accented – there is no disagreement there from any quarter – but also, if a word is accented, then it must somehow be focused, even if it appears to be part of a larger broad focus constituent. For example, in a sentence like *He took a BATH*, it is easy enough to argue that *bath* is the key to the meaning of the sentence, and that, given *bath*, the occurrence of *took* is (at least in American English!) very largely predictable. This is true whether the context is *He shaved and took a bath* (in which case we might speak of focus on the whole constituent *took a bath*) or *He didn't take a shower, he took a bath* (which clearly has a narrow focus on *bath*). In either case, *bath* can be seen as the most informative word in the sentence and hence the word most appropriately highlighted by an accent.

On the basis of examples like this, the radical FTA view maintains that there is no difference between the specific informativeness of narrow focus and the more general relative informativeness that depends on lexical meanings and knowledge about the world. However, in other cases this kind of explanation is, in my view, deeply implausible. In our example *five FRANCS*, for instance, the radical FTA theory must say that *francs* is accented in the broad focus case because it is somehow more informative or salient than *five*. It is hard to see how this could be so in an exchange like the following:

(5.5)   A: How much did they pay you for participating in the experiment?

B: Five francs.

In this case, *francs* is almost entirely predictable if the conversation takes place in a country where the unit of currency is the franc; *five* is the information of interest. Yet the accent is on *francs*. The best the radical FTA theory can do in a case like this is to say that other factors are at work in determining discourse salience and therefore focus. (For example, *francs* might be more salient because it is a noun, or because it stands last in the utterance.) But the argument is essentially circular, since the main evidence for the supposed greater salience of *francs* is the very fact that it is accented.

Despite such difficulties, a couple of partially independent current lines of research have nevertheless favoured the persistence of the radical FTA view. These lines of research are all in some sense concerned with the dynamic organisation of conversation and the flow of information between speaker and hearer (Grosz and Sidner 1986).[3] Among the specific issues considered are the different kinds of discourse statuses that entities may have (previously mentioned, newly introduced, etc.; see Prince 1981; Gundel, Hedberg, and Zacharski 1993); how long such discourse statuses last, and what causes them to change (e.g. in order to count as previously mentioned, must the earlier mention have taken place within a certain amount of elapsed time? a certain number of turns? a certain number of topic shifts?; see Grosz and Sidner 1986); the way in which entities are referred to depending on their discourse status (a full descriptive noun phrase, a noun with a definite article, a pronoun, etc.; see Gundel, Hedberg, and Zacharski, 1993); and, finally, the effect of discourse status on whether referring expressions are accented or not (Brown 1983; Nooteboom and Terken 1982; Nooteboom and Kruyt 1987; Terken and Hirschberg 1994). All this work is essentially concerned with exploring the reasons for which a speaker decides to focus on a constituent or not; in principle this work is compatible with either the structural FTA view or the radical FTA view. Yet because it tends to concentrate on single entities that can be referred to with single accented or unaccented words, attention is concentrated on the relation between the discourse status of words and the accentuation of words. The problem of where to locate accent *within* a focused constituent does not arise, and broad focus therefore receives little attention.

5.1.4 Breaking the deadlock

We may summarise the foregoing as follows. Even though everyone now accepts that accent signals focus, there is still a fundamental divide between what I have called the structural FTA view and the radical FTA view. Proponents of the latter view think that accents are directly meaningful signals of focus or discourse salience – unpredictable except with reference to speakers' intentions and specific contexts – and as such are part of some universal (and possibly prelinguistic) intonational highlighting function. Proponents of the former approach believe that focus involves language-specific constituent structure, and language-specific principles (or general structural principles: see Cinque 1993) relating individual accents to constituents of various sizes.

It appears that the only way to get beyond this debate is to demonstrate the existence of language-specific differences of accent pattern. Consider, for example, hypothetical data of the following sort:

(5.6) | *Language A* | *Language B* |
|---|---|
| This is book RED | This is BOOK red |
| I bought car NEW | I bought CAR new |
| He has nose BIG | He has NOSE big |

In language A alone, the radical FTA theory could argue that, in the absence of other influences, the accent goes to the end of the sentence (Bolinger's 'accents of power', widely observed in many contexts). In language B alone, the theory might suggest that nouns are intrinsically more informative than adjectives and are thus likely to attract the speaker's attention (Bolinger's 'accents of interest'). But the *comparison* between languages A and B makes it impossible to maintain that these principles are universal, or that conflicts between these principles are resolved by individual speakers in individual situations on the basis of universal principles. The difference between the two languages seems to point inevitably to language-specific – and hence possibly structure-dependent – principles for placing accent within broad focus constituents. This comparative approach is the general strategy adopted in the following section. On the basis of these comparisons, it is possible to demonstrate – conclusively, in my view – that there are consistent cross-language differences in patterns of sentence accentuation.[4] This in turn means that, whatever exactly the relation between focus and accent may be, it is not simply a matter of applying some universal highlighting gesture to individually informative words.

5.2   Prominence patterns across languages

The discussion of cross-language differences is organised as follows. First, I present three general types of cases in which I believe the evidence for cross-language differences is fairly clear. These are:

1   questions;
2   deaccenting and 'semantic weight';
3   predicates vs. arguments.

Following an extensive presentation of the data, I briefly discuss the ways in which these three general types of cases might be interrelated, and the question of which aspects of accentuation, if any, are governed by universal principles.

5.2.1   Questions
5.2.1.1   Yes–no questions
The most convincing cross-linguistic differences are those seen in yes–no questions (YNQs). These have already been alluded to in the preceding chapter (4.1.2 and 4.3.1). In some languages, like English, YNQs are treated exactly like statements for purposes of accent rules. Thus in 'citation form' we would expect

(5.7)   Statement: She bought a BOOK
         YNQ: Did she buy a BOOK?

Both of the following forms are distinctly non-neutral in some way:

(5.8)   Statement: She BOUGHT a book
         YNQ: Did she BUY a book?

English YNQs, like English statements, *can* be accented on the verb, but normally only if the verb is not followed by a lexical noun:

(5.9)   Statement: She's SLEEPING.
         YNQ: Is she SLEEPING?

In short, there is nothing in these data to suggest that the distinction between statements and questions is relevant to accentuation.

In other languages, however, such as Russian, the two sentence types pattern differently. Russian statements, like English statements, have the greatest prominence on the noun if there is one following the verb:

(5.10)   Ona kupila KNIGU
         (lit. she bought BOOK)

In YNQs, on the other hand, the neutral accent pattern or citation form has the greatest prominence on the verb, regardless of whether the verb is followed by a lexical noun:

(5.11)   a.   Ona SPIT?
              (lit. she SLEEPS?)

         b.   Ona KUPILA knigu?
              (lit. she BOUGHT book?)

A YNQ with greatest prominence on a noun is distinctly non-neutral; that is, the question

(5.12)   Ona kupila KNIGU?

is felt to focus narrowly on the book in the way that English *Did she BUY a book?* focuses on the buying. If we want to say something in Russian comparable to English *Did she BUY a book?* we must change the word order to (5.13):

(5.13)   Ona knigu KUPILA?

The method of comparing similar sentences across languages effectively precludes arguments about the nature of neutral sentence accent or the exact contexts in which one accent placement or another would be appropriate. The differences must be seen as genuine.[5] Languages like Russian accent YNQs on the verb, regardless of whether the sentence also contains nouns; languages like English accent the verb in YNQs only if there is no following lexical noun. In this case, 'languages like English' include all the Germanic and Romance languages with the exception of Romanian; 'languages like Russian' include Romanian, Hungarian, and many if not all of the Slavic languages. For most languages, the facts remain to be determined.

The existence of two neutral or default accentuation patterns for YNQs can be related to cross-linguistic facts about question particles. In languages that have question particles, there are two main locations for the particle. In one type of language, the question particle occurs at the edge of the sentence, either the beginning (e.g. Yoruba) or the end (e.g. Chinese); in these languages there is no relation between the location of the particle and the location of focus. In the other type of language, the particle attaches to the focus of the question, and if there is no special focused word, then the particle – like the accent in Russian – attaches to the finite verb. In Turkish, for example, the question particle normally occurs as one of the suffixes or enclitics on the finite verb or other predicate:[6]

(5.14)   a.   Gazete geldi mi?
                 'Did the newspaper come?' (lit. newspaper come.PAST Q-PART)

          b.   Yorgun musunuz?
                 'Are you tired?' (lit. tired Q-PART.PLURAL.you)

However, if there is a focus on some specific word or constituent other than the verb, the question particle is attached to the focus:

(5.15)   a.   Mehmet mi geldi?
                 'Was it Mehmet who came?'

          b.   Buraya uçakla mı geldiniz, vapurla mı?
                 'Did you come here by plane or by steamer?' (lit. here plane.by Q-PART come.PAST.PLURAL.you, steamer.by Q-PART)

In a number of other languages, the question particle has a fixed position – attached to the first word or constituent of the sentence – and the focused word may move into that position; if there is no special focused word, the word in first position is once again the finite verb. The following examples are from Russian:

(5.16)   a.   Mark li čitaet?
                 'Is MARK reading?' (lit. Mark Q-PART reads)

          b.   Čitaet li Mark?
                 'Is Mark reading?'

Analogous examples are possible in some Serbian varieties of Serbo-Croatian (Wayles Browne, personal communication) and in Latin. Once again, there seems to be a special connection between the focus of a question and the finite verb.

5.2.1.2 WH-questions

For YNQs, then, it appears that there are two different patterns of accentuation cross-linguistically: special neutral accent location for questions (on the verb), and neutral accent location similar in questions and statements. Similar conclusions seem to hold for questions containing question words like *who, how, what* (usually called WH-questions in English and here abbreviated WHQs). Various recent works on focus and accent deal uneasily with the accentuation of the WH-words in WHQs. Logic seems to suggest that the WH-word is the focus of the question, and yet, in English at least, the WH-word does not normally bear the most prominent accent. That is, English has

(5.17)   Where are you GOING?

rather than

(5.18)　WHERE are you going?

though the latter would seem to be demanded by a purely focus-based account of accent placement. (For an extensive discussion of this problem, see Culicover and Rochemont 1983: 139–44.)

Languages do exist, however, in which the WH-word is the most prominent in the unmarked accentuation. This appears to be the case, first of all, in languages without WH-movement (i.e. languages in which the WH-word does not stand at the beginning of the WHQ, as in most European languages, but instead occupies the same place in the WHQ as a lexical noun in the corresponding statement). Thus in Turkish we find:

(5.19)　Halil'e NE verdiniz?
　　　　'What did you give to Halil?' (lit. Halil-to WHAT you-gave)

And in Bengali we have:

(5.20)　Ram KAKE dekhlo?
　　　　'Whom did Ram see?' (lit. Ram WHOM saw)

Similarly, English WHQs without WH-movement – most often occurring as echo questions – have the accent on the WH-word:

(5.21)　a.　You did WHAT?

　　　　b.　They went WHERE?

and so on.

More relevantly for the comparison with ordinary English WHQs, there are languages with WH-movement that put the nuclear accent on the WH-word, so long as the sentence is fairly short. In Romanian, for example, one says:

(5.22)　a.　UNDE mergi?
　　　　　　'Where are you going?'

　　　　b.　CÂȚI bani ai?
　　　　　　'How much money do you have?'

　　　　c.　CÂND a plecat?
　　　　　　'When did it leave?'

　　　　d.　CINE a chemat?
　　　　　　'Who called?'

Essentially the same is true of Hungarian:

(5.23) a. KI az?
'Who is that?'

b. MIT vettél?
'What did you buy?'

c. MILYEN volt a vacsora?
'How was the dinner?'

On longer WHQs in these languages, there may be an accent later in the sentence. Thus in Romanian one would be likely to find either version of (5.24) and (5.25):

(5.24) a. Unde ai cumpărat cravata ACEASTA?

b. UNDE ai cumpărat cravata aceasta?
'Where did you buy that necktie?'

(5.25) a. Cu cine ai vorbit la FACULTATE?

b. Cu CINE ai vorbit la facultate?
'Who did you talk to at the university?'

The issue of sentence length and its effect on accentuation is discussed further in section 6.2.3. For short sentences, however, it appears that the correct phonological interpretation of the accentuation pattern is with the main accent on the WH-word. As with YNQs, then, we have two basic patterns cross-linguistically, one in which WHQs follow the same pattern as other sentences, and one in which there is a special rule for WHQs, whereby the neutral accent goes on the WH-word.

5.2.1.3 A note on question intonation

Before leaving the topic of accent placement in questions, it is important to draw attention to a potential difficulty in determining what the facts are. The problem has to do with the fact that in many cases, especially in questions, it is not a straightforward phonetic task to identify the most prominent word or syllable. I have tried to avoid this problem wherever possible in the discussion in this section, but it is important to sketch the issues briefly before going on.

First consider the accentuation of YNQs, and in particular the claim that the normal accentuation of YNQs in many languages puts the accent on the verb. The Russian data on this point are fairly clear, because the normal YNQ intonation in Russian involves a high accent peak on the most prominent syllable – $L+H^*..L$, or something of the sort. (Normal statement intonation is ${}^{!}$H*..L or H+L*..L; see section 4.2.4 for the difference between the two possible analyses.) In most other Eastern European languages, however (for example, Hungarian; section 4.1.2), the normal YNQ intonation is L*..H..L. Consequently, in these languages the syllable that I analyse as most prominent is phonetically low, and is followed later in the sentence by a peak-and-fall which is often acoustically more salient, at least to Western European ears, than the L*. I believe that my analysis of the prominence relations in these is correct (see my discussion of example (4.5)), but it means that such analysis is prerequisite to the kind of typological statements being attempted here. The situation is complicated still further by the existence of what I call 'postnuclear accent' in several Eastern European languages, including at least Romanian, Greek, and Czech. Postnuclear accent is discussed at greater length in section 6.1.3.

Similar problems arise in the case of the early accent on WHQs. Phonetically, there is a strong similarity between the contours on, for example, the Romanian and Italian phrases meaning 'Where are you going?':

(5.26)   a.   H*   L   L%
             Romanian: Unde mergi?

         b.   H* H+L* L%
             Italian: Dove vai?

However, I analyse the Romanian case as having the nuclear accent on the WH-word *unde* and the Italian case as involving a downstepped accent on *vai*. (That is, the Italian tune contains the same 'downstepping' accent – ${}^{!}$H*..L or H+L*..L – used in statement intonation in the Romance languages generally; see section 4.2.4.) This analysis is based on considerations of both phonetic detail and native-speaker intuition.

The phonetic considerations involve the course of F_0 on the unstressed second syllable of the WH-word (e.g. *unde* or *dove*). In Romanian (5.26a) the pitch comes down quickly on the unstressed syllable of *unde*, and there is no further movement on *mergi*. This suggests that there is only one accent on the phrase, on *unde*. In Italian (5.26b), by comparison, the pitch on *dove* stays relatively high and steps down to the following stressed syllable *vai*. The distinction between the two contours can be seen more clearly if we increase the number of unstressed syllables between the stressed syllable of the WH-word and the stressed syllable of the verb, as, for example, in the following sentences meaning 'Where did you buy it?' (the lexically stressed vowel of the verb is underlined):

(5.27)   a.   H* L   L%
              Romanian: Unde l-ai cumpărat?

          b.   H*   H+L*L%
          Italian: Dove l'hai comprato?

As for the matter of native-speaker intuitions, speakers of Romanian or Hungarian have firm intuitions that the WH-word bears the main accent in sentences like these. Italian or Portuguese speakers tend to be uncertain. Obviously, the situation would be clearer if Italian or Portuguese speakers had clear intuitions that the verb bears the main accent, but the difference is still noteworthy. In this connection it is worth noting that ordinary speakers of European languages generally seem inclined to equate high pitch with prominence, if asked to make metalinguistic judgements about which word is most prominent (see e.g. Bolinger 1958: 131–4 (1965: 38–43)). This may explain the uncertainty on the part of native speakers of Italian or Portuguese about the location of 'the' main accent in WHQs: the WH-word has the highest pitch even though, on the analysis proposed here, it is not the most prominent accent of the sentence. In any case, with WHQs as with YNQs, the typological discussion of accent placement depends to some extent on the validity of the phonological analysis.[7]

5.2.2   Deaccenting and 'semantic weight'

The data on accentuation in questions, as I have just presented them, are clearly difficult to reconcile with a universalist radical FTA theory. There seem to be two clear accentual patterns for both YNQs and WHQs, and there are clear similarities between the possible locations of accent in YNQs and the possible location of question particles. All these facts point to the conclusion that accentuation in questions is a matter of the grammar of specific languages rather than of universal principles of highlighting focused words. On the other hand, the data are admittedly limited, and potentially questionable in some cases. Accentuation has not been studied in questions anywhere near as much as in statements, and it is entirely possible that there are complexities beyond the brief presentation here that could be used to support a different interpretation. This section, therefore, concentrates on well-studied accentuation data from declarative sentences that form the heart of the case for the radical FTA view.

Specifically, in this section we consider cases in which, in English, accentuation can be influenced by the relative informativeness of words or constituents in a sentence. For example, it is well known that accent tends *not* to be placed on elements that are repeated or 'given' in the discourse, or on elements that are vague or generic. For adherents of the radical FTA view, this fact is a clear illustration of the general principles governing accentuation in any context: the speaker assesses the relative semantic weight or informativeness of potentially accentable words and puts the accent on the most informative point or points of the sentence. However, it is not hard to show that these observations, valid though they may be for English, do not apply in all languages. To back up the claim of non-universality, this section discusses structurally parallel examples from different languages, as in the discussion of questions. The discussion is divided into three sections, each dealing with one of three subcases: contextual deaccenting, indefinite pronouns, and 'semantically empty' words. In every instance the existence of cross-linguistic differences seems beyond dispute.

5.2.2.1 Contextual deaccenting
An important accentual difference between languages involves the treatment of repeated words or phrases, and more generally the treatment of 'given' information. A few examples from English follow:

(5.28)   a.   A: I found an article for you in a German journal.
                 B: I don't READ German.

          b.   I brought her a bottle of whisky, but it turns out she doesn't LIKE whisky.

In both of these, a word that we might expect to be accented (*German, whisky*) fails to be accented in a context where it has recently been used or where the entity to which it refers has recently been mentioned. In my own earlier work on this topic (Ladd 1980a), I used the term 'deaccenting' to describe this phenomenon, and this term has been widely used in more recent work.

The topic of deaccenting looms large in studies of accent and focus based on the West Germanic languages, particularly English. It represents crucial evidence for those who believe that accents occur on new or otherwise salient parts of the utterance more or less without regard to structure – the radical FTA view. However, there are many languages in which utterances like those in (5.28) do not have modified prominence patterns to reflect the repetition or 'givenness' of the normally accented word.

Within English, the absence of deaccenting has been noted in both Hawaiian pidgin (Vanderslice and Pierson 1967) and in Indian and Caribbean English (Gumperz 1982: ch. 5). Vanderslice and Pierson give the following example:

(5.29)   Forty-three per cent is government OWNED and fifty-seven per cent is privately OWNED.

(their example 8, with spelling standardised). One of Gumperz's examples from Indian English is:

(5.30)   If you don't give me that CIGARETTE I will have to buy a CIGARETTE.

(Gumperz's example 21, p. 125, with considerable discussion of prosodic detail omitted). Looking beyond English, Cruttenden (1993) has reported preliminary results from a large study of this and other cross-language differences of prominence patterns. His findings confirm that some languages (like English) more or less insist on deaccenting repeated material, while others (like Spanish, in his sample) quite strongly resist it.

I have elsewhere given examples from both Romanian and Italian (Ladd 1990a), which are certainly to be classed among the languages that resist deaccenting. One such case was the following Romanian sentence, which was spoken by a university employee who had come to inspect the contents of the apartment I was vacating after my year as a Fulbright scholar, and to check them against an inventory list that I had signed at the beginning of the year:

(5.31)   [. . . o să vedem] ce AVEŢI şi ce nu AVEŢI
          lit. [. . . we'll see] what you.have and what not you.have

An idiomatic translation that faithfully preserves the accent pattern would be something like *So let's see what you HAVE and what you don't HAVE* instead of the expected *So let's see what you HAVE and what you DON'T have*. The following more recent example, from Italian, is particularly convincing for speakers of Standard English. The speaker was Italian President Scalfaro, on the subject of the judicial investigations into massive bribery and corruption during the so-called 'Tangentopoli' scandal:

(5.32)   [le inchieste] servono a mettere a POSTO cose andate fuori POSTO
          [the investigations] serve to put to place things gone out-of place

Again, an idiomatic translation preserving the accent placement sounds decidedly odd:

(5.33)   The investigations are helping to put back in ORDER things that have got out of ORDER.

With such a rhetorical parallelism, the following accent pattern is more natural in English:

(5.34)   The investigations are helping to put BACK in order things that have got OUT of order.

Even in languages that resist deaccenting, accent *can* be shifted away from a neutral or default location under certain circumstances. In Italian or Romanian, which in general are strongly non-deaccenting, explicit meta-linguistic corrections can have paired accents on the corrigendum and the correction, irrespective of word order:

(5.35)   Non ho detto CASA bianca, ho detto COSA bianca.
         'I didn't say white HOUSE, I said white THING.'

Italian also fairly readily allows deaccenting of large constituents, especially where the resulting accent is on an auxiliary, and especially in negative sentences:

(5.36)   a. Non è la mia bici (l'ho presa in prestito).
             'It's NOT my bike (I borrowed it).'

         b. Non è intelligente.
             'He's NOT intelligent.'

         c. Non ti POSSO aiutare.
             'I CAN'T help you.'

         d. Non c'HA invitato.
             'He DIDN'T invite us.'

But there are clear syntactic restrictions on such accent shifts. I once encountered the following sentence in reading a children's story aloud in Italian (in the story, a young zebra is being instructed how to run):

(5.37)   Correre è come camminare in fretta, soltanto si deve andare molto più in fretta.
         'Running is like walking fast (lit. in haste), only you have to go much faster (lit. much more in haste).'

I used the following accent pattern, based on the pattern that would be appropriate on the literal translation:

(5.38)   Correre è come camminare in FRETTA, soltanto si deve andare molto PIÙ in fretta.
         cf. Running is like walking in HASTE, only you have to go much MORE in haste.

This pattern is unhesitatingly rejected by Italian native speakers, apparently because it deaccents only a part of the adverbial phrase *molto più in fretta*.

Another type of deaccenting that is not uncommon in English but which never occurs in the Romance languages involves the actual modification of lexical stress. A classic example is Bolinger's *This whisky wasn't EXported, it was* DEported (1961b: 83). An attested example from a BBC news broadcast is the following:

(5.39)   Greek divers have found the wreck of the British liner BritANNic, sister
          ship of the Titanic . . .

in which the lexical stress on *Titanic* is shifted to focus on the point of contrast between the two ships' names. A readily observable similar case involves the English *-teen* numbers, which have their lexical stress on *-teen* in citation form but normally have the stress shifted in counting:

(5.40)   FIFteen, SIXteen, SEVenteen, EIGHTeen, NINEteen, TWENty

Corresponding stress shifts in the Romance languages are impossible. In speaking Italian I once attempted the following utterance:

(5.41)   Moglie quaranTENne, marito CINquantenne.
          'Forty-year-old wife, fifty-year-old husband.'

shifting the normal lexical stress on *cinquanTENne* ('fifty-year-old') to the first syllable in order to emphasise the contrast between 'forty' and 'fifty'. The result, like my attempted deaccenting in (5.38), is completely unacceptable in Italian. I have elsewhere (Ladd 1990a) noted the Romanian analogue of the English teen-counting series, namely counting by tens to 100:

(5.42)   cinzECI, şaizECI, şaptezECI, optzECI, nouăzECI, o SUtă
          50, 60, 70, 80, 90, 100

The counting context is the same, the morphological transparency of the English teens and the Romanian multiples of ten is strikingly similar, but in Romanian there is no tendency whatever to shift the stress away from the repeated element *-zeci*. (Note that orthographic *-zeci* represents a single syllable.)

While the Romance languages mostly do not allow direct deaccenting, they all have a number of morphosyntactic strategies for achieving similar effects. The most common of these is right-dislocation, in which a constituent (usually but not always a noun phrase) is moved to the end of the sentence, leaving some sort of pronoun in its place. In these cases the right-dislocated constituent is always pronounced as an intonational tag (see section 6.1.4), which implies low pitch in ordinary statement intonation, and the phonetic effect of right-dislocation is thus very similar to the phonetic effect of deaccenting the last word in an English sentence. The following example from Italian illustrates both the syntactic device and the similarity of the phonetic effect to English deaccenting. The sentence was spoken to a child whose baby brother had just had his evening bath:

(5.43)   Adesso faccio scorrere il   TUO,   di bagnetto.
         now   I.make run   the yours, of bath.DIM

In English, in a comparable context, we would certainly have

(5.44)   Now I'll run YOUR bath.

A literal rendition of this in Italian would be

(5.45)   Adesso faccio scorrere il TUO bagnetto.

which is considerably less acceptable than (5.43). Right-dislocation is also an extremely common strategy for 'achieving deaccenting' in French; see section 4.3.3.

This brings up the question of the relation between accentuation and word order. Vallduví (1991; see also Vallduví and Zacharski 1994), basing himself primarily on comparisons between Catalan and English, proposes that some languages (like English) have 'plastic' accent patterns, and that other languages (like Catalan) do not. A language with a non-plastic intonation pattern is constrained to vary word order to shift words into sentence locations where they will appear with or without accent as appropriate. This word order variation can be accomplished either directly on the surface, or by the use of marked morphosyntax in the form of clefting, fronting, right-dislocation, etc. We will see numerous examples of this kind of comparison in the following sections.[8]

The conclusion from this brief survey must be that there is a difference between deaccenting and non-deaccenting languages – or more precisely, between (a) languages that permit, prefer, or virtually require the deaccenting of repeated and otherwise given material, and (b) languages in which such deaccenting is dispreferred or syntactically restricted, allowable mostly in cases of metalinguistic correction, and/or achievable primarily through word order modifications. This conclusion is difficult to reconcile with the radical FTA view that accent is used universally to highlight focused words.

5.2.2.2   Indefinite pronouns

Another specific point of disagreement between structure-based and radical FTA accounts of accentuation involves 'indefinite pronouns' such as *someone* and *nothing*. In English or Dutch, these often occur unaccented in positions where ordinary NP arguments would be accented:

(5.46)   a.   English
           (i) They've DISCOVERED something.
               (cf. They've discovered the DRUGS.)
           (ii) She can't EAT anything
               (cf. She can't eat FISH.)

         b.   Dutch
           (i) Ze hebben iets GEVONDEN. (lit. they have something found)
               (cf. Ze hebben de DRUGS gevonden.)
           (ii) Zij kan niks ETEN. (lit. she can nothing eat)
               (cf. Zij kan geen VIS eten.)

To the extent that such pronouns form an identifiable lexical class, it is tempting for a structure-based account to make special provision for them in accentuation rules on the basis of their 'part of speech'. Equally, however, the semantic vagueness or indefiniteness of these pronouns seems consistent with the radical FTA approach: they are unaccented because they contribute little semantic weight or interest. On the basis of data from English or Dutch alone, it is impossible to resolve this disagreement.

Cross-language comparison, though, suggests consistent differences in the way these items are handled. In some languages, indefinite pronouns such as *something*, *nobody*, etc. are treated for accentuation purposes like any other argument. In other languages, they are less accentable than other arguments. Some languages make a distinction between negative and non-negative indefinites, with only non-negative indefinites being given special treatment (Kefer 1986).

English treats negative indefinites rather like other arguments, while it treats non-negative indefinites as similar to personal pronouns. Thus we have *I saw NOBODY* analogous to *I saw MARY*, but *She HEARD something* comparable to *She HEARD it* and distinct from *She heard a FOOTFALL*. In Italian, unlike English, all indefinites are like other arguments, and no distinction is made between negatives and non-negatives. Thus we have:

(5.47)   a.   Ho sentito MARIA.
               'I heard Maria.'

         b.   Ho sentito QUALCUNO.
               'I heard someone.'

         c.   Non ho sentito NESSUNO.
               'I heard nobody.'

and the only interpretation for a sentence like, say, *Ho SENTITO qualcuno* is as a metalinguistic repair (i.e. 'I didn't see someone, I heard someone').[9] In certain syntactic contexts, we may nevertheless detect a difference between negative and non-negative indefinites in Italian, a difference that indirectly affects the accentuation. Specifically, the difference may be relevant to acceptability judgements about word order in Italian. Either of the following orders is acceptable:

(5.48) a. Ho sentito qualcuno parlare.
            'I heard someone talking.'

        b. Ho sentito parlare qualcuno.
            (lit. I heard talk someone)

but the verb-final order is much less acceptable with the negative indefinite:

(5.49) a. (?) Non ho sentito nessuno parlare.
            'I heard no one talking.'

        b. Non ho sentito parlare nessuno.
            (lit. I heard talk no one)

These are not, of course, just facts about word order, but have the consequence that *qualcuno* 'someone' may or may not occur in the accent-bearing location at the end of the sentence, whereas *nessuno* 'no one' must occur there. In some sense, then, negative indefinites are more likely to bear accent than non-negative indefinites, in Italian as in English. But the grammatical mechanism by which this comes about is different in the two languages: the notion of 'accent-bearing location at the end of the sentence' implicitly presupposes Vallduví's idea that some languages can modify their prominence pattern ('plastic') while others cannot ('non-plastic') and must modify their word order instead.

5.2.2.3 'Semantically empty' content words

The third type of case in which relative informativeness seems to affect accentuation involves intrinsically vague or general content words, such as *person, man, thing, stuff,* and so on. These often occur unaccented, again in ways that seem to favour the radical FTA view. Bolinger (1972b: 636) suggests that 'the [semantic] emptiness of certain nouns can be illustrated by comparing them with other nouns that are semantically richer'. His examples include pairs like:

(5.50) a. (i) He was arrested because he KILLED a man.
            (ii) He was arrested because he killed a POLICEMAN.

        b. (i) I've got to go SEE a guy.
            (ii) I've got to go see a FRIEND.

c.   (i) I'm going over to the DOCTOR'S place.
    (ii) I'm going over to the doctor's BARN.

He rightly criticises Bresnan (1971: 271) for suggesting that nouns like *man* and *guy* form a category of 'semi-pronouns'. As he points out (*ibid.*), this explanation is circular, because 'the only way . . . to identify such nouns is by their behavior under accent'. Moreover, Bolinger notes that these forms often exhibit variability: 'where the accentual behavior with true pronouns is predictable, that of empty nouns is only highly probable'. All of this evidence seems to weigh heavily in favour of the radical FTA view. (However, the charge of circularity is essentially the same criticism I directed at the radical FTA view in the discussion of the accentuation of *five FRANCS* in 5.1.2 above.)

A related type of case where semantic emptiness and predictability seem to influence accentuation involves Adjective + Noun phrases. Bolinger (1972b: 638) cites several examples in which the adjective rather than the noun is accented:

(5.51)   a.   I like it because it has a SILKY sheen.

b.   . . . I don't see how you could make it to OUR place in 45 minutes unless you went through every RED light.

Monaghan (1991: 149f.; 1992: 155ff.) identifies several combinations of Adjective + Noun that are likely to be accented on the adjective, including phrases with fairly unspecific nouns such as *meeting* and *committee* and those with deictic or ordinal adjectives such as *latter*, *second*, and *alternative*.

A final type of case in which accentuation is often said to depend on factors of informativeness involves sentence-final adverbs and prepositional phrases. For example, phrases denoting places and times that are effectively here and now often occur unaccented:

(5.52)   a.   I saw an ACCIDENT today.

b.   There's a FLY in my soup.

Chafe (1974, 1976) relies extensively on such cases in developing an account of how accentuation, pronominalisation, and various other phenomena depend on the speaker's assessment of what is likely to be in the hearer's consciousness or at the centre of the hearer's attention. This work may be seen as a forerunner of more recent work on discourse organisation and the form and interpretation of referring expressions by, for example, Prince (1981), Grosz and Sidner (1986), Gundel, Hedberg, and Zacharski (1993).

Bolinger's discussion of these cases shows that it is not just a matter of what is in the addressee's consciousness, but of even more general aspects of informativeness and predictability. As he notes, 'in the sentences

> They STRANGLED him to death.
> They hounded him to DEATH.
> They scared him to death.

(once more answering *What happened?*), the first de-accents *death* because strangulation normally involves *death*, the second accents *death* because hounding in itself is not fatal, and the third may be treated either way because figuratively there is a choice' (1972b: 639). Or again, he suggests that a semantic theory of accent 'predicts that [ordinary meals] will carry no particular semantic weight, hence *Peter had CLAMS for dinner*, but that something in between [meals] may well do so, hence *I had some nice CLAMS for my SNACK this afternoon*' (1972b: 638).

In all the cases just cited – semantically empty nouns like *person* or *thing*, relative semantic weight of adjective and noun in NPs like *silky sheen* and *the latter approach* and sentence-final adverbs and prepositional phrases – the evidence for the radical FTA view seems fairly compelling. However, cross-language comparison shows that the picture is not so clear. In languages like Italian, which resist deaccenting and which treat indefinite pronouns like any other argument, virtually none of the English examples just cited has a counterpart with accent patterns that reflect informativeness. For example, semantically empty nouns in Italian are treated for accentual purposes like any other argument:

(5.53)   a.   . . . perché ha ucciso un UOMO.
              '. . . because he killed a man.'

         b.   . . . perché ha ucciso un POLIZIOTTO.
              '. . . because he killed a policeman.'

In any context, *ha UCCISO un uomo* could only involve explicit contrast or metalinguistic correction (e.g. 'killed, not wounded'). Essentially the same is true of sentence-final adverbs and prepositional phrases. With these too we find very little tendency to deaccent and very little variability.

(5.54)   a.   C'è una mosca nella MINESTRA.
              'There's a fly in the soup.'

         b.   L'hanno spaventato a MORTE.
              'They scared him to death.'

As for analogues to English phrases like *silky sheen* or *the latter approach*, it is not possible to construct these in Italian, because the normal word order in NPs is Noun + Adjective. However, it is worth noting that there is no tendency at all for Italian Noun + Adjective phrases to be accented on the noun, regardless of relative semantic weight.

5.2.2.4   Lexical and syntactic effects on relative semantic weight

It thus appears that there are languages in which relative informativeness is relevant to accentuation and others in which it is not. However, those are not the only language-specific differences. Among languages that do take relative semantic weight into account, the details often differ unpredictably from language to language or even from dialect to dialect within the same language. The conditioning factors are both lexical and syntactic.

A good illustration of the complexity of such cases is provided by English phrases consisting of a proper name and a common noun, such as *George Square* or *Alzheimer's Disease*. As has been noted many times, when such phrases serve as names of thoroughfares (*Wellington Street, Chesley Drive, Dryden Road, Gillespie Crescent*, and so on), they have the main accent on the first part of the name if the second part is *Street* (i.e. *WELLINGTON Street*) but on the second part otherwise (i.e. *Chesley DRIVE, Dryden ROAD, Gillespie CRESCENT*). The explanation, proposed by an amateur observer of language well over half a century ago (see Mencken 1948) and repeated more than once since then, seems to be that in a town, *Street* is the least specific – and hence least informative – noun used in such names, and consequently can be deaccented.

In Ladd 1980b, I noted that the same sort of thing is true of several other sets of nouns, such as *Tompkins COUNTY, New York STATE, Baffin ISLAND*, but *GONDWANAland*. What I did not note is that there is consistent dialect variation in these cases. For example, in the set of nouns used in names of buildings, *House* is deaccented in American English (e.g. *FAUNCE House*, Brown University Student Union building, *BLAIR House*, Official US Government guest house in Washington; cf. *Morrill HALL, Carrie TOWER, Johnson MUSEUM*, etc.) but not in British English (e.g. *Adam HOUSE*, Edinburgh University examination hall, *Broadcasting HOUSE*, headquarters of BBC in London). Nor did I note that definiteness can have an effect: when such phrases are lexicalised with the definite article, they are more likely to deaccent the common noun (e.g. *Rockefeller CENTER* in New York but *the KENNEDY Center* in Washington). That is, while relative informativeness clearly plays a role, it does so within limits imposed by the lexicon and grammar of specific languages and dialects.

A good illustration of the interplay between relative informativeness and grammar is a common usage I observed while living in a rural area near Ithaca, New York. The official names of the rural roads almost all have *Road* rather than *Street* as the common noun (*Tunison Road, Townsendville Road, Lodi Center Road*, etc.), and as such should be accented on *Road* according to the rule of English just discussed. Yet in the rural context, the truly informative element of the name is the proper name. Accordingly, when they refer to roads by name, local residents frequently add a definite article, which allows them to deaccent *Road* and put the accent on the name (e.g. *the* TUNISON *Road, the* TOWNSENDVILLE *Road*). This example shows both the importance of relative informativeness and the importance of specific grammatical and lexical effects. If, as claimed by the radical FTA view, relative informativeness were the most important factor in accentuation, then it should be possible for speakers simply to say TUNISON *Road* and TOWNSENDVILLE *Road*. But those pronunciations create unwanted narrow focus: adding the definite article seems to sanction the shift *while retaining broad focus*. It is difficult to explain this effect with the radical FTA view.

A similar case is found in Icelandic. According to Arnason (ms.), the word for 'man' may be deaccented in *definite* Adjective + Noun phrases and still convey broad focus, but not in indefinite phrases. Other more informative nouns bear accent in Adjective + Noun phrases regardless of whether the phrase is definite or indefinite. Arnason's examples are the following:

(5.55) a. þarna er GAMLI maðurinn.
            'There's the old man.' (lit. there is old.DEF man.DEF)

        b. þarna er gamall MAÐUR.
            'There's an old man.' (lit. there is old man)

        c. þarna er gamla POSTHUSIÐ.
            'There's the old post office.' (lit. there is old.DEF post-office.DEF)

What is important about these sentences is that they can all be used to convey broad focus, despite the fact that the accent is on the noun in (5.55b) and (5.55c) and on the adjective in (5.55a). That is, Icelandic is like English in two respects: first, there are individual relatively uninformative nouns that may be deaccented and still convey broad focus; and second, definiteness favours this kind of deaccenting where indefiniteness does not. But there is no direct correspondence between English and Icelandic: we cannot use *the OLD man* in English without conveying some sort of narrow focus on *old*.

Another similar case involves English and Hungarian phrases denoting sums of money. As we saw above, in English sums of money are accented on the unit of currency: *five FRANCS, fifty CENTS*, and so on. In Hungarian, however, it is normal to deaccent the unit of currency.[10] Thus in contexts entirely comparable to ones discussed earlier, we might find:

(5.56)   A: Mennyit kaptál érte?
               'How much did you get for it?'

          B: Száz ötven forintot.
               '150 florins.'

This comparison between English and Hungarian is very nearly identical to the hypothetical cross-language comparison sketched in section 5.1.4. In comparable contexts we have phrases containing comparable words in the same order, yet we find one accent pattern in one language and another accent pattern in the other. A Bolingerian or radical FTA explanation for either pattern *on its own* is possible, but an explanation of the difference effectively destroys the predictive value of the FTA theory. Universal strategies for highlighting salient information simply do not explain all the facts about accent across languages. The Hungarian pattern makes Bolingerian sense as an 'accent of interest' (the number of florins is what counts, and the unit is predictable), while the English pattern makes sense as an 'accent of power' (other things being equal, put the accent at the end). What does not make sense is that English treats the relative informativeness of the number and the currency unit as equal, while Hungarian treats them differently. There seems no way to avoid putting this kind of difference in the grammar of individual languages.

5.2.2.5   Summary

The English data reviewed in this section, in my opinion, represent the best evidence there is for the radical FTA view. On the basis of the English cases alone, it is very clear that relative semantic weight is a key factor in the location of accent even in many broad focus cases. This fact is what drives the radical FTA view, and is what induces investigators to try to understand more about the nature of 'relative semantic weight' (discourse status, informativeness, etc.): if we understand relative semantic weight, we will automatically understand accent placement.

When seen in the light of cross-language comparison, however, the English data are less compelling. The totality of the evidence presented in this section suggests the rather less inspiring claim that relative semantic weight may play a role in accentuation in some syntactic contexts in some languages. This does not make it any less important to study the contextual factors that influence relative semantic weight – for those languages in which it is relevant – but it does mean that in all languages there is an important role for structural considerations as well.

The fact that the role played by relative semantic weight is language-specific has more general implications. As noted above, recent theorising about accent and information structure within cognitive science and artificial intelligence has attached much importance to accent placement and its relation to context and discourse structure. I think it is especially important for theorists in these fields not to ignore the data presented here. It would be unfortunate if models of human information processing turned out to be models of how to speak English.

5.2.3   Predicates and arguments

We now turn to the third area of potential cross-linguistic differences in accentuation patterns, namely the claim that in some languages there is a difference of accentability between arguments and predicates, with predicates (verbs and predicate nouns or adjectives) less accentable than arguments (noun phrases syntactically linked to a predicate). This claim, at least in the modern literature, seems to have been first made by Schmerling (1976: ch. 5). In origin it is a way of accounting for a long-standing and much-discussed problem with traditional normal stress rules.

In traditional syntax-based accounts of normal stress, the greatest prominence in a sentence is said to fall on the last content word. This rule encounters serious difficulties in English sentences with intransitive predicates. Some such sentences seem to be most naturally pronounced with the main accent on the subject, but others seem more appropriate with the main accent on the predicate, and for others there is no agreement even among proponents of the idea of normal stress. There has been much discussion in the literature of the conditions under which the two accent patterns occur, summarised briefly here.

In short sentences describing single events, accent on the subject is favoured:

(5.57)   a.   My UMBRELLA broke.

     b.   The SUN came out.

     c.   His MOTHER died.

This is particularly true if the predicate denotes appearance or disappearance or otherwise introduces the subject into the discourse (Allerton and Cruttenden 1979). By contrast, if the subject denotes a human agent and the predicate denotes an action over which the subject is likely to have some control, accent on the verb is more likely (Faber 1987):[11]

(5.58)   a.   My brothers are WRESTLING.

     b.   Jesus WEPT.

     c.   The professor SWORE.

Sentences with generic subjects, and sentences that state definitions, eternal truths, and grand abstractions are also often accented on the predicate (Gussenhoven 1983a: 403ff.; Faber 1987: 352f.):

(5.59)   a.   Wood FLOATS.

     b.   Penguins SWIM.

     c.   Hope FADED.

And accent on the verb is more likely if the subject is (in some sense that is not very clear) 'topicalised' or otherwise readily referrable to the context.[12]

These considerations account for Schmerling's often-cited pair of examples *Truman DIED* and *JOHNSON died*. These were the reports of the deaths of two former US presidents, addressed to Schmerling in both cases at the beginning of a conversation. Johnson's death was unexpected and the proposition is presented as a single event (over which, we may note, Johnson presumably had no control); by contrast, Truman's medical condition had been in the news for several days, and the accent pattern related the utterance to that prior context by treating *Truman* as a 'topic'. Similar subtly distinct pairs are discussed by Faber (1987) and Gussenhoven (1983a).

Given these data, Schmerling (1976) proposes that arguments are intrinsically more likely to be accented than predicates. She treats cases where the accent is on the intransitive predicate as special in some way – for example, what she calls 'topic–comment sentences', where the subject is somehow predictable or given in the context (like *Truman DIED*). Bing (1979), Ladd (1980a), and Gussenhoven (1983a) all follow Schmerling by building a basic difference between arguments and predicates into their accentuation rules, and Gussenhoven follows Schmerling still further by discussing pragmatically different sentence types (e.g. his 'eventive' and 'definitional' sentences) which favour accent on the subject or on the predicate.

Schmerling notes that the greater accentability of arguments also seems to hold in German: for example, object nouns are regularly more prominent than transitive verbs in main clauses (where the object follows the verb), in subordinate clauses (where the object precedes the verb), and in main clauses with non-finite forms of lexical verbs (where the object also precedes the non-finite verb). Thus:

(5.60)   a. Sie liest ein BUCH.
            'She is reading a book.'

         b. Er denkt, daß sie ein BUCH liest.
            'He thinks she is reading a book.'

         c. Sie hat ein BUCH gelesen.
            'She read a book.' (lit. she has a book read)

The literal translation of the second example is *He thinks that she a book reads*; as Schmerling points out, an English speaker reading such a literal translation aloud is likely to put the most prominent stress on *book*, not on *reads*. Selkirk (1984: section 5.2.2) makes similar observations about German, and Gussenhoven (1984: ch. 2) demonstrates at length that essentially the same is true of Dutch.

In all three languages, however, there is also a good case to be made that any apparent difference between nouns and verbs (or arguments and predicates) is simply a matter of the more general role of relative semantic weight or informativeness. That is, it can be argued that nouns generally carry more semantic weight than verbs, which are frequently rather predictable given a particular noun or nouns. If this is true, then data like Schmerling's actually support the radical FTA view, and any reference to structure (viz. to the predicate–argument distinction) is unnecessary. This case has been vigorously put by Bolinger (1972b; 1986: ch. 7; and especially 1989: ch. 9).

One type of evidence in favour of Bolinger's view is the existence of variability. There are many cases in which accent can plausibly occur on either a noun or a verb without necessarily signalling explicit contrast or narrow focus. For example, Bolinger points out that accent may be variable in cases where 'nouns are set against verbs that are comparably low in semantic content' (1972b: 637):

(5.61)   a.   I can't go with you; I've got too many THINGS to do.

          b.   . . . too many things to DO.

He notes that 'the same is true when noun and verb are equally rich' (1972b: 638):

(5.62)   a.   We're looking for a neighbourhood where there are other boys to PLAY with.

          b.   . . . where there are other BOYS to play with.

(5.63)   a.   It's too heavy a price to PAY.

          b.   It's too heavy a PRICE to pay.

Another piece of evidence for Bolinger's view involves the effects of definiteness. Such cases have been extensively discussed with reference to German, where it is well established that definiteness affects both word order and accentuation (e.g. Kiparsky 1966; Jacobs 1982). For example, in sentences that have a non-finite verb form at the end, the nuclear accent readily occurs on the verb if the preceding object noun phrase is definite, but not normally if the object is indefinite. The following examples are based on Cinque (1993):[13]

(5.64)   a.   Der Arzt wird einen PATIENTEN untersuchen.
                'The doctor will examine a patient.' (lit. The doctor will a patient examine)

          b.   (?) Der Arzt wird einen Patienten UNTERSUCHEN.

          c.   Der Arzt wird den PATIENTEN untersuchen.
          a.   'The doctor will examine the patient.'

          d.   (OK) Der Arzt wird den Patienten UNTERSUCHEN.

When the object noun phrase is indefinite, as in (a) and (b), it is likely to refer to an entity newly introduced into the discourse, and placing the main accent on the verb is odd. By contrast, when the object is definite, as in (c) and (d), it is likely to refer to a 'given' entity, and is correspondingly less informative. As a result it is much more acceptable to have the main accent on the verb.

In all these cases, if we consider only data from West Germanic languages, it is once again almost impossible to decide between the radical FTA view and a structure-based account that assumes language-specific rules. However, if we compare extensively across languages, it becomes apparent that certain languages are like English in treating arguments differently from predicates in accentuation rules, while other languages seem to treat arguments and predicates in the same way. Dutch and German, for example, are like English, while Italian and Spanish are not. It does not seem possible to account for the English or German data solely in terms of universal principles of informativeness.

Direct comparison of English or German with Spanish or Italian is unfortunately complicated by the fact that it is difficult to find analogues to sentences like *The* COFFEE *machine broke*. In general, in Spanish or Italian, such intransitive event sentences have verb–subject (VS) word order:

(5.65)   S'è rotta la CAFFETTIERA.
          'The coffee machine broke.' (lit. has broken the coffee machine)

That is, as with the difference between negative and non-negative indefinite pronouns (5.2.2.2), word order modifications in languages like Spanish or Italian may indirectly achieve the accentual effects that English accomplishes directly by manipulating the location of the nuclear accent.[14] This means that languages like Spanish or Italian, whose normal word order is subject–verb–object (SVO) and which allow VS word order in intransitives, are bad places to look for different accentual treatment of predicates and arguments.

There are constructions, however, that provide evidence of a difference between English or German and Italian or Spanish with regard to the relative accentability of nouns and verbs. These include infinitive 'small clauses', such as

(5.66)   a.   I have a BOOK to read.

          b.   They gave him a TUNE to play.

and short relative clauses containing no nouns, such as

(5.67)   a.   I don't like the SHIRTS he wears.

          b.   It was caused by some FISH she ate.

In English, these often have the main accent on the last noun rather than on the following verb. In Italian, corresponding sentences are accented on the verb:

(5.68)   a.   Ho un libro da LEGGERE.
                'I have a book to read.'

          b.   Gli hanno dato una musica da SUONARE.
                'They gave him a piece to play.'

   c. Non mi piacciono le camicie che PORTA.
      'I don't like the shirts he wears.'

   d. Fu causato da pesce che aveva MANGIATO.
      'It was caused by fish she had eaten.'

It is true, as Bolinger points out, that these kinds of structures are variable in English in phrases like *things to do* and *price to pay*, so it may be inappropriate to take the accent pattern in (5.66) and (5.67) as the neutral pattern for English. Nevertheless, there is clearly a cross-language difference, because this variability is absent in Italian: that is, Italian phrases like *cose da fare* ('things to do') or *prezzo da pagare* ('price to pay') can only be accented on the verb, except in cases of very explicit metalinguistic contrast. Unlike English, Italian really does put the main accent on the rightmost content word in the overwhelming majority of contexts. This in turn means that the apparent difference of accentability between predicates and arguments in English is not simply a specific instance of more general principles of accentual highlighting, but involves a language-specific, structure-based rule of sentence accentuation.

The examples just cited show that, in order to detect unambiguous differences between languages in the way they treat nouns and verbs in sentence accentuation, we need to find structures in which the verb is sentence-final. These are difficult to construct in comparing English and Italian. A more obvious place to look is in languages with subject–object–verb (SOV) word order. Specifically, one would predict that in an SOV language in which arguments are more accentable than predicates, unmarked accentuation would fall on the object, whereas in an SOV language that does not distinguish predicates and arguments accentually, unmarked accentuation would fall on the verb.

There does appear to be such a difference between SOV languages. In Turkish, especially with indefinite objects, the last accent normally falls on the object (see note 6 above):

(5.69)   Eski müdür bir KİTAP yazdı.
        'The former director wrote a book.' (lit. former director one BOOK wrote)

In Bengali, on the other hand, the last accent is generally on the verb (Hayes and Lahiri 1991):

(5.70)   Ram Shamoli DEKHLO.
        'Ram saw Shamoli.' (lit. Ram Shamoli SAW)

This difference would appear to confirm the existence of a difference between languages that treat arguments and predicates unequally and languages that do not. However, once again we are bedevilled by disagreements over the data. In a typological survey article by Kim (1988, cited in Cinque 1993), the claim is put forth that most SOV languages, including Bengali, have unmarked accentuation on the object. This directly contradicts the data from Hayes and Lahiri just cited. While we might grant *prima facie* credibility to Hayes and Lahiri on the grounds that Lahiri is a native speaker of Bengali, it is clear that this is a point on which further data are required. Languages with SOV word order need to be scrutinised for their broad focus prominence patterns.

5.2.4   *Constraints on cross-linguistic variation*
Given the existence of cross-linguistic differences of accentuation, it is obviously important to consider the extent of those differences. Can languages differ 'without limit and in unpredictable ways' (to use the often-quoted formulation of Joos 1957: 96)? Or is the range of variation constrained in principled ways? Or, for that matter, is the apparent variation all conditioned by some other property of the language?

The first possibility – that there are no principled limits on the way accentuation can differ from language to language – cannot be logically excluded, but it obviously runs counter to all recent views on language typology (in particular the principles-and-parameters approach),[15] as well as contradicting many long-standing observations about universal tendencies in intonation. The third possibility – that the apparent cross-linguistic diversity of accentuation is actually a reflection of something else – has recently been suggested by Cinque (1993). Cinque argues for a 'null theory of sentence stress', in which the most prominent accent of the sentence goes on the most deeply embedded element in the sentence's surface syntactic structure. I do not believe that this view can be maintained in light of the data presented in the foregoing subsections, though a point-by-point rebuttal of Cinque's arguments would take us too far afield here. This leaves us to search for principles that constrain the variability of accentuation from one language to another. In this section I offer some brief speculations on what those principles might be.

I propose, first, that there is a basic division between languages that normally require the main accent to occur on the rightmost content word and those that allow the main accent to be placed earlier in the sentence. In terms of a principles-and-parameters approach to language typology, we are dealing with a parameter [rightmost] (see Halle and Vergnaud 1987). In a [+rightmost] language, broad focus accent is rightmost in all or nearly all cases, and none of the factors we have been discussing – question vs. statement, relative informativeness, part of speech, definiteness, etc. – plays any important role in determining accent. These are Vallduví's [–plastic] languages. Such languages include Italian and Catalan.

In [–rightmost] languages, certain factors permit broad focus accent to occur further to the left. These factors include all the ones we have just been discussing – the differential treatment of predicates and arguments, the tendency to deaccenting, the accentuation of WH-words, and so on. In these languages, the obvious typological question is whether there is any systematic relationship among the various factors that draw accent to the left. For example, given the apparent parallel between YNQs and WHQs, it is obviously tempting to try to relate their behaviour – and indeed, this is what I have implicitly done by treating both types in the same section. With a parametric approach to cross-linguistic variation, we would express such a relation in terms of a parameter that constrains languages to two types of variation, one type treating questions and statements differently, and the other treating them alike. Romanian and Hungarian would be examples of languages that treat the two differently, while English and Italian would be examples of languages that treat them alike.

It is not clear whether the situation is so simple as that, though I know of no unambiguous counterexamples. There are obviously two possible types of counterexample in this case: one would be a language that has neutral accent on the verb in YNQs but treats WHQs like other sentence types, while the other would be a language that has neutral accent on the WH-word in WHQs but treats YNQs like statements. Superficially, it seems straightforward to determine whether such counterexamples exist, but there are plenty of complications, such as the fact that WHQs in Bengali require narrow focus intonation, or the fact that focus in YNQs in Turkish is marked in the first instance by the question particle and only secondarily by the location of accent. Furthermore, there is not much reliable information about question accentuation in many languages. At the very least, such a hypothesised 'parameter' of variation provides a focus for investigation of specific languages.

Similarly, we might speculate that all the factors relating to accentability and informativeness – contextual deaccenting, the special treatment of indefinite pronouns and 'empty' nouns, and effects of definiteness – are systematically related to the differential treatment of arguments and predicates. For example, we might predict that if a language treats predicates as less likely to be accented than arguments, it will also tend to deaccent contextually given material and exhibit variability in sentences involving indefinite pronouns or empty nouns. The basis for this speculation is primarily Bolinger's suggestion that the argument–predicate difference is a manifestation of the general relationship between accentuation and informativeness. As with the proposed question-related parameter, I know of no clear counterexamples, but as with that case it is also important to emphasise how little we know. Once again, the exemplification of cross-linguistic differences given here, combined with the general expectation that typological variation should be highly constrained, gives us a clear focus for empirical investigation.

5.2.5   Accent and phrasing

Before leaving the subject of cross-language comparison of sentence accent, we should discuss one further point: sentence accent, as a problem of linguistic description, is probably fairly restricted cross-linguistically. Meaningful variation of sentence accent clearly occurs in the European languages. For those languages I have argued for a view in which the variation is determined at least in part by language-specific grammatical rules (or by language-specific parameters in the principles-and-parameters sense), and against the universalistic view that focused words are highlighted by pitch accent in all languages. In a sense, though, there is an argument *a fortiori* against the universalist view, because in many languages there is not even a phenomenon that we can usefully identify as 'pitch accent'. The question of what determines its location consequently does not arise.

In a great many tone languages, for example, there seems to be no basis for identifying anything as pitch accent. In some such languages, we might find that the meaningful variation of pitch range provides an equivalent phenomenon. In Chinese, for example, as discussed in section 4.4.2, the point in the utterance at which pitch range narrows could be seen as analogous to the location of pitch accent. In Japanese, Pierrehumbert and Beckman (1988) have shown that pitch range can be expanded on individual lexically specified pitch accents to convey focus or emphasis effects similar to those conveyed by postlexical pitch accents in languages like English.

I think there is an even more basic – and clearly universal – phenomenon, however, to which we can relate the sentence accent data discussed in this chapter, namely the division of the utterance into prosodic phrases.

Sentence accentuation, in my view, is ultimately to be seen as one manifestation of prosodic structure. The correct question about sentence accent data is not 'Why is the main prominence in this sentence on word X rather than on word Y?' but rather 'Why is this sentence divided up into phrases the way it is?'

The most striking evidence for such a view comes from a comparison of European focus/accent data with data on the location of phrase boundaries in Japanese and Korean. This is the subject of recent work by Beckman and her students (e.g. Jun 1993; Venditti, Jun, and Beckman 1996). These studies introduce a notion of 'dephrasing' comparable to the European-language notion of deaccenting. Some of the nuances expressed by dephrasing in Korean are remarkably similar to corresponding differences of sentence accent in English, as can be seen from the following examples from Jun 1993:[16]

(5.71)   A: [satʃʰun-ənni] [irɨmi] [mwəni]
                'What is cousin's name?' (lit. cousin name what)

          B: [satʃʰun-ənni irɨmi] [suni-dʒi]
                'Cousin's name is Suni.' (lit. cousin name Suni)

(5.72)   a.   [na] [pap mək-ɨllejo]
                'I want to eat rice.' (lit. I rice eat-want)

          b.   [na] [pap] [pəri-lejo]
                'I want to throw out rice.' (lit. I rice throw out-want)

          c.   [na] [tol] [mək-ɨllejo]
                'I want to eat stone.' (lit. I stone eat-want)

In the question–answer sequence in (5.71), we see an analogue to contextual deaccenting: *irɨmi* ('name') forms a separate phrase when it is the point of the question and is 'dephrased' in the answer. Example (5.72) is more complicated; it illustrates effects of informativeness and predictability of the sort discussed in section 5.2.2.4. In (5.72a), 'rice' and 'eat' form a fairly predictable combination, and occur in a single phrase in Korean. In English, a corresponding sentence could completely deaccent *eat*. But when rice is to be thrown out or stones are to be eaten, the individual elements are more informative, and verb and object therefore form separate phrases in Korean. In English, to convey the same effect, the verb would certainly have an accent.

Given such similarities, it would obviously be desirable for a universally valid theory of the relation between prosody and focus to be able to relate data like these to data from English or Dutch. If we treat the relation between focus and accent in English as indirect, we are in a better position to draw such universal connections. That is, let us assume that in both English or Dutch and Korean or Japanese, focus is systematically signalled by prosodic structure. In Korean or Japanese, the main observable consequence of differences of prosodic structure is the presence or absence of accentual phrase boundaries (hence 'dephrasing'). In English or Dutch the most salient consequence of such differences is the presence or absence of pitch accents (hence 'deaccenting'). But dephrasing and deaccenting, in the view proposed here, are just different surface symptoms of the same deep structural effects.

This idea can be seen as a more general version of what I called the 'structural FTA' view in section 5.1.3. Recall that in the structural FTA view, the focus of the sentence is independently variable according to a variety of pragmatic and other considerations, but the location of the accent then follows by rule. Recall further that in Gussenhoven's version of the structural FTA view, the sentence is divided up into several 'focus domains', each of which receives an accent according to various accent rules. If we make it explicit that the 'focus domains' are also phonological domains of some sort (e.g. the 'Association Domains' of van den Berg, Gussenhoven, and Rietveld 1992), then we arrive at the conclusion that the location of accents is in some sense simply a reflection of the phonological structure of the sentence. I will return to this whole subject in chapter 6.

5.3 Some potential problems

The cross-language comparison undertaken in the preceding sections seems to suggest quite strongly that there are systematic differences of sentence accentuation from one language to another. Since this conclusion is so strongly at odds with universalist FTA assumptions, it is important to forestall certain objections that could be raised to some of my methods and assumptions. The following subsections discuss three such points.

5.3.1 *Are we just re-inventing 'normal stress'?*
The first potential problem has to do with the use of citation forms of sentences. It needs to be made clear that in using such citation forms we are not reverting to the old-fashioned notion of normal stress. Recall that normal stress, in the usage of structuralist and early generative writers, was seen as a single structurally determined accent pattern to which context is

by definition irrelevant. In context, one might get 'contrastive stress' anywhere in a sentence, but in principle one ought to be able to elicit the normal stress pattern without any context at all – that is, as citation forms of sentences. If we reject this notion of normal stress, we have to be suspicious of eliciting accent patterns out of context. In any case, it has often been suggested (e.g. by Bolinger 1972b) that it is methodologically unsound to try to determine how sentences are accented 'out of context' – for instance, when read as examples in a linguist's study – because speakers may imagine all kinds of contexts which will affect sentence accent in unpredictable ways.

The methodological aspect of this general line of argument obviously has some force: speakers may indeed imagine contexts which will affect their sentence accent patterns, and we must be careful not to base theories of sentence accent on data that may be distorted in this way. On the other hand, it is worth emphasising that with the FTA view – *any* version of the FTA view – we do not define anything in terms of contextlessness. If we preserve a notion of normal stress at all, we define it as the accent pattern that can convey broad focus. We make no claim that this pattern is contextless, but only 'unmarked' – that is, the pattern that is chosen when there is no compelling grammatical or contextual reason to choose some other. We continue to make reference to the communicative intention of the speaker and the context in which the utterance is used: the broad focus pattern *five FRANCS* is appropriate in a wide range of contexts, while the 'narrow focus' pattern *FIVE francs* is appropriate only in very few contexts, but nothing depends on any assumption of 'contextlessness'. This represents an important change of orientation from the structuralist and early generative view.

Obviously, we need to be wary of citation-form accent patterns: because of the methodological problems just cited, we may not succeed in eliciting broad focus accent patterns as citation forms. Yet in a sense this matters less for cross-language comparison than for the investigation of a single language. If we compare citation forms across languages and find consistent differences in the patterns of accentuation, it is difficult to explain away these differences with reference to theoretical or methodological problems with elicited citation forms; that is, it is difficult to imagine universal pragmatic principles that would account for consistent differences between languages in structurally parallel citation forms.

A related set of objections to the notion of neutral accent pattern is based on the difficulty of identifying a single neutral pattern for every sentence. The least problematic of these cases involves sentences that do not seem to allow neutral accentuation. Schmerling (1976), for example, found it some-what paradoxical that there are certain sentences that 'must have con-trastive stress' such as *Even a two-year-old could do that*. This objection applies only to the traditional structuralist conception of a single struc-turally determined 'normal stress' pattern for every sentence. As soon as we accept that accent signals focus (on constituents of some size) and that the use of certain words and constructions (such as *even*) crucially involves focus on single words or other small constituents, then there is no problem reconciling data like these with the notion of 'neutral' accent.

A potentially more serious problem is provided by cases that seem to allow more than one 'neutral' pattern. In some cases there is a clear differ-ence of meaning between the two patterns, yet neither seems to involve narrow focus. Gussenhoven (1983a) has extensively discussed a difference of meaning that arises from the choice of one accent pattern or the other: main accent on the verb gives a 'contingency' reading and main accent on the noun gives an 'eventive' reading. A humorous example of this difference is Halliday's report (1970: 38) of the man who saw a sign saying *Dogs must be carried* in the London underground 'and was worried because he had no dog'. The intended meaning of the sign is something like 'If dogs are brought into the underground, they must be carried', and the accent pattern that conveys this meaning is *Dogs must be CARRIED*. (This is Gussenhoven's contingency reading.) The meaning that the worried man inferred from the sign is something like 'If you are in the underground, you must carry a dog', and the accent pattern that conveys this meaning is *DOGS must be carried*. (Compare the sign *Shoes must be worn* commonly seen on the door of American shops and snack bars.) This is Gussenhoven's eventive reading. Neither of these readings seems to involve narrow focus, and it is consequently difficult to say which one is the 'neutral' pattern. However, so long as we are clear that what we mean by 'neutral' is 'broad focus', there is no reason to insist that there should be only one such pattern; the fact that there are two such patterns shows only that factors other than focus are involved in sentence accentuation. And once again, allowing the possibility of two broad focus patterns – like the possibility of having no broad focus pattern discussed in the preceding paragraph – shows that we are not simply re-inventing normal stress.[17]

5.3.2 Is the broad focus pattern really ambiguous?

The next potential issue has to do with our use of the transcription *five FRANCS* for both the broad focus reading and for narrow focus on *francs*.

Specifically, we need to justify equating the broad focus prominence pattern with one of the narrow focus patterns, and hence to justify the claim that the pattern notated this way is potentially ambiguous.

Some evidence for a genuine linguistic ambiguity comes from jokes and word play. One example is the exchange that is supposed to have occurred between a reporter and John Dillinger, a notorious American bank robber of the 1930s, shortly after Dillinger's arrest:

(5.73)   Reporter: Why do you rob banks?
         Dillinger: Because that's where the money is.

The reporter's question might be said to have broad focus on the entire verb-plus-object phrase *rob banks*, that is, the point of the question is why Dillinger engages in the anti-social activity of robbing banks. Dillinger's reply – which clearly works as a wisecrack or witty repartee – treats the question as if it focuses only on *banks*, that is, as if the questioner presupposes that Dillinger engages in robbing something, and wants to know why he robs banks rather than, say, grocery stores or filling stations. Essentially the same joke is found in a *Peanuts* cartoon (7 February 1994). Charlie Brown, in bed, says 'Sometimes I lie awake at night, and I ask, "Why am I here?".' In the next panel, he continues 'Then a voice answers, "Why? Where do you want to be?".' Charlie Brown's question is intended as a broad focus existential question that might be paraphrased as 'Why do I exist?', but the voice that answers treats the accent on *here* as if it signals narrow focus – as if Charlie Brown is asking why he is 'here' rather than somewhere else.[18]

It is not enough, however, to show that such ambiguities are possible. The story is more complicated than that, because there can be no doubt that it is also possible to pronounce the phrase *five francs* in such a way that it fairly *unambiguously* conveys narrow focus on *francs*. Such unambiguous narrow focus pronunciations involve what we may call 'emphatic stress'.

The acoustic cues to emphatic stress are a matter of considerable current interest (e.g. Bartels and Kingston 1994; Ladd and Morton, ms.; Rump and Collier 1996; Schmidt 1996); but are not really relevant here; what is important in the present context is that emphatic stress exists and that it can be used to eliminate ambiguity in the breadth of focus. Yet what is also important is that, despite the existence of emphatic stress, there is nevertheless also a considerable range of pronunciations that are potentially ambiguous between broad focus and narrow focus; that is, to convey narrow focus on *francs* it is not *necessary* to use emphatic stress, only pos-

sible. Narrow focus can be conveyed by pronunciations that are not phonetically distinct from broad focus readings.

Evidence for the view that we are dealing with a genuine ambiguity
includes the results of at least two experimental studies of the perception of
accent patterns. Gussenhoven (1983b) shows that, while English listeners
can distinguish prominence patterns analogous to the broad focus and contrastive stress version of *five* FRANCS under certain conditions, they are still
much more likely to confuse these patterns with each other than they are to
confuse them with patterns analogous to FIVE *francs*. Recent work by
Rump and Collier (1996) shows similar effects for Dutch.[19] One reasonable
conclusion from these findings is that the two patterns that we have been
writing as *five* FRANCS – viz. the broad focus reading and the reading with
narrow focus on *francs* – are in fact linguistically identical, as the notation
implies. Emphasis, in this view, would be a paralinguistic device that can
sometimes be brought into play: that is, on the one hand, we have the linguistic distinction between two categorically different accent patterns, FIVE
francs and *five* FRANCS; on the other hand, we have the paralinguistic possibility of gradiently modifying the realisation of those patterns so as to
single out individual words. 'Emphasis' and 'accent' may often go hand in
hand, but that does not mean they are the same thing.

This point of view can be made more plausible if we see the location of
accent as analogous to the location of focus particles. In many cases in
many languages, focus particles have a neutral or default location in the
sentence, but can be attached in other locations to convey narrow focus. If
the particle is in the neutral location, there is thus often a potential ambiguity between a broad and a narrow focus reading. In these cases, as with
focus conveyed by accent, different degrees of local emphasis may help
clarify the intended meaning. For example, in Russian the negative particle
ne occurs before a narrowly focused constituent if there is one but otherwise precedes the finite verb. If narrow focus is intended on the verb, this
can be made clear with emphatic accent (indicated by italic in the following example):

(5.74)　　a.　Ne MARK čitaet.
　　　　　　　'*Mark* isn't reading [someone else is].' (lit. not Mark reads)

　　　　　b.　Mark ne ČITAET.
　　　　　　　'Mark isn't reading.'

　　　　　c.　Mark ne *ČITAET*.
　　　　　　　'Mark isn't *reading*.' [he's doing something else].'

That is, the interpretation of the focus as broad or narrow is made clear by the presence or absence of local emphasis, not by the presence of accent or the presence of the negative particle alone.

When focus is conveyed by particles rather than accents, it is uncontroversial that the choice of focus pattern is categorical: either the focus marker is attached to one word or it is attached to another. It is also uncontroversial to distinguish the linguistic feature (the location of the focus particle) from the paralinguistic feature ('emphatic stress' to signal narrow focus), because the linguistic feature is segmental and the paralinguistic feature suprasegmental. The proposal here is that in languages like English, linguistic accent location and paralinguistic degree of emphasis – even though they are both phonetically suprasegmental – should be distinguished in the same way. It is then unproblematical to make the phonological idealisation that there is a single basic unmarked accent location, whose interpretation is ambiguous between broad and narrow focus, and which can be disambiguated by paralinguistic means.

All this evidence points to the conclusion that there are only two basic prominence patterns in a phrase like *five francs*, one with the main prominence on *five* and one with the main prominence on *francs*. (I am here ignoring the 'double-focus' cases, and will return to them in the next chapter.) The accent on either word can be exaggerated or made more prominent, by increasing pitch range, intensity, etc., in order to emphasise the individual accented word. This emphasis helps to make clear that the accent signals a narrow focus: if the accent on *five* is exaggerated in this way, the emphasis is redundant, but if the accent on *francs* is exaggerated, the emphasis helps to disambiguate the focus interpretation. In either case, the emphasis can be seen as a modification of one or the other basic pattern.

5.3.3   Is there a single 'main' accent?
Third, and perhaps most important, we need to justify the fact that we have implicitly – and at certain points even explicitly – been operating with a notion of 'main accent' or 'most important accent'. This is suspect on both phonetic and pragmatic grounds.

From the pragmatic point of view, the radical FTA theory assumes that any word is potentially accentable if it is sufficiently newsworthy, and, as a kind of corollary, the absence of accent on any word can be interpreted as signalling that it is less newsworthy than other words in the string. It is therefore unjustified to concentrate on some supposed 'main' accent – in particular, the last accent of a phrase or utterance – and ignore the presence or absence of accents on other words in the phrase. This point of view is discussed at some length by Bing (1980) and Bolinger (1986).

Phonetically, many have objected to the idea that the last accent is somehow more prominent than other accents. Bolinger has treated the intuition that the rightmost accent is somehow more prominent as a kind of illusion induced by its final position in the utterance (see Bolinger 1986: 58ff. and ch. 6 *passim*). The IPO tradition identifies the 'prominence' of an accent in explicitly phonetic terms, relating it to the size of the pitch excursion (e.g. 't Hart, Collier, and Cohen 1990; Terken 1991, Hermes and Rump 1994, Rump and Collier 1996), and allows no theoretical reason for regarding the final accent as anything special. It seems clear that phonetic data will provide no basis for the claim that the last accent is the most prominent.

It is, however, easy to show that in most contexts the last accent does have a special status in signalling focus: the location of the last accent determines whether a broad focus interpretation is possible. This can be illustrated by taking a short phrase and gradually expanding it.

Consider a phrase like *a cup of coffee*. The basic facts about prominence and focus in this phrase are completely comparable to those for the example *five francs* treated above. Broad focus can be conveyed by the pattern *a cup of* COFFEE, while only a narrow focus reading is available for the pattern *a* CUP *of coffee*: that is, the first pattern is potentially ambiguous between focus on the whole phrase (a cup of coffee as opposed to a sandwich or a piece of cake) and focus on *coffee* (a cup of coffee rather than a cup of tea or cocoa); the second unambiguously focuses on *cup* (i.e. a cup of coffee rather than a pot of coffee). As with the example *five francs*, it is not necessary for the accent on *coffee* to be the only accent of the phrase in the broad focus pattern: *cup* may be accented as well, without affecting the focus. But it is necessary for the accent on *coffee* to be the *last* accent of the phrase, and that is what is expressed in the notation *a cup of* COFFEE.

The importance of the location of the last accent can be seen by expanding the phrase, to something like *five francs and a cup of coffee*. A broad focus reading of this phrase would be appropriate in the context we cited earlier:

(5.75)　A:　What did they give you for participating in the experiment?

　　　　B:　Five francs and a cup of coffee.

In order to signal broad focus, there *must* be an accent on *coffee*. If the last accent is anywhere else (e.g. *five* FRANCS *and a cup of coffee* or *five francs and a* CUP *of coffee*), some sort of narrow focus is implied. As has often been observed, the number of accents may depend on the deliberateness of the speech and a number of other factors. If speaker B is answering hastily and matter-of-factly, it may be difficult to distinguish any accent other than the one on *coffee* and perhaps a H* accent on *five*. If speaker B thinks the experimenters were not very generous and wants to emphasise how little they gave her, she might put prominent H*+L accents on all four content words,

(5.76)   H*+L H*+L   H*+L   H*+L L L%
          FIVE FRANCS and a CUP OF COFFEE (can you believe it?)

If her questioner had already asked the question and been given the answer earlier, she might say impatiently:

(5.77)   L*   L*   L*   H*   L L%
          FIVE FRANCS and a CUP OF COFFEE (I already told you that!)

If speakers A and B are fellow students in a department that requires them to participate in experiments for minimal reward, she might say:

(5.78)   H*   ꞌH*   ꞌH*   ꞌH*   L L%
          FIVE FRANCS and a CUP OF COFFEE (. . . the usual.)

But none of these differences matters for the focus interpretation: all that counts is that there is an accent on *coffee*.

We can extend the example even further – perhaps stretching the bounds of plausibility a little – to something like *five francs seventy-five centimes and a cup of pretty tasteless coffee*. Again, in order for this phrase to serve as a broad focus response to the question about what the speaker was given for participating in the experiment, the last accent must be on *coffee*. As in the previous example, the overall number of accents and the details of any expressive intonational choices are irrelevant; but as in the previous example, any location of the last accent other than on *coffee* signals some fairly specific contextual presuppositions, and narrow focus.

The special significance of the last accent, then, lies not in any actual phonetic prominence it may have, but in the key role it plays in defining the *pattern* of prominence. It need not be specially prominent; it need only be present. This explains the emphasis on describing the location of the right-most accent in much previous work on sentence accentuation, and justifies our continuing to use a phonological notation that conveys the location of only a single accent. I believe it also shows the inadequacy of radical FTA accounts that treat the location of accents in terms of each individual word or small constituent, rather than in terms of an overall pattern. We will return to this whole issue again in the next chapter.

6 *Prosodic structure*

Throughout the book I have referred to the 'autosegmental–metrical' theory of intonation, but I have scarcely mentioned metrical phonology except in chapter 2. This is an accurate reflection of the state of the field. AM work on intonation has so far been overwhelmingly autosegmental, dealing with the phonological and phonetic properties of tones and pitch accents and of their association with the segmental string. There have been very few attempts at theoretical integration of this work with the findings of those who deal primarily with rhythm and timing, relative prominence, and hierarchical prosodic structure. What efforts there have been in this direction have failed, in my view, to realise the promise of the 'metrical' idea.

Metrical phonology is potentially a general theory of syntagmatic relations in phonology.[1] In developing the original version of this theory, Liberman (1975) concentrated specifically on rhythm and temporal relations, but as Beckman (1986: ch. 3) has argued, Liberman's work laid the foundation for a much more general account. This chapter sketches the outlines of an AM theory of intonational phonology in which 'metrical' aspects are central to the analysis. In accordance with Beckman's broad conception of what metrical phonology could become, the issues discussed in what follows are mostly about prosodic structure and abstract relative prominence, not about rhythm and timing.

I will deal with three main issues:

1   *The internal structure of tunes*: I will argue that tunes are not merely strings of pitch accents and edge tones, but that they have some sort of hierarchical constituent structure, including a distinction between nuclear and other accents.

2   *The phonological nature of sentence stress*: I will argue that sentence-level prominence is not primarily a matter of where pitch accents are located, but involves a specification of relative

prominence in the prosodic structure, which in turn determines the distribution of pitch accents.

3   *The nature of prosodic constituency*: I will argue that the 'Strict Layer Hypothesis', which is widely assumed to provide a valid characterisation of hierarchical structure in phonology, is too restrictive, and that, at least in the case of large prosodic chunks like intonational phrases, we need to recognise the existence of what I have called Compound Prosodic Domains.

I am well aware that these three topics will need to be better integrated than I have been able to do in what follows, but I hope that there is nevertheless some value in sketching my ideas here in their present form.

6.1   The structure of intonational tunes

6.1.1   Secondary accents in tune–text association

It is widely assumed that a language's intonational phenomena can be classified into contour *types* or 'tunes'. Many descriptions of many European languages contain references to 'neutral declarative' intonation, 'interrogative' intonation, and the like. Some descriptions of English go considerably further than this, positing specific tune types like the 'contradiction contour' (Liberman and Sag 1974) or the 'surprise–redundancy contour' (Sag and Liberman 1975). In the same way, the IPO description of Dutch identifies such tunes as the 'hat pattern' and the '3C', while Delattre's classification of French tune types (Delattre 1966) includes such tune types as 'major continuation', 'minor continuation', and 'implication'. Regardless of how many such types are recognised, one central goal of theories of intonational phonology is to be able to provide an explicit phonetic characterisation of all the tunes of a given language. In particular, we want to be able to make explicit predictions of how a given tune will be realised when it is applied to different texts.

A crucial ingredient of any such theory is an account of *tune–text association*. As we saw in section 2.2.2, this is the term employed by Liberman (1975) to describe the principles according to which the abstract phonological elements of the contour are lined up with the segmental features of the utterance. Consider the application of 'the same' contour to utterances with different numbers of syllables. Suppose, for example, we identify for English an 'emphatic' statement contour with an ordinary H* accent near the beginning of the utterance and a raised or emphatic H*..L..L%

sequence (here annotated *ad hoc* with an up-arrow ↑ before the H*) at the end:

(6.1)　　a.　H*　↑H* L L%
　　　　　　　Do it now.

　　　　　b.　　　　　H*　　　↑H* L L%
　　　　　　　Her mother's a lawyer.

Intuitively we are dealing with the same contour in both cases, despite the fact that the two utterances have different numbers of syllables. Pierrehumbert's tonal analysis (or indeed any analysis that treats the into-nation contour as a sequence of distinctive tonal events at particular points in the utterance) gives expression to this intuition: in both cases the contour is represented as H*..↑H*..L..L%. The association of the H* accents with *do* and *now* and the stressed syllables of *mother* and *lawyer* follows in a rule-governed way from their relative prominence. The autosegmental represen-tation of the tonal events and the metrical account of how the tonal events are associated with syllables give us a clear and explicit basis for describing the contours on the two texts as 'the same'.

　　Liberman's recognition of tune–text association as a problem gave an important impetus to the development of the general AM approach to into-national phonology.[2] However, any account of tune–text association based on current AM intonational phonology still falls short of capturing our intuitive understanding of what it means for two utterances to have the same intonation. One of the most serious problems involves secondary accents.

　　The secondary-accent problem arises whenever contours contain differ-ent numbers of accents. As we have just seen, it is straightforward to repre-sent a contrastive statement contour H*..↑H*..L..L% which can apply to texts with different numbers of *syllables*. However, if there are three H* accents, or only one, then standard AM assumptions provide us with no phonological abstraction that will allow us to refer to the resulting contours as 'the same', even though intuitively that seems appropriate. This can be seen from the following sentences.

(6.2)　　a.　(three H* accents)
　　　　　　　H*　　　H*　　　↑H* L L%
　　　　　　　Mary McKelvie's a lawyer.

　　　　　b.　(one H* accent)
　　　　　　　↑H* L L%
　　　　　　　Now!

Intuitively, these contours are the same as the ones in (6.1). The surface variations in (6.2a) and (6.2b) are just as lawful as those between (6.1a) and (6.1b): they are determined by the number and type of syllables in the text. Ultimately, then, they should be covered by a general theory of tune–text association; but given current AM assumptions, the representations H*..H*..↑H*..L..L% (6.2a) and ↑H*..L..L% (6.2b) must count as different, both from each other and from the H*..↑H*..L..L% in (6.1a) and (6.1b).

The same problem can be seen more clearly in the following pairs of sentences (from Ladd 1986):

(6.3)   (intonational nuance: relative neutral)

        H*   H*L L%
   a. I read it to Julia.

        H*   H*   H*L L%
   b. I wanted to read it to Julia.

(6.4)   (intonational nuance: ' . . . and that's that')

        H*   !H*L L%
   a. I read it to Julia.

        H*   !H*   !H*L L%
   b. I wanted to read it to Julia.

(6.5)   (intonational nuance: ' . . . as you ought to know')

        L*   H*L L%
   a. I read it to Julia.

        L*   L*   H*L L%
   b. I wanted to read it to Julia.

Both members of each pair appear to have the same intonation, in the sense that both convey the same pragmatic force suggested by the informal glosses of the intonational nuances. The number of accents preceding the final H*..L..L% seems to depend solely on the number of accentable syllables, and the categorical identity of those accents (H*, H* followed by downstep, L*) seems to represent a *single linguistic choice*, regardless of whether there are one or two such accents. Somehow, we want to be able to treat the final H*..L..L% sequence, which occurs only once, separately from the accent or accents that precede it, and to treat the exact number of preceding accents as a detail that is subject to predictable variation. That is, we want to be able to treat the phonological specification of the

'surprise–redundancy contour' in (6.5) as something like 'one or more L*
accents followed by a H*..L..L% sequence'.

6.1.2   *The nucleus and the hierarchical structure of tunes*

The idea that one part of the contour is both obligatory and potentially
unique can readily be related to the idea of the nucleus, which in one form
or another has been a part of theorising about intonational structure at
least since the beginning of the British tradition. (See Cruttenden 1992b for
an interesting discussion of pre-twentieth-century precursors to the nucleus
idea.) For those who are unfamiliar with this literature, a brief summary of
the traditional distinctions is in order.

According to the founding work in the British school, Palmer 1922, the
contour is divided into three parts, called head, nucleus, and tail. Only the
nucleus is obligatory, so that on a monosyllabic utterance the contour consists of the nucleus alone. In an utterance with more syllables, the nucleus
occurs on the most prominent stressed syllable, which is normally also the
last stressed syllable. One of a small set of different 'nuclear tones' (four in
Palmer's analysis) can be selected at the nucleus. The shape of the tail – the
stretch of contour following the nuclear syllable – is largely or entirely dictated by the choice of nuclear tone. The shape of the head, the stretch of
contour preceding the nuclear syllable, is an independent choice, though
many in the British tradition (e.g. O'Connor and Arnold 1973) have noted
that some combinations of head and nuclear tone are particularly favoured
or disfavoured.

With some variation, this basic plan has been part of the British
approach to describing intonation ever since. The inventory of contour
types for the 'head' has been the subject of considerable disagreement, as
has to a lesser extent the inventory of nuclear tone types, but the basic structure has scarcely been altered. Probably the most significant widely agreed
change to the structure outlined by Palmer has been the idea that the head
begins with a major stressed syllable (see Kingdon 1958), which entails the
addition of the 'prehead' – that is, any unstressed syllables preceding the
head – to the structure of the contour. Even Crystal (1969) and Halliday
(1967a), who provided penetrating theoretical criticisms of many of the
assumptions of the British tradition, retained the idea of the distinction
between the nucleus ('tonic' in Halliday's terminology) and other parts of
the contour. The basic plan of the division of the contour according to the
British school is shown in figure 6.1.

Similar ideas are found outside the British tradition as well: for example,

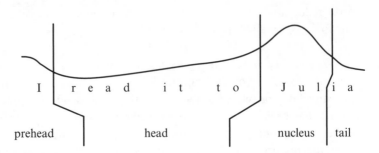

Figure 6.1 Division of the pitch contour in the typical analysis of the British school.

Pike (1945) drew a distinction between 'primary contour' and 'precontour' that almost exactly matches the distinction between nucleus (or nucleus-plus-tail) and head (or prehead-plus-head); both Hockett (1955, 1958) and Trager (1964) explored various versions of the same distinction in connection with the American structuralist theory of intonation; and the IPO tradition, though it originally had no such distinction, now incorporates a three-way distinction between prefix, root, and suffix which is comparable in many respects – though not identical – to the British distinction between head, nucleus, and tail ('t Hart, Collier, and Cohen 1990).

Pierrehumbert (1980), however, rejects the head/nucleus/tail division: contours are strings of accents, generated by the finite-state grammar in (3.1). Pierrehumbert does continue to refer informally to the last accent in the sequence as the 'nuclear' accent. She also acknowledges a substantial correspondence between the British taxonomy of nuclear tone types and what for her are sequences of the last accent and the following phrase tone and boundary tone (see section 3.2 and table 3.1 above). But she denies the notion of nucleus any formal status in the theory, with the consequences for tune–text association that we have just discussed in section 6.1.1.

It is worth noting, however, that Pierrehumbert's argument against the nucleus is in effect an argument against the 'head' of the British tradition, an argument that follows from her argument against global contour shapes; that is, she denies that the head is an identifiable component of contours primarily because traditional British descriptions of the head are often expressed in terms of global shapes ('scandent head', etc.). As I have argued elsewhere (Ladd 1986), it is important to distinguish arguments against the head as a global shape from arguments against the head *as a constituent or substring*. It is entirely possible to distinguish the nucleus from other accents – and hence to recognise in some way the existence of the head –

without abandoning Pierrehumbert's basic assumption that intonation contours are strings of pitch accents or tones. There is no deep incompatibility between AM assumptions and the idea that the nucleus has a special status.

Indeed, it is simple to modify Pierrehumbert's finite-state grammar for generating tunes so as to allow for a nucleus. The modified grammar might look like this:

(6.6)   Boundary   Prenuclear   Nuclear   Phrase   Boundary
          Tone   Accents   Accent   Tone   Tone

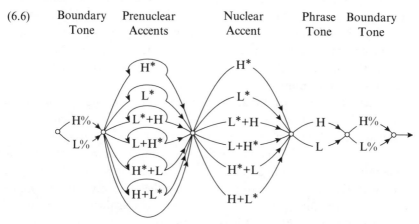

This grammar states that contours consist obligatorily of one accent, which corresponds to the nucleus. It states that the nucleus may be preceded by one or more accents, but that any preceding accents must be identical, as in examples (6.3)–(6.5).[3] This grammar thus gives us something corresponding to the head, but the 'something' is neither a global shape nor even a constituent in any strict sense – it is merely a substring of the contour. The British tradition's terminology is thus substantially redefined in accordance with AM assumptions, but the basic descriptive insight (which, as we have just seen, forms part of most traditions) is retained.

Note that this definition also defuses another of Pierrehumbert's arguments against assigning special status to the nucleus. She attaches considerable importance to the fact that there appears to be no phonetic difference between nuclear and prenuclear accents in English; the largest study of this question is by Silverman and Pierrehumbert (1990). Silverman and Pierrehumbert show that a number of phonetic conditioning factors on the alignment of H accent peaks affect nuclear and prenuclear accents in identical ways. While this means that the nuclear accent is not in any way *phonetically* distinct from prenuclear accents, it poses no obstacle to assuming that accents of a given type may play more than one *structural* role in the tune.

6.1.3   *Postnuclear accents*

If the nucleus is indeed merely the obligatory accent of the contour, then there is no necessary reason for it to be the last accent. As we have just seen, Pierrehumbert denies that the nuclear accent has any special status except as the last accent, and even those who assume the validity of the nucleus notion often take it for granted that it is the last accent of the phrase, and that a postnuclear accent is a contradiction in terms. In my view, this theoretical position is little more than a bias induced by the structure of intonation contours in Western European languages. This can be seen by considering more closely the facts of question intonation in several languages of Eastern Europe.

We saw in section 4.1.2 that the ordinary question tune in Hungarian consists of a L* nuclear pitch accent and a HL edge tone sequence. Given the general assumptions of the AM approach, it is clear that the HL sequence following the main accent involves only edge tones, and despite its acoustic salience is not a pitch accent. There are two reasons for saying this: first, the HL sequence does not make the word on which it occurs focused or prominent; and second, the HL sequence always occurs on the last one or two syllables and is completely indifferent to the location of lexical stress (which in Hungarian is always word-initial). However, in several other languages of Eastern Europe, a very similar question tune is found in which the status of the HL sequence is problematical: specifically, the line between edge tones and pitch accents is blurred.

We may illustrate with data from Romanian and Greek. In both of these languages, we see the same sequence of a L* accent and a following HL sequence at the end of the contour. Thus (lexical stress is marked by /'/ preceding the stressed syllable):

(6.7)   a.   Greek

       L* HL
       'ipjan?
       'Did they drink?'

    b.   Romanian

       L*H L
       'regele?
       'The king?'

There are slight differences of detail: most notably, the HL sequence always goes on the final syllable in Greek, rather than spreading itself over two unstressed final syllables as in Romanian and Hungarian. Nevertheless, it seems reasonable to treat this as the same tune as found in Hungarian.[4]

There are, however, other more significant differences in the way the HL sequence is associated with the text. In Hungarian, as we saw, the HL sequence never cares about lexical stress; it is always preferentially associated with the last two syllables of the phrase. In Romanian and Greek, by contrast, if there is enough lexical material following the main accent, then the H of the HL sequence will associate with the lexically stressed syllable of a following word. This is illustrated in the following examples.

(6.8)   a.   Greek

       (i)   L*   H   L
             xo'revi a'popse?
             'Is she dancing tonight?' (lit. she-dances tonight)

       (ii)   L*   HL
             tra'gudise xtes?
             'Did she sing yesterday?' (lit. she-sang yesterday)

     b.   Romanian

       (i)   L*   H   L
             Ai vă'zut a'fişul a'cesta?
             'Did you see this poster?' (lit. you-have seen poster-the this)

       (ii)   L*   H   L
             Ai vă'zut 'regele?
             'Did you see the king?'

The HL that clearly serves as an edge tone sequence in (6.7) associates with a stressed syllable in (6.8). In Hungarian, that is, the HL sequence is associated with the edge of the phrase regardless of the length of the post-accentual stretch, but in Romanian and Greek the HL sequence will associate with a lexically stressed syllable if one is available. More or less by definition, a tone that seeks to associate with a lexically stressed syllable is a *pitch accent*.

This H or HL accent – if that is what it is – remains in some important sense *subordinate to the L* accent*, however. In (6.8a), for example, the focus of the questions remains broad: the force of the utterances is not 'Is she dancing tonight as opposed to some other night?' or 'Did she sing yesterday as opposed to some other day?' The correct translation of (6.8ai) into English would clearly have the accent on the verb, not the adverb: that is, *Is she* DANCING *tonight?* In order to focus on the time adverb, we must move the L* onto it, with the resulting compression of the HL sequence.[5] Thus:

(6.9)   a.   H*   L* HL
xo'revi a'popse?
'Is she dancing *tonight?*'

b.   H*   L*HL
tra'gudise xtes?
'Did she sing *yesterday?*'

Much the same is true of (6.8b), although readers whose native language is Western European must remind themselves that, as in Hungarian, the neutral location of the main accent in Romanian yes–no questions is on the verb. That is, Romanian speakers feel that the main accent in (6.8b) is on *văzut*, not on *acesta* or *regele*, but they also feel that this is the normal way to pronounce these questions. The intonation contour in (6.8bi) certainly cannot be used to focus on the object noun phrase *afişul acesta*; to do that we would need to move the L* onto *acesta*, yielding the following contour:

(6.10)   H*   L* HL
Ai va̋'zut a'fişul a'cesta?
'Did you see *this* poster?'

In short, the only appropriate analysis of these data would appear to be as follows. In many Eastern European languages yes–no question intonation consists of a L* accent associated with the stressed syllable of the focused word, followed by a HL sequence. In some languages, such as Hungarian, the HL is invariably associated with the edge of the phrase. In others, such as Romanian and Greek, the HL is associated either with the edge of the phrase or with the stressed syllable of a word that follows the focused word; in the latter case, it must be regarded as a pitch accent. In all cases, however, the L* remains the main accent, in the sense that it is the one that signals the focus of the utterance. The HL (or H) pitch accent, where it occurs, is thus in some sense *postnuclear*.

Once we accept the notion of postnuclear accent, we find that it is useful in quite a number of languages. For example, both Grice (1995a) and Vella (1995), writing on Palermo Italian and Maltese respectively, show that in sentences where the main focus is early, there may be a secondary accent on a word that occurs after the focused word – a postnuclear accent. Both acknowledge that there is something odd about the notion of postnuclear accent, but both are led to the idea by their data. There are also phenomena in English which can most readily be explained if we recognise the existence of postnuclear accent, namely the distribution of postnuclear tones in the calling contour and in various 'fall–rise' tunes.

Recall that the English calling contour (see section 4.3.2) involves a H*
accent tone followed by a downstepped H tone. It has been noted by both
Leben (1976) and Haggo (1987) that the location of the step down to the ˈH
is sensitive to relative prominence; specifically, the ˈH 'prefers' to occur on
the most prominent postnuclear syllable. For example:

(6.11) H*   ˈH   H* ˈH   H*   ˈH
   a. Lunch is ready! (cf. Lu-unch! and Lunchtime!)

   H*   ˈH   H* ˈH
   b. Jonathan's turn! (cf. Jonathan!)

   H*   ˈH   H* ˈH   H*   ˈH
   c. Taxi's waiting! (cf. Taxi! or Taxi's here!)

The effect of postnuclear prominence in the Dutch calling contour is even
clearer: as we saw in section 4.3.2, there can be more than one postnuclear
ˈH in the Dutch calling contour, and Gussenhoven (1993) showed very
clearly that the steps occur at metrically strong syllables. This behaviour is
consistent with the idea that the postnuclear ˈH in the calling contour in
English or Dutch is in some sense an *accent*, not just an edge tone. Like the
postnuclear H in Greek or Romanian questions, the postnuclear step in the
calling contour occurs at a lexically stressed postnuclear syllable if there is
one, and only otherwise will it go to the edge of the phrase.

Similar observations can be made about the location of the postnuclear
L in English falling–rising tunes. In short utterances where the nuclear syllable is followed by at most a few unstressed syllables, it is not grossly inac-
curate to treat (rising–)falling–rising tunes as involving a single continuous
movement from the nucleus through the 'tail' to the end of the utterance.
This is what the British tradition does. As we have already seen, however,
when the number of postnuclear syllables increases, it becomes increasingly
obvious that the contour consists of a nuclear (rising–)falling accent and a
rising boundary movement (see the examples of *Sue* and *a driving instructor* discussed in section 2.1). In fact, as the number of syllables increases
even more, it becomes increasingly plausible to posit a L accent on the most
prominent postnuclear syllable. Consider the following example:

(6.12)

   I thought she was dancing tonight.

With the intonation intended, this has the most prominent stress on
thought, and the implication is 'I thought – despite what someone else may
have said – that she was dancing tonight, and it turns out I was right.' That

is, there is a (rising–) falling nuclear accent on *thought*, and a final boundary rise. Yet impressionistically there appears to be a L accent on *dancing* as well. In much traditional British work, for example, such a sentence would be transcribed *I ˋthought she was ˌdancing tonight*, that is, with a 'high fall' on *thought* and a 'low rise' on *dancing*. The problem with such a transcription is that it fails to indicate that the accent on *dancing* is somehow subordinate to the one on *thought*.

This point was clearly addressed by Halliday (1967a, 1970), who posited two 'compound tones' in English: a fall followed by a low rise (Halliday's tone 13) and a rise–fall followed by a low rise (Halliday's tone 53). According to Halliday, these compound tones have two tonic (i.e. nuclear) accents, with the second subordinate to the first. In Halliday's words (1970: 43):

> Tone groups with . . . tones 13 and 53 have the same general pattern of information as other tone groups, with the tonic marking new information. The difference is merely that there are two places where the speaker has decided to focus the information in the information unit, instead of one.
> The two tonics are unequal in value. The first tonic, with tone 1 or tone 5, is the 'major' one; the second, with tone 3, is the 'minor' one. The major tonic carries the principal new information in the tone group. The second tonic expresses information which is in some way secondary or subsidiary to it.

Ignoring the strong 'Focus-to-Accent' bias, these observations strike me as entirely accurate; translating them into the terms being used here, the compound tones involve a postnuclear accent. I find it remarkable that no one else in the British tradition has ever come up with similar ideas, despite the obvious problems with the taxonomy of falling–rising tunes.

Halliday's notion of compound tones, however, though it clearly foreshadows the idea of postnuclear accent, also misses an important point, because it makes no attempt to relate the two compound tones to the ordinary 'fall–rise' (Halliday's tone 4) (i.e. it makes no attempt to relate the tune on *Sue* in (2.1) on p. 44 to that on *I thought she was dancing tonight* in (6.12)). In the view advanced here, the L 'phrase tone' in the falling–rising contour in (2.1) is in some sense the same tonal element as the L postnuclear accent in the 'compound tone' in (6.12). As with the H tone in the Greek or Romanian question contour, the L postnuclear tone in English falling-rising contours attaches to a lexically stressed syllable if one is available, and otherwise merely forms the valley between the fall and the rise.[6]

6.1.4   Hierarchical structure for tunes?

Obviously, the idea that there can be pitch accents following the main accent causes problems for the idea that the nuclear accent is the last accent in the phrase. The data in the previous section show clearly that the essence of the nucleus is not its serial position but the fact that it is the most important accent from the point of view of focus. We might, of course, postulate a special category of pitch accent, which we could call a 'boundary accent' or perhaps 'phrase accent'. The nucleus would then be the last *ordinary* pitch accent of the phrase. If we use the term 'phrase accent' for this supposed special class of pitch accent, we deliberately recall the terminology used in Bruce's analysis of Swedish (see section 1.3.3), and we suggest that in both Swedish and languages like Romanian and Greek, there are pitch phenomena at the ends of phrases which are definitely accentual but also clearly distinct from the accentual phenomena in the main body of the phrase. Specifically, they behave like pitch accents when there is an accentable word available, but like edge tones when there is not. If we notate these special tones Tp, we could incorporate them into the modified finite-state grammar as follows:

(6.13)

Boundary Tone	Prenuclear Accents	Nuclear Accent	Phrase Accent	Boundary Tone

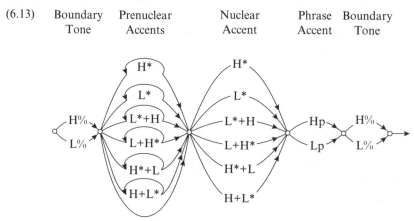

The problem with this proposal is that when such 'boundary accents' are associated with a lexically stressed syllable, there is nothing to distinguish them phonetically from any other accent. As with the distinction between nuclear and prenuclear accents discussed above, the distinction is structural, not phonetic. Unfortunately, though, we cannot handle postnuclear accents in the modified finite-state grammar as optional accents following the obligatory nuclear accent – which would be analogous to the way prenuclear accents are generated. This is because, unlike prenuclear accents, the postnuclear tones *are* in some sense obligatory: they are always present in the contour in one form or another. What is optional – and rule-governed – is whether they surface as accents or edge tones.

The essential structural feature of postnuclear accents in contexts like the Eastern European question tune or the English falling–rising tune is that they are *obligatory but secondary*. By implication, the essential properties of the nuclear tone are not only its obligatoriness and its potential uniqueness, but also the fact that it is primary: it is the accent that signals focus. This suggests that the difference between nuclear and postnuclear tones is essentially a matter of the relation between them in a metrical or other syntagmatic structure. For example, at a first approximation, we might indicate the tonal structure of the Eastern European question tune as follows:[7]

(6.14)

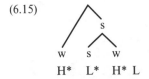

        s   w

     L*   H* L

   nuclear postnuclear

The similarity of this idea to Grice's proposals discussed in section 3.5.2 will be obvious.

Expanding the structure in (6.14) to include the prenuclear H* accent of the Eastern European question tune as well, we could write:

(6.15)

               s

     w   s   w

     H*   L* H* L

Such representations are consistent with a number of proposals, going back many decades, in which tunes have a constituent structure of some sort. For example, one early version (Chao 1932) of the head–nucleus–tail analysis sketched above suggested a hierarchical structure that could be represented in tree form as follows:

(6.16)

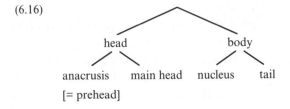

        head   body

  anacrusis   main head   nucleus   tail

  [= prehead]

Much more recently, in the part of his thesis dealing with tonal structure, Liberman (1975) proposed a structure for tunes identical to (6.15).

Updating these proposals in terms of the X-bar theory of constituent structure (Kornai and Pullum 1990), we might propose the following general structure for intonational tunes:

(6.17)

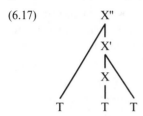

This treats the nucleus as the 'head' of the tune, the tail (redefined as the tone that surfaces variously as 'phrase tone' or postnuclear accent) as the 'complement', and the prenuclear accent as an 'adjunct'.[8] Such a structure is consistent with many of the observations that we have just been discussing:

1   A tune has one element – the nucleus – which is in some sense its central or most prominent point.
2   A tune has a constituent structure in which the most major break is that between the nucleus and all that precedes; the distinctive postnuclear elements of a tune are more closely bound to the nucleus than are the prenuclear elements.
3   Postnuclear elements in at least some languages may surface either as accents or as edge tones depending on the metrical structure of the segmental material to which they are associated.
4   The prenuclear element in a tune is a single linguistic choice. The occurrence of multiple prenuclear accents depends on the metrical structure of the segmental material to which the tune is associated.

By itself, of course, the structure proposed here does not actually describe in detail how prenuclear and postnuclear elements are associated with segmental strings of different metrical structure. (Indeed, even the association of the nuclear tone with the DTE is not clearly shown.) Obviously, therefore, in order to make any such proposal 'work', some formal mechanism will have to be provided to model these effects. For example, there might be tonal specifications of some sort on the parent intonational phrase node, specifications that percolate down to accent-bearing daughter nodes, yielding slightly different tonal strings depending on the metrical structure of the intonational phrase. But whatever mechanism is proposed, the idea that tunes have hierarchical structure has clear implications for a general theory of tune–text association. In particular, the principle that the tune is a property of a phrase, and is thus more abstract than a string of tones, seems inescapable. The elements of tunes are abstract tones, and they are not intrinsically either accent tones or edge tones (i.e. not intrinsically either starred or unstarred). Rather, what they are is intrinsically nuclear, prenuclear, or postnuclear. The prenuclear tones may surface as one or more accents or may be deleted/truncated. The postnuclear tones often surface as edge tones, and form a close group with the nuclear tone, but they may also surface as accents under certain circumstances.

Limitations of time and space make it impossible for me to pursue this topic in any depth here. However, it will be useful to mention two consequences of the notion of an abstract tune. The first is that it makes it possible to describe the restrictions on the pitch patterns of various kinds of tags. As has often been noted, for example, the pitch contour on tags such as *she said* or *he replied* is in some sense determined by (or at least consistent with) the pitch contour on the main part of the sentence:

(6.18)   H* H   H H%
        a.   Are you coming, she asked.

              L+H*   L   L L%
        b.   Get out of here, he yelled.

              L*+H L   L H%
        c.   I don't think   so, he said.

If the main sentence has a high-rising nucleus, the intonation on the tag continues high; if the main sentence has a falling nucleus, the intonation on the tag continues low; and – importantly – if the main sentence 'should' have a fall–rise nucleus, one possible pattern is for the falling accent to show up on the main sentence and the rise at the end of the tag. (Compare the similar behaviour of intonational tags in French, illustrated in example (4.40).) However, as has also often been noted, the tag generally has some sort of accent: there is a clear difference in the location of the valley in, for example, *he replied* and *he commented*, which have the greatest prominence on their final syllable and their antepenultimate syllable respectively. This kind of phenomenon should be readily accommodatable in a descriptive framework in which the postnuclear tone is not intrinsically either a pitch accent or an edge tone, and is associated with the most prominent syllable available.

A second consequence may be more far-reaching. If the tones in the abstract representation of a tune are not intrinsically starred or unstarred – if their status as accent tones or edge tones depends on the metrical structure of the text to which the tune is associated – it follows that sentence-level prominence must be defined in the metrical structure. The distribution of starred pitch accents is derived, not specified directly. This view is seriously inconsistent with many current theories of the relation between prominence and focus, which are expressed in terms of the placement of individual pitch accents rather than in terms of overall patterns of prominence. The implications of this are explored in the next section.

6.2   A metrical theory of sentence stress

The abstract view of tune structure just proposed has important implications for the 'Focus-to-Accent' (FTA) theory presupposed in chapter 5. According to the FTA view, focus is signalled by *pitch accents*, which are assigned directly to focused words or constituents. Yet the proposed general theory of tune–text association and abstract tune structure says that whether a tone surfaces as a pitch accent depends on its place in prosodic structure. If we adopt the idea of abstract tunes, we must relate both focus and accent to prosodic structure. This is the claim I wish to present. Specifically, in this section I will show that in many cases it is not pitch accent but *relative metrical strength* that is the essential signal of focus. In many cases, of course, metrical strength is reflected by pitch accent, but in a number of cases that I will discuss, it is necessary to recognise the priority of metrical strength, and more generally of syntagmatic relations in the phonology. This general view is consistent with the proposals in the preceding section, and with the overall attempt in this chapter to integrate metrical and autosegmental aspects of prosodic description.

The perspective presented here calls for some minor terminological and notational comments. In chapter 5 I talked fairly loosely about 'accent' or 'accentuation', and used the informal capital-letter notation to indicate the location of accents. Here I will refer to the phenomenon of interest as *sentence stress*, and reserve the term 'accent' to refer to actual pitch accents. For simplicity, I will retain the capital-letter notation to indicate sentence stress, but give it an explicitly metrical interpretation: the capitalisation of a word can be taken as a shorthand indicating that the word is the *Designated Terminal Element* (DTE; see section 2.2.2) of the utterance or of some relevant subconstituent. That is, the notations *five FRANCS* and

FIVE francs are equivalent to the metrical notations in (6.19a) and (6.19b) respectively:

(6.19)   a.   b.

This expresses the idea that sentence stress above all involves a syntagmatic relation between two constituents. In fact, as we shall see, there is still some role for non-relative 'paradigmatic' cues to focus. But prosodic structure remains at the heart of the account, and this is where we begin the exposition.

6.2.1   'Stress-first' and 'accent-first' theories

The difference between the FTA view and the view I wish to develop here is the difference between what Selkirk (1984: section 5.3) called 'accent-first' and 'stress-first' theories of sentence stress. Selkirk's own account of the focus–accent relation is what she calls an 'accent-first' account. In her model, a 'metrical grid' is constructed for each utterance, representing various features of the utterance's rhythm and stress pattern. Independently, pitch accents are assigned to individual words. The assignment of pitch accents pays no attention to the metrical grid, but is based purely on syntactic–semantic constituents ('sense groups') in accordance with the Focus-to-Accent theory.[9] In some cases this results in pitch accents being placed on words that do not have maximum (level 5) prominence in the metrical grid, in which case the grid must be adjusted so that pitch accents are only on maximally stressed syllables. (Among other things, this means that all pitch accents are equally prominent.) Apart from this adjustment of the metrical structure, there is no connection between pitch accent and stress, and Selkirk is at pains to insist that the string of pitch accents should not be seen as an additional level in the grid. She contrasts her approach with a 'stress-first' view, in which focus would be reflected directly in the metrical grid; the pattern of prominence in the metrical grid would in turn control the distribution of pitch accents in some way.

When Selkirk wrote, the question of whether stress or accent 'comes first' could be interpreted literally, within the context of a derivational model of phonology: pitch accents (or metrical structure) are assigned, 'and then' something else happens in the derivation. But this derivational interpretation – as Selkirk herself makes clear – is not essential. The dichotomy between accent-first and stress-first can still be understood in other ways that are more compatible with current ideas of what phonology is like. Stripped of its derivational overtones, the question boils down to something like the following. Assume that there is a phenomenon of postlexical or utterance-level prominence whose principal function is to signal focus. Is this postlexical prominence primarily a question of the distribution of pitch accents, or primarily a matter of relative prominence in the phonological structure of the utterance?

I believe that the evidence strongly favours the stress-first view. There are two kinds of cases that ought to be fatal counterexamples for any accent-first version of the FTA theory, namely accents that do not signal focus ('accent without focus'), and focus that is not signalled by accent ('focus without accent'). Both kinds of cases occur.

6.2.1.1 Accent without focus

In the preceding chapter (section 5.1.2) I alluded to the fact that there is normally a secondary accent on *five* in the broad focus reading of *five FRANCS*. Given the accent-first assumptions of recent FTA work, the existence of such secondary accents has been responsible for a certain amount of theoretical consternation. In a strict FTA interpretation, accents are supposed to signal focus. If there is no separate focus on *five* in *five FRANCS*, then there should be no accent either.

In some contexts it is possible to ignore the problem for phonetic reasons: on a phrase-initial monosyllabic word such as *five*, the secondary accent may be difficult to detect phonetically. However, if we replace the phrase *five francs* by *a million dollars*, the presence of such an accent on *million* is more or less indisputable, as can be seen in figure 6.2.

In the terminology proposed by Bolinger, the accent on *million* would be called a 'B accent', while that on *dollars* would be an 'A accent'. In Pierrehumbert's terms, both accents would be H*, but the second would be followed by a L phrase tone and the first would not. Whichever taxonomy we adopt, the secondary accent is clearly there, causing problems for a strict interpretation of the FTA view.

Selkirk (1984: 274) discusses just this point in connection with single-word utterances like *California*. Since this word constitutes the focus in a single-word utterance, it should have a pitch accent, and indeed it does. Unfortunately it frequently has *two* pitch accents, one on the primary stressed syllable *-for-* and one on the secondary stressed syllable *Cal-*. Selkirk admits that she has no explanation for the 'additional' accent.

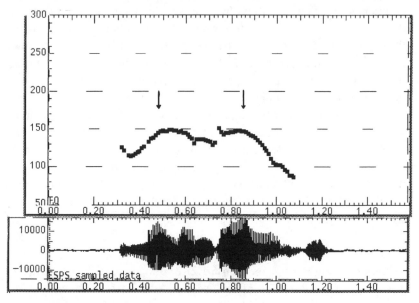

Figure 6.2 Non-emphatic American pronunciation of the phrase *a million dollars*, showing the clear secondary accent on *million*. The arrows mark the two accented vowels.

Similar observations apply to Steedman's recent work (Steedman 1991; Prevost and Steedman 1994). Steedman proposes an account of the relation between prosodic structure and the semantic interpretation of utterances that, like Selkirk's, is explicitly based on FTA principles. In particular, Steedman's whole model is based on the presumed *absence* of accent on any word that is not the head of a focus constituent. Actually, Steedman does allow for the possibility of additional accents within a focus constituent, but restricts this to cases where the accented words are 'new information'. Given information that is not focused (not 'thematic', in Steedman's terms) is assumed to bear what Steedman calls the 'null tone'. This leads him into complications to his analysis that include a 'virtual intermediate phrase boundary' which is not phonetically present. It is beyond the scope of this discussion to unravel these complications here, but it is clear that the phonetic accountability of his analysis is compromised by its dependence on entities whose presence cannot be independently verified.

In Gussenhoven's FTA-based analysis the presence of secondary accents is not even acknowledged. For example, as we saw in section 5.1.3, Gussenhoven's Sentence Accent Assignment Rule (SAAR) predicts that in a subject–verb–object sentence with broad focus, the verb and the object should form a single 'focus domain' that bears accent only on the object; the verb is, in his view, unaccented. In fact, Gussenhoven draws a clear distinction between cases where the verb is incorporated into a single focus domain with the object (and is hence 'unaccented'), and cases where the verb forms a separate domain from a following constituent and bears its own accent. For example, the SAAR predicts a prosodic difference between pairs like the following:

(6.20) a. He teaches linguistics. (subject–verb–object)

      b. He teaches in Ghana. (subject–verb–adverbial)

In a very interesting paper (1983b), Gussenhoven shows experimentally that listeners can distinguish accentual patterns of the sort on *teaches linguistics* from those on *teaches in Ghana*. Clearly, there is a difference to be accounted for here; but Gussenhoven expresses the difference in terms of the categorical presence or absence of accent: *teaches* is to be accented in one case, and not in the other. He never considers the possibility that there might be two different kinds of accent (Bolinger's B and A), or two different degrees of accent (secondary and primary), or that what is involved is the presence or absence of some sort of boundary (Pierrehumbert's L phrase tone). Like Steedman, he thereby weakens the phonetic accountability of his account.

6.2.1.2 Focus without accent

On the face of it, the secondary accent problem could be solved fairly readily without abandoning the basic ideas of an 'accent-first' account of sentence accentuation within the general framework of the FTA theory. Specifically, we lose little of substance if we abandon the insistence on equal pitch accents, and assume some kind of difference between primary and secondary accents. If we do this, many of the difficulties just discussed simply vanish. Focus will now be signalled by *primary* accent; secondary accents are distributed according to other criteria. Not only would this solve the accent-without-focus problem, but it would be consistent with the special status of secondary accents in tune–text association, discussed in section 6.1.

Selkirk anticipates some such solution in her discussion of the *California* example just cited:

> The additional pitch accents do not seem to modify the focus-related properties of the utterances . . . Whether additional pitch accents like these

have the same status in the grammar, and in particular whether they are assigned in (surface) syntactic structure and associated by [Selkirk's Pitch Accent Association Rule], we will leave open. [Selkirk's theory of the intonation-stress relation] does not require us to ascertain the status of these secondary pitch accents.

Gussenhoven's work could easily be recast in terms of primary accents rather than simply accents. With somewhat more difficulty, Steedman's model of accent and focus could also be revised to admit a distinction between primary and secondary accents as well. We would then be free to account for the distribution of primary accents in terms of the FTA theory, and secondary accents on 'low-level' prosodic grounds (e.g. the idea that prosodic phrases ideally have an early accent that somehow counterbalances the late primary accent; see Bolinger 1981; Shattuck-Hufnagel, Ostendorf and Ross 1994). An FTA solution along these lines is proposed by Kruyt (1985), who introduces a notion of 'half accent' roughly comparably to what I am calling secondary accent here.

Even if we recognise a distinction between primary and secondary accents, however, problems still remain. The most obvious is the occurrence of 'focus-without-accent': cases where focus is signalled by phonetic cues to prominence such as duration and vowel quality *without any pitch accent whatsoever*. Many such cases in English involve prepositional phrases with pronoun or adverb objects, such as *for him* and *in there*. These can of course occur with pitch accent on either word, but exactly the same focus distinctions can be made when the entire phrase is completely deaccented. This is, as far as I can see, impossible to reconcile with any version of the accent-first FTA view.

Consider the phrase *for him*. This can be pronounced with either word accented:

(6.21)   a.   I did it for HIM.

    b.   I did it FOR him.

Accent on *him* clearly conveys narrow focus – 'for him and not for someone else'. Accent on *for* apparently conveys broad focus, for example 'I did it for him because he wouldn't do it himself', in addition to the clearly narrow focus reading 'I did it for him, not with him'. However, it is not central to my argument whether accent on *for* conveys broad focus; what matters is that the two prominence patterns are distinct in form and in focus interpretation.

In addition to the location of the pitch accent, there are a number of other phonetic cues to stress in the phrase *for him*. When *for* is accented, it is likely to have a full vowel, and its final /r/ is likely to be realised even in non-rhotic varieties of English, since *him* is likely to be reduced to *'im* or *'m*. When *him* is accented, on the other hand, its initial /h/ is almost certain to be realised, and its vowel will be unreduced, whereas *for* will have a reduced centralised vowel and no /r/ in non-rhotic varieties. We might write these segmental variations informally as FOR *'im* and *f'r* HIM.

The key question for the accent-first account is whether these segmental differences are merely concomitants of pitch accent, or whether they are cues to a phenomenon of 'stress' which is independent of pitch accent (see section 2.2.1). It is not hard to show that they can occur independently, and can be used on their own to signal relative prominence: that is, the phrase can be pronounced in a context where neither word is accented, and yet it is still possible to distinguish the relative prominence of the preposition and the pronoun, and the intended focus reading, by the segmental and durational cues alone. For example, we might have the following dialogues, in which the last pitch accent is on *program*, and the prepositional phrase is unaccented:

(6.22) a. A: Bill says you haven't helped on his project very much.
            B: I don't know what he's complaining about. I wrote an entire
               PROGRAM for 'im.

        b. A: Bill seems to think you've been giving priority to other people in
               the department.
            B: I don't know what he's complaining about. I wrote an entire
               PROGRAM f'r him.

Cases like this are inexplicable if we assume that focus is signalled by accent. They seem to require a theory based on 'stress' (in the sense of section 2.2) or on relative strength in a metrical structure: in both (6.21) and (6.22) the focus distinction depends on whether *for* or *him* is the DTE of the phrase *for him*. As we saw in (6.21), the DTE may also bear a pitch accent, but that is not essential for conveying the focus distinction. The presence or absence of pitch accent is a separate question.[10]

Note that this point of view still acknowledges the overwhelming association of primary accent with focus: it states that focus is signalled in the first instance by the location of DTEs, not accents, but it also assumes that the DTE of any intermediate phrase will, by definition, have a primary accent. At the same time, however, it allows for cases of focus-without-accent, precisely because it treats the location of DTEs, not accents, as basic. Primary accents are often associated with focused words because focused words are often the DTE of intermediate phrases. Ultimately, however, accents do not respond directly to focus, but arrange themselves according to the demands of the metrical structure.

6.2.2   Evidence for a metrical view of sentence stress

Given the difficulties with an 'accent-first' view of the relation between focus and sentence stress, it seems worth developing the metrical alternative based on relative strength. This section outlines a possible stress-first theory that is consistent with the general ideas of metrical phonology. I will use Liberman–Prince metrical trees to exemplify metrical structure, but I leave open the question of whether this is the most appropriate representation. The main point – as in section 6.1 – is that some sort of metrical structure is at the heart of sentence prosody, and that pitch accents are essentially only one manifestation of the structure.

The first point to make is that, in many respects, the metrical interpretation of sentence stress makes the same predictions as an accent-first view. As we saw in section 2.2.2, the DTE of a short utterance is always accompanied by a pitch accent in any well-formed association of tune and text. This means that, given the metrical structures for *five FRANCS* and *FIVE francs* shown in (6.19) above, there must be a pitch accent on *francs* in one and on *five* in the other. In this short phrase, therefore, the metrical stress-first view may seem descriptively equivalent to the accent-first view. However, even in short phrases the empirical claims of the two views differ subtly. The most obvious difference concerns the broad focus pattern *five FRANCS*. In the metrical view, it makes no difference whether there is an accent on *five* or not: the w–s relation between *five* and *francs* can hold in either case. As we have just seen, the presence of a 'secondary' accent on *five* is at least somewhat problematical in a strict version of the FTA view. The metrical interpretation makes clear that the accentual pattern that we have been writing as *five FRANCS* need not have only a single pitch accent; what is important is only that the second accent is more prominent than the first.

Not only can the metrical interpretation of sentence accentuation accommodate the presence or absence of secondary stress on *five* in the broad focus case, but in some sense it also predicts the existence of the ambiguity of the pattern *five FRANCS* (i.e. the ambiguity between the broad focus reading and the reading with narrow focus on *francs*). This ambiguity is an inevitable consequence of the range of structurally distinct metrical representations: that is, the fact that there are only two possible metrical relations in a two-word phrase, namely the two shown in (6.19), predicts that there are only two phonologically distinct prominence patterns on a two-word phrase. Since there are three interpretations – two narrow focus readings and a broad focus reading – then one of the two patterns *must* be ambiguous. In an accent-first view this ambiguity is essentially an accident (although it is, as noted in section 5.3.2, comparable to the ambiguity of non-intonational focus markers). In a metrical account it follows naturally from the representation.

Further justification for a metrical account of sentence accentuation comes from a consideration of deaccenting. In Ladd 1980a, I discussed several aspects of deaccenting in English that are difficult to explain solely in terms of the distribution of pitch accents and seem to demand a syntagmatic account. I argued explicitly that deaccenting is fundamentally a matter of metrical structure, and only secondarily of pitch accent. Specifically, I showed that there are certain phenomena of deaccenting that are puzzling under an accent-shift analysis, but which can be readily explained if we treat deaccenting as a *reversal of relative strength in a metrical tree*. The clearest example is the case of rightward shift of accent in deaccenting.

In classic cases of deaccenting, accent shifts to the left compared to its neutral or non-deaccented position:

(6.23)   a.   A: Why didn't you read that article I gave you?
            B: I can't read GERMAN.

         b.   A: The only article on this is in German.
            B: I can't READ German.

In some cases, however, deaccenting causes accent to shift to the right:

(6.24)   a.   A: Where did you go just now?
            B: I took the GARBAGE out.

         b.   A: What happened to all the garbage?
            B: I took the garbage OUT.

(6.25)   a.   A: Anything happen while I was out?
            B: My PARENTS called.

         b.   A: Maybe we should call your parents and tell them.
            B: My parents CALLED – they already know.

In Ladd 1980, I suggested that both kinds of cases could be given a unified description in terms of reversed metrical nodes. So:[11]

(6.26)

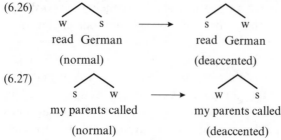

(6.27)

When one word is deaccented for pragmatic reasons, another word *must* be accented, because of the inherently relational or syntagmatic nature of prominence. But it is a matter of structure whether the word receiving the accent is to the left or the right of the deaccented word. It is difficult to account for this in terms of the linear shifting of pitch accents.

Finally, in addition to dealing easily with a wide range of deaccenting facts, a metrical interpretation of sentence accent also provides a natural account of the special status of the last accent discussed at the end of the preceding chapter (5.3.3). Specifically, the special status of the rightmost accent in phrases like *five francs and a cup of coffee* follows naturally from the claim that broad focus is normally signalled by the relation w–s (weak–strong) rather than s–w (strong–weak), because in metrical phonology we can define prominence relations *at any level of structure*. We start off with the w–s relation in *a cup of coffee* in order to signal broad focus in that constituent. As the focus constituent gets bigger and bigger, broad focus continues to be signalled by w–s relations at progressively higher levels of structure. This automatically makes the last accent of the largest phrase the strongest terminal element or DTE.[12]

This analysis is illustrated in the following set of trees. First we show the broad focus and narrow focus pattern for the short phrase *a cup of coffee*:

(6.28)

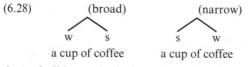

As we build progressively more complex phrases, the w–s relation between constituents continues to signal broad focus. Thus:

(6.29)

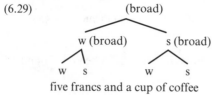

(6.30)

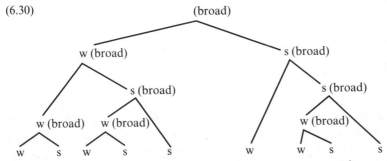

five francs seventy-five centimes and a cup of pretty tasteless coffee

In order to be interpreted as signalling broad focus, the strength relations in each constituent must be w–s.[13] As we saw in section 5.3.2, the resulting patterns can be realised in more and more different ways as the structure gets more complex, but the common element of all broad focus realisations is that *coffee* is the DTE and will always bear the last pitch accent.

6.2.3   *Limits of a syntagmatic account of sentence stress*

So far I have presented evidence that sentence stress is not essentially a matter of the location of pitch accents, but of *relative prominence within a metrical structure*. In the terms used at the beginning of the chapter, the prominence of any particular constituent in a structure is essentially *syntagmatic*: it depends crucially on the constituent's relation with other constituents in the same structure. While I think the case against an accent-first view of sentence stress is quite strong, it is ultimately not possible to treat prominence as a purely syntagmatic phenomenon either. The interplay of syntagmatic and paradigmatic factors is discussed in this section.

The first type of problematic cases are those of 'double focus', which I mentioned at the beginning of chapter 5 and have since carefully avoided. Example (5.3) is repeated and renumbered here for convenience:

(6.31)   I didn't give him SEVEN GUILders, I gave him FIVE FRANCS.

In both clauses, the noun phrases denoting sums of money each have two accents, indicating the presence of two points of focus or contrast in the sentence. The speaker in (6.31) is not simply opposing *five francs* to *seven guilders* (as in a broad focus case like *I didn't give him the car keys, I gave him five francs*), but is explicitly opposing both *francs* to *guilders* and *five* to *seven*.

Given the foregoing discussion of the nature of accentuation, the additional focus on *five* and *seven* is difficult to account for. If the last accent is indeed more prominent, as just suggested in section 6.2.2, then both the broad focus reading (with a secondary accent on *five*) and this double-focus reading will have the same weak–strong prominence relation:

(6.32)

$$\bigwedge$$
W   S

five francs

If the two versions have the same metrical structure, then the theory has no explanation of why they should have different interpretations. Intuitively it seems clear that, in the terms suggested in section 6.2.1.2, the basis of the extra focus is that *five* has a primary accent rather than a secondary accent. Somehow, the prominence is signalled by a difference of accent *type* – a paradigmatic distinction, rather than the purely syntagmatic contrasts to which we have attributed sentence prominence so far. Perhaps, as suggested in section 6.2.1.2, there is a deep connection between primary accent and focus after all.

The nature of this connection can be made somewhat clearer by considering an ostensibly unrelated problem. In English, as we saw in 5.2.3, many intransitive sentences have the main accent on the subject rather than on the verb:

(6.33)   a.   The COFFEE machine broke.

          b.   JOHNSON died.

However, as we also noted, this accent pattern is less likely when the subject is very long, or when there are adverbial expressions intervening between subject and verb:

(6.34)   a.   ??The coffee machine in the ANTHROPOLOGY office broke down this morning.

          b.   ??Former President JOHNSON unexpectedly died today.

Instead, we would be more likely to find accents on both subject and predicate, with the latter accent – presumably for the reasons just discussed in section 6.2.2 – perceived as strongest or most prominent:

(6.35)   a.   The coffee machine in the ANTHROPOLOGY office broke DOWN this morning.

          b.   Former President JOHNSON unexpectedly DIED today.

As we noted in section 5.2.1.2, a comparable effect of sentence length is seen in Romanian or Hungarian WH-questions, which would normally be accented on the WH-word at the beginning of the sentence, but which may have a later nucleus when the sentence is long.

The difference between the short and long sentences can be analysed as follows. When the sentences are short, the predicate need not constitute an intermediate phrase of its own. Instead, subject and predicate are combined in a single intermediate phrase, with a single primary accent. In English, under these circumstances, subject and predicate are in the relation strong–weak (see section 5.2.3), and the result is that the primary accent – the DTE of the single intermediate phrase – occurs on the subject. By contrast, when the sentences are longer, it is difficult to treat the whole sentence as a single intermediate phrase, and the subject phrase and the predicate phrase therefore form separate intermediate phrases. Within these phrases the expected strength relations apply, yielding DTEs (and accents) on *Johnson* and *died*:

(6.36)

Former President Johnson unexpectedly died today

At the highest level of structure, however, these two primary accents are in the relation weak–strong, exactly as in the case of *five francs and a cup of coffee* just discussed above. This means that the DTE of the sentence – and hence the last pitch accent – is the DTE of the *predicate* phrase.

(6.37)

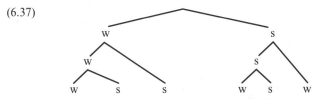

Former President Johnson   unexpectedly died today

This example suggests that the connection between primary accent and focus has something to do with the division of the utterance into intermediate phrases. That would be very interesting if it were true, because it would provide a kind of explanation for the cross-linguistic similarity of phrasing facts and accentual facts noted in section 5.2.5 above. Indeed, the connection between phrasing and accent can easily be shown to apply in other cases. Specifically, a similar account can be given for sentences that have 'two normal stress locations', such as the following (see section 5.3.1):

(6.38)   a.   DOGS must be carried.

        b.   Dogs must be CARRIED.

As we saw, this has two interpretations, (6.38a) meaning roughly 'You must have a dog and carry it' and (6.38b) meaning roughly 'If you have a dog, you must carry it'. If we approach these from the point of view of accent – and particularly if we approach them from the point of view of the location of a single main accent – we will ask 'Why is the accent on *dogs* in one case and on *carried* in the other?' However, if we assume that accent reflects phrasing or prosodic structure, we will analyse the accentual difference as a difference between a version in which the whole sentence is grouped into a single prosodic phrase and one in which the sentence is divided into two phrases, *dogs* and *must be carried*. In the first case, where subject and predicate form a single intermediate phrase, there is a single primary accent; this accent is on *dogs*, in accordance with the principle of English that treats arguments as more accentable than predicates (see section 5.2.3). In the second case, where subject and predicate each form a separate intermediate phrase, each has its own DTE and therefore its own accent (on *dogs* and *carried*, respectively). The accent on *carried* then becomes the main accent of the sentence for the reasons sketched in section 6.2.2.

This approach has the advantage of taking full account of the phonetic facts – in particular, the additional accent on *dogs* in (6.38b) – while at the same time allowing for the intuition that the accent on *carried* is the main accent of the sentence. In a sense it still leaves one central question unanswered, namely the question of why there should be two patterns and why they should match up with interpretations as they do. Yet even that question becomes more tractable when the two patterns are seen as 'one domain vs. two' rather than 'accent on subject vs. accent on predicate'. The various discussions of these cases by Schmerling (1976), Gussenhoven (1983a), and Faber (1987) all suggest that in the one-phrase pattern the subject and predicate in some sense form a single unit of new information ('news sentence', 'eventive reading'), while in the two-phrase pattern the subject is in some sense separated out and presented as a reference point in the discourse and the really new information is in the predicate ('topic–comment sentence', 'definitional reading'). Faber's terms 'integrative' and 'non-integrative' for the two patterns make the same basic point in a slightly different way.

In any case, when we consider cases like *Dogs must be carried* together with the effects of constituent length in sentences like *Johnson died* and the effects of double focus in sentences like *Five francs*, it seems fairly clear that much of the reason for dividing sentences into two phrases or keeping them as one has to do with a general phenomenon of phonological or semantic 'weight'. *The heavier a constituent is, the more likely it is to constitute its own intermediate phrase*. The sources of 'weight' are admittedly not very clear. In these three examples alone, constituents become heavy enough to form intermediate phrases for three different reasons: the 'weight' can result from mere length, as in (6.37), or from semantic separateness, as in (6.38), or from contrastive focus. In the long run it will be necessary to be more explicit about what kinds of factors can contribute to the weight of constituents. But the phonological effect is unambiguous: if a constituent is heavy enough, it will form its own intermediate phrase and, in languages like English, will contain its own primary accent.

6.3   The nature of prosodic constituency

If we define primary accent as the DTE of the 'intermediate phrase', we immediately run up against the problem that the definition of prosodic phrases of all types is notoriously elusive. It is universally assumed that one of the functions of prosody is to divide up the stream of speech into chunks or phrases of one sort or another – for the moment, informally, let us call these chunks intonational phrases or IPs. Despite the apparent universality of the chunking function, however, IPs and IP boundaries are remarkably difficult to define and to identify consistently. IP boundaries seem to take on a bewildering variety of manifestations, from a clear pause accompanied by a local F_0 fall or rise, to a subtle local slowing or pitch change that defies unambiguous definition. As a result, there is often disagreement about whether a particular IP boundary is or is not present, and definitions of IP boundaries in the literature are frequently circular or vague. For more discussion of this problem, see Crystal (1969: section 5.4), Liberman (1975: 9ff.), and Ladd (1986: section 1.1).

In my view, the difficulty of identifying IP boundaries has less to do with the inherent subtlety of the phonetic cues involved than with the fact that their definitions involve conflicting criteria. IPs are supposed to be set off by audible boundaries: if IP boundaries were not audible, then much of the point of the chunking function would be lost. At the same time, IPs are frequently assumed to have an internal prosodic structure of some sort – an intonational tune, a DTE, etc. The details of the supposed internal structure vary from analysis to analysis, but the effect is the same: the assumption of internal prosodic structure creates a potential for *theoretically incompatible observations*. We may find stretches of speech that appear to be delimited by prosodic boundaries but do not exhibit the expected internal structure; conversely, we may find stretches of speech that appear to have the internal structure of an IP but whose edges are not marked by audible boundaries.

The most important – and most complex – conflict of criteria arises from the twin assumptions that (a) the division of sentences into IPs in some way reflects syntactic, semantic, or discourse constituency, but that (b) prosodic structure is somehow fundamentally simpler than syntactic structure. Exploring the relationship between syntactic/semantic and prosodic structure has been a major area of research in prosody for at least two or three decades now (e.g. Halliday 1967b; Downing 1970; Langendoen 1975; Selkirk 1981, 1984, and especially 1986; Nespor and Vogel 1982, 1983, 1986; Chen 1987; Steedman 1991; Croft 1995). Obviously, the assumed existence of a broadly grammatical system underlying prosodic phrasing places still another potentially conflicting constraint on where we may observe IP boundaries (and indeed, a major part of what the works just referred to attempt to do is to explain – or explain away – 'mismatches' between prosodic structure and syntactic/semantic constituency). If we hear an audible break in a syntactically or semantically 'impossible' location, we may be tempted to say that it is a hesitation rather than an IP boundary; conversely, if we fail to observe a clear boundary where our rules lead us to expect one, we may be tempted to conclude that one is present anyway, but that it is hard to hear.

Yet considered purely as a problem of phonetics and phonology, boundaries are demonstrably not difficult to define and identify. In the ToBI transcription system, for example, the definitions of boundaries are expressed quite clearly in phonetic terms, and there is good inter-transcriber agreement on the location of accents and boundaries. (Admittedly, as noted in section 3.3.3, the system itself has an explicit mechanism – break index 2 – for dealing with theoretically incompatible observations.) In a recent study by de Pijper and Sanderman (1995), non-expert listeners showed good agreement in rating the 'strength' of prosodic boundaries on a ten-point scale, even when the segmental content of the utterances was rendered unintelligible. In the face of results like these, it is hard to maintain that prosodic boundaries are especially elusive or mysterious. Rather, I believe that the problem arises from conflicting criteria when we attempt to reconcile clear phonetic and phonological definitions with independent ideas about prosodic structure and its relation to syntax; that is, I believe that, as with stress (see section 2.2), the alleged elusiveness of the phenomenon is primarily a theoretical problem. This is the topic of this section.

6.3.1 The Strict Layer Hypothesis

The differences between prosody and syntax – and the problems these differences pose for phonetic definitions of prosodic constituents – are illustrated by the well-known case of the children's poem 'The house that Jack built', first discussed in this connection by Chomsky and Halle (1968: 371ff.). As Chomsky and Halle pointed out, the syntactic structure of each verse is indefinitely right-branching:

(6.39)   [This is [the dog that chased [the cat that killed [the rat that ate [the malt that lay in [the house that Jack built]]]]]].

The prosodic structure, however, involves a succession of phrases in which this depth does not appear to be reflected in any way.

(6.40) | This is the dog | that chased the cat | that killed the rat | that ate the malt | that lay in the house that Jack built |

Moreover, as can be seen, the boundaries between these prosodic phrases 'come in the wrong place' from the point of view of the syntax: not at the beginning of each noun phrase, but somewhere in the middle. Such mismatches are generally taken as the inevitable result of attempting to map one kind of structure (indefinitely branching syntactic structure) onto another fundamentally simpler kind (the intuitively 'flatter' or 'shallower' prosodic structure).

There is widespread agreement that the prosodic structure of utterances involves a hierarchy of well-defined domain types (syllables, phrases, etc.), such that the boundaries at each level of structure are also boundaries at the next lower level. This idea was first explicitly discussed by Halliday (1960, 1967a). For example, in Halliday's analysis of English phonological structure, utterances are composed of tone groups, tone groups of feet, feet of syllables, and syllables of phonemes. This means that every tone group boundary is simultaneously a foot boundary and a syllable boundary. Such a structure can be represented in a tree diagram of the sort that is now generally familiar:[14]

(6.41)

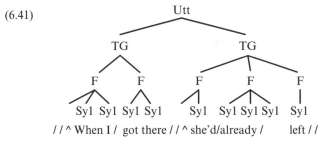

More recent investigators have proposed rather different inventories of categories or domain types, but the principle that they can be arranged in a hierarchy of size or inclusiveness is accepted by nearly everyone.

One property of trees like (6.41), much discussed by Halliday and his followers and critics (Huddleston 1965; Halliday 1966; Matthews 1966) and more recently by, for example, Selkirk (1984) and Nespor and Vogel (1986), is that they are *non-recursive*. No node may dominate another node of the same category. This property has been incorporated into several recent theoretical discussions in the form of a specific constraint on prosodic structure that Selkirk (1984) has dubbed the 'Strict Layer Hypothesis'. The Strict Layer Hypothesis (SLH) may be stated as follows:

(6.42)   *Strict Layer Hypothesis (SLH)*
          There is a hierarchy of prosodic domain types such that, in a prosodic tree, any domain at a given level of the hierarchy consists exclusively of domains at the next lower level of the hierarchy.

This abstract statement translates into some of the concrete prohibitions shown graphically in table 6.1. More importantly for the point under discussion, it entails that *prosodic trees are of fixed depth*. Any tree constructed according to the constraints stated in (6.42) can have only as many levels of structure as there are distinct domain types: for example, in Halliday's model shown in (6.41), with four domain types *Utt*, *TG*, *F*, and *Syl*, every *Syl* node will always be exactly three levels down from the root *Utt* node. The Strict Layer Hypothesis thus gives expression to the intuitive 'flatness' of prosodic trees by equating flatness with fixed depth. By restricting the set of prosodic trees to those of fixed depth, it also – as just noted above – makes it inevitable that there will be certain types of syntactic structures (such as repeated right branching) that cannot be reproduced in the corresponding prosodic trees. It thereby provides a reason why there should be 'mismatches' between prosody and syntax.

The SLH is widely taken to be self-evident. Four years after Selkirk formulated it as a 'useful working hypothesis' (1984: 26), Pierrehumbert and Beckman (1988: ch. 6) incorporated it into their formal system as an axiom in the literal sense – and making no reference to Selkirk, Nespor and Vogel, or the term 'Strict Layer Hypothesis'. But this rapid acceptance can hardly be attributed to overwhelming empirical evidence that prosodic structure is of fixed depth, or to clear data supporting the prohibitions in table 6.1. On the contrary, the SLH clearly causes empirical problems. For example, both Hyman *et al.* (1987) and Chen (1987) point to bracketing paradoxes that arise from assuming the SLH in languages with complex tone sandhi.

Table 6.1. *Some consequences of the Strict Layer Hypothesis. The category labels A, B, C in the diagrams are intended to represent prosodic domain types (intonational phrase, phonological word, foot, syllable, etc.), where A is a larger domain than B and B is a larger domain than C*

a. No multiple domination

b. No heterogeneous sisters

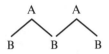

c. No skipping of levels

d. No unlabelled nodes

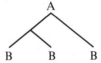

e. No recursion

The problems I wish to discuss revolve around the notion of *boundary strength*. It has been shown in several studies that clear IP boundaries may have different acoustic properties that in some way reflect the structural strength or depth of the boundary (see e.g. Cooper and Sorensen 1981; Thorsen 1985 and 1986; Ladd 1988). It has even been found, as noted above, that listeners are able to detect such differences reliably when segmental content is acoustically masked (de Pijper and Sanderman 1995). This evidence for boundary strength cues conflicts with the idea that the prosodic structure of an utterance is of fixed depth.

The nature of the conflict can easily be demonstrated. In (6.40) I marked the last phrase of the utterance as *that lay in the house that Jack built*. What I really hear when I say the verse to myself is that there is another boundary after *house*, but that it is weaker or more subtle than the ones I marked in (6.40). Under the usual assumptions about prosodic phrasing, there is no good way to indicate this percept of a 'weaker' boundary; either it is there (and I perceive it as weaker because I am aware of syntactic differences between it and the other boundaries) or it is not there (but I perceive it anyway because I know it is there syntactically).

There are only two ways to reconcile evidence for phonetic cues to boundary strength with the SLH. One is to interpret different boundary strengths as different *probabilities* with which a given syntactic boundary will be marked prosodically. This is the approach taken in Pierrehumbert and Liberman's re-interpretation of Cooper and Sorensen, discussed in section 1.3.1 above. The other is to express the perceived weakness of a given boundary directly, by saying that it is a *different kind of boundary* – specifically, a lower or more minor boundary. Under the SLH, as a moment's reflection will make clear, the only possible differences of boundary strength are differences of boundary type.

The idea that there are two different kinds of IPs has been proposed independently a number of times over the past half-century. These proposals include those of Trim (1959; major and minor tone groups), O'Connor and Arnold (1973; single and double bar boundaries), and Beckman and Pierrehumbert (1986; intonation phrases and intermediate phrases). In all cases, the theoretical proposal amounts to distinguishing between big IPs and little IPs, with big ones consisting of one or more little ones – as required by the SLH. Unfortunately, there is no clear correspondence among the various proposals for two levels of IP. For example, as I noted in Ladd 1986, Trim's big IPs are roughly comparable to O'Connor and Arnold's little IPs. If we were to credit the observations of both, we would therefore end up with three levels of IP; and detailed comparison with other proposals could lead us to posit even more. In order to avoid positing too many different types of boundaries, investigators more often resolve the implicit conflict of criteria by simply ignoring certain boundary cues, and falling back on the 'elusiveness' of prosodic phrasing as an explanation for their difficulties. This is in effect what I did when I marked the location of IP boundaries in example (6.40).

A more extended illustration of the empirical problems caused by the SLH is provided by the development of ideas on phonological structure within metrical and prosodic phonology. If we trace this history we repeatedly observe preliminary proposals that admit indeterminate depth; after the SLH is made an explicit part of the theory, however, these proposals are replaced by alternative analyses. For example, Selkirk (1980) allowed (or at least considered the possibility of) structures like (6.43), which violate the SLH, but Selkirk (1984) proposed to ban them:

(6.43)

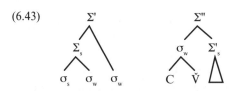

Similarly, the 'grid-only' models of prosodic structure proposed by Prince (1983) and developed by Selkirk (1984) may be said to differ from the grids of Liberman and Prince (1977) precisely by incorporating the SLH: Liberman and Prince's purely relational grid is of indeterminate depth, whereas the Prince/Selkirk grid has exactly five well-defined levels. Or again, in developing their model of Prosodic Phonology, Nespor and Vogel started out (1982, 1983) allowing (indeed, making crucial use of) structures like (6.44),

(6.44)

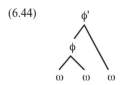

but by the time of their monograph (1986), these structures are explicitly proscribed, and the SLH (as stated in their principles 1 and 2, p. 7) is said to be 'relatively uncontroversial'.

These developments point to the conclusion that fixed depth of prosodic structure, far from being one of the empirical foundations of the SLH, has rather been forced on theorists by the SLH itself. Close inspection of any given phonological phenomenon repeatedly seems to 'reveal' additional layers of structure. In my view, what is really happening is that close inspection reveals differences of boundary strength. Investigating prosodic structure while maintaining the SLH therefore involves a balancing act in interpreting observed differences of boundary strength: on the one hand, one wants to allow for one's careful observations, but on the other hand, a steady increase in the number of prosodic categories makes for implausible depth of structure in simple cases, and, worse, it significantly weakens the independent definability of the prosodic categories one posits.[15]

6.3.2   *Evidence for the indeterminate depth of prosodic structure*
So long as the observations of boundary strength differences are impressionistic, it is possible to dismiss them as syntactically induced illusions or explain them away in other ways. But as we have just seen, there is also an increasing amount of instrumental evidence for such differences. Perhaps

the clearest illustration of the effect of the SLH on the interpretation of boundary strength data is provided by the results of a study that I carried out some years ago (Ladd 1988).

The study involved sentences of the form *A and B but C* and *A but B and C*, where *A*, *B*, and *C* are clauses of roughly similar syntactic and accentual structure, such as:

(6.45)a. Warren is a stronger campaigner, and Ryan has more popular policies, but Allen has a lot more money.

  b. Warren is a stronger campaigner, but Ryan has more popular policies, and Allen has a lot more money.

The most natural interpretation of these sentences treats the *but* boundary as stronger – that is, in (6.45a) it opposes the conjunction of *A and B* to *C*, while in (6.45b) it opposes *A* to the conjunction of *B and C*. Graphically:

(6.46) a.   b.

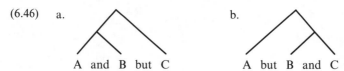

In multiple readings of these sentences by four speakers, I found evidence of F_0 declination during each clause and across the entire sequence of three clauses; each clause ended with a clear boundary tone. It therefore seems appropriate to treat each clause as an intonational phrase, and the whole thing as an Utterance. Given standard assumptions about prosodic structure including the SLH, we might therefore diagram the structure of these utterances as follows:

(6.47)

In line with the standard motivations for the SLH, this structure is 'flatter' than the structures in (6.46).

In addition to the clear phonetic evidence for dividing up the Utterance into three intonational phrases, however, I also found phonetic differences that reflect the hierarchical organisation shown in (6.46). Specifically, the initial peaks of clauses B and C were higher after a *but* boundary than after an *and* boundary. Moreover, the pauses preceding *but* boundaries were by and large longer than those preceding *and* boundaries. That is, both the F_0 cues and the pause-duration cues agree in signalling that the *but* boundaries are 'stronger'.

Unfortunately, the most obvious ways of representing this difference of boundary strength are both ruled out by the SLH:

(6.48)   Recursive node

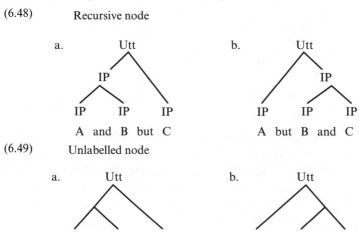

a.   Utt

IP

IP IP IP

A and B but C

b.   Utt

IP

IP IP IP

A but B and C

(6.49)   Unlabelled node

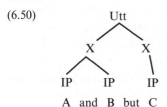

a.   Utt

IP IP IP

A and B but C

b.   Utt

IP IP IP

A but B and C

This is because, as we noted earlier, the only differences of boundary strength permitted by the SLH are differences of boundary type. In order to represent the hierarchical organisation of (6.46) without violating the SLH, we must come up with a new domain type for the intermediate layer of structure between the root Utterance node and the string of three IP nodes:

(6.50)   Utt

X   X

IP IP IP

A and B but C

If we restrict our analysis to recognised domain types, we must as it were slide them up or down the tree in order to accommodate the demands of the SLH. For example, we might treat the conjunction of clauses A and B as an Utterance, and analyse the whole structure as a Paragraph:

(6.51)   Para

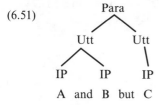

Utt   Utt

IP IP IP

A and B but C

Alternatively, we could treat the conjunction of clauses A and B as an IP, which then forces us to treat the individual clauses as intermediate phrases (ip):

(6.52)

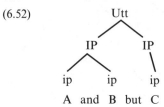

A   and   B   but   C

But there is no independent motivation for any of these solutions. They all weaken the independent phonetic definitions of prosodic domain types: (6.51) makes it difficult to give a consistent definition of Utterance: (6.52) makes it difficult to give a consistent definition of intermediate phrase; and (6.50) posits an intermediate phonetic category for which there is no independent evidence – and *a fortiori* no phonetic definition. In all cases the justification for the intermediate layer of structure is entirely theory-internal – to avoid building a tree that violates the SLH.

6.3.3   Compound prosodic domains

If we wish to account for the evidence of fine differences of boundary strength while at the same time keeping the number of prosodic domain types to a minimum of independently motivated categories, then we have no choice but to get rid of the SLH in its present form. I propose to take this conclusion at face value, and to show that the SLH can be modified to accommodate observed differences of boundary strength. The key to making any such modification work is to allow for the existence of phonetic cues to indeterminate depth of structure while at the same time preserving the intuition that prosodic structure is somehow flatter than the syntatctic structure to which it corresponds. That is, I believe it is important to express the intuition that there is some essential difference between syntactic and prosodic structure; I take it that what we need to do is to weaken or relax the SLH, not (as I proposed in Ladd 1986) to abandon it altogether. The theoretical construct that makes this balancing act possible is what I have elsewhere (Ladd 1992b) called a Compound Prosodic Domain (CPD).

A CPD is a prosodic domain of a given type X whose immediate constituents *are themselves of type X*:

(6.53)   X
          ╱‾‾╲
        X   X

This is precisely the structure usually assumed for compounds in morphosyntax, and the analogy is intentional. A compound noun like *telephone call* is made up of two independently occurring nouns *telephone* and *call*, but at the same time functions exactly like a single noun; the definition of noun is not compromised by the existence of such compounds. In the same way, [*A and B*] in (6.46) can be treated for certain purposes as a single IP, even though at the same time we recognise that it is composed of the two IPs *A* and *B*. As with morphosyntactic compounds, this analysis need not compromise the definitions of domain types: in particular, definitions in terms of boundaries can apply to simple and to compound domains in exactly the same way. That is, the right edges of both the simple IP [*B*] and the compound IP [*A and B*] are marked by a single boundary tone, as specified by Pierrehumbert and Beckman's definition of an IP. The fact that it is the very same boundary tone and the very same edge is of no consequence to the definitions. We may therefore diagram the prosodic structures corresponding to the two readings of (6.46) as in (6.48), that is, with a compound IP dominating either [*A and B*] or [*B and C*].

Strictly speaking, the notion of CPD involves recursive structure. If prosodic domains can be compound, then the depth of prosodic trees cannot be determinate, and this is clearly incompatible with the SLH. However, compounding is a limited kind of recursiveness. So long as the indeterminate depth of prosodic trees arises only through compounding and in no other way, then prosodic structure is still crucially different from syntactic structure, because the devices that create indeterminate depth in syntactic trees are richer and more powerful than compounding alone. There is no prosodic analogue to the sort of recursiveness seen in syntax whereby, for example, a sentence can contain noun phrases which in turn can contain sentences. Under the CPD proposal, there remains a clear sense in which phrases are 'higher' or more inclusive than feet, and feet are higher than syllables. *The categories of the prosodic hierarchy are still strictly ranked.* This means that, even if we allow CPDs, we are still able to express the 'flatness' of prosodic structure relative to syntax, and therefore do not lose the only important empirical advantage of the SLH.

On the other hand, if we allow CPDs, the empirical basis of the overall theory of prosodic phrasing is considerably strengthened. The notion of CPD allows us to accommodate decades of observations that have been forced into the straitjacket of 'big IPs vs. little IPs', and to reconsider the early proposals by Liberman and Prince, Selkirk, and Nespor and Vogel on the ways in which prosodic domains can be related to each other. It almost certainly means that the number of prosodic domain types can be reduced rather than continually expanded: for example, Nespor and Vogel's 'clitic group' might be treated as a 'compound phonological word'. More relevantly for the topic of this book, we might also consider the possibility that the 'intermediate phrase' is nothing more than the smallest prosodic unit that can have a tune, and that the distinction between the intermediate phrase and the intonational phrase can be eliminated. Lack of space unfortunately prevents me from exploring these possibilities here.

In any case, such a reduction in the number of prosodic domain types would substantially strengthen the definitions of prosodic domains. It would allow us to identify any given boundary as being of one category or another on purely phonetic and phonological grounds, without as it were looking over our shoulder at the theoretical consequences for prosodic structure or for syntax–prosody mapping. For example, it would allow us to treat the boundary after *house* in (6.40) above as being of the same type as the others (because it is marked by the same fall in pitch after the H* accent, and the same preboundary lengthening of the segments), but to recognise that it is also 'weaker' than the others, in the sense that it demarcates two domains (*that lay in the house* and *that Jack built*) that form a compound domain.

6.3.4   *Some descriptive consequences*
In this section I briefly sketch two specific cases where recognising the existence of CPDs helps resolve a descriptive dilemma. The first has to do with the application of 'the same' tune to utterances with different metrical structures, which we discussed in section 6.1. The second returns to the relation between primary accent and focus, which we dealt with in section 6.2.

6.3.4.1   Abstract tunes revisited
One of the most widely ignored problems in intonational phonology is the problem of *dependencies* between intonational phrases, such as the intonational dependency between main sentences and tags briefly mentioned in section 6.1.4 above. Various writers have alluded to these problems (e.g. my own very brief discussion in Ladd 1980a: section 7.5); the most extensive discussion is Crystal's discussion of 'intonational subordination' (Crystal 1969: section 5.10, reprinted in Bolinger 1972a: 126–35), but there is no convincing account of how such dependencies work anywhere in the literature. As I argued in Ladd 1986, relaxing the Strict Layer Hypothesis makes it possible to consider a range of possible prosodic structures that

may help to make sense of these dependencies.[16] Here I wish to discuss one case that seems to exemplify the relevance of CPDs to the understanding of tune–text association, namely the case of what I call *compound contours*.

It is not hard to demonstrate that 'compound contour' is a useful notion. Consider the contrast between the following two English contours, illustrated on a single short phrase:

(6.54) a. L*   H* L L%
         Mary and Peter

     b. H*   !H* L L%
          Mary and Peter

The context might be a discussion of whom to invite as the fourth couple for a dinner party: (6.54a), with the 'surprise-redundancy contour' (Liberman 1975) suggests a sudden inspiration ('Why, I know who we can invite!'), while (6.54b), with extreme 'final lowering' of the nuclear accent on *Peter*, suggests rather the final decision of the person with the final say on the matter ('I say this is who we'll invite'). The same distinction applies to the following two utterances, each of which consists of two phrases:

(6.55) a. L* H H% H* L   L%
        If Mary goes, Peter can go.

     b. H* H H% !H* L   L%
        If Mary goes, Peter can go.

Here the context might be a discussion of a children's outing of some sort. In (6.55a), the problem is that Peter is too young to go on his own; the speaker has had the sudden inspiration that Peter's big sister Mary could go, which in turn solves the problem ('Why, this makes it possible for Peter to go'). In (6.55b), the problem is rather that Peter thinks he is too old for whatever is being planned and does not want to go with his little sister Mary; the speaker – as in the previous example, someone with the final authority – is fed up with dealing with the siblings' disputes and makes a determination that Peter is to accompany Mary ('I say Peter should go'). If, at some level of description, we can treat the contours on (6.55a) and (6.55b) as being the same as those on (6.54a) and (6.54b), then this similarity of intonational nuance poses no theoretical problem. If, on the other hand, the phonology is prevented in principle from treating the contours in (6.55) as compound units that are identical to the simple units in (6.54), then the similarity of meaning is, in rigorous theoretical terms, accidental.

The significance of compound contours to these two problems of tune–text association is to show clearly that the abstract identity of the tune does not reside in the string of tones. If the surprise-redundancy tune can be manifested either as a sequence L*..H*..L..L% (on a single phrase), or as a sequence L*..H..H%..H*..L..L% (on the two constituent phrases of a compound phrase), then the surface differences between the two sequences of tones must be seen as low-level differences conditioned by prosodic structure. Once we admit the notion of CPDs, and specifically compound tunes, that is, we have further evidence that tonal specifications are abstract properties of IPs, and that the surface string of accents and edge tones is a concrete and quite predictable consequence of a general process of tune–text association.

6.3.4.2   Primary accent and focus

The notion of CPDs also sheds some light on the most notable remaining problem in striking a balance between the paradigmatic and syntagmatic aspects of prominence. Recall that in section 6.2, I drew attention to the deep connection among focus, primary accent, and the division into intermediate phrases. What I did not point out is that there are plenty of cases where primary accent fails to signal focus. One such case involves the distinction between 'epithet' and 'literal' interpretations of words like *butcher* and *bastard*. In Ladd (1980a: 64ff.), I discussed a series of examples showing that one function of deaccenting is to favour the 'epithet' reading.[17] This is seen in the following example:

(6.56)   A: Everything OK after your operation?

B: Don't talk to me about it! I'd like to STRANGLE the butcher!

Deaccenting makes it possible to treat *butcher* in this exchange as an epithet referring to the doctor who performed the operation. Absence of deaccenting – that is, the sentence stress pattern that in most contexts would be interpreted as signalling neutral broad focus – turns B's contribution into an incoherent rant about a literal butcher, someone who sells meat:

(6.57)   A: Everything OK after your operation?

B: Don't talk to me about it! I'd like to strangle the BUTCHER!

As I also noted in Ladd 1980a, the same distinction between epithet and literal meanings can be signalled by the *type* of accent, when the word in question is not sentence-final. With a secondary H* accent (what I called a 'B accent' in my original discussion, following Bolinger), the noun can have the epithet reading:[18]

(6.58)   A: Everything OK after your operation?

        B: Don't talk to me about it!

> H*   H* L L%
> The butcher charged me a thousand bucks!

With a primary accent (a Bolinger 'A accent'; in Pierrehumbert's terms a H* accent followed by an intermediate phrase boundary and a L phrase tone), we again have the reference to the man who sells meat:

(6.59)   A: Everything OK after your operation?

        B: Don't talk to me about it!

> H* L   H*   H* L L%
> The butcher charged me a thousand bucks!

So far, these observations are consistent with a modified FTA view whereby focus is signalled only by *primary* accent. In Pierrehumbert's terms, we might say that in (6.58), B's entire sentence *The butcher charged me a thousand bucks* is a single intermediate phrase, and the accent on *butcher* is therefore secondary. In (6.59), on the other hand, *The butcher* is a separate intermediate phrase, so that *butcher* by definition bears a primary accent, which in turn means that it cannot be interpreted as deaccented.

This analysis breaks down, however, in a very emphatic rendition of the sentence. If we put primary accents on all four content words – that is, if we divide the sentence into four intermediate phrases – then the epithet interpretation of *butcher* is once again favoured:

(6.60)   A: Everything OK after your operation?

        B: Don't talk to me about it!

> H* L   H*   L   H* L   H* L L%
> The butcher charged me a thousand bucks!

Here, *primary* accent is being used to signal the *epithet* reading. Intuitively, what seems to be happening is that in (6.59), *butcher* is separate enough from the prosody of the rest of the sentence that it counts as its own local maximum – this is essentially the same explanation as saying that it occurs as its own intermediate phrase – whereas in (6.58) and (6.60) the prominence of the accent on *butcher* is evaluated relative to the accents elsewhere in the sentence, and the local maximum for the sentence as a whole is on *bucks*.

There is no way to incorporate this intuition into a revised accent-first theory in which focus is signalled by primary accent. The intuitive explanation in terms of 'separateness' is readily identifiable with the notion of 'boundary strength': somehow the boundary between *butcher* and the rest of the sentence is 'stronger' in (6.59) than it is in (6.58) and (6.60). What all the epithet cases have in common is that *butcher* bears a degree of prominence that is in some sense *relatively less prominent* than some other accent in the utterance; but that idea cannot be reconciled with the observation that the boundary between *butcher* and the rest of the sentence is an intermediate phrase boundary in (6.59) and (6.60) but not in (6.58).

The traditional solution to this kind of problem, as I noted in section 6.3.1, is to say that the phonetic cues to phrase boundaries are mysterious and elusive. If we take refuge in the difficulty of identifying prosodic boundaries, we can salvage some kind of account of focus based on primary accent. Specifically, we can say that the accents in (6.60), which fail to signal focus, are not really primary; they are not really primary because the valleys we identified as phrase boundaries are not really phrase boundaries. (They could instead be the manifestation of a 'sagging transition' (see section 3.5.2).) The problem with this solution is, once again, that it weakens the independent phonetic basis of our whole analysis.

With the notion of CPD, we are not forced into this position. Instead, we simply treat each emphatic accent in (6.60) as the primary accent of a *local* intermediate phrase, but at the same time treat the entire sentence as a compound intermediate phrase in which *bucks* is the nucleus and *butcher* is prenuclear. That is, we would diagram (6.58)–(6.60) as follows:

(6.61)   (corresponds to (6.58))

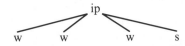

The butcher charged me a thousand bucks

(6.62)   (corresponds to (6.59))

The butcher charged me a thousand bucks

(6.63)   (corresponds to (6.60))

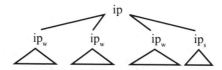

The butcher charged me a thousand bucks

This allows us both to maintain the definition of intermediate phrase and to express the differences of syntagmatic structure that seem to be involved in determining the interpretation of *butcher*. Obviously, if this proposal is to have real explanatory value, it will be necessary to constrain the range of circumstances in which we can posit compound intermediate phrases; ideally, we will be able to identify phonetic characteristics of compound domains as well as simple domains. The point here is to suggest the notion of CPDs as a way forward, a basis for future research.

7 Pitch range

Pitch is an anomalous phonetic feature. In dealing with segmental speech sounds, we have many points of reference that are essentially valid for all speakers, and there are well-established taxonomic frameworks for both articulatory and acoustic aspects of segmental sounds. There is a measure of inter-speaker variability, but it does not affect the usefulness – or the explicitness – of descriptions like 'high back unrounded vowel' or 'bandwidth of second formant 80 Hz'. For pitch, such fixed terms of reference are largely lacking: pitch differs conspicuously from speaker to speaker (e.g. male vs. female speech), from occasion to occasion (e.g. bored vs. angry speech), and even from one part of an utterance to another (e.g. 'declination' and other similar effects). This appears to mean that we must provide characterisations that are explicitly *relative*.

The question is, relative to what? There are two obvious ways of thinking about the relative nature of pitch features: they may be relative to the speaker's voice, or they may be relative to other parts of an utterance. For reasons that will become clear presently, I will refer to these two approaches as *normalising* and *initialising* respectively. The proper balance between these two points of view has long been a point of contention – or just plain confusion – in theoretical discussions of the phonology of pitch.

7.1 The relativity of pitch in phonological theory

7.1.1 *'Suprasegmental' features and the initialising approach*
The need for some relativity in the characterisation of pitch features is the source of the idea that pitch is somehow an intrinsically relational or syntagmatic feature, which can be correctly interpreted only when there is movement or change. This idea, widespread in phonology as well as in phonetics, was explicitly discussed by Jakobson, Fant, and Halle (1952). Their influential scheme of distinctive features posited a fundamental divide between *inherent* features (the vowel and consonant features, which

252

are supposed to be characterisable in absolute acoustic terms) from *prosodic* features (features of pitch, stress, and duration, which depend for their definition on acoustic change or contrast within the context of the utterance). Jakobson, Fant, and Halle claim that any 'opposition of inherent distinctive features [is] definable without any reference to the sequence. No comparison of two points in a time series is involved. Prosodic features, on the other hand, can be defined only with reference to a time series' (p. 13). With specific reference to pitch, they approvingly quote Pike (1948: 18), who says that 'the important feature is the relative height of a syllable in relation to the preceding or following syllables'.

Jakobson, Fant, and Halle's distinction between inherent and prosodic features corresponds almost perfectly with the American structuralist distinction between segmental and suprasegmental phonemes (e.g. Lehiste 1970). Among other things, the general understanding of pitch features implied by the segmental–suprasegmental (or inherent–prosodic) split is what underlies the 'configurations' position in the 'levels-vs.-configurations' debate (cf. section 2.3.1). The 'configurations' point of view describes pitch contours in terms of elements that are intrinsically relational, like 'rise early in the stressed syllable': a rise is a rise, and remains a rise whether it moves from 90 Hz to 120 Hz in a low male voice or from 200 Hz to 450 Hz in an animated female voice. There is no need to refer to pitch level, and hence no need to deal with range differences anywhere in the description.

More generally, the Jakobson–Fant–Halle phonological theory can best be implemented in what I am calling an 'initialising' description of pitch phonetics. Such a description attempts to provide invariant characterisations of all tones in terms of *what has preceded in the utterance*. (To give an oversimplified illustration, it might state that H tone is realised 6 semitones higher than an immediately preceding L and half a semitone lower than an immediately preceding H.) The only thing such a model requires in order to derive actual F_0 values is an initial state for each utterance. It does not ever need to refer to characteristics of the speaker's range; all it needs is a starting point, and each successive target can be specified with respect to what has gone before. For example, in such a model low rise could be distinguished from high rise by the fact that the former starts lower than what precedes and the latter starts higher. This was an explicit part of Bolinger's definitions of English pitch accent types or 'profiles' (Bolinger 1958, 1986), which are all expressed in terms of pitch change to or from the accented syllable.

The initialising approach is clearly capable of modelling many aspects of F_0: for example, it can readily be used to describe local modifications of pitch range for emphasis, changes of topic, and the like. This idea was developed extensively by Crystal (1969: 143–52). In Crystal's transcription system, each syllable bears one of either five or seven possible relations to the immediately preceding syllable: same level, slightly higher, slightly lower, much higher, much lower, and (for stressed syllables only) very much higher, and very much lower. Furthermore, these distinctions can cooccur with what Crystal calls 'step-up' and 'step-down', which affect the overall level of a whole stretch of speech (such as a parenthetical phrase). In addition, each distinctive pitch movement (the nuclear tones) may span a range that is classed as normal, wide, or narrow, according to the distance between its beginning point and its endpoint. By combining these dimensions of variation, Crystal is able to transcribe a remarkable amount of phonetic detail without any reference to absolute F_0 levels or to the limits of the speaker's range.

7.1.2   *Problems with the initialising approach*

There are well-known problems with the Jakobson–Fant–Halle point of view, however, and with the notion of a fundamental split between 'suprasegmental' and 'segmental' phenomena. The most important of these problems is the existence of languages with level tone phonemes, like Yoruba. If we adopt a syntagmatic view, then we will have to define these tone phonemes relative to each other: for example, within some domain to be identified, H is higher than M, which is higher than L. But this definition cannot always be applied in a given utterance. In many such languages it is quite possible to have utterances that consist of only a single syllable with a single tone, or of a string of syllables all having the same tone. The following Yoruba examples are from Connell and Ladd 1990:

(7.1)   a.   (all-high)
Wón tún gbé túwó wá.
'They brought tuwo again.'

b.   (all-mid)
Omo wọn ni e lo fi se oko.
'It is their son that you marry.'

c.   (all-low)
Èwù ònà Àrà ò tàn.
'The colour of the garments on the way to Ara is dull.'

Such cases pose a problem for the formal distinction between inherent and prosodic features: if H can only be defined as locally higher than M or L, then it remains undefined in an utterance with only H tones.[1]

A second phenomenon that suggests the usefulness of defining pitch level relative to the speaker's voice range is the existence of distinctions like 'high rise' vs. 'low rise'. Such distinctions are posited in many intonational descriptions which in theory are based on pitch movement alone. The IPO model of Dutch intonation, for instance, draws a distinction between a Type A Fall, which falls to the bottom of the range, and a Type E Fall, which is a partial or incomplete fall. Many traditional British descriptions of English intonation (beginning with Palmer 1922) distinguish high rise from low rise, and some (notably O'Connor and Arnold 1973) distinguish high fall from low fall. Although, as we just saw, Bolinger and others have tried to define these in syntagmatic terms, we will probably have to acknowledge that, for example, a 'low rise' is low relative to the speaker's overall voice range, and that therefore some way of phonetically characterising levels within the speaker's range is ultimately needed.[2]

These and other problems formed the basis of Leben's extensive critique (1973) of the suprasegmental concept. In many respects, autosegmental phonology, building on Leben's work, has abandoned the idea of a fundamental distinction between segmental and suprasegmental. One obvious illustration of this is the fact that autosegmental analyses of lexical tone do not assume that the primitives of pitch systems must involve change or movement. If anything, they strive to express all pitch contrasts in terms of static level tones. Even in the description of languages like Chinese, where the motivations for referring to pitch movements are strong (Pike 1948; Wang 1967; Gandour 1978), autosegmental analyses have always favoured treating contour tones as sequences of level targets like H and L (e.g. Woo 1969; Anderson 1978). Only recently have autosegmental analysts (notably Yip 1989) begun to look for ways of referring to the contour as a unit, while still retaining the notion of level targets (roughly speaking, this analysis treats contour tones as analogous to diphthongs, affricates, and other 'complex segments') – and even this idea has recently come under attack (Duanmu 1994).

There is also a more fundamental way in which autosegmental and metrical theory have moved away from Jakobson, Fant, and Halle's view. In autosegmental representations, pitch features are exactly like segmental features. This can be seen in the use of the term 'melodic' to refer to both kinds of features, as well as in the analogy between contour tones and diphthongs just mentioned. Stress and duration, on the other hand, are treated in current non-linear phonology in terms of the structural properties of phonological strings, rather than as features or elements of the strings themselves. Traditional suprasegmentals – or the Jakobsonian prosodic features – do not form any sort of natural class within this theoretical picture: if we were to express autosegmental views in Jakobsonian terms, then we would certainly say that pitch is an inherent feature, and that the only prosodic features are stress and duration.

7.1.3   Normalising models

The theoretical considerations just discussed suggest that we should explore the possibilities of a normalising rather than an initialising model of pitch range. A normalising model reifies the notion of 'pitch range' in terms of some speaker-specific reference points, such as upper and lower F_0 values. Such a model attempts to abstract away from differences between speakers, paralinguistic effects, and so on, and expresses the invariant characterisations of tones in terms of the *idealised speaker range* that results from this process of factoring out sources of variation. For example, instead of stating that H tone is realised some distance higher than L, it might state that H tone is realised at the top of the speaker's current range. The tonal specifications in such a model will make no reference to the phonetic context of the utterance: the beginning of a low-rise configuration will have its lowness defined relative to the idealised range, not – as in an initialising model – to some preceding pitch level.

Probably the simplest possible normalising model would specify the highest and lowest values of an individual's overall speaking range, and define the phonetics of F_0 relative to these points. This was the approach taken by Earle (1975) in his study of lexical tones in monosyllabic Vietnamese words. Assigning a value of 100 to the top of each speaker's 'average F_0 range' and 0 to the bottom, Earle defines the citation forms of each of the six lexical tone contours in terms of movement along the percentage scale defined for each speaker. Rose (1987), in his study of Wu Chinese, takes a somewhat different approach: his normalised speaker-specific scale is based on a z-score transform[3] rather than on the top and the bottom of the range, and indeed he argues that such a normalisation is superior to Earle's. In both cases, however, the conclusion is essentially the same. *Normalised descriptions of the tone contours show a high degree of inter-speaker agreement.* Results from Earle and Rose are shown in figure 7.1.

What both normalisations provide is a phonetic description that is not based on the utterance context but is nevertheless *quantitative* and *explicit*. For example, in Earle's definition, Vietnamese Tone 3 starts at about 28 per cent, rises slightly to about 30 per cent by the midpoint of the syllable, and then rises sharply to about 80 per cent by the end of the syllable. This compares to Tone 2, which starts about 35 per cent, rises to above 50 per cent by the midpoint, and reaches 100 per cent at the end. Both are 'rises' and both span much of the speaking range, but the normalised description makes it possible to state precisely how they differ in terms that are valid for all speakers.

Slightly adapting the terminology of Chomsky and Halle (1968), one might refer to such normalised descriptions of pitch levels within a speaker's range as *systematic phonetic* representations.[4] Perhaps the most obvious objection to the idea of a 'systematic phonetics' of pitch range is that it is not clear how listeners might identify phonetic specifications like 'top of current range'. But as we saw above (see note 1), listeners in at least some languages can do this kind of thing, and there are lots of obvious candidates for what the acoustic cues might be (e.g. subtle phonation differences at different parts of the overall range). And in any case, the theoretical problems with initialising models suggest that trying to construct a normalising model may be worth the effort.

In the context of the discussion in this book, there is an even more obvious reason to be sceptical of normalising models. Earle's and Rose's studies deal only with monosyllabic citation forms in tone languages, which is probably the likeliest place to find regularities of this sort, and our main concern here is intonation. Yet numerous studies of longer utterances in European intonation languages point to the same conclusion reached by Earle and Rose: the scaling of pitch targets is highly systematic. For this reason I think it is worth pursuing the goal of trying to give quantitative description of tonal realisation on some speaker-specific normalised scale. The next section reviews some of the empirical findings on which any such approach to normalisation will have to be based.

7.2   The phonetics of pitch range variation

In this section we will consider two principal sources of pitch range variation that have been investigated experimentally. These are inter-speaker differences and within-speaker paralinguistic range modification. It is worth briefly sketching what is involved in both, and why it seems appropriate to try to model them using some sort of normalisation.

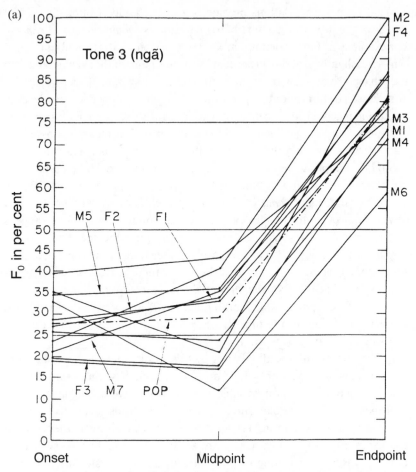

(a)

Figure 7.1 Normalised lexical tone contours. Panel (a), from Earle 1975, shows average starting, middle, and ending points for the Vietnamese tone 3, based on multiple readings by twelve different speakers, plotted on a normalised percentage scale that treats the bottom of each speaker's range as 0 and the top as 100. Panel (b), from Rose 1987, shows pitch traces for Wu Chinese tones 1 and 3 for seven different speakers, plotted on a normalised z-score scale that treats the speaker's mean F_0 as 0 and defines scale units in terms of the standard deviations around each speaker's mean.

A conspicuous difference between pitch and other phonetic phenomena, as we have already seen, is that it shows a great deal of meaningful inter-speaker variation. Inter-speaker differences do exist in segmental phonetics as well (e.g. average formant values differ slightly between adult

(b)

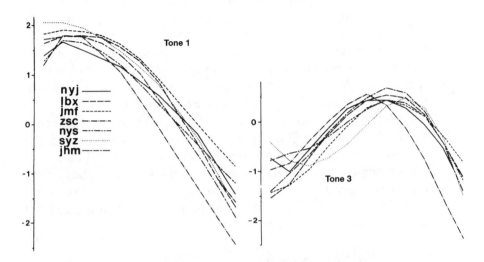

males, adult females, and children), but ordinary listeners (or even trained listeners) are generally unaware of them, and for many purposes they can be completely ignored. Inter-speaker differences of pitch, by contrast, are well known to everyone, and in some cultures may be exaggerated as markers of gender or status. Yet in some sense, none of this variation affects the linguistic message: in principle, anybody can say anything, irrespective of sex, age, or any other physical characteristics. It is therefore reasonable for a phonetic description of intonation to incorporate some sort of normalisation that abstracts away from differences due to this source.

The search for a normalisation is complicated, however, by the fact that the pitch range can also be *modified* within the speech of any one speaker, for a variety of paralinguistic or other communicative purposes. For example, the voice can be raised in anger, or to express surprise, or simply to make oneself heard in a noisy room; it can be lowered if the speaker is depressed, or to express confidentiality, or simply to keep from waking the children. As with inter-speaker differences, it would seem that at least some of this variation is independent of the linguistic message: it seems possible to say anything with the voice raised that can be said with the voice lowered. Some normalisation of these differences also therefore seems appropriate.

In trying to normalise away from such modification, however, we quickly run into difficulties distinguishing what is linguistic from what is paralinguistic. It is by no means clear that differences in pitch range that result from deliberately raising the voice to be heard in noise are the same – either acoustically or semiotically – as the changes in pitch range that accompany the expression of anger. In this case, interpreting the results of experimental work not only requires us to see if a normalisation is possible, but also to decide which features should be abstracted away from in the normalisation, and which should be preserved in the linguistic analysis.

I will return to the issue of what is linguistic and what is not in section 7.3. In this section I will concentrate on differences that are unarguably extralinguistic – differences between speakers – and on global differences of pitch range within speakers that result from the deliberate raising or lowering of the voice. I hope to show that, for these sources of variation, a normalising model is both possible and well supported empirically, and that the broad outlines of such a model are clear.

7.2.1   Overall level and span

The first thing to point out is that 'pitch range' is not a single variable. Inspection of comparable F_0 data from different speakers reveals two partially independent dimensions of variation: differences of overall level, and differences in what I propose to call *span* (the range of frequencies used). If we compare a low male voice with a normal female voice, we may find no overlap at all in the F_0 ranges – say 60–140 Hz for the male and 180–340 for the female. Whatever other differences analysis may reveal, the female voice is unambiguously *higher*: the most conspicuous difference between the two is one of *overall level*. But if we compare male with male or female with female, it is often difficult to say which is higher, because the range of one may be entirely included in the range of another. For example, suppose male speaker A has a range of 100–160 Hz and speaker B has a range of 80–200 Hz. Whether we have a difference of overall level is a matter of definition: if we compare the lower extremes, then A has the higher range; if we compare upper extremes, then B has the higher range; and if we compare means, they would come out about the same. The difference between them is above all one of *span*: 60 Hz (or 8.1 semitones) for speaker A, and 120 Hz (or 15.9 semitones) for speaker B.

One of the reasons why level and span are often not clearly distinguished is that they co-vary: broadly speaking, the higher the level, the wider the span. This covariation is often taken to justify logarithmic transformation of F_0 values, especially in comparing male and female voices. For example, given a male speaker whose normal range spans 80 Hz, 80–160 Hz, and a female speaker whose range spans 160 Hz, 160–320 Hz, we will say that the female speaker's range is twice that of the male speaker's if we express the range in Hz (160 Hz vs. 80 Hz), but that they are the same width – one octave or 12 semitones – if we express the range logarithmically (160/80 = 320/160 = 2). Nevertheless, as we shall see in more detail below, not all of the observable differences of span can be mathematically transformed out of existence. Whatever their differences in F_0 level, some speakers use a fairly wide span and others a comparatively narrow one. Any pitch range model must therefore treat the two separately; the choice of measurement unit is a separate issue.[5] Moreover, by distinguishing level and span in this way I do not mean to imply that they are the only relevant differences between speakers; see, for example, Henton's discussions (1989, 1995) of 'pitch dynamism' in female and male speech.

A related reason that level and span are often conflated is that *modifications* of level may be difficult to distinguish from modifications of span, and 'raising the voice' may involve modifications of both. For example, in a language like English where most accents are marked by pitch peaks (or H tones), raising and widening will be difficult to distinguish empirically, since the effect of both is to raise high tones. Furthermore, if the appropriate scale for pitch range is logarithmic or otherwise non-linear, then the top of the range will be more greatly affected by raising the overall level than the bottom, and on a linear scale will appear to involve span expansion as well. However, we can show that the distinction is clear in principle on the basis of a hypothetical lexical tone language with three invariant level tones H, M, and L. If the overall level is raised, the realisation of all three tones will go up. If the span is expanded while holding M constant, then H will go up and L will go down. If overall level is raised and span widened at the same time, L may stay the same or even go up, and M and H will go up even more. This is shown in figure 7.2.

7.2.2   *Experimental studies of pitch range*

This section reviews the findings of several experimental studies of pitch range variation in European intonation languages. Before considering these studies in detail, it will be useful to outline in a general way what such studies are looking for, and in particular to sketch what we might expect to find if Earle's or Rose's results for tonal citation forms can be generalised to intonation.

As we saw, Earle compared the scaling of three points in each tone

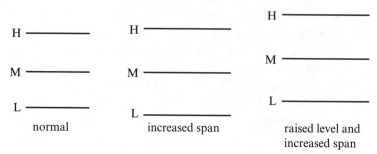

Figure 7.2 Distinction between level and span, illustrated with respect to a hypothetical tone language with three invariant level tones H, M, and L.

contour – three targets, to use the terminology of chapters 2 and 3. He found that, by defining a speaker-specific percentage scale, he could give a quantitative definition of the scaling of the targets that was approximately valid for all speakers. If the idea of 'the unity of pitch phonology' (section 4.4) is valid, then we would expect to find similar consistencies in the scaling of targets across speakers in utterances in the European languages. For example, consider the sentence

(7.2)

I've been there before.

spoken with the neutral declarative intonation shown. We might identify four targets, an initial L, an accentual H* on *been* and an immediately following L that creates the 'elbow' on *there*, and a final L%. Hypothetical non-normalised data for these four targets as spoken by three speakers are shown in figure 7.3. It can be seen that there is one male speaker and two female speakers, one of whom has a wide span and the other of whom has a narrow span. However, if we normalise the three individual pitch ranges so that the H* represents 100 per cent and the L% represents 0 per cent, then for all three speakers the four target points come out the same, as shown in figure 7.4. This is the kind of finding that would support a normalising model.

With this introduction, let us now turn to some experimental results. First let us look at studies of the same contour spoken by different speakers. If certain targets are scaled by all speakers at the same level on their own speaker-specific scale, then we would expect to find a high correlation between the target values of one speaker and those of another. This expectation is borne out by data from several studies, including Thorsen 1980b, 1981, Liberman and Pierrehumbert 1984, and Ladd and Terken 1995.

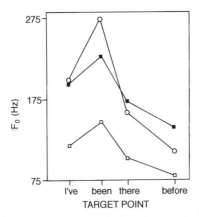

Figure 7.3 Hypothetical average data for four target points in three speakers' pronunciation of the English declarative sentence *I've been there before*. The contours are impressionistically similar despite differences of level and span.

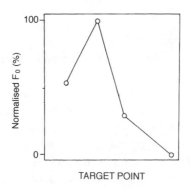

Figure 7.4 The hypothetical data from figure 7.3, replotted on a normalised percentage scale of the sort used by Earle 1975. The normalisation abstracts away from the differences of level and span seen in figure 7.3.

Here I consider in detail data from two studies of Standard Danish by Nina Grønnum (published as Thorsen 1980b, 1981; I am grateful to Nina Grønnum for making the raw data available to me). In both studies Grønnum recorded six readings by four different speakers of eight different sentences. The sentences range in length from one pitch accent to eight pitch accents. For each sentence, I have taken the targets to be the beginning and ending F_0 values, and the valley and peak associated with each pitch accent. For each speaker I have thus considered 160 targets (2 studies × (2 targets per accent for (1+2+3+4+5+6+7+8) accents + a beginning

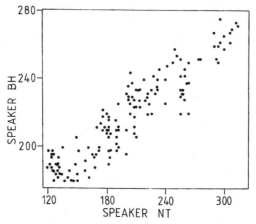

Figure 7.5 Correlation between target F_0 values in two speakers' readings of the same sentences in Grønnum's studies of Danish sentence intonation (Thorsen 1980b, 1981). Each value plotted is the mean of six repetitions. For more detail see text.

and an end target for each of 8 sentences)). For each target I have taken the mean of a speaker's six repetitions to represent the intended F_0 level for that target for that speaker.

Figure 7.5 plots all the average target values for one speaker against those for another speaker. In a general way, what this plot shows is that a target that is very low in one speaker's range will be very low in another's; a target that is moderately high for one will be moderately high for another; and so on. The correlation between the target values for the two speakers shown in figure 7.5 is an extremely high 0.92. For all pairs of speakers in Grønnum's two studies the correlations are never below 0.89.

In collaboration with Elizabeth Shriberg and Jacques Terken, I have recently undertaken a large-scale study of this kind of cross-speaker consistency, based on fifteen speakers of Standard Dutch. Preliminary results are reported in Ladd and Terken 1995. The overall picture is identical to the picture suggested by Grønnum's results. Inter-speaker correlations are all about 0.90.

Similar regularities can be seen when we look at paralinguistic within-speaker variation in pitch range – that is, the raising and lowering of the voice by an individual speaker. The use of experimentally induced modifications of overall pitch range as a means of studying the systematic relations between tonal targets was pioneered by Liberman and Pierrehumbert (Pierrehumbert 1980; Liberman and Pierrehumbert 1984), and the

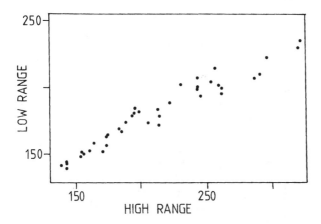

Figure 7.6 Correlation between target F_0 values in one speaker's 'involved' and 'detached' readings of the same sentences, in Bruce's study of sentence-level pitch range effects in Swedish. Each value plotted is the mean of six repetitions.

technique has since been used in several other studies, including Bruce 1982, Pierrehumbert and Beckman 1988, Liberman *et al.* 1993, and Ladd and Terken 1995. If we assume that inter-speaker differences and within-speaker paralinguistic modification are comparable,[6] we would expect them to be comparable in their quantitative manifestations. In particular, we would expect a speaker's target scaling in a normal speaking voice to correlate with his or her own target scaling with a raised or lowered voice.

This expectation is borne out by all the studies just cited. If we calculate correlations between different pitch ranges in the same way as we calculated correlations between speakers in Grønnum's data, we get similar results. Figure 7.6 is based on a study by Bruce (1982), in which a speaker produced the same contours in a low range (as if 'detached') and a high range (as if 'involved'). It shows the two sets of target points – from the detached and involved readings – plotted against each other. Once again the correlation is about 0.90. Results from Ladd and Terken 1995 and from the work in progress by Ladd, Terken, and Shriberg yield the same picture; figure 7.7 shows results for two speakers.

7.2.3 *Modelling pitch range*

While all this evidence indicates in a preliminary way that it may be possible to define speaker-specific scales for use in a normalising model of the phonetics of pitch, quite a number of problems – both theoretical and

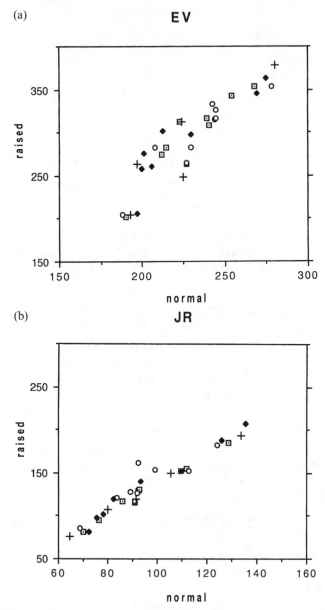

Figure 7.7 Correlation between target F_0 values in normal voice and raised voice for two speakers' readings of the same sentences in Ladd, Terken, and Shriberg's work on cross-speaker range comparison in Dutch (Ladd and Terken 1995). Each value plotted is the mean of between ten and sixteen repetitions. Different plot symbols are used for different texts.

empirical – remain. The most obvious is that correlation coefficients are too crude to reveal a number of fairly clear quantitative properties of any speaker-specific scale, and a number of fairly clear quantitative regularities in studies of pitch range. In order to capture these regularities, more sophisticated models of pitch range are required.

The most obvious quantitative regularity not captured by a correlation coefficient is the fact that the bottom of the speaking range is a fairly constant feature of an individual's voice. As we saw in section 2.3.3.1, numerous studies of both read and spontaneous speech, in a variety of languages including lexical tone languages, have shown that an utterance-final fall in pitch reaches a low F_0 level that is largely unaffected by raising or lowering the voice or by other within-speaker range changes. What this means is that raising the voice, broadly speaking, involves *expanding the pitch span from the bottom up*.

This being the case, the simplest quantitative model of within-speaker pitch range modifications would take the utterance-final low as a speaker-specific zero level or reference frequency (Fr), express normal target values as a function of Fr, and then scale all target values up or down by a constant factor when the voice is raised or lowered. For example, suppose we determined that in normal speaking voice the average contour onset F_0 value is 1.5 times the value of Fr (i.e. 7 st above Fr), while the value of an average high peak is twice as high as Fr (i.e. 12 st or one octave higher). We then assign those targets abstract pitch values of 1.5 and 2, respectively. If raising the voice increases the onset value to 1.75(Fr) – that is, by a factor of 1.167 – the model would then predict that the peak value would be increased proportionally, to 2.33(Fr). This kind of model is shown graphically in figure 7.8.

Mathematically, the model can be expressed as

(7.3) $F_0 = Fr \cdot T \cdot r$

where Fr is the Hz value of the bottom-of-the-range reference level, T is the abstract pitch value for any given target in normal range, and r is a range multiplier whose value is 1.00 for normal range. This model could readily be extended to the description of range differences between speakers as well, in something like the following:

(7.4) $F_0 = Fr \cdot T \cdot N \cdot r$

In this, we assign an *invariant* abstract pitch value T to each target, and the factor N normalises across speakers by adjusting the T values for each speaker's span. Thus, building on the example just given, we might treat 1.5

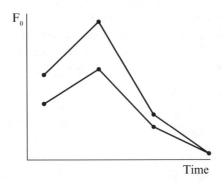

Figure 7.8 A simple model for normalising pitch range modifications within a single speaker. The bottom of the range remains constant and all other target values are scaled up or down when the voice is raised or lowered, in such a way as to maintain constant proportion between target values.

and 2 as invariant abstract pitch values for contour onset and typical high peak. A speaker whose actual onset and peak values were 1.5 and 2 times his or her Fr value would be said to have an N of 1.00. A speaker with a narrow span whose actual onset and peak values were on 1.125(Fr) and 1.5(Fr) respectively would be assigned an N of 0.75; a speaker with a wide span and an N of (say) 1.15 would be predicted to have onset and peak values of 1.725(Fr) and 2.3(Fr) respectively.

There are, however, at least three reasons why such a model is inadequate. First, the apparent constancy of the utterance-final low has been called into question on at least two counts: Ladd and Terken (1995) have shown that in most speakers the utterance-final low is affected slightly by extreme raising of the voice; Hirschberg and Pierrehumbert (1986) suggest that the constancy of the utterance-final low is at least in part an artifact of measurement difficulties, and state that manipulating the precise value of the utterance-final low to reflect discourse structure gives better-sounding synthetic speech. Second, a number of experiments by Gussenhoven and his colleagues (summarised in Gussenhoven *et al.*, ms.) have shown that manipulating the utterance-final low in a stimulus sentence has no effect whatever on the perceived prominence of accent peaks; this suggests that the notion 'reference frequency' or 'bottom of speaker-specific scale' cannot be identified in any simple way with the actual utterance-final low in a given utterance. And third, even if there were not such objections, a simple multiplicative model of the sort shown in (7.4) *does not work*, in the very basic sense that it fails to make accurate predictions

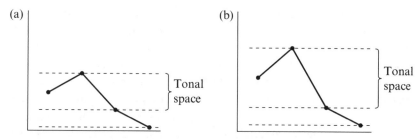

Figure 7.9 One possible model of pitch range modification, in which the width of the 'tonal space' is expanded or contracted partly independently of the height of the tonal space above the bottom of the range. This independent variability means that the proportions between targets do not remain constant; for example, the 'elbow' in the contour is proportionally closer to the bottom of the range in raised voice (b) than in normal or lowered voice (a).

about the quantitative regularities that have been observed in range-modification and range-comparison experiments of the sort described above. A more complicated quantitative model is required.

Various attempts at such a model have been made by e.g. Ladd (1987, 1990), Clements (1990), and Traunmüller and Eriksson (1994), but the most extensive line of work in this area is undoubtedly that of Liberman, Pierrehumbert, and their coworkers (Pierrehumbert 1980; Liberman and Pierrehumbert 1984; Pierrehumbert and Beckman 1988; Liberman *et al.* 1993). The details are different in each case, but the basic idea in all of them, as expressed by Liberman *et al.* 1993, is that pitch range modification involves some *additive* component in addition to the multiplicative factors in (7.4). Informally speaking, what this means is that raising the voice is *not* just a matter of scaling targets up proportionally from a fixed reference level at the bottom of the range, but involves some modification of the fixed reference level as well. One possible pattern of pitch range modification along these lines is shown in figure 7.9. There are a variety of ways in which this informal idea can be expressed mathematically; unfortunately, present data are insufficient to distinguish between them, and it therefore seems appropriate to omit further mathematical discussion from this brief review.

7.3   The phonology of pitch range effects

7.3.1   *Intrinsic and extrinsic factors*
The studies reviewed in the previous section suggest that it may be possible to distinguish fairly clearly between what we might call *intrinsic* and

extrinsic factors in the phonetics of pitch. Intrinsic factors have to do with the relative height of tonal targets on a 'vertical scale' of pitch, while extrinsic factors refer to modifications of the scale itself. But the distinction is by no means clear, and in this section I will attempt to make it clearer.

A clear example of an intrinsic difference is that between a H tone and a M tone. 'Other things being equal' (an innocent-sounding phrase that gives a great deal of trouble in the study of pitch range), H is higher than M, intrinsically, by the very nature of the two tones in a language that has both. Differences of the sort documented by Earle and Rose in their tone normalisation studies are also intrinsic: the endpoint of a Vietnamese Tone 2 is – again, 'other things being equal' – higher than the endpoint of a Tone 3.

A clear example of an extrinsic factor is the difference between different speakers' overall speaking ranges. The actual F_0 values corresponding to H tone and M tone will depend on whether they are spoken by a man or a woman, by a person with a monotonous voice or a person with a lively voice; that is, the acoustic realisation of the pitch scale depends crucially on the speaker and the paralinguistic context, but neither the position of the tones on the scale, nor their linguistic identity, is affected by this speaker dependence. In terms of the kind of quantitative model given in (7.4) above, intrinsic factors are expressed by the term T of the equation, while extrinsic factors are the speaker variables for level and span (Fr and N) and the utterance variable for overall range (r).

I believe the distinction between intrinsic and extrinsic factors provides a useful way of thinking about the general problem of the phonetics of pitch, in part because it immediately highlights the existence of phenomena that do not fit comfortably into either category. The clearest example of an intermediate phenomenon is downstep, particularly the kind of 'non-automatic' downstep seen in some African languages. In two-syllable words in Efik, for example, after H tone on the first syllable there is a three-way distinction between H, ᶦH (downstepped H), and L, as in the following example from Connell and Ladd 1990:

(7.5)   H H
     a.   ọbọng 'mosquito'

          H ᶦH
     b.   ọbọng 'chief'

          H L
     c.   ọbọng 'cane'

Recognition that the second syllable in (7.5b) is a downstepped H and not a M dates from Winston 1960; the most important evidence for this analysis involves the fact that the tone in question establishes a new ceiling for following tones that are unambiguously H. Similar cases of such 'tone terracing' can be found throughout sub-Saharan Africa (for a thorough discussion see Clements 1979).

Downstep of this sort seems 'intrinsic' in the sense that it is both categorical and linguistically distinctive. Either a given tone is downstepped or it is not, and if it is, it conveys a different meaning than if it is not. Yet at the same time, downstep is clearly 'extrinsic' in that it does not involve specification of a scale value, but a modification of the scale itself: downstep 'happens' at an identifiable point in the utterance, and the resulting scale modification affects subsequent non-downstepped tones. Indeed, the whole point of describing a given tone as 'downstepped H' rather than 'M' is precisely that the linguistic identity of subsequent H tones at the level of the downstepped H is clearly H, not M. Consequently, I believe it makes sense to regard downstep as extrinsic.

If we treat downstep as extrinsic, however, it means we must further distinguish between two kinds of extrinsic effects: categorical local 'shifts' such as downstep, and overall expansions or contractions such as those discussed in section 7.2. The two kinds need to be distinguished partly on the basis of their function: the local shifts are clearly linguistic, while the overall expansions and contractions are paralinguistic or extralinguistic. The two kinds also need to be distinguished because they are phonetically distinct: the local shifts can be nested inside the global modifications. Downstep, if it occurs, occurs on linguistic grounds, and it does so irrespective of whether the speaker's voice is raised or lowered. The local and the global operate independently. This can be seen from, for example, Pierrehumbert and Beckman's data on downstep in Japanese (1988: esp. ch. 3), in which the same patterns of downstep following lexically accented syllables are seen in sentences spoken with lowered, normal, and raised voice.

We therefore draw two intersecting distinctions: intrinsic vs. extrinsic, and linguistic vs. paralinguistic or extralinguistic. Together, these two distinctions give us a three-way classification of pitch range effects:

(7.6)

intrinsic	extrinsic	
H vs. M	downstep	raising the voice
linguistic		para- or extralinguistic

This three-way classification is relevant to several specific issues in AM intonational phonology and to the more general question of how to draw the line between linguistic and paralinguistic effects in intonation, as we shall see in the following sections.

7.3.2   Pitch range in AM intonational descriptions

As we saw in chapter 2, and in section 7.2 above, the general problem of pitch range manifests itself within the AM approach as the specific problem of *tone scaling*. Given a string of tones – which is the ultimate representation of the pitch contour in the AM approach – the task of providing explicit phonetic realisation rules for pitch contours is primarily a matter of establishing the F_0 level at which each tone is realised. The rest of the contour can then be filled in as transitions between tones.

Stated as a problem of tone scaling, the problem of pitch range seems relatively straightforward. Though refinements remain to be made, it is clear that a system with two abstract levels and a moderately elaborate set of phonetic realisation rules can successfully model intonation contours in languages like English. In one fairly obvious approach, which is developed in some detail in Pierrehumbert 1980, Liberman and Pierrehumbert 1984, and Ladd 1987b, there are several independent but interacting factors affecting each tone: if the speaker's voice is raised all tones will be higher than normal; if a tone is downstepped it will be lower than it would otherwise be; and so on. This approach to tone scaling clearly 'works', in the sense that it can be used as the basis of an intonation model for speech synthesis (e.g. Pierrehumbert 1981; Anderson, Liberman, and Pierrehumbert 1984; Ladd 1987b, 1990b); indeed, the simple model in (7.4) above formed the starting point for developing the quantitative model used in my own synthesis work.

Despite this empirical success, however, and despite the well-defined nature of the descriptive task, the AM theory still has important theoretical and empirical problems with pitch range – just like every other approach to intonational phonology. I believe that the three-way classification of pitch range effects just proposed can help us to understand why.

First let us consider the way pitch range effects are handled in Pierrehumbert's description of English intonation. Pierrehumbert clearly recognises the existence of extrinsic effects. These include local emphasis and 'relative prominence' generally, which is discussed briefly by Pierrehumbert (1980: ch. 1) and then left largely unexplored. They also include the constant quantitative relations between the accent peaks in 'answer–background' and 'background–answer' sentences discovered by Liberman and Pierrehumbert in the *Anna/Manny* experiment, discussed at some length in section 2.3.3.1. Liberman and Pierrehumbert's treatment of these kinds of factors clearly presupposes a notion of 'extrinsic' scaling effects, which are specified in the detailed phonetic realisation model, but are *not reflected in the tonal string*. In the *Anna/Manny* sentences, for example, the accents in all cases are L+H*, and the 'answer/background' relation is specified separately. The nature of this separate specification is never made very clear, but it is certainly not phonological; in fact, Beckman and Pierrehumbert (1992) seem to suggest that it is not any sort of linguistic specification at all, but merely a consistent way of controlling paralinguistic pitch range that speakers adopt in response to a particular experimental task.

Downstep, on the other hand, is clearly phonological in Pierrehumbert's model, and involves something very close to an 'intrinsic' scaling factor. Pierrehumbert, as we have seen, treats downstep as the result of a phonetic realisation rule that operates on certain specific strings of tones and not on others. Unlike the 'extrinsic but linguistic' classification of downstep suggested just above, the difference between a downstepped accent and a non-downstepped accent in Pierrehumbert's analysis is at least to some extent a difference of accent *type*, almost like the difference between a H tone and a M tone in a language like Yoruba. This can be seen in particular from the H+L* accent, which, as we saw in chapter 3, scales the *low* (L*) tone at what might otherwise be considered to be the level of a downstepped *high*. To be sure, Pierrehumbert's treatment of downstep – especially the version presented in Pierrehumbert and Beckman 1988 – does also include some 'extrinsic' aspects, and in any case the precise match-up between Pierrehumbert's categories and the ones proposed in the previous section is not the point. But what is clear is that Pierrehumbert's account of pitch range draws a *two-way* distinction – between those effects that are represented in the tonal string and those that are not. In my opinion, this two-way distinction is both empirically inadequate and the source of considerable theoretical problems.

Nowhere are these problems seen more clearly than in the history of the H*+H accent. It will be recalled that Pierrehumbert's original analysis posits seven pitch accent types, but that one of them – the H*+H – is eliminated in the revised version presented in Beckman and Pierrehumbert 1986. As we saw in chapter 3, H*+H was used in the original analysis to represent a high accent that is followed by a sustained high level transition to a following high accent, in contrast with the H* accent, which is followed by a 'sagging' transition when the next accent is high (see figure 3.6). Informal experiments with synthetic speech have suggested to me that the difference between these two is extremely salient to listeners and involves a quasi-categorical abrupt shift in percept as the transition changes from high level to slightly sagging; similar results based on more formal experiments are reported for Italian by Grice and Savino (1995). It thus seems clear that any analysis of English intonation must provide a way of representing this distinction.

Pierrehumbert's proposal to use the H*+H accent for this purpose is entirely in keeping with the rest of her analysis. First, it treats the distinction as involving a difference in the tonal string: like Pierrehumbert's treatment of downstep, that is, the difference between the sustained and sagging transitions is a matter of quasi-intrinsic scaling factors. Second, the specific tonal representation H*+H makes use of an independently needed principle in her description as a whole, namely the idea that 'unstarred' tones – in this case, the trailing H tone – may be subject to tone spreading (see section 3.2.2.2). It is this spreading that yields the sustained transition.

For various reasons, however, the combination H*+H sits uneasily with the other bitonal pitch accents. The most obvious problem is the fact that it appears to violate the Obligatory Contour Principle[7] by having two identical specifications adjacent in a phonological representation: that is, the other bitonal accents all involve a combination of a H and a L; only the H*+H contains two tones of the same type. There are thus theoretical reasons for wanting to eliminate it from the inventory of pitch accents. The wider application of extrinsic scaling effects provides a way to do so. Beckman and Pierrehumbert (1986: 306, n.2) state that 'we would now analyse [the sustained transition between H* accents] as involving ordinary H* accents produced in an elevated but compressed pitch range'. In other words, the phonetic details that led Pierrehumbert to posit the H*+H accent in the first place are reanalysed as extrinsic scaling factors. The phonetic basis of the new analysis is shown in figure 7.10.

No justification is given for the reanalysis, however. Beckman and Pierrehumbert state, in an aside, that 'recently the H*+H pitch accent has been [*sic*] eliminated as a possible pattern' (1986: 256), and, in a footnote, that 'this reanalysis was [*sic*] a natural outcome of the new treatment of pitch range introduced by Liberman and Pierrehumbert (1984)'. This aside and this footnote are to my knowledge the full extent of published discussion of the change. No reference is provided for the elimination of the

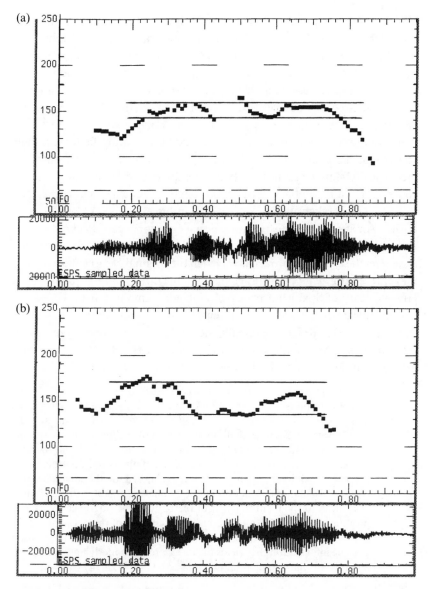

Figure 7.10 Pierrehumbert's reanalysis of the H*+H..H* sequence. Panel (a) shows the contour originally analysed as H*+H..H* and panel (b) that originally analysed as H*..H*. (The contours are identical to those in figure 3.6, panels (a) and (c) respectively.) In the new analysis, both contours are said to be H*..H*, but with the range 'elevated and compressed' in the panel (a) and presumably unmodified in panel (b).

H*+H, though this change is referred to only in past-tense forms, and there is no elaboration on the claim that this is a 'natural outcome' of Liberman and Pierrehumbert 1984 – where the H*+H is never mentioned. I know of no subsequent reference to the H*+H in published work by Pierrehumbert and her colleagues. No detail is ever provided about when the pitch range can be 'elevated and compressed'.[8] No other intonational distinctions are analysed in exactly such terms, although as I noted above, Liberman and Pierrehumbert do introduce the idea of extrinsic scaling factors in their analysis of the distinction involved in the *Anna/Manny* experiment. The theoretically embarrassing H*+H is thus done away with, but the more general lack of theoretical clarity about pitch range remains unaddressed.

This issue is taken up by Sosa (1991), in his extensive AM analysis of Latin American Spanish intonation. Sosa rejects Beckman and Pierrehumbert's reanalysis of the English H*+H. Indeed, he argues for *extending* the type of approach involved in the original H*+H analysis, and for representing *more* pitch range distinctions directly in the tonal string. His inventory of Spanish accent types includes, among others: H*+L, to trigger downstep in a following accent, as in Pierrehumbert's analysis of English; H*+H, which represents the same sort of accent type as in Pierrehumbert's original analysis of English; and H+H*, which indicates extra height on a high nuclear accent in a question. Of the H+H* he says:

> The reason we consider this pitch accent necessary is phonetic: this pitch accent is responsible for raising the tone of this syllable to higher levels than a simple H* tone could do. It would not take account of the melodic facts to say, for example, that the suspension of declination is responsible for the horizontal contour of the [prenuclear contour], and that then the H* pitch accent takes care of the last raising of pitch on the nucleus, since ... there are differences between Caracas dialect and other dialects which have suspension of declination but do not have a notable raising of pitch in relation to the relative height of the body of the utterance. Thus, our positing of the H+H* pitch accent takes account of the phonetic details of [yes–no] questions in this dialect, and in addition it has the implication that the information that yields the rise is present underlyingly, and is different from what happens in other dialects. (1991: 123; my translation)

Sosa's guiding principle might be stated as follows: if an intonational distinction is phonological, then it must be represented in terms of different tonal strings. Except for clearly extralinguistic effects such as inter-speaker differences of range, there is no place in Sosa's analysis for extrinsic scaling factors anywhere. Even the higher overall pitch of yes–no questions is analysed by Sosa as involving a difference of tonal sequence, though such a phenomenon is reported or assumed for many languages and might arguably be treated as paralinguistic and hence as an extrinsic scaling factor. The overall raising in questions, according to Sosa, reflects the occurrence of an initial high boundary tone (H%), restricted to questions, which triggers an initial upstep. This initial upstep 'increases the frequency of the first syllable (accented or unaccented) to a higher level than the normal level of the utterance. On the basis of this initial height, the phonetic implementation rules assign numerical values in Hz to the later tones, which results in the effect of greater pitch height for the whole interrogative utterance all the way to the nucleus' (1991: 120; my translation).[9]

As will be clear from the discussion in the previous section, I do not agree with Sosa's approach. I think there is an important role for 'extrinsic but linguistic' scaling factors in the description of intonation, which will, among other things, simplify the tonal representations of languages like Spanish or English. But Sosa's work is relevant to the discussion here in two important ways. First, it has the virtue of making its theoretical criteria about pitch range explicit. It proceeds from a kind of analytical null hypothesis, which is that intonational distinctions are assumed to be phonological *and represented in the tonal string* unless there is a clear basis for treating them otherwise. Second, Sosa's work shows that the proper treatment of pitch range phenomena in AM intonational phonology is by no means settled. Pierrehumbert's solution – to treat downstep as a quasi-intrinsic effect represented in the tonal string, and to treat all other scaling effects as extrinsic and essentially non-phonological – is not the only reasonable possibility within the general framework of AM assumptions.

7.3.3   'Structural' pitch range effects

Having reached the intermediate conclusion that the place of pitch range factors in the AM approach is problematical, we may now return to the issue of English downstep, which we discussed extensively in chapter 3. The story so far is as follows. Pierrehumbert (1980) proposed that downstep is the result of local phonological rules operating on specific sequences of tones, which has the effect of modifying the pitch range at specific points in the contour. Ladd (1983a) argued that this phonological analysis fails to express the fact that downstep in a language like English has a certain functional unity, regardless of the accent type to which it applies, and proposed a downstep 'feature' that can apply to any accent type. In their rejoinder, Beckman and Pierrehumbert (1986) pointed out that such a downstep feature could apply not only to any accent type, but also to accents in any position, creating presumably meaningless tonal specifications in which the first accent in a series is downstepped.

In order to deal with this problem, while at the same time preserving what I believe to be the correct assumption that downstep is an extrinsic scaling factor orthogonal to accent type, I subsequently proposed (Ladd 1988, 1990b, and especially 1993b) that downstep involves a *syntagmatic relation* of pitch level between two accents or other prosodic constituents. This proposal, inspired by similar work on African tone languages by Clements (1983) and Huang (1980), is based directly on the notion of relative strength in metrical phonology. Just as two phonological constituents or domains can be related as either weak–strong or strong–weak (see section 2.2.2), so I proposed that at least certain kinds of prosodic constituents can be related as either *low–high* or *high–low*. Thus:

(7.7)

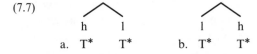

The relation in (7.7a) is that between an accent and a following downstepped accent; the relation in (7.7b) is that between an accent and a following non-downstepped one.[10]

This 'metrical' representation of downstep fits nicely with the three-way classification of pitch range effects proposed in the previous section, because it means we have three different kinds of representations corresponding to three different kinds of effects. Intrinsic effects are those represented in the tonal string in terms of H and L tones. Global extrinsic effects – those based on the overall level and range of the speaker's voice – are non-phonological, and should ideally be normalised out of phonetic data once we understand the appropriate basis for such a normalisation. In between these two kinds of effects lies the 'extrinsic but linguistic' category identified in the previous section. Such effects are not represented in the tonal string, but instead involve abstract relations between tones and between higher-level phonological constituents – including the downstep relation just outlined, and the *Anna/Manny* relation discovered by Liberman and Pierrehumbert.

One obvious argument in favour of recognising an intermediate category of 'extrinsic but linguistic' pitch range effects is the fact that these effects can apparently be controlled independently of the clearly extrinsic global range modifications; that is, when speakers modify their overall range, the pitch range relations within the utterances remain the same. Indeed, if this were not the case, all the systematic relations discovered so far would never be observed, and there would have been nothing to write about in section 7.2!

The appropriateness of the metrical representation is further suggested by the fact that relations of pitch level apply between phrases (and probably even larger constituents) as well as between individual accents. Several studies have demonstrated that it is possible to have downstep within a series of short phrases, superimposed on an overall downward trend across the utterance as a whole. (For example, this was clearly shown in the Ladd 1988 study discussed in connection with the indeterminate depth of prosodic structure in section 6.3.2 above; see also van den Berg, Gussenhoven, and Rietveld 1992.) In a metrical analysis of downstep, it is easy to express such 'nested' or 'embedded' downstep by extending the relations shown in (7.7) to constituents at a higher level, as in the following:

(7.8)

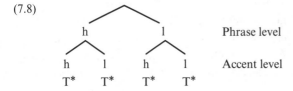

That is, the metrical proposal makes it possible to treat nested downstep as a natural consequence of the phonological nature of downstep within phrases.

By allowing for pitch range relations to be nested like prominence relations, the metrical analysis treats downstep as only one of a group of what we might call 'structural' pitch range effects, in which pitch range shifts are used to signal syntactic and textual structure. For example, Ladd (1990a) presents preliminary evidence that the *Anna/Manny* relation can be nested in the same way as downstep. The metrical analysis also makes sense of 'declination reset', the upward modification of the pitch range at the beginning of a new stretch of declination, and 'final lowering', the corresponding downward modification of the pitch range at the end. These are related to 'paragraph cues', whereby paragraphs or other larger chunks of text often begin quite high and end quite low (e.g. Lehiste 1975; Silverman 1987), and to discourse level resettings of the sort noted by Brown, Currie, and Kenworthy (1980), whereby speakers tend to begin new topics high in their speaking range. In the view presented here, such resettings are simply the phonetic manifestation of phonological pitch range relations that can hold between prosodic constituents at different levels of structure.

7.4   Gradience, pitch range, and paralanguage

An important aspect of my critique of Pierrehumbert's treatment of down-step has to do with the fact that it treats linguistically important pitch range effects in inconsistent ways. For Pierrehumbert, downstep within intermediate phrases is the quasi-intrinsic effect of a phonological rule operating on certain specific sequences of accents. Other pitch range effects are explicitly classed as paralinguistic: for example, Beckman and Pierrehumbert (1986) claim that downward trends from phrase to phrase are paralinguistic, generated by a series of independent pitch range choices that merely 'mimic' downstep. Beckman and Pierrehumbert (1992) go further, suggesting that the constant patterns in the experimental data discussed in section 7.2 are merely the consequence of ill-defined 'speaker strategies' for making paralinguistic choices in the experimental situation: it is only a remarkable coincidence that all these choices bear the same quantitative relation to one another whether the voice is raised or lowered. If we recognise the existence of an intermediate 'extrinsic but linguistic' category of pitch range effects, which we represent in terms of metrical relations between prosodic constituents, we are not forced to adopt this view.

Yet Beckman and Pierrehumbert obviously have a point. It is implausible to assume that the global paralinguistic effects and what I have called structural effects are completely unrelated. As Bolinger repeatedly pointed out (e.g. 1986: ch. 9), 'resetting' the pitch range at the beginning of a new topic is too obviously related to the paralinguistic function of raising the voice for the two to be completely separate systems. While I believe that the notion of pitch range effects that are 'extrinsic but linguistic' may go some way to clarifying the issues, the problem of the relationship between the linguistic and the paralinguistic still has not gone away. In the final section I wish to discuss the relevance of the metrical proposal for this perennial question.[11]

As noted above, I first proposed treating downstep as an extrinsic scaling effect in Ladd 1983a, where I discussed the problem in terms of a possible downstep 'feature'. In the same article, I also suggested that certain other distinctions in the height of H accent peaks might reflect the existence of another feature, which I called 'raised peak'. Specifically, I proposed to distinguish between 'normal' and 'raised' H accent peaks in pairs like the following (as in examples (6.1) and (6.2), the raised H peak is indicated with a preceding up-arrow):

(7.9)　　　　H*　　　H* L L%
　　a.　Where's the hammer.
　　　　(businesslike; peremptory)

　　　　H*　　　↑H* L L%
　　b.　Where's the hammer?
　　　　(repeating previous question; also in a context that implies 'You've
　　　　asked me to nail this up, but you haven't told me where the hammer is')

(7.10)　　　　H*　　H*LL%
　　a.　They won't do it.
　　　　(neutral; expressing certainty; etc.)

　　　　H*　↑H*LL%
　　b.　They won't do it.
　　　　(surprised; irritated; repeating previous statement)

(7.11)　　　　H*　　　　H*LL%
　　a.　Give it to Mary.
　　　　(straightforward imperative; answer to question 'What should I do
　　　　with this?'; etc.)

　　　　H*　　↑H*LL%
　　b.　Give it to Mary.
　　　　(contrastive, i.e. 'Mary, not Anna'; repeating previous statement; etc.)

As I noted at the time, this distinction recalls the difference between High and Overhigh pitch levels in the American structuralist phonemic analysis of intonation (see chapter 2, note 10). As I also noted, '[raised peak] covers some of what has often been called "contrastive stress"; but as the approximate intonational glosses show, the distinction involves much more than mere logical contrast' (1983a: 736).

The idea of such a distinction had been comprehensively rubbished by Bolinger in the 1950s. Instead, Bolinger argued that intonation involves a small number of categories (e.g. the pitch accents) and that the categories can be *gradiently varied* for expressive purposes (see section 1.4 above). Specifically in the case of High and Overhigh, Bolinger argued that what is involved in all cases is a single category of falling pitch accent, and that the pitch range – the extent of the fall – can be wider or narrower depending on the speaker's emotional involvement and expressive intent (or more prosaically on the degree of 'prominence' of the pitch accent). This view found wide acceptance and was explicitly incorporated into Pierrehumbert's notion of prominence (1980: section 1.3). Indeed, so uncontroversial is the idea of gradiently variable pitch range that Beckman and Pierrehumbert

(1986), who devoted considerable space to arguing against my proposal for a downstep feature, simply dismissed the suggestion of a raised-peak feature in a footnote. However, it is worth pursuing the issue here at least briefly, because it draws attention to an important assumption about pitch range that I believe is incorrect.

As we have seen, much AM discussion of pitch range effects has been in terms of whether a given phenomenon is to be represented in the tonal string or treated as an 'extrinsic' scaling factor. In the case of downstep, I have argued that the phenomenon is extrinsic, while Pierrehumbert and Sosa treat it as part of the tonal description. In the case of the H*+H accent, Pierrehumbert originally analysed the phenomenon as part of the tonal string and now treats it as extrinsic, whereas Sosa maintains the original view. Discussed in this way, these issues are the latest in a long string of 'paralinguistic stalemates', of the sort discussed in section 1.4: one analyst treats a given intonational phenomenon as linguistic and makes provision for it in the phonological analysis (in this case, the tonal string), while another analyst – or the same analyst a few years later – argues that the phenomenon is outside the system of linguistic contrasts and consequently should not be represented phonologically at all. The underlying question – paralinguistic vs. linguistic, extrinsic vs. intrinsic – is in all cases the same.

In the context of such stalemates, my proposal for a raised peak 'feature' is different, because in this case *everyone agrees* that the phenomenon is extrinsic to the tonal description. Instead, the disagreement is whether the extrinsic variability of pitch range in this case is gradient (as in the received Bolinger–Pierrehumbert view) or categorical (as implied by my proposal for a raised peak 'feature'). For Pierrehumbert, this disagreement makes no theoretical sense. Her approach involves the clear but unstated assumption that if a pitch range scaling factor is extrinsic, it must be paralinguistic, and therefore it must be gradient. Since I agree that raised peak is extrinsic, it seems incoherent for me to argue that it might also be linguistic and categorical. But the basis of the incoherence is nothing more than the premise that extrinsic = paralinguistic = gradient. If we allow other possible combinations of attributes, the incoherence disappears.

This brings us back to the metrical pitch range effects. By proposing a category of pitch range effects that is intermediate between clearly intrinsic and clearly extrinsic, and by proposing a metrical representation of pitch range relations, I am proposing that it is theoretically coherent to recognise the existence of factors that are *categorical and linguistic* but nevertheless extrinsic or *orthogonal to the tonal string*. In English, I believe that these factors include at least downstep – both within and between intermediate phrases – and the *Anna/Manny* relation. As it happens, further work (Hayes 1993; Ladd, Verhoeven, and Jacobs 1994; Ladd and Morton ms.) has convinced me that Bolinger and Pierrehumbert were probably right about 'raised peak' – emphatic peak raising probably is gradient and paralinguistic, though it sometimes gives rise to nuances that appear categorically distinct. Nevertheless, the more general point behind the raised peak proposal is in my view still valid: extrinsic pitch range effects do not have to be paralinguistic and gradient.

The book ends, therefore, where it began: trying to untangle the linguistic and the paralinguistic. I believe that the three-way classification of pitch range effects proposed here provides the theoretical basis we need for designing empirical studies that will advance our understanding. I also believe that, more generally, the AM approach to pitch range as a problem of target scaling will make it possible to interpret the results of such studies in revealing ways. But I concede that we must stop short of drawing a clear boundary between language and paralanguage. For now, that question remains open.

Notes

1 Introduction to intonational phonology

1 For excellent tutorial reviews of the literature on pitch and loudness as they are relevant to the study of intonation, see Beckman (1986: chs. 4 and 5).

2 The term 'postlexical' has a specific meaning within the theory of Lexical Phonology (e.g. Kaisse and Shaw 1985), in which 'lexical' phonological rules are supposed to apply within words, and then 'postlexical' rules apply to strings of words that are assembled by the syntax. Readers who object to the derivational metaphor implicit in the term, or who simply find it unenlightening, may be assured that nothing crucial depends on my use of it here.

3 The use of final rises in statements has recently been termed 'uptalk'. An early comment in the popular press was Gorman 1993. Recent discussions in the linguistics and phonetics literature include Ching 1982, Britain 1992, and Cruttenden 1994. I will return to this whole topic in chapter 4.

4 It is possible for the weak–strong pattern to be used in an analogous way to focus on *pounds*, for example in reply to a question like *Did you say five francs?* That is, there is a clear asymmetry in the linguistic effects of the two prominence patterns. Again, however, this does not undermine the basic point being made here, that we are dealing with two distinct patterns. The asymmetry of prominence patterns will be discussed at some length in chapter 5.

5 The informed reader will notice that I do not draw a clear distinction, either here or (especially) in chapter 6, between 'metrical phonology' (e.g. Liberman and Prince 1977) and 'prosodic phonology' (e.g. Nespor and Vogel 1986), but have considered them both to be aspects of an eventual general theory of prosodic structure.

6 In the standard IPO notation, the pointed hat is actually represented as *1&A* and the flat hat as *1 A*. In effect, the stretches of ∅ and 0 are regarded as an option that is always available, while the absence of a stretch of ∅ (i.e. the occurrence of 1 and A on the same syllable) must be specified.

7 The principal microprosodic phenomena are (a) the intrinsic F_0 of vowels (see Lehiste 1970: 68–71; Whalen and Levitt 1995); (b) rapid F_0 movements in the vicinity of obstruents (see Lehiste 1970: 71–4; Reinholt Petersen 1986); and (c) gaps in the contour during periods of voicelessness. It has been demonstrated very clearly by, for instance, Silverman (1986) and by Kohler and his coworkers (e.g. Gartenberg and Panzlaff-Reuter 1991; Kohler 1991) that these phenomena

behave acoustically and perceptually like local perturbations of an idealised underlying F_0 course. There seems little doubt that an overlay model is the best way to treat them in generating F_0 for synthetic speech (see Hirst 1983; Beckman 1995).

8   A related problem with Fujisaki's model bears on its claim to be generalisable beyond Japanese. Both Liberman and Pierrehumbert (1984) and Taylor (1994) have attempted to apply Fujisaki's model to English, but have been unable to reproduce certain English contour types – without, again, arbitrarily locating certain phrase commands and/or arbitrarily specifying the size of the phrase commands. The principal difficulty is in modelling low or low-rising accentual contours (as in a common pronunciation of English *Good morning*) – a feature that is completely absent from Japanese. The quantitative details of Fujisaki's model are such that negative accent commands yield contours of the wrong shape. It is possible to approximate the low-rising contours by negative phrase components, but this is inconsistent with the intended function of the phrase component.

9   Since the distribution of the two accents is almost entirely predictable on the basis of phonological and morphological properties of words, there are not many minimal pairs, and most, like *anden/anden*, involve segmental sequences that can be analysed morphologically in more than one way. This is true in the other European 'pitch accent' languages as well.

10 The only clear exception to this statement – that is, the only clear cases where intonation does affect truth value – involves accent and the scope of quantifiers. For example, the following pair of sentences (from Vallduví 1990 [1992: 142]) will be true or false under different conditions, depending on what the speaker sprinkled where:

> I only sprinkled SALT in the stew.
> I only sprinkled salt in the STEW.

The following pair (from Rooth 1985: 164) is comparable:

> In Saint Petersburg, officers always escort BALLERINAS.
> In Saint Petersburg, OFFICERS always escort ballerinas.

11 We may also identify the 'paralinguistic gambit', in which one description is presented as superior to some other on the grounds that it correctly distinguishes the intonational contrasts from the paralinguistic variation, while the rival description has been misled into attempting categorical descriptions of things that are really paralinguistic, or vice versa. Good examples of the paralinguistic gambit include Lieberman (1967: 175, criticising the British 'nuclear tone' tradition), Bolinger (1951, criticising the American 'pitch phoneme' tradition), Crystal (1969: ch. 4, criticising much previous work, but in particular distancing himself from the rest of the British nuclear tone tradition), and Beckman and Pierrehumbert (1986: 307, criticising Ladd 1983a).

2 Fundamental concepts of the autosegmental–metrical theory

1   The term 'edge tone' is offered here as a general term referring to any tone associated with the periphery of a prosodic domain. It covers Pierrehumbert's

'phrase tone' and 'boundary tone'. Edge tones do not necessarily have to occur phonetically at the very edge of a domain, that is, associated with the first or last segment, syllable, etc. Pierrehumbert and Beckman (1988: 126ff.) have shown that, in Japanese, such tones can occur some time after the beginning or before the end of the domain with which they are associated, and for this reason they propose to associate such tones with nodes in a tree rather than with 'edge' elements in the segmental string. What is crucial is that these tones must occur 'outside' the pitch accents in the domain on whose edge they occur. See further section 4.4 below.

2 The terminology in the general area of 'accent' is really a mess, and readers should be alert to possible confusions arising from differences between their own usage and my attempt at a standardised usage here. The first problem to which attention should be drawn is that the term *pitch accent* has two distinct meanings. In one sense, it refers to the lexically specified pitch features of languages like Japanese, some Bantu languages, and some European languages including Swedish, Norwegian, and Serbo-Croatian. In the other sense, which is more relevant for our discussion here, it refers to a pitch feature (normally a localised pitch movement) associated with a prominent syllable: in this sense pitch accent is simultaneously a building-block of an intonation contour and an important cue to the prominence of the syllable with which it is associated. See further notes 4 and 5 below.

3 Note that Bolinger's and Abercrombie's use of the terms 'stress' and 'accent' are almost the reverse of each other. The lexical abstraction is 'stress' for Bolinger and 'accent' for Abercrombie; the actual utterance prominence is 'accent' for Bolinger and 'stress' for Abercrombie.

4 I have had to normalise everyone's terminology here. For what I am calling 'stress' and 'accent', Halliday uses 'salience' and 'tonicity' respectively; Vanderslice and Ladefoged use 'accent' and a cover feature [± intonation] respectively; and the Ladefoged textbook uses 'stress' and 'tonic accent'. Also, note that my distinction between stress and accent should not be confused with either Bolinger's or Abercrombie's; see note 3.

5 Note also in this connection that melodic features in music can influence the way in which temporal and other acoustic cues are interpreted: temporally identical sequences of tones will be grouped in three or in four depending on the apparent harmonic progression. For example, sequence (a) will be heard with a prominent beat every three notes, while sequence (b) will be heard with a prominent beat every four:

(a)

(b)

I am grateful to Dik Hermes for this example.

6 'Right-dislocation' refers to the occurrence of a constituent (normally a noun phrase) following a clause, with a pronoun or other grammatical marker indicating the grammatical place that the constituent 'would have' occupied had it occurred inside the clause. A possible English example is *She's clever, that lass*, in which *that lass* is right-dislocated and *She* indicates its grammatical role. Outside Celtic-influenced varieties right-dislocation is not very common in English. It is, as suggested in the text, widespread in all the Romance languages.

7 This analysis appeared in two versions, both of which used numbers to label the pitch levels. Pike's original version (Pike 1945, but presented in teaching materials for English as a foreign language as early as 1942) numbered the levels from top to bottom, so that Overhigh was 1, High was 2, and so on. The version first published in Wells 1945, which became the standard pre-generative American analysis when it was adopted by Trager and Smith (1951), numbered the levels from 1 at the bottom to 4 at the top. The essence of both analyses – in particular, the restricted distribution and special status of the highest level – is captured by the labels Low, Mid, High, and Overhigh given in the text.

8 For example, the idea that intonation involves distinctive movements between relatively low and relatively high was developed independently during the 1960s by both Isačenko and Schädlich (1970) and the IPO researchers (see section 1.2). However, Isačenko and Schädlich's work emphasised the two levels, while the IPO work emphasised the movements between the two levels, and the IPO researchers seem not to have appreciated the extent of the common ground between their work and Isačenko and Schädlich's (see Cohen and 't Hart 1967: 189; 't Hart and Cohen 1973). While the isolation of Eastern European scholars during that period undoubtedly played a role in this, it seems reasonable to suggest that the levels-vs.-configurations debate was primarily responsible for Cohen and 't Hart's belief that their approach and Isačenko and Schädlich's were fundamentally opposed. In this connection I should note that the levels-vs.-configurations issue was the basis of my own initial (and, I would now agree, mistaken) rejection of the autosegmental approach to tonal structure (Ladd 1978).

9 This point echoes one made by Bolinger himself (1951: 210 (1965: 16)), though of course Bolinger was arguing *for* a configurations approach, not just *against* a four-level approach: '"231 and 241" (plus a note on synonymy) is less efficient than "rise-fall" (plus a note on pitch range), because the qualifying note in the latter can be generalized for all configurations and does not have to be repeated.'

10 The elision of the /o/ is probably a grammatical phenomenon rather than a synchronic phonological/phonetic process (see Rowlands 1969: 34f.), but that does not affect the point being made here.

11 In their model of these data, Liberman and Pierrehumbert attempt to show that in fact the two contours exhibit the same underlying relationship between the two peaks, despite the superficial difference. Specifically, they suggest that the surface patterns result from the combined effects of the answer–background ratio (which specifies that the 'answer' accent peak is higher than the 'background' accent peak by some fixed proportion) and 'final lowering' (which lowers the last accent in a sequence by a certain factor). That is, in the BA

contour the second peak is underlyingly quite a bit higher than the first, but is lowered by final lowering to the point where the two are almost the same; in the AB contour, the second accent is already underlyingly lower than the first, and is lowered even more by final lowering. I think this is a mistaken interpretation; see Ladd 1990b. Clearly, however, the issue of whether we are dealing with one constant relationship or two does not affect the point being made here.

12 Beckman and Pierrehumbert (1986), following Poser (1984), replace Pierrehumbert's term 'downstep' with the coinage *catathesis*, but in Beckman and Pierrehumbert 1992 they return to 'downstep', and this usage now appears to be well established. The neologism was originally motivated by a desire to steer clear of disagreements within the Africanist literature over distinctions like *downstep – downdrift* and *automatic vs. non-automatic downstep*.

13 Actually, there is nothing in principle to rule out the existence of both downstep and 'true' (i.e. time-dependent) declination, and Pierrehumbert and Beckman (1988: ch. 3) incorporate this possibility into their model of Japanese. However, the empirical difficulties of testing such a model – distinguishing downstep from declination, and distinguishing both from natural variability in F_0 – are rather considerable, and the issue is by no means settled.

14 In fact, there is a potential empirical issue here between a declination model and a downstep model, which arises from the fact that the downward trend in a declination model is a function of time, while in the downstep model it is a function of the number of accents. This is only a 'potential' empirical issue, however, because it is quite difficult to design an experiment using realistic-sounding speech materials without confounding time and number of accents. Both Jacques Terken and Liberman and Pierrehumbert have informally presented the results of simple experiments along these lines, and in both cases the results seem to go against the idea that downtrends are a simple function of time, but in neither case can the results be called conclusive. Nevertheless, it is clear that a downstep model 'works' phonetically at least as well as a declination model.

3 Phonological representation of pitch in the autosegmental–metrical theory

1 The terms 'leading tone' and 'trailing tone' were not originally used as such by Pierrehumbert, who talks only of unstarred tones that 'lead' or 'trail' the starred tone (1980: 23ff. [1988: 9ff.]). The technical usage seems to have become established in informal discussion since the mid-1980s. The terms are used extensively by Grice (1995a, 1995b); Féry (1993) uses 'lead tone' and 'trail tone'.

2 Table 3.1 identifies both L*..H..H% and L*+H..H..H% as equivalent to the British low rise. In the original Pierrehumbert (1980) analysis, the difference between the two is said to reside in the details of the trajectory from the L* to the H%: fairly straight in the case of the L*..H..H%, and with an elbow (rapid rise followed by more slowly rising plateau) in the case of the L*+H..H..H%. The two are of course difficult to distinguish unless there are many syllables following the nuclear syllable. In the Beckman and Pierrehumbert 1986 version of the analysis, this distinction is not made. For Beckman and Pierrehumbert, L*+H..H..H% represents a type of British rise–fall–rise nucleus, because the

L*+H pitch accent is said to trigger downstep of the H phrase tone. The distinction made in the original 1980 version of the analysis is reanalysed as involving a 'gradient' difference in the alignment of the H phrase tone.

3 In British terms the Pierrehumbert taxonomy provides for three kinds of nuclear falling accents, with H*, L+H*, and L*+H as the three possible representations of the rise and peak that precede the fall. In the British tradition only 'fall' and 'rise–fall' are conventionally distinguished. If we treat this as a matter of how the peak is aligned in time with the stressed syllable (see 2.3.3), the Pierrehumbert analysis claims that there are three distinctive alignment positions and the British analysis only two. In any case it seems fair to say that this is an unresolved point in the taxonomy. Confusion data from evaluations of inter-transcriber consistency in ToBI show that the distinction between H* and L+H* is a frequent point of disagreement (Pitrelli, Beckman, and Hirschberg 1994).

4 This use of H+L* is certainly one of the more problematic aspects of Pierrehumbert's original analysis, as can be seen by two subsequent developments. First, in the ToBI version of the Pierrehumbert analysis, the H+L* analysis is dropped and this accent type is more transparently notated H+!H*, that is, as a downstepped high accented syllable that is marked by a local drop from the immediately preceding context (see section 3.3.3). Second, in essentially all AM analyses of Romance languages (Frota 1995 on European Portuguese; Post 1993 on French; Grice 1995a on Palermo Italian; and Sosa 1991 on American Spanish), the H+L* notation is used for the sentence-final accent in a common neutral statement intonation. Phonetically, the pattern involves an accented syllable which is (a) stepped down to from the preceding syllable (hence H+) and (b) more or less at the bottom of the speaker's range (hence L*). That is, unlike Pierrehumbert's English H+L*, the 'low' target of the Romance H+L* in these analyses is independently characterisable as low, not merely lower than the preceding syllable (see 4.2.4). The whole question of downstep in the Pierrehumbert analysis will be dealt with in more detail in section 3.3, and again in chapter 7. See also section 4.2.4.

5 Bruce actually used the term 'sentence accent' but Pierrehumbert revises this without comment to 'phrase accent'. This revision can readily be justified by the already existing polysemy of the term 'sentence accent' in English.

6 In fact, it may not be entirely meaningless to talk about downstepping the first accent, if we assume that there is comparability of pitch level across utterances. That is, we might in principle find that, other things being equal, some utterance-initial H tones are systematically lower than others. (How we might find this in practice is not altogether clear, given the conceptual problems with the notion of pitch range and the consequent difficulties with the phrase 'other things being equal'; see chapter 7.) However, it is worth noting that both Connell and Ladd (1990) and Laniran (1992) independently looked for evidence of 'initial downstep' in Yoruba – where it is relatively simple to compare the average pitch of initial H tone with that of the H of an initial LH sequence – and failed to find any. It does not seem far-fetched to suggest that, at least in some languages, downstep 'happens' between a H and a L, rather than between a L and a H. See Poser (1984: 319) for some discussion of this point.

7 It may be worth noting that Hayes and Lahiri accept Pierrehumbert's analysis of falling nuclear accents as involving a H* accent followed by a L phrase tone, while Grice does not. Grice does make the distinction between two types of edge tone – her T_b and T_B – but this is motivated by other problems of tonal analysis in Palermo Italian; she analyses the statement fall as H*+L in all cases. See section 4.2.4.

8 The details of Gussenhoven's phonological analysis are somewhat different from mine but the basic approach is the same. The two analyses were developed at more or less the same time, and with a good deal of discussion between us over a period of a couple of years, so it is difficult to say exactly which ideas are whose. Despite the differences, the shared history of the two analyses will be apparent to anyone.

9 One explanation for all this activity might be that ambitious young researchers are expediently adopting a fashionable theory, for essentially sociological reasons. A more idealistic view would be that the theory offers genuinely new insight into old problems, that it 'asks the right questions'. There is some reason for taking the latter view, because at least two of the authors just cited – Grice and King – started their investigations using 'tonetic stress marks' and other notions from the traditional British approach to intonational description, and switched to the AM theory only after discovering that it made sense of problems that had seemed intractable under their earlier assumptions.

10 In this connection we might note recent work by Cabrera-Abreu (1996), who proposes that there are no L tones in English intonation at all, only H tones and the absence of H tones. This work is motivated in part by comparable claims for various accentual systems of Africa, particularly among the Bantu languages (see Stevick 1969). I will not pursue this suggestion here, but it provides another illustration of a way in which we might plausibly deviate from the principle of identifying turning points with tones.

11 As noted earlier, the H*+H accent – and consequently the H*+H..H* sequence – was eliminated in Beckman and Pierrehumbert's revision of the original analysis. This does not affect the point being made here, which applies with equal force to the comparison between the two remaining sequences H*..H* and H*..L+H*.

12 To make the discussion in the following chapters as useful as possible for those who are familiar with Pierrehumbert's analysis of English, I will generally use a notation based on Pierrehumbert for English tunes. In particular, despite the discussion in this chapter, I will separate the 'phrase tone' from the last accent – for example, transcribing a falling nuclear contour as H*..L rather than H*+L. However, in some cases the status of the postaccentual tones is precisely what is at issue. In case of doubt I have tried to err in the direction of a phonetically transparent transcription in which tones correspond to turning points or clear target levels, and in which as little phonological organisation as possible is specified.

4 Cross-language comparison of intonation

1 All uses of intonation not covered by Lieberman's analysis were to be regarded as 'emotional' (i.e. paralinguistic, in the terms used here) and hence justifiably

excluded from any linguistic account. This is one of the instances of the 'paralinguistic gambit' cited in chapter 1, note 11.

2 The use of the terms 'nucleus (of the intonation contour)' and 'nuclear accent' for the most prominent accent of the phrase – called elsewhere 'focal accent' or 'sentence accent' or simply 'primary stress' – is discussed in chapter 6. The whole notion of 'neutral' accent signalling that there is 'no special focus' is discussed extensively in chapter 5, as is the fact that the nucleus is located on the verb in yes–no questions in some languages.

3 The interaction of nucleus shift and word order change in these examples to convey different pragmatic messages is typical of Hungarian. The details are beyond the scope of this discussion, but it is worth pointing out that the fourth logical possibility, namely *vettél szódát* with the L* question nucleus on *szódát*, strikes native speakers as odd. The problem is that the intonation signals narrow focus (see section 5.1.2) on *szódát*, but the syntax requires narrow focus constituents to occur before the verb; there is thus a mismatch between the syntax and the intonation. For more on this general topic see, for example, Kiefer 1967, Vogel and Kenesei 1987, Horvath 1986.

4 The possibility of describing intonational variation in terms explicitly analogous to Wells's was suggested by Francis Nolan in discussion at the third ToBI workshop on prosodic transcription held at Ohio State University in June 1993.

5 It is important to note that both of A's utterances remain statements, in the sense that the propositions 'I have an appointment with Dr Macmillan' and '[My name is] William Jarvis' are being asserted, not questioned. The questioning nuance conveyed by the intonation applies to the interaction as a whole, but not to the proposition itself. Compare this with the situation in, for example, French, where question intonation on the utterance *J'ai rendez-vous avec le docteur Desmoulins* would yield the pragmatically rather odd meaning 'Do I have an appointment with Dr Desmoulins?' This means that we cannot simply say that American or Australian utterances with rising intonation like this are a kind of question; the situation is considerably more subtle than that.

6 Given how distinctively British this contour is, it is remarkable to find little discussion of it in the traditional British literature on intonation. Halliday, the only one who unambiguously treats it, calls it a 'Tone 2̲', which he distinguishes both from a 'Tone 2' (the ordinary rising question tune, L*..H..H% or H*..H..H%), and from 'Tone 4' (the English (rise–)fall–rise contour, L*+H..L..H% or L+H*..L..H%). In the rest of the British tradition the contour under discussion is not clearly distinguished from the non-interrogative fall–rise.

7 These varieties of English share a number of peculiarities, which are sometimes attributed to Irish influence (see Wells 1982, vol. II: 371; Bolinger 1989: 34). This explanation is not implausible, as the three English cities named, together with Glasgow, were major destinations of Irish immigration during the nineteenth century. However, Cruttenden (1994) provides evidence suggesting that the intonational peculiarities typical of Newcastle were already present in the eighteenth century.

8 Close-range uses seem especially limited in American English. One striking difference between British and North American intonation is the British use of

the calling contour on *Bye* at the close of telephone conversations, compared to the normal declarative fall used in North America. The British usage sounds facetious to American English listeners.

9 After a seminar presentation on this general topic, I was once told a supposedly true anecdote of two girls named Louise, one French-speaking and one English-speaking, who were good friends when they grew up in a bilingual area of Ottawa. The two often played together outdoors, and could always tell which one was being summoned home, by the association of tune and text in the parental call!

10 The fact that the postnuclear ꜛH tone can be repeated in this way recalls the Dutch version of the calling contour discussed in the previous section. I return to the topic of accent-like postnuclear tones in more depth in section 6.1.3.

11 In Yoruba, final lexical L tones are realised with a fall to the bottom of the speaker's range (L edge tone?), while final H and M tones are realised as sustained levels or very slight rises (H edge tone? absence of edge tone?), but there is no difference between statements and questions or any other obvious effect of sentence-level pragmatics.

12 This is related to another 'realisational' difference between languages, which is quite independent of the distinction between tone languages and intonation languages, namely the fact that languages may have different typical overall pitch ranges: for example, Russian is reported to have a wider overall pitch range than English (Holden and Hogan 1991). Interestingly, in both languages expansion of pitch range has similar paralinguistic effects (signalling greater arousal, interest, annoyance, etc.), so that Russian sounds more animated than English – not only to English speakers but also, according to Hogan and Holden's results, to Russians themselves. Presumably differences in overall pitch range are similar to other paralinguistic differences between cultures (Americans talk louder than British speakers, Germans stand closer in social interaction than Americans, etc.): different cultures set different *norms* along these dimensions, which can lead to cross-cultural misunderstanding, but a *change* in either direction along a paralinguistic dimension (raising or lowering the voice, moving closer or backing off, etc.) carries much the same meaning in any culture. This interpretation is supported by the recent findings of van Bezooijen (1995), who compared the reactions of Dutch and Japanese listeners to Dutch and Japanese female speakers with different pitch ranges. Dutch and Japanese listeners drew very similar inferences about the speakers' physical size and personality, but differed significantly in their evaluation of the attractiveness of the voices: the Japanese listeners found higher-pitched voices more attractive than the Dutch listeners did.

13 A question that arises here is whether pitch range modifications for emphasis and focus are linguistic or paralinguistic. I would be inclined to treat them as paralinguistic – bearing in mind the idea that paralinguistic cues can be extremely localised in an utterance; see section 1.4.2 – but I admit that they are clearly borderline cases. Evidence bearing on this issue would include the extent of variability or gradience: if the pitch range is regularly narrowed by a fixed amount after the focus, that might constitute evidence for a clearly linguistic use

of pitch range modification, whereas if the occurrence of the pitch range modification and the amount of modification were variable, that would represent evidence for a paralinguistic interpretation.

14 The numbering of the tunes in Shen's figure disagrees with that in her prose definitions. Herman's definitions – and my usage on page 155 – are based on the numbering in Shen's figure.

15 The idea that a phonological feature – accent in this case – might be realised in different ways phonetically is well established in segmental phonology: for instance, many languages have a voicing distinction that is manifested in different ways (e.g. Kohler 1984; Keating 1984; Kingston and Diehl 1994). Even a feature as specific and concrete as 'labiovelar' can be shown to have a variety of differences of detail from language to language (Connell 1994).

5 Patterns of prominence

1 To avoid misunderstanding, I should make explicit that this example involves 'broad focus' only with respect to the specific phrase *five francs*. In the context of the sentence as a whole, one might reasonably talk about paired narrow focus on the first phrase (*a sandwich*, *the car keys*, etc.) and on the second phrase (*five francs*). Among other things, cases like this show that we are not dealing with two essentially different kinds of focus, narrow and broad; rather, breadth of focus is a matter of degree, and it is probably meaningful to talk about focus on a wide range of constituent types, from individual morphemes such as prefixes to whole clauses or sentences.

2 In Ladd 1980a, I used the term 'default accent' to refer to the location of the accent in cases where the normally accented word was deaccented; the idea was that the accent pattern signals the emptiness or predictability of the deaccented word rather than the salience of the accented word, which receives the accent only 'by default'. However, I acknowledge that this term has been caught up in the march of lexical change, and that it needs to be withdrawn. Computer jargon is far more widespread now than it was in the mid-1970s, when I coined the term, and nowadays anyone encountering the term for the first time would assume that it meant an accent that occurs on a particular word in the absence of specific reasons to occur somewhere else – in other words, unmarked or normal stress.

3 It is important to point out that the term *focus* is used in two essentially incompatible ways in the recent literature. In the tradition that begins with Grosz and Sidner (1986), a discourse entity is said to be 'in focus' if it is the current topic of conversation, that is, if it is the most salient or activated in the speakers' awareness. Such entities are obviously 'given' rather than 'new', and as such are likely to be referred to with *unaccented* expressions in English. This usage of the term contrasts with the older usage originated by Bolinger, which is carried forward into both the formal semantics tradition of, for example, Jackendoff (1972) and Rooth (1985) and the intonational work of, for example, Ladd (1980a), Gussenhoven (1983a), and Selkirk (1984). In this usage, focus attaches to the most informative parts of the sentence, which are accordingly

likely to be pronounced *accented* in English. It is extremely unfortunate that such a terminological confusion has been allowed to arise.

Part of the problem may be that, even if we confine ourselves to the Bolinger/Jackendoff/Ladd sense of focus, work on this topic frequently conflates two different phenomena: the logical/semantic aspects of narrow and broad focus, and the discourse/pragmatic aspects of newness, givenness, and informativeness or predictability more generally. The latter aspects are obviously related to the Grosz and Sidner sense of focus, which feeds the confusion and the cross-fertilisation. The distinction between the logical and discourse-related aspects of focus has recently been discussed by Kiss (1996), who shows that the two kinds of focus have distinct syntactic consequences in Hungarian. For more general discussion of the different kinds of focus, see Hajičova 1987 and Gundel 1994.

4 This approach was first taken in a very interesting paper by Michel Kefer (Kefer 1986), which has unfortunately never been published.

5 In his last letter to me (10 June 1990), Bolinger conceded that this case 'is a puzzler, certainly, for what I would want to claim', though I think it is fair to say that he nevertheless remained convinced of the ultimate validity of the radical FTA view that he had held for so long.

6 The accentual data from Turkish here and below are based on class notes from a structure-of-Turkish seminar held at Cornell in 1976–7. Most of the sentences are from Underhill 1976 and the patterns of prominence are based on the speech of Vedia Ceranoğlu, the seminar's native-speaker consultant.

7 Kefer (1986) attempts to sidestep this problem by using a pretheoretical phonetic definition of prominence and by concentrating his typological study on statements. While such an approach is probably more convincing in the short run, I believe it is ultimately necessary to acknowledge that our conclusions depend on our phonological analysis, which is why I have discussed the matter at some length here.

8 Not all Romance languages are equally non-plastic: Catalan and French seem to be the most strongly resistant to moving accent out of phrase-final or sentence-final position. In any case, detailed comparison clearly suggests that languages resist deaccenting to different degrees: for example, the Italian sentences involving accent on auxiliaries in (5.36) have no direct counterparts in Catalan, which must use right-dislocation in all such cases (E. Vallduví, p.c.).

9 The discussion of indefinite pronouns in Haspelmath 1994 claims that patterns like *Ho VISTO qualcuno* are possible even in neutral contexts. This claim is not borne out by my own observations of Italian or by the intuitions of those native speakers I have consulted.

10 In Hungarian this may actually be a general fact about noun phrases, not a specific fact about sums of money: that is, noun phrases generally may normally be accented on the first element (e.g. the adjective in an adjective-noun sequence such as *nehéz nyelv* 'difficult language'). Note that in the present example the number *száz ötven* itself is stressed on the first element; contrast English *a hundred and FIFTY*. The uncertainty over whether this is a valid generalisation for all noun phrases and number names is due to factors of the sort discussed in

section 5.2.1.3 above, namely to the interaction of one's decisions about the accent placement with one's analysis of the intonational tune. I will leave this question for further investigation.

11 To use a term that has become rather more common than when Faber wrote, the cases in which the predicate is commonly deaccented involve *unaccusative* predicates. See Perlmutter 1978 and Levin and Rappaport-Hovav 1995.

12 Accent on the predicate is also more common in sentences with longer constituents, and in sentences with additional adverbial constituents in the verb phrase.

> Former President Johnson unexpectedly DIED today.
> The dog's mysteriously DISAPPEARED.

We shall return to the problem of constituent length in section 6.2.3.

13 I have expanded Cinque's example a bit to show that what is at issue is the *relative* acceptability of accent on the verb, depending on the definiteness of the noun phrase. Cinque himself presents these examples as if the only possibilities were accent on the verb when the object is definite and accent on the object when it is indefinite. For more on the notion of relative acceptability and its theoretical implications see Bard, Robertson, and Sorace 1996 and some of the references cited there.

14 VS word order in Spanish or Italian occurs in circumstances that are uncannily parallel to those in which unaccusative verbs are unaccented in English, and in any given context the nuances of VS vs. SV word order in Spanish or Italian are generally extremely similar to the nuances of unaccented vs. accented unaccusative verbs in English (for examples of this see Bolinger 1954; Hatcher 1956; Ortiz-Lira 1994). This observation gives some comfort to a radical FTA view of accent placement, because it means that 'accent on the noun' or 'accent on the verb' appear to have similar pragmatic effects in different languages. At the same time, however, the FTA account of these similarities provides no explanation for the fact that some languages (like English) can readily move accent away from the last content word, while others (like Italian) must modify word order to get the appropriate content word into accented position. See Vallduví 1991.

15 The principles-and-parameters view is an influential approach to describing constraints on typological variation within generative grammar. The basic idea is that there are a number of 'parameters' or dimensions of variation on which languages can vary in specified ways; in many cases these parameters are said to have a 'default setting' which can be overridden in a particular language. A simple example is the 'pro-drop' parameter, according to which languages either normally drop subject pronouns (the default setting, as in Spanish, Hungarian, Japanese, and many other languages) or normally require them (as in English and Russian). An early statement of this idea is Chomsky 1986; for a textbook presentation see the introduction to Haegeman 1994.

16 These examples are based on Jun's examples 7 and 8, pp. 197ff. I have simplified the glosses, and indicated phonological phrase boundaries by square brackets.

17 It is likely that in *DOGS must be carried* we are dealing with a single prosodic domain (intermediate phrase or something similar), whereas in *Dogs must be CARRIED* we have two such domains, and an accent on *dogs* in addition to the

one on *carried*. The difference of two prosodic patterns would therefore be, in the first instance, a difference of phrasing rather than accent placement *per se*. See sections 5.2.5 and 6.2.3.

18 I consign still another example, a classic dirty limerick, to this note: There once was a man from Darjeeling / Who journeyed from London to Ealing / The sign on the door / Said 'Don't pee on the floor' / So he carefully peed on the ceiling.

19 Rump and Collier's own account of their data emphasises the potential distinctiveness of the narrow and broad focus readings rather than their confusability, and I must explicitly exempt them from any responsibility for the interpretation I have put forward here.

6 Prosodic structure

1 'Syntagmatic' distinctions in the phonology of a language are those that intrinsically involve some comparison in the context of an utterance. For example, in order for a segment to be the nucleus of a syllable, it must be the syllable's most sonorous segment, and relative sonority can only be established in context. In *psst*, /s/ is the peak of sonority and may be termed the syllable nucleus, whereas in *passed*, /s/ is less sonorous than /a/, which is therefore the nucleus. By contrast, 'paradigmatic' distinctions are those between independently definable features in a set of possibilities. The opposition between English voiced and voiceless consonants is paradigmatic: a given segment can be assigned to one category or the other without reference to any other segment. However, the difference between syntagmatic and paradigmatic is not as clear as it might appear from these two examples, and it is possible to define certain phenomena in ways that look more syntagmatic or more paradigmatic: for example, if 'primary accent' is defined as 'most prominent accent in a phrase', that is a syntagmatic definition, whereas if it is defined as 'one of a set of possible combinations of pitch accent and phrase tone', that is paradigmatic. Striking the right balance between these kinds of definitions is one of the main goals of this chapter. See further section 7.1.1 below.

2 I do not of course mean to suggest that the principles that Liberman identified as principles of tune–text association were absent from earlier descriptions, but only that such principles operated almost entirely out of the awareness of researchers. The only important exception to this generalisation known to me is 't Hart and Collier's discussion of contour identity (1975).

3 In a limited number of cases, there may be prenuclear accents of different types. One possible example of this is the English 'contradiction contour' (Liberman and Sag 1974), which may be analysed as beginning with a prenuclear L*+H followed by one or more prenuclear L* accents before the nuclear L*. Another example is an alternating sequence of H* and L* prenuclear accents, which is very common in German reading style. It is a simple matter to modify the finite-state grammar in (6.6) to accommodate such cases, though it is naturally of interest to know what kinds of constraints there may be on the occurrence of non-identical prenuclear accents in the same tune. This is a topic for future investigation.

4 This is an appropriate place to remake a point I made in Ladd 1981. The fact that geographically contiguous but unrelated (or only distantly related) languages should share an unusual intonational feature suggests strongly that we are dealing with an areal feature (like clicks in Southern African languages, sex-based grammatical gender in the European languages, etc.). The very existence of areal features is difficult to reconcile with the strong universalist notion that intonation is basically the same in all languages, and suggests rather that we are dealing with linguistic structures and linguistic distinctions that can be borrowed from one language to another.

5 In cases of multiple tones on a single syllable, Greek seems to compress rather than truncate (see section 4.3.1). However, when the L*..HL question tune is compressed onto a single syllable, as in (6.9b), the Ls are scaled higher than they would be otherwise: that is, the range spanned by the rise-fall pitch movement is considerably reduced.

6 A complete analysis along these lines will require some account of the 'spreading' of the L tone between the accentual H* and the boundary H%. Developing such an account is beyond the scope of this chapter.

7 Like Liberman (1975) and Pierrehumbert and Beckman (1988), I am assuming that the boundary tone is in some way outside the main structure of the tune, and in this diagram of the 'metrical relation' between the accent tone and the phrase tone have simply left the boundary tone out of account.

8 The terminological confusion between 'head' in the X-bar sense and 'head' in the traditional British sense of 'prenuclear stretch of contour' is unfortunate but cannot be helped. The only solution appears to be to avoid the term 'head' in discussing intonation altogether. The British sense of 'head' can be replaced with 'precontour' or 'prenuclear accents'; for the X-bar sense of 'head' we can retain the traditional term 'nucleus'. This is the solution I have adopted here.

9 In the terms introduced in section 5.1.3, Selkirk's version of the FTA theory should be described as 'structure-based' rather than 'radical', since she discusses various aspects of focus projection and clearly attempts to account for broad focus. Her account differs crucially from Gussenhoven's structure-based account, in that hers is firmly anchored in a generative analysis of syntactic structure, while Gussenhoven's is ostensibly concerned with 'semantic constituents' rather than syntactic ones and depends considerably on linear order rather than constituent structure.

10 Note also that cases like these make it difficult to maintain the IPO/Bolinger view of the relation between stress and accent, discussed in section 2.2.1. In that view, stress is nothing but an abstract lexical property of certain syllables, realised in actual utterances – if at all – by pitch accent. Stress distinctions in unaccented stretches of contour are supposedly perceived only by recognising a word and identifying the location of its abstract lexical stress (see example (2.5)). However, this explanation clearly breaks down here: in an unaccented stretch of speech we are able to distinguish relative prominence, and yet the prominent syllable is not the lexically stressed syllable of an unaccented word, but the post-lexically stressed syllable of an unaccented phrase.

11 The presence of the discontinuous constituent *took . . . out* makes this analysis

difficult to apply to (6.24) unless we resort to three-dimensional metrical trees – a proposal that it is unquestionably beyond the scope of this book to explore. However, ignoring the discontinuity, the basic explanation advanced in the text for (6.23) and (6.25) works equally well for (6.24). In the neutral version, the argument (i.e. object noun) *garbage* is strong and the predicate (i.e. discontinuous verb) *took . . . out* is weak. In the deaccented version, this prominence relation is reversed, so that *took . . . out* is strong. Within that strong constituent, in turn, *took* is weak and *out* is strong. In short, the primacy of arguments over predicates (see section 5.2.3) and the idea that deaccenting involves prominence reversal both apply just as well to this case as to (6.23) and (6.25). The only problem is diagramming the way in which these principles apply.

12 More generally, the metrical analysis in all these examples expresses the implication that every phrase, and perhaps every utterance, has a single peak of prominence. This is the Trubetzkoyan idea that stress is a 'culminative' feature, that is, a feature that distinguishes one unit from the other similar units (e.g. singles out one syllable as most prominent) within some stretch of speech (see the illuminating discussion by Beckman 1986: 19–27). More or less by definition, no such notion of culminativeness figures in 'accent-first' generative accounts of sentence-level prominence, nor generally in the FTA view. By contrast, culminativeness can be readily accommodated in a metrical view, and indeed, one might argue, with Beckman, that the property of culminativeness is precisely what is formalised in the idea of the DTE.

13 Some provision will of course have to be made in this statement for the stress shift or 'iambic reversal' (Liberman and Prince 1977) that is possible on the constituent *seventy-five*: a strong–weak pattern on this constituent in this context does not normally signal narrow focus on *seventy*.

14 In the text of this example the TG boundaries are marked by // and the foot boundaries by /, while ^ marks a 'silent ictus'. The latter is a hypothetical beat at the beginning of TG-initial feet; it stands in place of the stressed (Halliday's 'salient') syllable with which feet normally begin. In the case of the foot ^ *she'd*, the silent ictus is said to be manifested phonetically by a pause whose duration is governed by the rhythm of the sentence as a whole (see Halliday 1970); there is some experimental evidence for this idea (Scott 1982). However, in the case of the foot ^ *When I*, the motivation for the silent ictus is purely theoretical. Utterance-initial unstressed syllables must be assigned to a foot, and a foot by definition must have an 'ictus' or salient beat; since there is no observable ictus, it must be silent. Nowadays cases like this might be discussed in terms of 'extrametricality' (e.g. Hayes 1981; Pierrehumbert and Beckman 1988: ch. 6) or 'degenerate feet' (Halle and Vergnaud 1987). The 'silent ictus' remains a nice example of the kind of construct that is likely to arise from theoretically incompatible observations.

15 I take it as self-evident that it is important for prosodic domain types to have phonetically explicit definitions. However, I have found this point to be responsible for a certain amount of misunderstanding: several people with whom I have discussed these issues seem to assume that the various prosodic domain types are defined by descriptions of how syntactic structure is mapped onto

prosodic structure – such as those of Nespor and Vogel 1986 or Selkirk 1986. (For example, they might say that a phonological phrase is defined as the head of a maximal projection and everything to its left.) To my way of thinking, it makes no sense to treat accounts like Nespor and Vogel's or Selkirk's as *definitions* of phonological domains; rather, they are hypotheses about the correspondence between one type of independently definable structure and another. For example, we may want to define a phonological phrase as the domain whose DTE bears a nuclear pitch accent, or as the stretch between two phrase tones, or in some other way, but the adequacy of the definition must be evaluated in the first instance on phonological and phonetic grounds. It is then an empirical matter whether Nespor and Vogel's account or Selkirk's account successfully predicts the correspondence between syntactic maximal projections and phonological phrases as independently defined. Unless the syntactic and the phonological structures are defined in their own terms, the whole exercise becomes purely circular.

16 Some of the specific analyses in Ladd 1986 would not be permitted under the proposals outlined here, but the basic idea is the same.

17 While the distinction between the epithet and literal readings is not transparently a matter of focus, it seems clear that deaccenting and focus are part of the same cluster of phenomena, and I will therefore treat the epithet/literal distinction as equivalent to the non-focus/focus distinction for purposes of the point being made here.

18 I have taken this example directly from Ladd 1980a, complete with its twenty-year-old assumptions about what counts as an outrageous medical expense.

7 Pitch range

1 On this problem, Jakobson and Halle (1971: 37) suggest the following:

> both alternatives of a prosodic feature co-exist in the code as two terms of an opposition and, moreover, co-occur and produce a contrast within the message. If the message is too brief to include both contrasting units, the feature may be inferred from the substitutive cues offered by the sequence; e.g., . . . the register of a monophonemic message [may be inferred] from the modulation span at the onset and/or decay of the vowel.

In fact, to the extent that we understand how pitch perception works in languages with level tones, we know that syntagmatic considerations are involved in some way: for example, in many African languages L tones normally fall somewhat, which helps to distinguish them from M and H tones (see e.g. LaVelle 1974). Nevertheless, Jakobson and Halle's statement seems tantamount to acknowledging that there are phonetic cues to distinctive pitch level even in the absence of syntagmatic contrast, and it is therefore not clear why pitch level is treated as fundamentally different from other phonological distinctions.

2 This issue was aired in the early days of the levels-vs.-configurations debate. Sledd (1955) argued that any distinction like low rise vs. high rise effectively undermines the levels-vs.-configurations dichotomy; see further below. However, some British descriptions (notably Schubiger 1958 and especially

Crystal 1969) have treated such distinctions as paralinguistic or otherwise orthogonal to the basic distinction between rise and fall, and may thereby be said to maintain a purely 'configurations'-based description.

3 A z-score normalisation is based on the statistical distribution of data points – in this case the F_0 values of each individual analysis frame in an utterance or a longer corpus of a speaker's speech. The mean F_0 value is assigned a normalised score of 0, and the size of the units on the normalised scale is determined by the standard deviation: an F_0 value that is 2 standard deviations above the mean has a normalised scale value of +2.00; an F_0 value that is 1 standard deviation below the mean has a scale value of -1.00; and so on.

4 An important theoretical point of Pierrehumbert 1980 is that for F_0 there is no analogue to a 'systematic phonetic' level of description. She argues that it is necessary to map from phonological representations of the sort we have discussed throughout the book directly to actual F_0 values. In my opinion, there are actually two separate issues here: first, whether a 'systematic phonetic' level of description can be a formally defined part of *any* phonetically complete phonological description, and second, whether F_0 is any different from segmental phonetics in this regard. The discussion in Pierrehumbert and Beckman 1988 can be taken as suggesting that the answer to the first question is negative: it seems fair to say that Pierrehumbert (and many others) would now cast more general doubt on the formal theoretical status of systematic phonetics. I do not wish to enter this debate here; my point is rather that F_0 is no different from segmental phonetics. There is an unquestionable practical usefulness to descriptions like 'high back unrounded vowel', whatever status they may have in the theory, and I believe that such descriptions can be matched by comparable descriptions of F_0.

5 More or less the same thing can be said of the results of Dik Hermes and his collaborators (Hermes and van Gestel 1991; Hermes and Rump 1994), who have argued that the most appropriate scale for measuring speech F_0 is an 'Equivalent Rectangular Bandwidth' (ERB) scale based on psychophysical research by Glasberg and Moore (1990). Hermes and his coworkers have shown very clearly that for certain kinds of simple pitch movements resynthesised in different overall ranges from the same voice source, the perceptual equality of the size of the pitch movement is best expressed on an ERB scale, which is approximately midway between a linear Hz scale and a logarithmic semitone scale. However, for comparing production data across speakers, the ERB scale is no more successful than the semitone scale at normalising away differences of span.

6 Though the two kinds of pitch range differences are comparable in theory, they raise somewhat different methodological problems, because in order to get 'the same' contour spoken in different ranges we have to instruct speakers to deliberately raise or lower their voices – with uncertain effects on the naturalness of the resulting speech. Also, if we instruct speakers to sound angry or surprised or bored or whatever, we may get a variety of other effects (on speech rate, on voice quality, and possibly on the tune itself), so that we cannot be sure that we are dealing with 'the same' contour. Despite these difficulties, however, results from the studies cited in the text suggest that they have succeeded in getting speakers to produce the same contours in different pitch ranges.

7 The Obligatory Contour Principle, or OCP, was formulated by Goldsmith (1976; see also Leben 1973). According to the OCP, phonological representations are ill formed if they contain adjacent identical tones or other adjacent identical features. (The name 'Obligatory Contour Principle' refers to the fact that any sequence of *non*-identical tones will be realised as a change of pitch or 'contour'.) It was originally suggested that the OCP might be a universal principle of phonological organisation, but it is now generally accepted that it can be violated in some languages under some circumstances. For an extended discussion of the OCP see Goldsmith (1990: 309–18).

8 As we saw in section 7.2, when pitch range is raised it normally causes the tonal space to widen, not narrow. Thus the idea of an 'elevated but compressed' pitch range, though obviously not impossible *a priori*, may be difficult to reconcile with the general direction of findings on pitch range modification.

9 Note the strong 'initialising' bias in Sosa's approach to pitch range.

10 In order to clarify a point that has sometimes led to misunderstanding, I should emphasise that the relations h–l and l–h are not intended to supplant the relation w–s; that is, constituents may enter into relations of relative pitch level *in addition to* relations of relative prominence. The whole point of recognising downstep in a language like English, as we discussed in section 2.4, is that a given accent may be 'nuclear' (and hence structurally more prominent than a preceding accent) even though it is 'downstepped' (and hence scaled at a lower pitch than the preceding accent). For more discussion of this point see Ladd 1989.

11 For a somewhat different approach to untangling the various effects on pitch range, see Ayers (1994), who tries to distinguish between effects that are related to dialogue management and those that are related to the topic structure of the discourse.

References

Abbreviations

AIPUK	*Arbeitsberichte, Institut für Phonetik und digitale Sprachverarbeitung, Universität Kiel*
ARIPUC	*Annual Report, Institute of Phonetics, University of Copenhagen*
BLS	*Proceedings of the Berkeley Linguistics Society*
ICPhS	*Proceedings of the International Congress of Phonetic Sciences*
IEEE	Institute of Electrical and Electronics Engineers
IJAL	*International Journal of American Linguistics*
IPO	Institute for Perception Research
IULC	Indiana University Linguistics Club
JASA	*Journal of the Acoustical Society of America*
JIPA	*Journal of the International Phonetics Association*
JL	*Journal of Linguistics*
JPhon.	*Journal of Phonetics*
Lg.	*Language*
LgSp.	*Language and Speech*
LI	*Linguistic Inquiry*
MIT	Massachusetts Institute of Technology
NELS	*Proceedings of the North-East Linguistic Society*
NLLT	*Natural Language and Linguistic Theory*
OSU	Ohio State University
UCL	University College London

Abe, Isamu. 1962. Call contours. *ICPhS* 7 (Helsinki): 519–23. Mouton.

Abercrombie, David. 1991. *Fifty years in phonetics*. Edinburgh University Press.

Abramson, Arthur. 1962. The vowels and tones of Standard Thai: acoustical measurements and experiments. *IJAL* 28, no. 2 part 3.

Adriaens, L. M. H. 1991. Ein Modell deutscher Intonation: eine experimentell-phonetische Untersuchung nach den perzeptiv relevanten Grundfrequenzänderungen in vorgelesenem Text. PhD thesis, Eindhoven University of Technology.

Allerton, David and Alan Cruttenden. 1979. Three reasons for accenting a definite subject. *JL* 15: 49–53.

Altmann, Hans (ed.). 1988. *Intonationsforschungen*. Tübingen: Niemeyer.

Anderson, Anne H., Miles Bader, Ellen Gurman Bard, Elizabeth Boyle, Gwyneth Doherty, Simon Garrod, Stephen Isard, Jacqueline Kowtko, Jan McAllister, Jim Miller, Catherine Sotillo, Henry S. Thompson and Regina Weinert. 1991. The HCRC Map Task Corpus. *LgSp*. 34: 351–66.

Anderson, Mark, Janet Pierrehumbert, and Mark Liberman. 1984. Synthesis by rule of English intonation patterns. *Proceedings of the IEEE International Conference on Acoustics, Speech, and Signal Processing*, 2.8.2–2.8.4.

Anderson, Stephen R. 1978. Tone features. In Fromkin 1978: 133–75.

Anderson, Steven W. and William E. Cooper. 1986. Fundamental frequency patterns during spontaneous picture description. *JASA* 79: 1172–4.

Apple, W. and K. Hecht. 1982. Speaking emotionally: the relation between verbal and vocal communication of affect. *Journal of Personality and Social Psychology* 42: 864–975.

Arndt, W. 1960. 'Modal particles' in Russian and German. *Word* 16: 323–43.

Arvaniti, Amalia. 1994. Acoustic features of Greek rhythmic structure. *JPhon*. 22: 239–68.

Arvaniti, Amalia and D. Robert Ladd. 1995. Tonal alignment and the representation of accentual targets. *ICPhS* 13 (Stockholm), vol. 4: 220–3.

Ashby, Michael. 1978. A study of two English nuclear tones. *LgSp*. 21: 326–36.

Ayers, Gayle M. 1994. Discourse functions of pitch range in spontaneous and read speech. *OSU Working Papers in Linguistics* 44: 1–49.

Bard, Ellen, Daniel Robertson, and Antonella Sorace. 1996. Magnitude estimation of linguistic acceptability. *Lg*. 72: 32–68.

Bard, Ellen Gurman, Lynn Cooper, Jacqueline Kowtko, and Chris Brew. 1991. *Psycholinguistic studies on the incremental recognition of speech: a revised and extended introduction to the messy and the sticky*. ESPRIT Basic Research Action BR3175, DYANA: Dynamic Interpretation of Natural Language, Deliverable R1.3B/C.

Bartels, Christine, and John Kingston. 1994. Salient pitch cues in the perception of contrastive focus. In Peter Bosch and Rob van der Sandt (eds.), *Focus and natural language processing*, vol. 1: *Intonation and syntax*. IBM Working Papers of the Institute for Logic and Linguistics, pp. 11–28.

Batliner, Anton and Matthias Reyelt. 1994. Ein Inventar prosodischer Etiketten für VERBMOBIL. Memo 33–1994.

Beaugendre, Frédéric. 1994. Une étude perceptive de l'intonation du français. PhD thesis, Université de Paris XI.

Beckman, Mary E. 1986. *Stress and non-stress accent*. (Netherlands Phonetic Archives 7.) Dordrecht: Foris.

1995. Local shapes and global trends. *ICPhS* 13 (Stockholm), vol. 2: 100–7.

Beckman, Mary E. and Gayle M. Ayers. 1994. Guidelines for ToBI labelling, vers 2.0. Ms. and accompanying speech materials, Ohio State University.

Beckman, Mary E. and Julia Hirschberg. 1994. The ToBI annotation conventions. Ms. and accompanying speech materials, Ohio State University.

Beckman, Mary E. and John Kingston. 1990. Introduction. In Kingston and Beckman 1990: 1–16.

Beckman, Mary E. and Janet B. Pierrehumbert. 1986. Intonational structure in English and Japanese. *Phonology Yearbook* 3: 255–310.
    1992. Comments on chapters 14 and 15. In Docherty and Ladd 1992, pp. 387–97.
Bing, Janet Mueller. 1979. Aspects of English prosody. PhD thesis, University of Massachusetts.
    1980. The given/new distinction and the unmarked stress pattern. In V. Burke and J. Pustejovsky (eds.), *NELS* XI, University of Massachusetts, Amherst.
Bolinger, Dwight. 1951. Intonation: levels versus configurations. *Word* 7: 199–210. Reprinted in Bolinger 1965: 3–16.
    1954. English prosodic stress and Spanish sentence order. *Hispania* 37: 152–6.
    1958. A theory of pitch accent in English. *Word* 14: 109–49. Reprinted in Bolinger 1965: 17–56.
    1961a. Generality, gradience, and the all-or-none. The Hague: Mouton.
    1961b. Contrastive accent and contrastive stress. *Lg.* 37: 83–96. Reprinted in Bolinger 1965: 101–17.
    1964. Intonation: around the edge of language. *Harvard Educational Review* 34: 282–96. Reprinted (slightly abridged) in Bolinger 1972a: 19–29.
    1965. *Forms of English: accent, morpheme, order*. Cambridge, MA: Harvard University Press.
    (ed.). 1972a. *Intonation*. Harmondsworth: Penguin.
    1972b. Accent is predictable (if you're a mind-reader). *Lg.* 48: 633–44.
    1978. Intonation across languages. In J. Greenberg (ed.) *Universals of human language*, vol. II: *Phonology*. Palo Alto, CA: Stanford University Press, pp. 471–524.
    1981. Two kinds of vowels, two kinds of rhythm. IULC.
    1982. Intonation and its parts. *Lg.* 58: 505–33.
    1986. *Intonation and its parts*. Palo Alto, CA: Stanford University Press.
    1989. *Intonation and its uses*. Palo Alto, CA: Stanford University Press.
Brazil, David. 1975. *Discourse intonation*, vol. I. Birmingham University, Department of English.
Brazil, David, Malcolm Coulthard, and Catherine Johns. 1980. *Discourse intonation and language teaching*. London: Longman.
Bresnan, Joan. 1971. Sentence stress and syntactic transformations. *Lg.* 47: 257–80.
    1972. Stress and syntax: a reply. *Lg.* 48: 326–42.
Britain, David. 1992. Linguistic change in intonation: the use of high rising terminals in New Zealand English. *Language Variation and Change* 4: 77–104.
Brown, Gillian. 1983. Prosodic structure and the given/new distinction. In Cutler and Ladd 1983: 67–77.
Brown, Gillian, Karen Currie, and Joanne Kenworthy. 1980. *Questions of intonation*. London: Croom Helm.
Browne, E. W. and James D. McCawley. 1965. Serbo-Croatian accent. In Erik C. Fudge (ed.) *Phonology*. Harmondsworth: Penguin, pp. 330–5.
Bruce, Gösta. 1977. *Swedish word accents in sentence perspective*. Lund: Gleerup.
    1982. Developing the Swedish intonation model. *Working Papers*, Department of Linguistics and Phonetics, University of Lund 22: 51–116.
Bruce, Gösta and Eva Gårding. 1978. A prosodic typology for Swedish dialects. In

E. Gårding, G. Bruce, and R. Bannert (eds.) *Nordic prosody.* Gleerup, pp. 219–28.

Cabrera-Abreu, Mercedes. 1996. A phonological model for intonation without low tone. PhD thesis, UCL.

Campbell, W. N. 1993. Automatic detection of prosodic boundaries in speech. *Speech Communication* 13: 343–54.

Caspers, Johanneke. 1994. Pitch movements under time pressure: effects of speech rate on the melodic marking of accents and boundaries in Dutch. PhD thesis, University of Leiden.

Chafe, Wallace. 1973. Language and memory. *Lg.* 49: 261–81.

1974. Language and consciousness. *Lg.* 50: 111–33.

1976. Givenness, contrastiveness, definiteness, subjects, topics, and points of view. In C. Li (ed.) *Subject and topic.* New York: Academic Press, pp. 25–56.

Chang, Nien-Chuang. 1958. Tones and intonation in the Chengtu dialect (Szechuan, China). *Phonetica* 2: 59–84. Reprinted in Bolinger 1972a: 391–413.

Chao, Y. R. 1932. A preliminary study of English intonation (with American variants) and its Chinese equivalents. T'sai Yuan Pei Anniversary Volume, supplementary vol. 1 of *Bulletin of the Institute of History and Philology of the Academica Sinica, Peiping.*

Chen, Matthew. 1987. The syntax of Xiamen tone sandhi. *Phonology Yearbook* 4: 109–49.

Ching, Marvin K. L. 1982. The question intonation in assertions. *American Speech* 57: 95–107.

Chomsky, Noam. 1972. Deep structure, surface structure and semantic interpretation. In Noam Chomsky, *Studies on semantics in generative grammar.* The Hague: Mouton, pp. 62–119.

1986. *Knowledge of language: its nature, origin, and use.* New York: Praeger.

Chomsky, Noam and Morris Halle. 1968. *The sound pattern of English.* New York: Harper and Row.

Cinque, G. 1993. A null theory of phrase and compound stress. *LI* 24: 239–97.

Clements, G. N. 1979. The description of terraced-level tone languages. *Lg.* 55: 536–58.

1983. The hierarchical representation of tone features. In I. Dihoff (ed.) *Current approaches to African linguistics*, vol. I. Dordrecht: Foris.

1990. The status of register in intonation theory. In Kingston and Beckman 1990: 58–71.

Cohen, A., René Collier, and Johan 't Hart. 1982. Declination: construct or intrinsic feature of speech pitch? *Phonetica* 39: 254–73.

Cohen, A. and J. 't Hart. 1967. On the anatomy of intonation. *Lingua* 19: 177–92.

Cole, Sarah. 1991. The rising tone phenomenon: a preliminary look at rising tones in the Johnstone accent of English. MA Honours dissertation, Edinburgh University.

Collier, René and J. 't Hart. 1981. *Cursus Nederlandse Intonatie.* Louvain: Acco/De Horstink.

Connell, Bruce. 1994. The structure of labial-velar stops. *JPhon.* 22: 441–76.

Connell, Bruce and D. Robert Ladd. 1990. Aspects of pitch realisation in Yoruba. *Phonology* 7: 1–30.

Cooper, William, Stephen J. Eady, and Pamela R. Mueller. 1985. Acoustical aspects of contrastive stress in question-answer contexts. *JASA* 77: 2142–55.

Cooper, William and Jeanne Paccia-Cooper. 1980. *Syntax and speech*. Cambridge, MA: Harvard University Press.

Cooper, William and John Sorensen. 1981. *Fundamental frequency in sentence production*. Heidelberg: Springer.

Croft, William. 1995. Intonation units and grammatical structure. *Linguistics* 33: 839–82.

Cruttenden, Alan. 1986. *Intonation*. Cambridge University Press.

1992a. Review of 't Hart, Collier, and Cohen 1990. *JL* 28: 522–6.

1992b. The origins of nucleus. *JIPA* 20: 1–9.

1993. The de-accenting and re-accenting of repeated lexical items. *Working Papers*, Department of Linguistics and Phonetics, University of Lund (= Proceedings of the ESCA Workshop on Prosody, Lund, 27–29 September 1993), vol. 41: 16–19.

1994. Rises in English. In J. Windsor Lewis (ed.) *Studies in general and English phonetics: Essays in honour of Professor J. D. O'Connor*. London: Routledge, pp. 155–73.

Crystal, David. 1969. *Prosodic systems and intonation in English*. Cambridge University Press.

Culicover, Peter and Michael Rochemont. 1983. Stress and focus in English. *Lg.* 59: 123–65.

Cutler, Anne and D. Robert Ladd (eds.). 1983. *Prosody: models and measurements*. Heidelberg: Springer.

Daneš, Frantisek. 1967. Order of elements and sentence intonation. In *To honour Roman Jakobson: essays on the occasion of his seventieth birthday*. The Hague: Mouton, pp. 499–512. Reprinted in Bolinger 1972a: 216–32.

Delattre, Pierre. 1965. *Comparing the phonetic features of English, German, Spanish and French*. Heidelberg: Julius Groos.

1966. Les dix intonations de base du français. *French Review* 40: 1–14.

Dell, François. 1984. L'accentuation dans les phrases en français. In F. Dell, J.-R. Vergnaud, and D. Hirst (eds.) *Les Représentations en phonologie*. Paris: Hermann, pp. 65–112.

de Pijper, Jan Roelof. 1983. *Modelling British English intonation*. (Netherlands Phonetic Archives 3.) Dordrecht: Foris.

de Pijper, Jan Roelof, and Angelien Sanderman. 1995. On the perceptual strength of prosodic boundaries and its relation to suprasegmental cues. *JASA* 96: 2037–47.

Docherty, Gerald and D. Robert Ladd (eds.). 1992. *Papers in laboratory phonology*, vol. II: *Gesture, segment, prosody*. Cambridge University Press.

Downing, Bruce T. 1970. Syntactic structure and phonological phrasing in English. PhD thesis, University of Texas.

Duanmu, San. 1994. Against contour tone units. *LI* 25: 555–608.

Eady, S. J. and W. E. Cooper. 1986. Speech intonation and focus location in matched statements and questions. *JASA* 80: 402–15.

Eady, S. J., W. E. Cooper, G. V. Klouda, P. R. Mueller, and D. W. Lotts. 1986. Acoustical characteristics of sentential focus: narrow vs. broad and single vs. dual focus environments. *LgSp.* 29: 233–51.

Earle, M. A. 1975. An acoustic phonetic study of Northern Vietnamese tones. Speech Communications Research Laboratory (Santa Barbara).

Ebing, E. F. 1994. Towards an inventory of perceptually relevant pitch movements for Indonesian. In Odé and van Heuven 1994: 181–210.

Faber, David. 1987. The accentuation of intransitive sentences in English. *JL* 23: 341–58.

Fant, Gunnar and Anita Kruckenberg. 1994. Notes on stress and word accent in Swedish. *Speech Transmission Laboratory Quarterly Status Report*, 15 October, 1994. Department of Speech Communication and Music Acoustics, Royal Institute of Technology, Stockholm.

Féry, Caroline. 1993. *German intonational patterns*. Tübingen: Niemeyer.

Fónagy, I., J. Fónagy, and J. Sap. 1979. A la recherche de traits pertinents prosodiques du français parisien. *Phonetica* 36: 1–20.

Fowler, Carol A. and J. Housum. 1987. Talkers' signaling of 'new' and 'old' words in speech and listeners' perception and use of the distinction. *Journal of Memory and Language* 26: 489–504.

Fromkin, Victoria (ed.). 1978. *Tone*. New York: Academic Press.

Frota, Sónia. 1995. On the prosody of intonation of focus in European Portuguese. Ms., University of Lisbon.

Fry, D. B. 1955. Duration and intensity as physical correlates of linguistic stress. *JASA* 27: 765–8.

1958. Experiments in the perception of stress. *LgSp.* 1: 126–52.

Fujisaki, Hiroya. 1983. Dynamic characteristics of voice fundamental frequency in speech and singing. In Peter F. MacNeilage (ed.) *The production of speech*. Heidelberg: Springer-Verlag, pp. 39–55.

Fujisaki, Hiroya and Keikichi Hirose. 1982. Modelling the dynamic characteristics of voice fundamental frequency with applications to analysis and synthesis of intonation. In *Preprints of Papers, Working Group on Intonation, Thirteenth International Congress of Linguists, Tokyo*, pp. 57–70.

Gandour, Jackson T. 1978. The perception of tone. In Fromkin 1978: 41–76.

Gårding, Eva. 1983. A generative model of intonation. In Cutler and Ladd 1983: 11–25.

1987. Speech act and tonal pattern in standard Chinese – constancy and variation. *Phonetica* 44: 13–29.

Gartenberg, Robert and Christa Panzlaff-Reuter. 1991. Production and perception of F_0 peak patterns in German. *AIPUK* 25: 29–114.

Gay, Thomas. 1978. Physiological and acoustic correlates of perceived stress. *LgSp.* 21: 347–53.

Gibbon, Dafydd. 1976. *Perspectives of intonation analysis*. Bern: Lang.

Glasberg, B. R. and Brian Moore. 1990. Derivation of auditory filter shapes from notched-noise data. *Hearing Research* 47: 103–38.

Goldsmith, John. 1976. Autosegmental phonology. PhD thesis, MIT. Distributed by IULC and published 1979 by Garland Press, New York.

1990. *Autosegmental and metrical phonology*. Oxford: Basil Blackwell.

Gorman, James. 1993. On language. *New York Times Magazine*, 20 August.

Gósy, Mária and Jacques Terken. 1994. Question marking in Hungarian: timing and height of pitch peaks. *JPhon.* 22: 269–81.

Grice, Martine. 1995a. *The intonation of interrogation in Palermo Italian: implications for intonation theory*. Tübingen: Niemeyer.

1995b. Leading tones and downstep in English. *Phonology* 12: 183–233.

Grice, Martine and Ralf Benzmüller. 1995. Transcription of German intonation using ToBI-Tones: the Saarbrücken System. *PHONUS* (Research Report, Institute of Phonetics, University of the Saarland) 1: 33–51.

Grice, Martine and Michelina Savino. 1995. Low tone versus 'sag' in Bari Italian intonation; a perceptual experiment. *ICPhS* 13 (Stockholm), vol. 4: 658–61.

Grønnum, Nina. *See also* Thorsen.

1991. Prosodic parameters in a variety of regional Danish standard languages, with a view towards Swedish and German. *Phonetica* 47: 188–214.

1992. *The groundworks of Danish intonation: an introduction*. University of Copenhagen/Museum Tusculanum Press.

Grosz, Barbara and Candy Sidner. 1986. Attention, intention, and the structure of discourse. *Journal of Computational Linguistics* 12: 175–204.

Grundstrom, Allan W. 1973. L'intonation des questions en français standard. In A. Grundstrom and P. Léon (eds.) *Interrogation et intonation en français standard et français canadien*. (Studia phonetica, 8.) Montreal: Didier, pp. 19–51.

Gumperz, John. 1982. *Discourse strategies*. Cambridge University Press.

Gundel, Jeanette. 1994. On different kinds of focus. In Peter Bosch and Rob van der Sandt (eds.) *Focus and natural language processing*, vol. III: *Discourse*, IBM Working Papers of the Institute for Logic and Linguistics, pp. 457–66.

Gundel, Jeanette, Nancy Hedberg, and Ron Zacharski. 1993. Cognitive status and the form of referring expressions in discourse. *Lg.* 69: 274–307.

Gussenhoven, Carlos. 1983a. Focus, mode, and the nucleus. *JL* 19: 377–417.

1983b. Testing the reality of focus domains. *LgSp.* 26: 61–80.

1984. *On the grammar and semantics of sentence accents*. Dordrecht: Foris.

1985. Two views of accent: a reply. *JL* 21: 125–38.

1993. The Dutch foot and the chanted call. *JL* 29: 37–63.

Gussenhoven, Carlos and Toni Rietveld. 1988. Fundamental frequency declination in Dutch: testing three hypotheses. *JPhon.* 16: 355–69.

1991. An experimental evaluation of two nuclear-tone taxonomies. *Linguistics* 29: 423–49.

Gussenhoven, Carlos and P. van der Vliet. MS. The phonology of tone and intonation in the Dutch dialect of Venlo. Submitted to *JL*.

Hadding-Koch, K. and M. Studdert-Kennedy. 1964. An experimental study of some intonation contours. *Phonetica* 11: 175–85. Reprinted in Bolinger 1972a: 348–58.

Haegeman, Liliane. 1994. *Introduction to Government and Binding theory* (2nd edn). Oxford: Basil Blackwell.

Haggo, Douglas C. 1987. The structure of English tonal morphemes. PhD thesis, University of Canterbury (NZ).

Hajičova, Eva. 1987. Focussing: a meeting point of linguistics and artificial intelligence. In P. Jorrand and V. Sgurev (eds.) *Artificial intelligence*, vol. II: *Methodology, systems, applications*. Amsterdam: North-Holland, pp. 311–21.

Halim, A. 1984. Intonation in relation to syntax in Indonesian. The Australian National University, Materials in Pacific Linguistics D36.

Halle, Morris and Jean-Roger Vergnaud. 1987. *An essay on stress*. Cambridge, MA: MIT Press.

Halliday, M. A. K. 1960. Categories of the theory of grammar. *Word* 17: 241–92.

1966. The concept of rank: a reply. *JL* 2: 110–18.

1967a. *Intonation and grammar in British English*. Mouton.

1967b. Notes on transitivity and theme in English (part II). *JL* 3: 199–244.

1970. *A course in spoken English: intonation*. Oxford University Press.

Halliday, M. A. K. and Ruqaiya Hasan. 1976. *Cohesion in English*. London: Longman.

Haspelmath, Martin. 1993. A typological study of indefinite pronouns. PhD thesis, Free University of Berlin.

Hastings, Ann. 1990. Intonation in a Scottish accent. Ms., Edinburgh University Linguistics Department.

Hatcher, Anna G. 1956. Theme and underlying question: two studies in Spanish word order. *Word* 12 (Monograph no. 3).

Haugen, Einar and Martin Joos. 1952. Tone and intonation in East Norwegian. *Acta Philologica Scandinavica* 22: 41–64. Reprinted in Bolinger 1972a: 414–36.

Hawkins, Sarah and Paul Warren. 1991. Factors affecting the given-new distinction in speech. *ICPhS* 12 (Aix-en-Provence), vol. 4: 66–9.

Hayes, Bruce. 1981. A metrical theory of stress rules. PhD thesis, MIT. Distributed by IULC.

1993. 'Gesture' in prosody: comments on the paper by Ladd. In Keating 1993: 64–75.

Hayes, Bruce and Aditi Lahiri. 1991. Bengali intonational phonology. *NLLT* 9: 47–96.

Henton, Caroline. 1989. Fact and fiction in the description of female and male pitch. *Language and Communication* 9: 299–311.

1995. Pitch dynamism in female and male speech. *Language and Communication* 15: 43–61.

Herman, Rebecca. 1995. Final lowering in Kipare. *Ohio State University Working Papers in Linguistics* 45: 36–55.

Hermes, Dik and Joost van Gestel. 1991. The frequency scale of speech intonation. *JASA* 90: 97–102.

Hermes, Dik and H. H. Rump. 1994. Perception of prominence in speech intonation induced by rising and falling pitch movements. *JASA* 96: 83–92.

Hirschberg, Julia and Janet Pierrehumbert. 1986. Intonational structuring of discourse. *Proceedings of the twenty-fourth meeting of the Association for Computational Linguistics, New York*, pp. 136–44.

Hirst, Daniel. 1983. Structures and categories in prosodic representations. In Cutler and Ladd 1983: 93–109.

Hobbs, Jerry. 1990. The Pierrehumbert–Hirschberg theory of intonational meaning made simple: comments on Pierrehumbert and Hirschberg. In P. R. Cohen, J. Morgan, and M. E. Pollack (eds.) *Intentions in communication*. Cambridge, MA: MIT Press, pp. 313–23.

Hockett, Charles F. 1955. *A manual of phonology*. Baltimore: Waverley Press.

1958. *A course in modern linguistics*. Macmillan.

Holden, K. T. and J. T. Hogan. 1993. The emotive impact of foreign intonation: an experiment in switching English and Russian intonation. *LgSp.* 36: 67–88.

Horvath, Julia. 1986. *Focus in the theory of grammar and the syntax of Hungarian*. Dordrecht: Foris.

Huang, C.-T. James. 1980. The metrical structure of terraced-level tones. In J. Jensen (ed.) *NELS 11* (Cahiers Linguistiques d'Ottawa 9), Department of Linguistics, University of Ottawa, pp. 257–70.

Huddleston, Rodney. 1965. Rank and depth. *Lg.* 41: 574–86. Reprinted in M. A. K. Halliday and J. R. Martin (eds.) *Readings in systemic linguistics*. London: Batsford.

Huffman, Adem. 1993. Rising F_0 contours in Glasgow speech. MSc. dissertation, University of Edinburgh.

Huss, Volker. 1978. English word stress in the postnuclear position. *Phonetica* 35: 86–105.

Hyman, Larry, Francis Katamba, and Livingstone Walusimbi. 1987. Luganda and the strict layer hypothesis. *Phonology Yearbook* 4: 87–108.

Inkelas, Sharon and William Leben. 1990. Where phonology and phonetics intersect: the case of Hausa intonation. In Kingston and Beckman 1990: 17–34.

Inkelas, Sharon and Draga Zec. 1988. Serbo-Croatian pitch accent. *Lg.* 64: 227–48.

Isačenko, A. and H.-J. Schädlich. 1970. *A model of Standard German intonation*. The Hague: Mouton.

Jackendoff, Ray. 1972. *Semantic interpretation in generative grammar*. Cambridge, MA: MIT Press.

Jacobs, Joachim. 1982. Neutraler und nicht-neutraler Satzakzent im Deutschen. In Th. Vennemann (ed.) *Silben, Segmente, Akzente*. Tübingen: Niemeyer, pp. 141–69.

Jakobson, Roman, Gunnar Fant, and Morris Halle. 1952. *Preliminaries to speech analysis*. Cambridge, MA: MIT Press.

Jakobson, Roman and Morris Halle. 1971. *Fundamentals of language* (2nd edn). The Hague: Mouton.

Jarman, E. and Alan Cruttenden. 1976. Belfast intonation and the myth of the fall. *JIPA* 6: 4–12.

Joos, Martin. 1957. *Readings in linguistics*, vol. I. University of Chicago Press.

Jun, Sun-Ah. 1993. The phonetics and phonology of Korean prosody. PhD thesis, Ohio State University.

Kaisse, Ellen M. and Patricia A. Shaw. 1985. On the theory of Lexical Phonology. *Phonology Yearbook* 2: 1–30.

Keating, Patricia. 1984. Phonetic and phonological representation of stop consonant voicing. *Lg.* 60: 286–319.

(ed.). 1993. *Papers in laboratory phonology*, vol. III: *Phonological structure and phonetic form*. Cambridge University Press,

Kefer, Michel. 1986. Some sentence accent universals referring to noun phrases. Ms, University of Liège.

Kendon, Adam. 1972. Some relationships between body motion and speech: An analysis of an example. In Aron Siegman and Benjamin Pope (eds) *Studies in dyadic communication*, London: Pergamon Press.

Kiefer, Ferenc. 1967. *On emphasis and word order in Hungarian*. The Hague: Mouton.

Kim, A. H. 1988. Preverbal focusing and type XXIII languages. In M. Hammond, E. Moravcsik and J. R. Wirth (eds.), *Studies in syntactic typology*. Amsterdam: Benjamins, pp. 147–69.

King, Heather B. 1994. *The declarative intonation of Dyirbal: an acoustic analysis*. MA. thesis, The Australian National University. (To be published in Lincom Studies in Australian Linguistics, Munich: Lincom Europa.).

Kingdon, Roger. 1958. *The groundwork of English intonation*. London: Longman.

Kingston, John and Mary E. Beckman (eds.). 1990. *Papers in laboratory phonology*, vol. I: *Between the grammar and physics of speech*. Cambridge University Press.

Kingston, John and Randy L. Diehl. 1994. Phonetic knowledge. *Lg.* 70: 419–54.

Kiparsky, Paul. 1966. Uber den deutschen Akzent. *Studia Grammatica* 7: 69–98.

Kiss, Katalin. 1996. Focus is a non-uniform phenomenon. In I. Kohlhof, S. Winkler, and H. B. Drubig (eds.), *Proceedings of the Göttingen Focus Workshop*, University of Tübingen.

Knowles, G. O. 1974. Scouse: the urban dialect of Liverpool. PhD thesis, University of Leeds.

Kohler, Klaus J. 1984. Phonetic explanation in phonology: the feature fortis/lenis. *Phonetica* 41: 150–74.

1987. Categorical pitch perception. *ICPhS* 11 (Tallinn), vol. 5: 331–3.

1991. Terminal intonation patterns in single-accent utterances in German: phonetics, phonology and semantics. *AIPUK* 25: 115–85.

König, Ekkehard. 1991. *The meaning of focus particles: a comparative perspective*. London: Routledge.

Koopmans-van Beinum, F. J. and D. R. van Bergem, 1989. The role of 'given' and 'new' in the production and perception of vowel contrasts in read text and in spontaneous speech. *Proceedings of Eurospeech 1989*, pp. 113–16.

Kori, S. 1987. The tonal behavior of Osaka Japanese: an interim report. *Working Papers in Linguistics, Ohio State University* 36: 31–61.

Kornai, Andras and Geoffrey K. Pullum. 1990. The X-bar theory of phrase structure. *Lg.* 66: 24–50.

Kramer, E. 1964. Elimination of verbal cues in judgments of emotion from voice. *Journal of Abnormal and Social Psychology* 68: 390–6.

Krifka, Manfred. 1991. A compositional semantics for multiple focus constructions. In S. Moore and A. Wyner (eds.) *Proceedings of SALT I, Cornell*, pp. 127–58.

Kruyt, J. G. 1985. Accents from speakers to listeners. An experimental study of the production and perception of accent patterns in Dutch. PhD thesis, University of Leiden.

Kubozono, Haruo. 1989. Syntactic and rhythmic effects on downstep in Japanese. *Phonology* 6: 39–67.

Ladd, D. Robert. 1978. Stylized intonation. *Lg.* 54: 517–39.

1980a. *The structure of intonational meaning: evidence from English.* Bloomington: Indiana University Press.

1980b. English compound stress. *NELS* 10. Repr. in D. Gibbon and H. Richter (eds.) *Intonation, accent and rhythm.* Berlin: Walter de Gruyter, pp. 253–66.

1981. On intonational universals. In T. Myers, J. Laver, and J. Anderson (eds.) *The cognitive representation of speech.* Amsterdam: North Holland, pp. 389–97.

1983a. Phonological features of intonational peaks. *Lg.* 59: 721–59.

1983b. Levels versus configurations, revisited. In F. B. Agard, G. B. Kelley, A. Makkai, and V. B. Makkai (eds.) *Essays in honor of Charles F. Hockett.* Leiden: E. J. Brill, pp. 93–131.

1983c. Even, focus, and normal stress. *Journal of Semantics* 2: 157–70.

1984. Declination: a review and some hypotheses. *Phonology Yearbook* 1: 53–74.

1986. Intonational phrasing: the case for recursive prosodic structure. *Phonology Yearbook* 3: 311–40.

1987a. Review of Bolinger 1986. *Lg.* 63: 637–43.

1987b. A phonological model of intonation for use in speech synthesis by rule. In *Proceedings of the European Conference on Speech Technology, Edinburgh,* pp. 21–4.

1988. Declination 'reset' and the hierarchical organization of utterances. *JASA* 84: 530–44.

1989. Review of Pierrehumbert and Beckman 1988. *JL* 25: 519–26.

1990a. Intonation: emotion vs. grammar. (Review of Bolinger 1989). *Lg.* 66: 806–16.

1990b. Metrical representation of pitch register. In Kingston and Beckman 1990: 35–57.

1992a. An introduction to intonational phonology. In Docherty and Ladd 1992: 321–34.

1992b. Compound prosodic domains. Edinburgh University Linguistics Department Occasional Paper.

1993a. In defense of a metrical theory of intonational downstep. In H. v. d. Hulst and K. Snider (eds.) *The representation of tonal register.* Dordrecht: Foris, pp. 109–32.

1993b. Constraints on the gradient variability of pitch range (or) Pitch Level 4 lives! In Keating 1993: 43–63.

1993c. On the theoretical status of 'the baseline' in modelling intonation. *LgSp.* 36: 435–51.

Ladd, D. Robert and Rachel Morton. Ms. The perception of intonational emphasis: continuous or categorical? Submitted to *JPhon.*

Ladd, D. Robert, K. R. Scherer, and Kim Silverman. 1986. An integrated approach to studying intonation and attitude. In C. Johns-Lewis (ed.) *Intonation in discourse*. London: Croom Helm, pp. 125–38.

Ladd, D. Robert, Kim Silverman, Frank Tolkmitt, Gunther Bergmann, and K. R. Scherer. 1985. Evidence for the independent function of intonation contour type, voice quality and F_0 range in signalling speaker affect. *JASA* 78: 435–44.

Ladd, D. Robert and Jacques Terken. 1995. Modelling intra- and inter-speaker pitch range variation. *ICPhS* 13 (Stockholm), vol. 2: 386–9.

Ladd, D. Robert, Jo Verhoeven, and Karen Jacobs. 1994. Influence of adjacent pitch accents on each other's perceived prominence: two contradictory effects. *JPhon.* 22: 87–99.

Ladefoged, Peter. 1967. Linguistic phonetics. *UCLA Working Papers in Phonetics*, 6.

1982. *A course in phonetics* (2nd edn). New York: Harcourt Brace Jovanovich.

1983. The linguistic use of different phonation types. In D. Bless and J. Abbs (eds.) *Vocal fold physiology: contemporary research and clinical issues*. San Diego: College Hill Press, pp. 351–60.

Laksman, Myrna. 1994. Location of stress in Indonesian words and sentences. In Odé and van Heuven 1994: 108–39.

Langendoen, D. Terence. 1975. Finite-state parsing of phrase structure languages and the status of readjustment rules in the grammar. *LI* 6: 533–54.

Laniran, Yetunde Olabisi. 1992. Intonation in tone languages: the phonetic implementation of tones in Yoruba. PhD Thesis, Cornell University.

LaVelle, C. R. 1974. An experimental study of Yoruba tone. *Studies in African Linguistics*, supplement 5, pp. 185–94.

Laver, John. 1980. *The phonetic description of voice quality*. Cambridge University Press.

1994. *Principles of phonetics*. Cambridge University Press.

Leben, William. 1973. Suprasegmental phonology. PhD thesis, MIT. Published 1980 by Garland Press, New York.

1976. The tones in English intonation. *Linguistic Analysis* 2: 69–107.

Lee, W. R. 1956. Fall–rise intonations in English. *English Studies* 37: 62–72.

Lehiste, Ilse. 1970. *Suprasegmentals*. Cambridge, MA: MIT Press.

1975. The phonetic structure of paragraphs. In A. Cohen and S. G. Nooteboom (eds.), *Structure and process in speech perception*. Cambridge, MA: Springer, pp. 195–203.

Lehiste, Ilse and Pavle Ivić. 1980. The intonation of yes-and-no questions: a new Balkanism? *Balkanistica* 6: 45–53.

1986. *Word and sentence prosody in Serbo-Croatian*. Cambridge, MA: MIT Press.

Levin, Beth and M. Rappaport-Hovav. 1995. *Unaccusativity: at the syntax–lexical semantics interface*. Cambridge, MA: MIT Press.

Levy, E. T. and D. McNeill. 1992. Speech, gesture, and discourse. *Discourse Processes* 15: 277–301.

Liberman, Mark. 1975. The intonational system of English. PhD thesis, MIT. Distributed 1978 by IULC.

Liberman, Mark and Janet Pierrehumbert. 1984. Intonational invariance under changes in pitch range and length. In M. Aronoff and R. Oerhle (eds.) *Language sound structure*. Cambridge, MA: MIT Press, pp. 157–233.

Liberman, Mark and Alan Prince. 1977. On stress and linguistic rhythm. *LI* 8: 249–336.

Liberman, Mark and Ivan Sag. 1974. Prosodic form and discourse function. *Proceedings of the Chicago Linguistics Society*: 10: 416–27.

Liberman, Mark, J. Michael Schultz, Soonhyun Hong, and Vincent Okeke. 1993. The phonetic interpretation of tone in Igbo. *Phonetica* 50: 147–60.

Liddell, Scott. 1977. An investigation into the syntactic structure of American Sign Language. PhD thesis, University of California, San Diego.

Lieberman, Philip. 1960. Some acoustic correlates of word stress in American English. *JASA* 32: 451–4.

1965. On the acoustic basis of the perception of intonation by linguists. *Word* 21: 40–54.

1967. *Intonation, perception, and language*. Cambridge, MA: MIT Press.

Lieberman, Philip and Sheldon B. Michaels. 1962. Some aspects of fundamental frequency and envelope amplitude as related to the emotional content of speech. *JASA* 34: 922–7. Reprinted in Bolinger 1972a: 235–49.

Lindau, M. 1986. Testing a model of intonation in a tone language. *JASA* 80: 757–64.

Lindsey, Geoffrey. 1985. Intonation and interrogation: tonal structure and the expression of a pragmatic function in English and other languages. PhD thesis, University of California, Los Angeles.

1992. Quantity and quality in British and American vowel systems. In S. Ramsaran (ed.) *Studies in the pronunciation of English: a commemorative volume in memory of A. C. Gimson*. London: Routledge, pp. 106–18.

McCawley, James D. 1978. What is a tone language? In Fromkin 1978: 113–32.

McClure, J. Derrick. 1980. Western Scottish intonation: a preliminary study. In L. Waugh and C. van Schooneveld (eds.) *The melody of language*. Baltimore: University Park Press, pp. 201–17.

McNeill, David. 1992. *Hand and mind*. University of Chicago Press.

Maeda, Shinji. 1976. A characterization of American English intonation. PhD thesis, MIT.

Matthews, Peter H. 1966. The concept of rank in Neo-Firthian linguistics. *JL* 2: 101–9.

Mencken, H. L. 1948. American street names. *American Speech* 23: 81–8.

Menn, Lise and Suzanne Boyce. 1982. Fundamental frequency and discourse structure. *LgSp.* 25: 341–83.

Mennen, Ineke and Els den Os. 1993. Intonation of Modern Greek sentences. *Proceedings of the Institute of Phonetic Sciences, University of Amsterdam* 17: 111–28.

Möbius, B. 1993. Perceptual evaluation of rule-generated intonation contours for German interrogatives. *Working Papers*, Department of Linguistics and Phonetics, University of Lund (= Proceedings of the ESCA Workshop on Prosody, Lund, 27–9 September 1993), 41: 216–19.

Möbius, B., M. Pätzold, and W. Hess. 1993. Analysis and synthesis of German F_0 contours by means of Fujisaki's model. *Speech Communication* 13: 53–61.

Monaghan, A. I. C. 1991. Intonation in a text-to-speech conversion system. PhD thesis, Edinburgh University.

1992. Heuristic strategies for the higher-level analysis of unrestricted text. In G. Bailly, G. Benoit, and T. R. Sawallis (eds.) *Talking machines: theories, models, and designs.* Amsterdam: Elsevier, pp. 143–61.

Nespor, Marina and Irene Vogel. 1982. Prosodic domains of external sandhi rules. In Harry van der Hulst and Norval Smith (eds.) *The structure of phonological representations,* vol. I. Dordrecht: Foris, pp. 225–55.

1983. Prosodic structure above the word. In Cutler and Ladd 1983: 123–40.

1986. *Prosodic phonology.* Dordrecht: Foris.

Newman, Stanley. 1946. On the stress system of English. *Word* 2: 171–87.

Nooteboom, S. G. and J. G. Kruyt. 1987. Accents, focus distribution and the perceived distribution of given and new information: an experiment. *JASA* 82: 1512–24.

Nooteboom, S. G. and J. M. B. Terken. 1982. What makes speakers omit pitch accents? An experiment. *Phonetica* 39: 317–36.

O'Connor, J. D. and G. F. Arnold. 1973. *Intonation of colloquial English* (2nd edn). London: Longman.

Odé, Cecilia. 1989. *Russian intonation: a perceptual description.* Amsterdam: Rodopi.

1994. On the perception of prominence in Indonesian. In Odé and van Heuven 1994: 27–107.

Odé, Cecilia and Vincent J. van Heuven (eds.). 1994. *Experimental studies of Indonesian prosody.* Department of Languages and Cultures of Southeast Asia and Oceania, University of Leiden.

Ohala, John. 1975. Review of Lehiste 1970. *Lg.* 51: 736–40.

Öhman, S. E. G. 1967. Word and sentence intonation: a quantitative model. *Speech Transmission Laboratory (Stockholm) Quarterly Progress and Status Report* 2: 20–54.

Ortiz-Lira, Hector. 1994. A contrastive analysis of English and Spanish sentence accentuation. PhD thesis, University of Manchester.

O'Shaughnessy, Douglas and Jonathan Allen. 1983. Linguistic modality effects on fundamental frequency in speech. *JASA* 74: 1155–71.

Palmer, Harold. 1922. *English intonation, with systematic exercises.* Cambridge: Heffer.

Perlmutter, David. 1978. Impersonal passives and the unaccusative hypothesis. *BLS*: 157–89.

Pierrehumbert, Janet. 1980. The phonology and phonetics of English intonation. PhD thesis, MIT, published 1988 by IULC.

1981. Synthesizing intonation. *JASA* 70: 985–95.

Pierrehumbert, Janet and Mary E. Beckman. 1988. *Japanese tone structure.* Cambridge, MA: MIT Press.

Pierrehumbert, Janet and Julia Hirschberg. 1990. The meaning of intonational contours in the interpretation of discourse. In P. R. Cohen, J. Morgan, and M. E. Pollack (eds.) *Intentions in communication.* Cambridge, MA: MIT Press, pp. 271–311.

Pierrehumbert, Janet and Mark Liberman. 1982. Modelling the fundamental frequency of the voice. (Review of Cooper and Sorensen 1981.) *Contemporary Psychology* 27: 690–2.

Pike, Kenneth L. 1945. *The intonation of American English.* Ann Arbor: University of Michigan Press.

    1948. *Tone languages: a technique for determining the number and type of pitch contrasts in a language, with studies in tonemic substitution and fusion.* Ann Arbor: University of Michigan Press.

Pitrelli, J. F., Mary E. Beckman, and Julia Hirschberg. 1994. Evaluation of prosodic transcription labeling reliability in the ToBI framework. *Proceedings, 1994 International Conference on Spoken Language Processing*, 1: 123–6. Yokohama, Japan.

Poser, William J. 1984. The phonetics and phonology of tone and intonation in Japanese. PhD thesis, MIT.

Post, Brechtje. 1993. A phonological analysis of French intonation. Master's thesis, University of Nijmegen.

Prevost, Scott and Mark Steedman. 1994. Specifying intonation from context for speech synthesis. *Speech Communication* 15: 139–53.

Price, P. J., M. Ostendorf, S. Shattuck-Hufnagel, and C. Fong. 1991. The use of prosody in syntactic disambiguation. *JASA* 90: 2956–70

Prince, Alan. 1983. Relating to the Grid. *LI* 14: 19–100.

Prince, Ellen. 1981. Toward a taxonomy of given-new information. In Peter Cole (ed.) *Radical pragmatics.* New York: Academic Press, pp. 223–56.

Reinholt Petersen, Niels. 1986. Perceptual compensation for segmentally conditioned fundamental frequency perturbation. *Phonetica* 43: 21–42.

Rietveld, A. C. M. and Carlos Gussenhoven 1985. On the relation between pitch excursion size and prominence. *JPhon.* 13: 299–308.

Roach, Peter. 1994. Conversion between prosodic transcription systems: Standard British and ToBI. *Speech and Communication* 15: 91–9.

Rooth, Mats. 1985. Association with focus. PhD thesis, University of Massachusetts.

Rose, Phil. 1987. Considerations in the normalisation of the fundamental frequency of linguistic tone. *Speech Communication* 6: 343–51.

    1989. Phonetics and phonology of Yang tone phonation types in Zhenhai. *Cahiers de Linguistique Asie Orientale* 18: 229–45.

    1990. Acoustics and phonology of complex tone sandhi. *Phonetica* 47: 1–35.

Rowlands, E. C. 1969. *Teach yourself Yoruba.* Sevenoaks, Kent: Hodder and Stoughton.

Rump, H. H., and René Collier. 1996. Focus conditions and the prominence of pitch-accented syllables. *LgSp* 39: 1–15.

Sag, Ivan and Mark Liberman. 1975. The intonational disambiguation of indirect speech acts. *Proceedings of the Chicago Linguistic Society* 11: 487–97.

Scherer, K. R., D. Robert Ladd, and K. Silverman. 1984. Vocal cues to speaker affect: testing two models. *JASA* 76: 1346–56.

Schmerling, Susan F. 1976. *Aspects of English sentence stress.* Austin: University of Texas Press.

Schmidt, Mark. 1996. Acoustic correlates of encoded prosody in written conversation. PhD thesis, Edinburgh University.

Schubiger, Maria. 1958. *English intonation: its form and function*. Tübingen: Niemeyer.

1965. English intonation and German modal particles: a comparative study. *Phonetica* 12: 65–84. Reprinted in Bolinger 1972a: 175–93.

1980. English intonation and German modal particles, II: a comparative study. In L. R. Waugh and C. H. van Schooneveld (eds.) *The melody of language*, Baltimore: University Park Press, pp. 279–98.

Scott, Donia R. 1982. Duration as a cue to the perception of phrase boundary. *JASA* 71: 996–1007.

Selkirk, E. O. 1980. The role of prosodic categories in English word stress. *LI* 11: 563–605.

1981. On prosodic structure and its relation to syntactic structure. In T. Fretheim (ed.), *Nordic prosody II* (Trondheim: Tapir), pp. 111–40.

1984. *Phonology and syntax: the relation between sound and structure*. Cambridge, MA: MIT Press.

1986. On derived domains in sentence phonology. *Phonology Yearbook* 3: 371–405.

Sharp, Alan E. 1958. Falling–rising intonation patterns in English. *Phonetica* 2: 127–52.

Shattuck-Hufnagel, S., M. Ostendorf, and K. Ross. 1994. Stress shift and early pitch accent placement in lexical items in American English. *JPhon.* 22: 357–88.

Shen, Xiao-nan Susan. 1990. *The prosody of Mandarin Chinese*. (University of California Publications in Linguistics 118.) Berkeley: University of California Press.

Shields, L. W. and D. A. Balota. 1991. Repetition and associative context effects in speech production. *LgSp.* 34: 47–55.

Shore, John. 1988. Interactive signal processing with UNIX. *Speech Technology* 3 (March/April).

Silverman, Kim. 1986. F_0 segmental cues depend on intonation: the case of the rise after voiced stops. *Phonetica* 43: 76–91.

1987. The structure and processing of fundamental frequency contours. PhD thesis, Cambridge University.

Silverman, Kim, Mary E. Beckman, John Pitrelli, Mari Ostendorf, Colin Wightman, Patti Price, Janet Pierrehumbert, and Julia Hirschberg. 1992. ToBI: a standard for labeling English prosody. *Proceedings, Second International Conference on Spoken Language Processing* 2: 867–70. Banff, Canada.

Silverman, Kim and Janet Pierrehumbert. 1990. The timing of prenuclear high accents in English. In Kingston and Beckman 1990: 71–106.

Sledd, James. 1955. Review of Trager and Smith 1951. *Lg.* 31: 312–35.

Sluijter, Agaath, and Vincent van Heuven. Forthcoming. Spectral balance as an acoustic correlate of linguistic stress. To appear in *JASA*, 1996.

Sosa, Juan Manuel. 1991. Fonética y fonologia de la entonación del Español Hispanoamericano. PhD thesis, University of Massachusetts, Amherst.

Steedman, Mark. 1991. Structure and intonation. *Lg.* 67: 260–96.

Stevick, Earl. 1969. Tone in Bantu. *IJAL* 35: 330–41.

Sugito, Miyoko and Hajime Hirose. 1988. Production and perception of accented devoiced vowels in Japanese. *Annual Bulletin of Research Institute of Logopedics and Phoneatrics* 22: 21–39.

Talkin, David. 1989. Looking at speech. *Speech Technology*, 4 (April/May).

Tartter, V. 1980. Happy talk: perceptual and acoustic effects of smiling on speech. *Perception and Psychophysics* 27: 24–7.

Taylor, Paul A. 1994. A phonetic model of English intonation. PhD thesis, University of Edinburgh, distributed by IULC.

Terken, Jacques. 1991. Fundamental frequency and perceived prominence of accented syllables. *JASA* 89: 1768–76.

Terken, Jacques and Julia Hirschberg. 1994. Deaccentuation of words representing given information: effects of persistence of grammatical function and surface position. *LgSp.* 37: 125–45.

't Hart, Johan. 1979. Explorations in automatic stylization of F_0 curves. *IPO Annual Progress Report* 14: 61–5.

    1981. Differential sensitivity to pitch distance, particularly in speech. *JASA* 69: 811–21.

't Hart, Johan and A. Cohen. 1973. Intonation by rule: a perceptual quest. *JPhon.* 1: 309–27.

't Hart, Johan and René Collier. 1975. Integrating different levels of intonation analysis. *JPhon.* 3: 235–55.

't Hart, J., René Collier, and A. Cohen. 1990. *A perceptual study of intonation: an experimental-phonetic approach.* Cambridge University Press.

Thorsen, Nina. *See also* Grønnum.

    1980a. A study of the perception of sentence intonation: evidence from Danish. *JASA* 67: 1014–30.

    1980b. Intonation contours and stress group patterns in declarative sentences of varying length in ASC Danish. *ARIPUC* 14: 1–29.

    1981. Intonation contours and stress group patterns in declarative sentences of varying length in ASC Danish: supplementary data. *ARIPUC* 15: 13–47.

    1983. Two issues in the prosody of standard Danish. In Cutler and Ladd 1983: 27–38.

    1985. Intonation and text in Standard Danish. *JASA* 77: 1205–16.

    1986. Sentence intonation in textual context: supplementary data. *JASA* 80: 1041–7.

Trager, George L. 1958. Paralanguage: a first approximation. *Studies in Linguistics Occasional Papers* 13: 1–12.

    1964. The intonation system of American English. In David Abercrombie, D. B. Fry, P. A. D. MacCarthy, N. C. Scott, and J. L. M. Trim (eds.) *In honour of Daniel Jones*. London: Longman. Reprinted in Bolinger 1972a: 83–6.

Trager, George L. and H. L. Smith. 1951. *An outline of English structure*. Norman, OK: Battenburg Press. Reprinted 1957 by American Council of Learned Societies, Washington.

Traunmüller, H. and A. Eriksson. The perceptual evaluation of F_0 excursions in speech as evidenced in liveliness estimations. *JASA* 97: 1905–15.

Trim, J. L. M. 1959. Major and minor tone-groups in English. *Le Maître Phonétique* 112: 26–9.

Uhmann, Susanne. 1988. Akzenttöne, Grenztöne und Fokussilben: zum Afbau eines phonologischen Intonationssystems für das Deutsche. In Altmann 1988: 65–88.

1991. *Fokusphonologie: eine Analyse deutscher Intonationskonturen im Rahmen der nicht-linearen Phonologie.* Tübingen: Niemeyer.

Uldall, Elizabeth. 1964. Dimensions of meaning in intonation. In D. Abercrombie, D. B. Fry, P. A. D. MacCarthy, N. C. Scott, and J. L. M. Trim (eds.) *In honour of Daniel Jones.* London: Longman. Reprinted in Bolinger 1972a: 250–9.

Underhill, Robert. 1976. *Turkish grammar.* Cambridge, MA: MIT Press.

Vaissière, Jacqueline. 1983. Language-independent prosodic features. In Cutler and Ladd 1983: 53–66.

Välimaa-Blum, Riita. 1993. Intonation: a distinctive parameter in grammatical constructions. *Phonetica* 50: 124–37.

Vallduví, Enric. 1990. The information component. PhD thesis, University of Pennsylvania, published 1992 by Garland Press, New York.

1991. The role of plasticity in the association of focus and prominence. *Proceedings of the Eastern States Conference on Linguistics* (ESCOL) 7: 295–306.

1992. *The informational component.* New York: Garland.

Vallduví, Enric and Ron Zacharski. 1994. Accenting phenomena, association with focus, and the recursiveness of focus-ground. In P. Dekker and M. Stokhof (eds.) *Proceedings of the Ninth Amsterdam Colloquium* (Department of Philosophy, University of Amsterdam), pp. 683–782.

van Bezooijen, Renée. 1995. Sociocultural aspects of pitch differences between Japanese and Dutch women. *LgSp.* 38: 253–65.

van den Berg, Rob, Carlos Gussenhoven, and Toni Rietveld. 1992. Downstep in Dutch: implications for a model. In Docherty and Ladd 1992: 335–58.

Vanderslice, Ralph and Peter Ladefoged. 1972. Binary suprasegmental features and transformational word-accentuation rules. *Lg.* 48: 819–38.

Vanderslice, Ralph and Laura S. Pierson. 1967. Prosodic features of Hawaiian English. *Quarterly Journal of Speech* 53: 156–66. Reprinted in Bolinger 1972a: 439–50.

Varga, László. 1989. The stylized fall in Hungarian. *Acta Linguistica Hungarica* 39: 317–30.

Vella, Alexandra. 1995. Prosodic structure and intonation in Maltese: influence on Maltese English. PhD thesis, Edinburgh University.

Venditti, Jennifer, Sun-Ah Jun, and Mary Beckman. 1996. Prosodic cues to syntactic and other linguistic structures in Japanese, Korean and English. In James L. Morgan and Katherine Demuth (eds.), *Signal to syntax: bootstrapping from speech to grammar in early acquisition*, Part IV: *Speech and the acquisition of phrase structure* (Hillsdale, NJ: Lawrence Erlbaum), pp. 287–311.

Verhoeven, Jo. 1994. The discrimination of pitch movement alignment in Dutch. *JPhon.* 22: 65–85.

Vogel, Irene and Istvan Kenesei. 1987. The interface between phonology and other components of grammar: the case of Hungarian. *Phonology Yearbook* 4: 243–63.

von Stechow, Arnim and Susanne Uhmann. 1986. Some remarks on focus projection. In W. Abraham and S. de Meij (eds.) *Topic, focus, and configurationality.* Amsterdam: Benjamins, pp. 295–320.

Wang, William. 1967. The phonological features of tone. *IJAL* 33: 93–105.

Ward, Ida C. 1933. *The phonetic and tonal structure of Efik.* Cambridge: Heffer.

Ward, Gregory and Julia Hirschberg. 1985. Implicating uncertainty. *Lg.* 61: 747–76.

Weinreich, Uriel. 1954. Stress and word structure in Yiddish. In Uriel Weinreich (ed.) *The field of Yiddish: studies in Yiddish language, folklore and literature.* Linguistic Circle of New York, pp. 1–27.

Wells, J. C. 1982. *Accents of English*, vol. I: *An introduction*; vol. II: *The British Isles.* Cambridge University Press.

Wells, Rulon. 1945. The pitch phonemes of English. *Lg.* 21: 27–40.

Welmers, William 1973. *African language structures.* Berkeley: University of California Press.

Whalen, D. H. and Andrea Levitt. 1995. The universality of intrinsic F_0 of vowels. *JPhon.* 23: 349–66.

Wilbur, R. B. 1994a. Eyeblinks and ASL phrase structure. *Sign Language Studies* 84: 221–40.

1994b. Foregrounding structures in ASL. *Journal of Pragmatics* 22: 647–72.

Willems, Nico, René Collier, and Jan Roelof de Pijper. 1988. A synthesis scheme for British English intonation. *JASA* 84: 1250–61.

Williams, Carl E. and Kenneth N. Stevens. 1972. Emotions and speech: some acoustical correlates. *JASA* 52: 1238–50.

Williams, Edwin. 1976. Underlying tone in Margi and Igbo. *LI* 7: 463–84.

Winston, F. D. D. 1960. The 'mid' tone in Efik. *African Language Studies* 1: 185–92.

Woo, Nancy. 1969. Prosody and phonology. PhD thesis, MIT. Distributed by IULC.

Wunderlich, Dieter. 1988. Der Ton macht die Melodie: zur Phonologie der Intonation des Deutschen. In Altmann 1988: 1–40.

Yip, Moira. 1989. Contour tones. *Phonology* 6: 149–74.

Index of names

Names are not included in the following list if the only reference to them is as second or subsequent author of a work with three or more authors.

Index of languages

African languages 2, 61–3, 74, 89, 104, 135, 147, 151, 270f., 278, 288 n. 12, 299 n. 1

Bantu 286 n. . 2, 290 n. 10
Bengali 102, 127, 156f., 171, 192

Catalan 179, 194, 294 n. 8
Celtic languages 287 n. 6
Chinese 1f., 7, 25, 27, 35, 148ff., 150, 152f., 155, 159, 169, 195
  Chengtu Chinese 150
  Mandarin Chinese 2
  Wu Chinese 256, 258
Chuchkee 149
Czech 173

Danish 25, 27, 29, 115, 128, 133, 152, 263f
Dutch 14–17, 42, 45f., 49, 58f., 61, 74, 77, 87, 102, 117, 138f., 157, 159, 180, 189, 191, 197, 201, 206, 215, 255, 264, 266, 292 n. 10, 292 n. 12
  Venlo Dutch 157, 159
Dyirbal 102, 131

Eastern European languages 173, 212, 214, 218
Efik 62, 270
English 2ff., 7, 9, 12, 14, 25, 36f., 40, 42–50 *passim*, 54, 58-61, 65-7, 70, 74f., 77, 79–112 *passim*, 115, 117–38 *passim*, 140, 148ff., 155ff., 168–71, 174–97 *passim*, 206, 211–18 *passim*, 226f., 229, 232–5, 237, 247, 253, 255, 261, 272, 274, 276, 277, 283, 285 n. 8, 287 n. 6, 287 n. 7, 290 n. 12, 292 n. 9, 294 n. 10, 295 n. 15, 296 n. 1, 296 n. 3
  American English 9f., 119–23, 125–8 *passim*, 131, 136, 143–7, 184, 224, 291 n. 8
  Australian English 120f., 123, 125, 128
  Belfast English 123
  British English 119–26, 143–7, 184, 291 n. 6, 291 n. 8
  Caribbean English 175

  Hawaiian Pidgin English 175
  Indian English 175f
  Irish English 120, 123
  New Zealand English 121, 123, 125
  North American English 121ff., 144, 291 n. 8
  RP (Received Pronunciation) 119f., 122, 126
  Scottish English 120, 123f., 144–7
  Urban North British 123–6, 143–7, 291 n. 7

Finnish 127
French 2, 14, 56–9, 66, 102, 115, 127, 138, 140-3, 179, 206, 220, 289 n. 4, 291 n. 5, 292 n. 9, 294 n. 8

German 7, 14, 30, 35, 54, 102, 111, 122f., 128f., 133–9, 175, 189f., 296 n. 3
Germanic languages 169, 175, 190
Greek 69, 102, 144, 169, 173, 178, 212–17, 297 n. 5

Hausa 74, 150ff.,
Hawaiian pidgin 175
Hindi 37
Hungarian 102, 115–18, 123, 125, 132f., 135, 138, 169, 171, 173f., 186, 194, 212ff., 232, 291 n. 3, 294 n. 10, 295 n. 15

Icelandic 185f
Indo-Aryan 37
Indonesian 14, 59
Italian 116, 128–31, 135, 140, 142f., 173f., 176–81, 183f., 191f., 194, 214, 257, 274, 294 n. 9, 295 n. 14
  Palermo Italian 102, 109, 127, 133, 214, 289 n. 4

Japanese 3, 50, 58, 75, 90, 93, 102, 105, 148f., 155ff., 159, 195, 197, 271, 285 n. 8, 286 n. 2, 292 n. 12, 295 n. 15
  Osaka Japanese 149
  Tokyo Japanese 149

325

Subject index